The ECHR and Human Rights Theory

The European Convention on Human Rights (ECHR) has been relatively neglected in the field of normative human rights theory. This book aims to bridge the gap between human rights theory and the practice of the ECHR. In order to do so, it tests the two overarching approaches in human rights theory literature: the ethical and the political, against the practice of the ECHR 'system'. The book also addresses the history of the ECHR and the European Court of Human Rights (ECtHR) as an international legal and political institution.

The book offers a democratic defence of the authority of the ECtHR. It illustrates how a conception of democracy – more specifically, the egalitarian argument for democracy developed by Thomas Christiano on the domestic level – can illuminate the reasoning of the Court, including the allocation of the margin of appreciation on a significant number of issues. Alain Zysset argues that the justification of the authority of the ECtHR – its prominent status in the domestic legal orders – reinforces the democratic process within States Parties, thereby consolidating our status as political equals in those legal and political orders.

Alain Zysset is a Max Weber Fellow at the European University Institute (EUI) in Florence, Italy.

Routledge Research in Human Rights Law

Available titles in this series include:

Children's Lives in an Era of Children's Rights
The Progress of the Convention on the Rights of the Child in Africa
Afua Twum-Danso Imoh & Nicola Ansell

China's Human Rights Lawyers
Advocacy and Resistance
Eva Pils

The Right to Equality in European Human Rights Law
The Quest for Substance in the Jurisprudence of the European Courts
Charilaos Nikolaidis

Business and Human Rights in South East Asia
Risk and Regulatory Turn
Mahdev Mohan & Cynthia Morel

Indigenous Peoples, Title to Territory, Rights and Resources
The Transformative Role of Free Prior and Informed Consent
Cathal M. Doyle

Challenging Territoriality in Human Rights Law
Building Blocks for a Plural and Diverse Duty-Bearer Regime
Wouter Vandenhole

Comparative Executive Clemency
The Prerogative of Mercy in the Commonwealth
Andrew Novak

Human Rights Law and Personal Identity
Jill Marshall

Shifting Centres of Gravity in Human Rights Protection
Rethinking Relations between ECHR, EU, and National Legal Orders
Edited by Oddný Mjöll Arnardóttir and Antoine Buyse

Developing the Right to Social Security – A Gender Perspective
Beth Goldblatt

The ECHR and Human Rights Theory

Reconciling the Moral and
the Political Conceptions

Alain Zysset

LONDON AND NEW YORK

First published 2017
by Routledge
2 Park Square, Milton Park, Abingdon, Oxon OX14 4RN

and by Routledge
711 Third Avenue, New York, NY 10017

Routledge is an imprint of the Taylor & Francis Group, an informa business

© 2017 Alain Zysset

The right of Alain Zysset to be identified as author of this work has been asserted by him in accordance with sections 77 and 78 of the Copyright, Designs and Patents Act 1988.

All rights reserved. No part of this book may be reprinted or reproduced or utilised in any form or by any electronic, mechanical, or other means, now known or hereafter invented, including photocopying and recording, or in any information storage or retrieval system, without permission in writing from the publishers.

Trademark notice: Product or corporate names may be trademarks or registered trademarks, and are used only for identification and explanation without intent to infringe.

British Library Cataloguing in Publication Data
A catalogue record for this book is available from the British Library

Library of Congress Cataloging in Publication Data
A catalog record for this book has been requested

ISBN: 978-1-138-64103-7 (hbk)
ISBN: 978-1-315-63080-9 (ebk)

Typeset in Times New Roman
by Swales & Willis Ltd, Exeter, Devon, UK

Printed and bound by CPI Group (UK) Ltd, Croydon, CR0 4YY

To my parents, Frédy and Gabrielle.

Contents

Acknowledgements	xi
Abbreviations	xii

**1 Introduction: human rights theory and the challenge
of the ECHR**   1

  1.1 The need for determinacy 2
     1.1.1 Griffin and the conception of personhood 4
     1.1.2 The moral dimension of human rights 5
  1.2 The need for practice-responsiveness 7
     1.2.1 Beitz and the rejection of moral reasoning 9
     1.2.2 The political dimension of human rights 10
  1.3 The main argument 11
     1.3.1 Claim one 12
     1.3.2 Claim two 14
     1.3.3 Claim three 15
     1.3.4 Claim four 17
  1.4 The neglect of the ECHR in human rights theory 19
  1.5 The ECHR: ethical and political? 22
  1.6 The justificatory deficit of human rights qua *law 23*
  1.7 The plan of the book 25

**2 Ethical theories of human rights and their
practice-independence**   28

  2.1 Griffin's moral conception 29
     2.1.1 Griffin's diagnosis of indeterminacy 30
     2.1.2 Griffin's practice-independent account 31
     2.1.3 Practicalities 34
     2.1.4 Equality 34
     2.1.5 Personhood and normative ethics 35

viii *Contents*

2.2 *Griffin's normative scope 36*
    2.2.1 Personhood and international law 38
    2.2.2 The external critique 40
    2.2.3 The internal critique 41
    2.2.4 The rights-based critique 42
2.3 *Forst's variant 44*

3 Political theories and their practice-dependence   47

3.1 *The global perspective 48*
3.2 *The emerging global practice of human rights 52*
3.3 *Beitz's analytical account 54*
    3.3.1 The limits of the global standpoint 54
    3.3.2 Beitz's practical inferences 55
3.4 *Beitz's normative model 57*
    3.4.1 The Rawlsian roots of practice-dependence 58
    3.4.2 The Rawlsian basis in Beitz and Raz 59
3.5 *The practice-based distinction 62*

4 Theorizing human rights: a constructivist proposal   64

4.1 *Constructivism* qua *justification 66*
    4.1.1 The third way of constructivism 66
    4.1.2 Constructivism in Rawls 67
4.2 *Constructivism* qua *method of justification 70*
4.3 *Theorizing human rights: a constructivist proposal 72*

5 The ECHR in historical perspective   76

5.1 *The "alarm bell" against totalitarianism 77*
5.2 *The Convention proposal at the legislative and
    intergovernmental levels 79*
5.3 *The embryonic practice of the ECtHR 83*
5.4 *The 1970s: the slow establishment of a supranational
    judicial authority 85*
5.5 *The explosion of human rights and the need for
    structural reform 88*

6 The normativity of ECHR law   92

6.1 *Normativity and authority 94*
6.2 *Human rights norms* qua *international legal norms 96*
    6.2.1 The normative legitimacy of international law 98
    6.2.2 The normative legitimacy of international
        human rights 100

Contents ix

6.3 *The ECHR qua international human rights treaty 102*
    6.3.1 Monism and dualism 103
    6.3.2 Effect, validity and rank 104
    6.3.3 The constitutionalist argument 108
6.4 *The ECtHR qua international judicial organ 111*
    6.4.1 The execution of judgments 113
    6.4.2 The binding force of judgments 117
    6.4.3 Decisional and jurisprudential authority 117

7 Interpretation at the ECtHR: setting the stage   **120**

7.1 *The semantic exercise 121*
7.2 *From the VCLT principles to the quest for moral truths 124*
    7.2.1 The rejection of intentionalism in *Golder* 125
    7.2.2 The rejection of textualism in *Engel* 128
    7.2.3 The ambivalent role of consensualism 130
7.3 *The "teleological" doctrine: a quest for moral truths? 133*

**8 Balancing and justification at the ECtHR: the pivotal
concept of "democratic necessity"**   **139**

8.1 *The balancing test and the margin of appreciation doctrine 140*
    8.1.1 The margin of appreciation doctrine 143
    8.1.2 The *ad hoc* balancing 148
    8.1.3 The pivotal concept of "democratic society" 151
    8.1.4 The practical reason of the ECtHR 153
8.2 *"Democratic society" and the internal concept of
sovereignty: Article 10 (expression) 154*
    8.2.1 Why pluralism? 156
    8.2.2 The normative basis 158
    8.2.3 The prominent rights-holders of Article 10 159
    8.2.4 The limits of Article 10 167
8.3 *Article 11 (assembly and association) 174*
    8.3.1 The normative basis restated 175
    8.3.2 The prominent rights-holders of Article 11 177
    8.3.3 The limits of Article 11 178
8.4 *Article 3 Protocol 1 (free elections) 180*
    8.4.1 The specification of "legislative body" 181
    8.4.2 The interest protected 183
    8.4.3 The limits of Article 3 Protocol 1 186
8.5 *"Democratic society" and the external concept of
sovereignty: Article 9 (freedom of thought and religion) 189*
    8.5.1 The interest protected 192
    8.5.2 The limits of Article 9 194

x   *Contents*

8.6   *Article 8 (Privacy) 199*
    8.6.1   The interest protected 199
    8.6.2   The limits of Article 8 202

9   Conclusion: constructing the normative foundations of the ECHR   207

9.1   *Three steps towards reconciliation 209*
9.2   *Step one: the resources of the political conception 211*
    9.2.1   The limits of Beitz's global standpoint 212
    9.2.2   The relevance of Beitz's three-pronged model 213
9.3   *Step two: the resources of the moral conception 215*
    9.3.1   Equality in deliberation 218
    9.3.2   The scope of disagreement 219
    9.3.3   The normative claim in the face of disagreement 219
    9.3.4   Equality in representation 229
9.4   *Step three: the reconciliation thesis 236*

Bibliography   241
Index   251

Acknowledgements

I wish to thank two professors whose teaching, expertise, support and friendship will accompany me, I hope, for the rest of my academic endeavours.

First, I am immensely grateful to Michael Esfeld, Professor of Philosophy of Science and Epistemology at the University of Lausanne. Michael taught me the basics of philosophy that are necessary to any intellectual investigation. Michael's help and support were also crucial to my project of studying at the London School of Economics, a school whose true commitment to overcome disciplinary boundaries has had an enormous influence on me.

Second, I am deeply grateful to Samantha Besson, Professor of International and European Law at the University of Fribourg. I could not imagine having had a better supervisor for my doctoral project. Samantha examined every line of my dissertation with the utmost rigor. She set the standards I will aspire to in future projects.

I am also very grateful to Thomas Christiano, Professor of Philosophy at the University of Arizona, who kindly supported my visit to the Department of Philosophy in 2012 and whose work is central to the argument I defend in this book. I am also indebted to Francis Cheneval, Professor of Political Philosophy at the University of Zurich, for continuously discussing various draft chapters.

I would also like to express my gratitude to the Swiss National Science Foundation for financing my doctoral and my postdoctoral research. Last but not least, I wish to thank Katie Carpenter and Olivia Manley at Routledge and Colin Morgan and Liz McElwain at Swales & Willis for their superb editing assistance, and two anonymous reviewers for their constructive and helpful comments.

Abbreviations

ACHR	American Convention on Human Rights
CAT	Convention Against Torture and Other Cruel, Inhuman or Degrading Treatment or Punishment
CEDAW	Convention on the Elimination of All Forms of Discrimination
CERD	Committee on the Elimination of Racial Discrimination
CoE	Council of Europe
ECHR	European Convention for the Protection of Human Rights and Fundamental Freedoms
ECtHR	European Court of Human Rights
ECJ	European Court of Justice
EU	European Union
HRC	Human Rights Committee
ICCPR	International Covenant on Civil and Political Rights
ICESCR	International Covenant on Economic, Social and Cultural Rights
ICJ	International Court of Justice
UN	United Nations
VCLT	Vienna Convention on the Law of Treaties

1 Introduction

Human rights theory and the challenge of the ECHR

The ordinary discourse on human rights is premised on the claim that those rights are inherent in our condition as human beings. The "inherence view"[1] suggests that those rights capture something that is fundamentally binding, "dignity". In the words of Perry, "the inherent dignity has a normative force for us, in this sense: we should live our lives in accordance with the fact that every human being has inherent dignity".[2] At first sight, it seems as if "dignity" requires no theoretical defence. It is obvious. "Dignity" is used not only to *identify* human rights among other rights and values; it also allows us to *justify* them normatively. "Dignity" illuminates the binding force that human rights have upon us.

One implication of "dignity" as a grounding concept for human rights immediately follows. If being human entails having dignity, then human rights are rights we owe to every single human being. As such, human rights matter to both *political* and *interpersonal* moralities. As Valentini puts it, "on this view, if Sarah gets mugged on her way home and is badly injured as a result, she can be said to have suffered a human-right violation".[3] Another implication follows from the premise of "dignity" as a grounding concept for human rights: if human rights bind us just because of our inherent "dignity", then human rights are independent for their existence from any conventional norm (social, political, legal). As Pogge puts it, they have a normative existence "whose validity is independent of any political or legal authority".[4] In particular, *legal* recognition and enforcement may be ways of making those rights effective, but are not necessary for their conditions of existence.

The inherence view of human rights has other attributes that may be captured intuitively. One is their *minimal* character. Human rights seem to differ from other moral values in that their provisions do not go beyond a core of basic entitlements. As Nickel explains, "human rights aim at avoiding the terrible rather than achieving

---

1 This term is owed to Morsink, *Inherent Human Rights: Philosophical Roots of the Universal Declaration.*
2 Perry, *Toward a Theory of Human Rights: Religion, Law, Courts*, 5.
3 Valentini, "In What Sense Are Human Rights Political? A Preliminary Exploration", 182.
4 Pogge, *World Poverty and Human Rights: Cosmopolitan Responsibilities and Reforms*, 52.

2 Introduction

the best. Their modality is 'must do' rather than 'would be good to do'".[5] This premise is also explicit in Shue's seminal account of "basic rights":

> "Security" and "subsistence" are equally essential basic entitlements that secure the enjoyment of other, non-basic rights such as freedom of expression: "basic rights" are "the morality of the depths. They specify the line beneath which no one is to be allowed to sink".[6]

Human rights are not elaborate moral goods such as justice or virtue. They capture a "core" of the values we ascribe to human life, those that are "fundamental" or "essential" to a "decent" human life.

In the same vein, human rights strike us with an idea of *urgency*. Human rights are not long-term social and political goals to contemplate. Given the stringency of "human dignity", it is urgent that human rights are respected. As Nussbaum suggests, human rights are conceived as "a list of urgent items that should be secured to people no matter what else we pursue. . . . We are doing wrong to people when we do not secure to them the capabilities on this list".[7] Human rights refer to a set of urgent, minimal and pre-institutional rights stemming from the "dignity" of human beings that should be given priority against other normative considerations. This intuitive characterization suggests that human rights are not just a semantic creation. They capture a fundamental moral category.

1.1 The need for determinacy

Pre-institutional, urgent, minimal. These are just intuitive attributes of the inherence view of human rights underlying the ordinary discourse. How do we move from this basic *concept* to a *conception*?[8] We may all understand the basic concept of human rights but strongly disagree about its underlying normative content. As Griffin puts it:

> The term "human right" is nearly criterionless. There are unusually few criteria for determining when the term is used correctly and when incorrectly – and not just among politicians, but among philosophers, political theorists, and jurisprudents as well. The language of human rights has, in this way, become debased.[9]

---

5 Nickel, *Making Sense of Human Rights*, 36.
6 Shue, *Basic Rights: Subsistence, Affluence, and U.S. Foreign Policy*, 18.
7 Nussbaum, "Capabilities and Human Rights", 143.
8 This distinction used here is owed to Rawls' distinction between the concept and the conception of justice. The concept of justice refers to "the role of its principles in assigning rights and duties and in defining the appropriate division of social justice" while "a conception of justice is an interpretation of this role": Rawls, *A Theory of Justice*, 9.
9 Griffin, *On Human Rights*, 15.

Introduction 3

This is also what Buchanan terms the "justificatory deficit"[10] of human rights. The grounding concept of "dignity" pervading lists of international human rights[11] is particularly concerning. We often hear worries about its ontological and epistemological status: is "dignity" an inalienable property of human beings? If so, how can we lose it and thereby have our rights infringed? Surely, the "fact" of human "dignity" cannot be understood as the regularity of behavioural patterns or dispositions. Its binding force lies somewhere in the *normative* realm. We may agree that it is a normative status entitling rights-holders to be treated in certain ways independently of institutional relations,[12] but to what extent do human rights overlap with the broader Kantian concept of autonomy? A number of prominent legal and political theorists have also incorporated "dignity" into their concept of rights,[13] but to what extent does it overlap with "human" rights? On pain of infinite regress, such a special moral status needs to be specified. We may also agree that "dignity" grounds our rights, while disagreeing about what these rights are rights *to*. Rosen rightly notes that:

> Where John Paul II, for example, believes that dignity requires the inviolability of all human life from the moment of conception to the expiration of all vital functions, the well-known Swiss organization Dignitas is famous for assisting those who wish to "die with dignity" to end their own lives.[14]

10 Buchanan, "Human Rights and the Legitimacy of the International Order". See also Buchanan, "The Egalitarianism of Human Rights". The indeterminacy is not just troubling to "armchair" philosophers. In his thorough study of the legal and judicial practice of "human dignity", Christopher McCrudden concludes that "there is no common *conception* of dignity, although there seems to be an acceptance of the concept of *dignity*": McCrudden, "Human Dignity and Judicial Interpretation of Human Rights", 712.

11 The Preamble to the Universal Declaration of Human Rights (UDHR) states: "Whereas recognition of the inherent dignity and of the equal and inalienable rights of all members of the human family is the foundation of freedom, justice and peace in the world . . .". The Declaration itself says: "Whereas the people of the United Nations have in the Charter reaffirmed their faith in fundamental human rights, in the dignity and worth of the human person and have determined to promote . . .". Arts 1, 22, 23(3) of the UDHR also mention "human dignity". In his wide study of the status of dignity in international and constitutional law, McCrudden explains that "at the international level, dignity is now routinely incorporated in human rights charters, both general and specific". He also explains that by 1986, dignity had become the central guiding concept in the framing of new human rights instruments in international law: McCrudden, "Human Dignity and Judicial Interpretation of Human Rights", 668–70. The concept of dignity is also central in the post-1945 European constitutional tradition, as seen in the German Basic Law (1949), Art. 1.

12 As Michael Perry notes, we may agree on the negative implications of human rights: "To say that every human being has inherent dignity is to say that the dignity of every human being does not inhere in – it does not depend on – anything as particular as a human being's race, colour, sex, language, religion, political or other opinion, national or social origin, property, birth or other status. But to say that is not to say what the human dignity of every human being depends on. What is the source, the ground, of this dignity – and of the normative force this dignity has for us?": Perry, *Toward a Theory of Human Rights*, 5.

13 See e.g. Gewirth, "Rights and Virtues", 743. See also Buchanan, "Human Rights and the Legitimacy of the International Order", 45–6.

14 Rosen, *Dignity: Its History and Meaning*, 6–7.

4   *Introduction*

The room for disagreement is exponential. It may arise in the middle of our ordinary rights claims. Does the right against inhumane or cruel treatment prohibit corporal punishment in all of its forms or only some? Should human rights lists include a right to free elections? As Letsas suggests, "we cannot inflate the concept of human rights so much that it covers the whole realm of justice. Human rights would then lose their distinctive moral force".[15] Furthermore, human rights are not just the rights of *human beings*. They are also *rights*. How do we understand the concept of rights within the concept of human rights? Are we justifying rights or just values or interests? As Nickel explains, "the fragment of intension we have – namely, a claim that we have on others simply in virtue of our being human – holds of moral claims in general and not all moral claims are rights-generated".[16] The concept of *rights* is expected to preserve a certain structure. Finally, one may draw on the history of ideas to fill the normative vacuum. However, the inherence view has a long and controversial history and may be justified by antagonistic conceptions of the deeper reasons for having and protecting rights.[17] Indeed, the concept of "dignity" may find a place in Christian theology, in early liberal thought or later in Kant.

The philosophical task before us is significant. In this introductory chapter, I want to present two distinct and predominant ways in which this task has been envisioned in the recent literature in normative human rights theory: the *moral* conception of James Griffin, on the one hand, and the *political* conception of Charles Beitz, on the other. To construct the distinction, I present how each of those theorists understands the role of normative facts and practices associated with human rights in the enterprise of normative theorizing. Roughly put, normative facts and practices are the actions for which human rights give reasons for in the social world. I argue that this role differs radically in Griffin and Beitz: while the structure and content of human rights can be attained by moral reasoning in Griffin, that structure and content can be apprehended only through an interpretation of political facts and practices in Beitz. On the basis of that distinction, I suggest a way to move forward.

1.1.1 Griffin and the conception of personhood

In *On Human Rights*, James Griffin makes a seminal contribution to the field of normative human rights theory in arguing that human rights protect our status of normative agents. Griffin defends an account of human rights based on the value of "personhood",[18] understood as the inherent capacity for normative agency. This conception best captures the binding force of human rights and thereby *justifies* them. As Griffin explains:

---

15 Letsas, *A Theory of Interpretation of the European Convention on Human Rights*, 129.
16 Nickel, *Making Sense of Human Rights*, 16.
17 See Rosen, *Dignity: Its History and Meaning*, Chapter 1.
18 Griffin's account is critically examined in detail below in Chapter 4.

Anyone who has the capacity to identify the good, whatever the extent of the capacity and whatever its sources, has what I mean by "a conception of a worthwhile life"; they have ideas, some of them reliable, about what makes a life better or worse.[19]

The value of personhood specifically aims to remedy the justificatory deficit of human rights.

The exercise of this distinctively human capacity for agency requires three things:

- first, an *autonomy* condition: one must "choose one's path through life – that is, not be dominated or controlled by someone else";[20]
- second, a *minimum provision condition*: one must "at least have a certain minimum education and information; and, having chosen one's path, one must be then able to act – that is, one must have at least the minimum provision of resources and capabilities that it takes";[21]
- third, a *liberty condition*: "others must also not forcibly stop one from pursuing what one sees as a worthwhile life".[22]

If those three conditions are fulfilled, the value of personhood is realized. Further, personhood helps to determine in a straightforward manner the duties and correlative to rights are determined and allows for the evaluation of "most of the conventional lists of human rights":[23] life, torture, security of person, political decision, free expression, assembly, free press, worship, education and minimum provision. The "generative capacities"[24] of personhood therefore constitute the *substantive* basis of Griffin's moral account. It is a *substantive* account of human rights in that the evaluative content should help us in distinguishing "human" rights among all sorts of rights and values and illuminate the inherence view outlined above.

1.1.2 The moral dimension of human rights

There is a more methodological way to distinguish Griffin's moral conception. It lies in how Griffin's moral account obtains independently from the legal and political practices that we routinely observe in association with (international) human rights. When we turn to the most salient practices and discourses connected with human rights, we may observe that the concept plays a more circumscribed role than that suggested by Griffin. The concept seems appropriate to *describe* and *evaluate* some situations and not others. Most clearly, the concept is routinely employed as a normative standpoint to morally condemn states and governments that mistreat their subjects. The prototypical addressee of human rights remains

---

19 Griffin, *On Human Rights*, 46.
20 Ibid., 33.
21 Ibid.
22 Ibid.
23 Ibid.
24 Ibid.

6 Introduction

the modern nation state and that normative relation is taken to be valid across states around the world. The international dimension of human rights is also relevant to the prototypical actions that those rights justify: human rights justify some forms of international action and actions but not others. Human rights justify the signing, ratifying and amending of international treaties. They justify a range of international interventions (from military attack against the state violator to the imposition of sanctions upon that state), but there are also actions that human rights do not justify. For instance, there is currently no human rights court on a global scale despite the fact that those rights were first recognized in law. In other words, human rights generate some duties but not others.

While those features of the practice are addressed in Griffin's inquiry, they do not arrive at the structure and content of those rights. As Besson suggests (for moral conceptions more generally), "when read carefully indeed, they refer to human rights practice at most as a test case for their theoretical proposal or as something to criticize or guide from that perspective".[25] This is because for Griffin human rights speak for a fundamental moral category that requires an independent form of moral reasoning. "Personhood" fills a vacuum in our moral repertoire. Consequently, the form of justification developed by Griffin operates from a *first person* perspective. As Valentini puts it, the personhood account "captures the sense in which human rights are fundamental moral claims whose validity is independent of contingent empirical facts".[26] This is also why Griffin almost exclusively focuses on the *interests* and *values* that those rights may protect. Those interests are sufficient to derive the rights enshrined in "most of the conventional lists of human rights"[27] such as life, torture, security of the person, political decision, free expression, education or minimum provision.

The strongly moral dimension of "personhood" does not imply that Griffin's account is esoteric, however. Rather, Griffin simply assumes that the relevant standpoint to construction of the concept is our ordinary life as human beings. The need to abstract from this practice is justified in the face of the persisting disagreement over the content and scope of those rights. The proliferation of rights[28] in human rights discourse reinforces the need for determinacy in this sense.[29] Indeed, human rights are

---

25 Besson, "Human Rights: Ethical, Political . . . or Legal? First Steps in a Legal Theory of Human Rights", 216.

26 Valentini, "Human Rights, Freedom, and Political Authority", 576.

27 Griffin, *On Human Rights*, 33.

28 Historically, social and economic rights were the first provisions to enlarge the scope of human rights and made them contingent upon economic and social conditions, moving the concept beyond the core of civil and political rights that were their primary concern. Some rights were rapidly targeted, starting with the right to work contained in the UDHR (Art. 23.1). In the same vein, Art. 7(c) of the Additional Protocol to the American Convention (1969) asserts that every worker has a right to promotion or upward mobility in his employment. More significantly, the International Covenant on Economic, Social and Cultural Rights (ICESCR) (1966) claims that we have a right to the highest attainable standard of physical and mental health.

29 The two grounds should, however, be clearly distinguished. As Tasioulas points out, "whether a particular conception of human rights validates 'too many' or 'too few' human rights – and how

Introduction   7

not only becoming more recognized worldwide, they are also proliferating in number. As Raz nicely puts it, "human rights practice is not only becoming more established, it is also spreading its wings".[30] Beyond the continuously growing number of international treaties in which human rights are enshrined, an ever-growing number of rights are claimed to be human rights. It is, for instance, declared that all persons should have a right to a secure, healthy and ecologically sound environment.[31] A pressing threshold is therefore needed to help us attain "the significance of a right's being a human right"[32] and the use of independent moral reasoning may respond to that need.

1.2 The need for practice-responsiveness

To adopt an independent moral standpoint *à la* Griffin may nonetheless come at a price. It may fail to explain the confinement of human rights claims and practices to particular contexts of use. As Tasioulas puts it, "it runs the risk of changing the subject by failing to engage adequately with the understanding of human rights that has emerged historically and which plays such a prominent role in contemporary political and legal life".[33] Human rights were recognized primarily in international law. From this standpoint, reconstructing the concept of human rights first requires addressing the factual and practical context in which those rights have been recognized and identifying the kind of action for which they give reasons. The overarching role of human rights *qua* international legal norms is to specify the limits of what modern nation states may do to their citizens. As Letsas explains:

> To assert, in the aftermath of the Second World War, that individuals have rights "by virtue of being human" was simply to assert that states have obligations by virtue of being members of the international community, with respect to how they treat individuals within their jurisdiction.[34]

It is therefore difficult, on this basis, to infer that human rights invest both political and interpersonal moralities with the same normative weight or that they refer to a fundamental moral category. Unlike the case of Sarah's mugging, "arbitrary expropriation or confinement on the part of the state intuitively strikes us as human-right violation".[35]

---

    that is to be decided – is a separate question from that of giving a determinate account of their identification, specification, and normative weight": Tasioulas, "Taking Rights out of Human Rights", 648.

30 Raz, "Human Rights Without Foundations", 322.
31 See Draft Principles on Human Rights and the Environment, available at www1.umn.edu/humanrts/instree/1994-dec.htm; quoted in Raz, ibid.
32 Ibid., 323.
33 Tasioulas, "Taking Rights out of Human Rights", 649.
34 Letsas, *A Theory of Interpretation of the European Convention on Human Rights*, 19.
35 Valentini, "In What Sense Are Human Rights Political?", 182.

8 Introduction

Similarly, it is difficult to hold that human rights *qua* international norms do not depend for their existence on any prior norm. The institution of international law, together with the post-1945 international state system, remains a central premise. Beyond the Universal Declaration of Human Rights (UDHR), the following are the main conventions that have consolidated the international legal dimension of human rights in the second half of the twentieth century:

- American Convention of Human Rights (ACHR) (adopted in 1968);
- European Convention on Human Rights (ECHR) (1950);
- International Convention on the Elimination of all Forms of Racial Discrimination (ICERD) (1965);
- International Covenant on Civil and Political Rights (ICCPR) (1966);
- International Covenant on Economic, Social and Cultural Rights (ICESCR) (1966);
- African Charter on Human and People's Rights (The Banjul Charter) (1981);
- Convention against Torture and other Cruel, Inhuman or Degrading Treatment or Punishment (CAT) (1984);
- Convention on the Rights of the Child (CRC) (1989).

Those treaties have also established (quasi-)judicial organs in charge of supervising the implementation of human rights norms. In order to effectively shape the life of rights-holders, those treaties need mechanisms of incorporation in national legal orders and this, therefore, requires addressing the status of international law in their jurisdictions. International law is a normative construct of its own, and so is human rights law.

Is independent moral reasoning fundamental to reconstructing this practical dimension of human rights? It seems that such ordering puts the cart before the horse. Conceptualizing human rights along those lines is still *normative* but not in the same sense as the moral conception. It appears to be *sociological* rather than *moral*, in that it first requires us to identify with the range of actors and structures involved in this circumscribed context and understand how human rights norms give those reasons for action. The reasons may not be those that are authoritative from an independent and privileged moral standpoint. This is reminiscent of the circumstances in which founding treaties of human rights law were signed. As Buchanan explains:

> The urgent priority was to get as much agreement as possible on a set of minimal standards for how states should treat their own peoples, and this appeared to require three things: a highly abstract set of rights, avoidance of potentially divisive debates about their foundations, and assurance that these "rights" were not enforceable against states.[36]

---

36 Buchanan, "Human Rights and the Legitimacy of the International Order", 40–1.

Introduction 9

From this practical standpoint, human rights do not seem as if they necessarily refer to a fundamental moral category.

1.2.1 Beitz and the rejection of moral reasoning

Charles Beitz is a prominent defender of the political approach to human rights. It must be clear that his approach does not simply require taking the practices of human rights more seriously. More importantly, Beitz argues that addressing and interpreting those practices directs us to the core content and structure of those rights:

> Human rights claims are supposed to be reasons-giving for various kinds of political actions which are open to a variety of agents. We understand the concept of human rights by asking for what kinds of actions, in what kinds of circumstances, human rights claims may be understood to give reasons.[37]

According to Beitz, therefore, the foundations that ethical theorists seek to construct by moral reasoning should be found in an interpretation of the practices associated with those rights: human rights "do not appear as a fundamental moral category . . . . Human rights operate at a middle level of practical reasoning, serving to organize these further considerations and bring them to bear on a certain range of choices".[38] The content of global human rights cannot derive from "a single, more basic value or interests such as those of human dignity, personhood, or membership. The reasons we have to care about them vary with the content of the right in question . . . . Human rights protect a plurality of interests and require different kinds and degrees of commitment of different agents".[39] In sharp contrast to Griffin, therefore, human rights do not constitute a distinctive moral category.

The same goes for their legal dimension. Beitz notices that the legal practice of human rights (on a global scale) is restricted to mechanisms of "consultation, reporting, and public censure".[40] Until today human rights have lacked anything close to a supranational judicial organ delivering authoritative decisions similar to those found in constitutional regimes. Similarly, there is no legal sanction mechanism in the event of non-compliance. This is typical of human rights *qua* international legal norms. As Besson and Tasioulas note, the only sanctions triggered by official coercion are "rare, diverse in character, and often non-systematically applied".[41] The existence of a court with general and compulsory

---

37 Beitz, *The Idea of Human Rights*, 8–9.
38 Ibid., 127–8.
39 Ibid., 128.
40 Ibid., 32.
41 Besson and Tasioulas, "The Emergence of the Philosophy of International Law", 12.

10 *Introduction*

jurisdiction is conventionally taken as a necessary condition of a legal system.[42] Consequently, for Beitz human rights are neither *legal* nor *moral* rights. In fact, Beitz even rules out the concept of *rights* to interpret the practice of human rights. A Razian interest-based approach, for instance, would frame human rights as intermediaries between the interests of some and the duties of others. Although human rights imply interests, Beitz does not draw on rights theory to account for the normativity of human rights. He knows "no good systematic method of interpretation for social practices".[43] If human rights are neither moral nor legal rights, nor rights *tout court*, what are they?

1.2.2 The political dimension of human rights

Surely, human rights do not stand in a normative vacuum; but their normativity is distinctively *political*, Beitz suggests. The typology of actions that human rights generate (their violation) goes from coercive intervention to change a regime and assistance and pressure from civil society. What do all those actions have in common? Beitz's concept of human rights modelled upon the practice has three main components. The first concerns the interest protected by those rights. It must be "sufficiently important when reasonably regarded from the perspective of those protected that it would be reasonable to consider its protection to be a political priority".[44] The model must accommodate the importance of the interest in such a way that it can "be recognized even by those who do not share it (e.g. 'being able to follow one's religion')".[45] The second component concerns the advantageous protector of the interest, that is, the state. This element derives from "more-or-less substantial empirical generalizations about human social behavior and the capacities and dynamics of social institutions".[46] Finally, any plausible human rights "must be suitable objects of international concern".[47] This third component further constrains the set of possible interests that may count as global human rights:

> Whatever its importance regarded from the perspective of potential beneficiaries and however appropriate it would be as a requirement for domestic institutions, a protection cannot count as a human right if it fails to satisfy a requirement of this kind.[48]

The third component remains the core of Beitz's idea: human rights violation provides a *pro tanto* reason for external actors to take action.

---

42 See e.g. Raz, "On the Nature of Law", 1–25.
43 Beitz, *The Idea of Human Rights*, 107.
44 Ibid., 137.
45 Ibid., 138–9.
46 Ibid., 139.
47 Ibid., 140.
48 Ibid.

Introduction 11

Now, one may think that capturing the salient practices of human rights is the task of the social sciences. It is the perspective of the impartial observer, employed to retrieve the internal point of view. The best account would be the one that best resists falsification. However, Beitz makes clear that we cannot get to the very content and structure of human rights other than through a careful reconstruction of the political practices associated with human rights: "A practical approach does more than notice that a practice of human rights exist; it claims for the practice a certain authority in guiding and thinking about the nature of human rights."[49] This leads to the conclusion that the moral conception of Griffin and the political conception of Beitz are *mutually exclusive* as far as the role of normative facts and practices is concerned. On the one hand, moral conceptions identify a stringent moral category (such as "personhood") through independent moral reasoning, which helps them to navigate from the moral to the political and the legal dimensions of human rights (unidirectional). Not only does the personhood account determine the human rights we have; it also pervades the very structure of rights in determining their correlated duties, and serves as a standard of criticism to "clean" the conventional lists of human rights in international law. As Tasioulas puts it, "on the interest-based account, they are rights grounded in universal interests significant enough to generate duties on the part of others".[50] To this extent, the moral conception is "practice-independent".

On the other hand, the political conception makes the nature, structure and content of human rights fully dependent upon the interpretation of global political practice as it contingently presents itself – that is, the "system" designed by the typical actors of the international scene (such as sovereign nation-states, international organizations (IOs) and non-governmental organizations (NGOs)). Implicit in this political practice is an international state system thath is profoundly structured by the sovereign equality of states resistant to intrusive judicial mechanisms of review. As Besson puts it, human rights are here conceived as "politically adopted norms that constitute recognized limits on state sovereignty in current international relations".[51] What drives normative theorizing here is the political dimension of human rights. The reconstruction of the concept is, as such, "practice-dependent".[52]

1.3 The main argument

Having identified the role of normative facts and practices as distinguishing the moral and the political conceptions, I turn now to the preliminary claim of my

---

49 Ibid., 10.
50 Tasioulas, "The Moral Reality of Human Rights", 77.
51 Besson, "Human Rights: Ethical, Political . . . or Legal? First Steps in a Legal Theory of Human Rights", 223.
52 As we shall see later, this approach resembles that adopted by John Rawls in stressing that his account does not seek to derive human rights from a 'theological, philosophical, or moral conception of the nature of the human person': Rawls, *The Law of Peoples: With "The Idea of Public Reason Revisited"*, 81.

12 *Introduction*

investigation. To recall, both the ethical and political conceptions of human rights are *normative* conceptions. They serve the same objective of distinguishing "human" rights among all sorts of rights and values. Beitz does not rule out the normative purpose of human rights theorizing – but, as he explains, "we cannot think about this further question without first understanding the practice in which these claims are made and responded to".[53] Moreover, Beitz firmly argues that understanding this practice inevitably implies ascribing to human rights a thin moral content. In my investigation, I aim to contest this inference. The general and preliminary argument runs as follows. Reconstructing their practical role does not necessarily exclude moral reasoning. The key to this reconciliation is to be found, I argue, in another characterization of human rights practice. By contrast to the political conception that captures the global political practice of human rights, I argue that human rights are better captured in *legal* and *judicial* terms in view of the reconciliation between the two conceptions. This other interpretation of the practice of human, I argue, can avoid the limitations of the two conceptions: the foundationalism of Griffin, which ends up irresponsive to the practice of human rights and to the pervasive disagreement of ordinary modern politics, on the one hand, and the anti-foundationalism of Beitz, denying them any basis in a moral layer of reasoning, on the other. Interpreting the practice in legal and judicial terms opens a conceptual space in which both conceptions become complementary. Four more specific claims can help us in clarifying this argument.

1.3.1 Claim one

The first claim applies to the practice-dependent dimension of Beitz's account. I want first to argue that the *factual* premises that Beitz uses are not exhaustive. They result from a selection as to what constitutes the relevant and meaningful practices of human rights. Surely, Beitz's conception aims to be as *inclusive* as possible. As Beitz explains, "the aim is to describe the most important features of this practice in a schematic and reasonably charitable way, if possible without prejudging the outcome of some interpretative and normative issues that arise when one thinks critically about it".[54] However, "global political life" is not the only standpoint one may take when one interprets the practice of human rights from an evaluatively neutral perspective. It is one thing to notice that the current practice of international human rights lacks anything close to a supranational and authoritative organ in charge for their recognition, specification and allocation, and that human rights give reasons for a number of distinctively political actions. Yet nor does it follow that human rights stand in a legal and judicial vacuum. True, Beitz notices that the legal and judicial dimensions of human rights are restricted to

53 Beitz, *The Idea of Human Rights*, 105.
54 Ibid., 13.

Introduction 13

mechanisms of "consultation, reporting, and public censure",[55] but he fails to account for the nature and scope of this practice such as the quasi-judicial practices of UN treaty bodies.[56] It is the absence of the *legal effects* in national legal orders of both the rights enshrined in treaties and the views and recommendations of UN treaty bodies that Beitz targets here, not the adjudication that is inherent in the quasi-judicial function of treaty bodies, regional human rights courts and to the national implementation of those norms. A limited number of states have indeed established special procedures to apply the decisions of the bodies. It is reported, however, that 70 per cent of the Views delivered by the Human Rights Committee (HRC) established by the ICCPR are not implemented.[57]

It is therefore correct to point out that the *authority* of international human rights law is weak. In fact, the treaty bodies are not judicial organs *stricto sensu*. International human rights law lacks anything close to a central supranational judicial organ for authoritatively adjudicating state/individual disputes similar to the system we have in constitutional regimes. As far as the HRC is concerned,

> the general perceptions of states that Views do not impose legal obligations on them has a substantial impact on decisions not to implement them . . . . Even states that have proved generally respectful of the work of the treaty bodies do at times insist on their discretion to either implement or reject the outcome of individual communication procedures.[58]

However, it is incorrect to infer that international human rights stand in a normative vacuum *qua* legal norms. Since human rights are irremediably thick and abstract, judicial organs play a crucial role in specifying their normative content. This is true of both UN treaty bodies and, more importantly, of regional courts such as the European Court of Human Rights (ECtHR). A quick look at the case law of the ECtHR shows how the ECtHR needs to identify the interest(s) that the right serves, how it identifies rights-holders whose contribution to the interest(s) underlying the right is central, or how it accords a margin of appreciation to respondent States Parties depending on the circumstances. In addition, the *subsidiarity* of international human rights implies that their legal and judicial dimension is also and primarily to be found at the level of internal state practices independently of the international level. As Besson explains, "international human rights need to be contextualized and specified before they can be applied and interpreted. As a result, their interpretation cannot but be domestic in priority".[59]

---

55 Ibid., 32.
56 For a recent overview of this judcial practice, see Schlütter, "Aspects of Human Rights Interpretation by the UN Treaty Bodies".
57 For a recent analysis of the effects of the decisions of UN treaty bodies, see Van Alebeek and Nollkaemper, "The Legal Status of Decisions by Human Rights Treaty Bodies in National Law".
58 Ibid., 372.
59 Besson, "The 'Erga Omnes' Effect of the European Court of Human Rights", 174.

14 *Introduction*

International human rights are frequently implemented at the level of domestic law only. Again, this applies to the reception of judgments and decisions of the ECtHR and, surprisingly, of UN treaty bodies. Some national courts have also given effect to the Views of the HRC in the absence of adopted legislation and may attach interpretive authority to treaty body decisions. As a result, one may wonder if the global standpoint is optimal to grasp the practice of human rights – in particular, its legal and judicial dimension.

Beitz's scrupulous analysis of the global political practices of human rights is not thereby ruled out. The point is that it falsely conveys the idea that this practice of human rights is all that there is to the practice of human rights and that the object of theorizing is *exhaustively* captured. When Beitz argues that human rights is a global concern in that it provides a *pro tanto* reason for external actors to take action (not necessarily military intervention) when a state violates a right, only one pattern (Beitz uses the word "form"[60]) among others is captured. As a result, the thin moral content of Beitz's account is contingent upon the practice it aims to cover. This is not a direct attack on political approach as a conception and method for human rights theorizing, but rather an invitation to apply and adjust it to another dimension of the practice of human rights – the legal and judicial dimension.

1.3.2 Claim two

In order to envision how to reconcile the ethical and political conceptions of human rights, I suggest continuing with a thought experiment. Let us imagine that human rights were the product of a firmer agreement on their normative foundations. Instead of "agreeing on disagreement", as Beitz and others insist, drafting states had a fruitful discussion and happened to agree on what human rights are. They did not have a very firm philosophical idea of what those foundations are, but imagine that the "reflecting equilibrium"[61] was sufficient to articulate, in broad terms, the purpose of the treaty. Let us also imagine that states did not just articulate and justify those rights in an abstract manner, but managed to establish an impartial, efficient and reliable international judicial organ in charge of reviewing, on the basis of this international treaty, whether States Parties respect those rights internally. Following the principle of subsidiarity, which regulates the allocation of the right to rule, those rights are interpreted and enforced primarily by States Parties, so that the established world court would work as a supplementary organ.

Finally, imagine that states abided by the judgments of this court (not with great reluctance sometimes) and engaged with the necessary adjustments in their internal legal orders. This world court would by now have operated for more than 50 years. In its ordinary judicial function, the world court would have expressed, specified

---

60 Beitz, *The Idea of Human Rights*, 40.
61 I use the concept of "reflective equilibrium" in a descriptive sense. As T.M. Scanlon explains, "on the descriptive interpretation, the rationale is rather that those judgments are the most accurate representation of the 'moral sensibility' of the person whose conception is being described": Scanlon, "Rawls on Justification", 142.

Introduction 15

and justified the duties correlative to human rights within a sustainable institutional arena. In interpreting those rights, the imaginary world court would have needed to appeal to the interests and values that those rights protect. Here is my second claim. If we were to apply the methodological framework of Beitz to this legal and judicial practice, we would naturally address the layer of reasons that operates in the judgments rendered by the court. This additional layer of reasons has the epistemic virtues that the objects of theorizing of both Beitz and Griffin do not have. Since human rights are thick and abstract, the adjudication of those rights by the established world court specifies their normative content. In doing so, one does not take a definitive stand about the nature of law or the nature of human rights law as a social object. It simply suggests that the justificatory dimension inherent in the judicial practice of human rights – its reasons-giving nature – lends itself to moral evaluation because those rights refer to highly abstract properties of human beings. As such, the question of the normative legitimacy of international human rights is inextricably connected with the localized legal and judicial practice of human rights. I here follow Besson in her characterization of the relationship between human rights and the corresponding duties as "justificatory and dynamic".[62]

1.3.3 Claim three

My third claim is that the legal and judicial practice of the ECtHR exemplifies the model of the world court just outlined. As we know, there is no global judicial organ – no "world court" – for the review of human rights records on a global scale. Things are very different, however, at the European level. The ECHR – which was promulgated by the CoE in 1953 and entered into force in 1959 – protects the basic civil and political rights of more than eight hundred million people in the 47 States Parties that to date have ratified the ECHR. The most distinctive feature of the ECHR "system" is clearly the ECtHR in Strasbourg (France) in charge of reviewing whether the rights enshrined in the ECHR are respected in the jurisdictions of the 47 States Parties. Abstractly conceived, the ECtHR is an authoritative judicial organ in charge of determining what States Parties owe to individuals living within their jurisdictions as a matter of ECHR law. The ECtHR is a creation of the ECHR itself whose subsidiary review of ECHR rights is its sole legal function. For the ECtHR to perform its subsidiary function, the right of individual application, established in 1998 in Protocol 11 to the ECHR, must be used. An individual may file a case at the ECtHR if, and only if, that person has exhausted the internal remedies in his or her domestic jurisdiction. As Besson explains, the result of this pre-eminence of the national level is that the "national judges remain the primary judges of the conformity of domestic law to the Convention. This has actually given rise to a rich inter-judicial dialogue between national and ECtHR judges in the past".[63]

62 Besson, "The Human Right to Democracy – A Moral Defence with a Legal Nuance", 17.
63 Besson, "European Human Rights, Supranational Judicial Review and Democracy – Thinking Outside the Judicial Box", 107.

16   *Introduction*

By contrast to the UN human rights treaties, therefore, the law of the ECHR is shaped by an accomplished, well-respected and quasi-constitutional judicial organ. The ECtHR does not have the power to strike down a piece of domestic legislation, but it holds the ultimate say over the interpretation, and therefore the content, of ECHR rights. As Letsas puts it:

> The European Court has the final authority to rule on whether a state (through its statutory provisions, case law, or executive acts) violates abstract moral principles. What it rules on is inevitably an abstract issue of principle which it then must apply to all Europeans.[64]

True, the ECHR is formally an international human rights treaty that does not require States Parties to implement its rights in a uniform fashion. The judgments of the ECtHR are *declaratory* and leave it to the State Party to select the appropriate measure by which to conform with the judgment. Moreover, states are bound only by the *decisional* content of the judgment. Yet the authority of the judgments of the ECtHR within the States Parties make the ECHR "system" closer to those of constitutional regimes. Indeed, national courts routinely give direct effect to the rights of the ECHR and the judgments of the ECtHR. Direct effect means that the rights and the judgments are binding within national law and may be invoked by individuals against all state institutions, whether legislative, executive or judicial. The authority of the ECHR remains exceptional in international human rights law to that extent at least. As Letsas rightly points out, "unlike the role of human rights in the work of international human rights bodies, the purpose of the ECHR is not to set acceptable political goals that all states have a reason to promote".[65] ECHR rights as human rights are not, as Beitz argues, *pro tanto* reasons for action. Rather, in light of their authority in national legal orders, they are *conclusory* reasons for its subjects (public institutions) to take action.

Further, the "practice" of the ECHR cannot be reduced to its special status in national legal orders. In addition, one must address the adjudicatory function of the ECtHR. This function implies that the content of those rights is specified in the course of the applications lodged by individuals throughout Europe. The ECtHR not only must specify the interest(s) that those abstract rights protect in light of the claims made by the applicant; it must also balance them against normative considerations put forward by the respondent state. In the words of Waldron, a court is an "adversarial institution",[66] so that the balance of reasons defended by the court must be responsive to various kinds of argument provided by the parties. I would like to suggest that this component offers the appropriate conditions for the ethical approach to human rights. This supranational judicial arena provides us with

---

64 Letsas, *A Theory of Interpretation of the European Convention on Human Rights*, 10.
65 Ibid., 36.
66 Waldron, *Law and Disagreement*, 23.

Introduction 17

an additional layer of justificatory reasons *within* the practice and therefore an optimal "material of construction"[67] for normative theorizing.

1.3.4 Claim four

There is a further premise that should be clarified before starting the investigation. The project of normatively theorizing the practice of the ECtHR supposes that one can address the specificities of an institution while maintaining that some form of normative objectivity may be reached in doing so. Yet if human rights are moral properties the elucidation of which is conceptually prior to the specification of their duties, one has then to explain why we should address the legal and judicial practice of human rights in the first place. The objective status of the moral "ought" of human rights must therefore be properly accounted for if one wants to address the practice while leaving their normative force in the dark.

My fourth claim is that the *constructivist* framework in moral and political theory has the resources to justify addressing the (legal and judicial) practices first. Two central features of constructivism may be mentioned as a matter of introduction. On the one hand, constructivism as a meta-ethical framework can adopt the premise that human rights are primarily a political, legal and institutional construct that plays a specific and contingent role in social and political (and therefore international) relations. This is because constructivists assign priority to justifying the practical role of public norms. As for Rawls' conception of justice, the primary role of human rights theory is practical, not theoretical. As Freeman puts it, "this contrasts with an epistemological point of view of the detached observer who seeks moral truth by inquiring into the way the world (or all possible worlds) really is or ought to be".[68] As such, the constructivist framework can account for the need to interpret and conceptualize an independent normative practice *pace* Beitz. In the case of the ECHR, this step notably implies capturing the status of the ECHR in domestic legal orders as this status reveals how the ECHR has been domesticated by the democratic process.

On the other hand, and as indicated above, the normativity of the ECHR cannot be reduced to its special status in national legal orders. In addition, one must address the adjudicatory function of the ECtHR as the content of those rights is specified in the course of the applications lodged by individuals from throughout Europe. This is because adjudication by the ECtHR authoritatively supports the normative role that the ECHR plays domestically. Since constructivism conceives normative principles as those that would obtain if we were to engage in an "idealized process of deliberation"[69] from within our institutional

---

67 Street, "Constructivism About Reasons", 210.
68 Freeman, "Constructivism, Facts, and Moral Justification", 49.
69 Bagnoli, "Constructivism in Metaethics".

18 *Introduction*

practices,[70] the reasoning of the ECtHR (its justificatory dimension) has to be selected as the relevant practical standpoint. However, the ultimate aim of constructivism remains: to provide individuals with norms which they can find reasonably acceptable and with which they can regularly comply for genuinely moral reasons – that is, norms they would not endorse simply because it is the best compromise to pursue their own interests. Consequently, the attention devoted to concrete legal and judicial practices comprises the deeper aim of reconciling free and rational individuals with the institutions that govern their social relations – to "actualize" our freedoms within a given institutional legal and political ordering. As Song puts it:

> The task of political philosophy is to help us see the way in which our political institutions are reasonable and rational, and when this is clear to us, we need not be simply resigned to them, but can embrace them as meeting our fundamental human needs.[71]

In the case of the ECHR, this step requires an examination of how the ECtHR justifies the enlargement or the restriction of the scope of ECHR rights, and how this *legal* justification could be sustained by a *moral* justification acceptable to all. Legal and judicial practice provides us with a space of reasons – a practical standpoint that lends itself to moral reconstruction and evaluation in the constructivist sense.

If Rawls seminally developed constructivism in contemporary political theory, ethical theorists have more recently elaborated on the process of justification on which constructivism relies and how it may be used in other practical contexts. Following Sharon Street's account, constructivism does not just imply a hypothetical procedure to establish normative truths. It also implies that "the truth of a normative claim consists in that claim's being entailed from within the practical point of view".[72] The very fact of making a normative claim – to take a sufficient reason to act – itself sets standards by which other reasons for action may possibly be endorsed from within a practical standpoint. Her account offers us a fruitful framework for reflecting normatively from *within* the space of reasons that judicial practice implies. Note that this constructivist project is independent of the

---

70 Rawls famously defined an institution as "a public system of rules which defines offices and positions with their rights and duties, powers and immunities, and the like. These rules specify certain forms of action as permissible, others as forbidden; and they provide for a certain penalties and defences, and so on, when violations occur. As examples of institutions, or more generally social practices, we may think of games and rituals, trials and parliaments, markets and systems of property. An institution may be thought of in two ways: first, as an abstract object – that is, as a possible form of conduct expressed by a system of rules; and, second, as the realization in the thought and conduct of certain persons at a certain time and place of the actions specified by these rules": Rawls, *A Theory of Justice*, 48.

71 Song, "Rawls' Liberal Principle of Legitimacy", 171.

72 Street, "What Is Constructivism in Ethics and Metaethics?", 371.

Introduction 19

theorization of human rights law as a social object – a theory that would account for the conditions of its existence *qua* law.[73] Human rights may be justified by moral reasoning without necessarily being themselves understood as moral values. As such, the ECtHR can be subject to moral exploration in the constructivist sense without assuming strong stands in analytic jurisprudence.

1.4 The neglect of the ECHR in human rights theory

Having introduced the object of investigation and the overall aim of justification in constructivist terms, I now return to the current standing of human rights theory and its limitations. Despite their contradictions, ethical and political conceptions of human rights share an under-noticed commonality: they are locked in a global perspective. True, human rights theorists engaging with practice acknowledge the diversity of "practices" and the resulting difficulty of delimiting their object. As Valentini puts it:

> Should we look at international covenants and charters? Should we take what activists think of as human rights as definitive of the concept? It immediately appears that what may legitimately be defined as a public culture of human rights is not an easy task.[74]

Still, the core norms against which philosophical accounts are judged typically consist either of the lists of rights enshrined in global covenants (such as the UDHR and the UN covenants) or of some salient overarching pattern – most prominently, coercive or soft external intervention (such as the imposition of sanctions, military invasions, occupation by multilateral organizations or states). Beitz's "global political life" and the list of "paradigms of implementation" are a salient illustration of this tendency.[75] Beitz's contention that human rights are better understood as political rather than legal ("most international and transnational efforts to promote and defend human rights are more accurately understood as political rather than legal"[76]) irremediably tends to discard the search for an evaluatively rich account of their foundations. Otherwise put, this descriptive standpoint inevitably shapes the normative *desideratum* of human rights. Yet the normative content derived directly depends on the descriptive standpoint adopted and one may question the relevance of Beitz's model here too – that is, in the selection of facts and practices from which the concept of human rights is inducted.

Indeed, given the localized and dynamic character of human rights practice outlined above, the global standpoint is incomplete. This applies, in particular,

---

73 For the premises of such a project, see Besson, "Human Rights: Ethical, Political . . . or Legal? First Steps in a Legal Theory of Human Rights". See also Besson, "Human Rights and Democracy in a Global Context: Decoupling and Recoupling".
74 Valentini, "In What Sense Are Human Rights Political?", 186.
75 Beitz, *The Idea of Human Rights*, Chapter 5.
76 Ibid., 40.

20   *Introduction*

to the legal and judicial dimension of human rights. The *subsidiary* nature of international human rights law implies that their normativity is found at both the national and supranational levels without any necessary connection. Indeed, "the enforcement of human rights is in principle a domestic responsibility and only subsidiarily an international one".[77] The regional regime of the ECHR is an instance of that localized and dynamic practice of human rights. Of course, the absence of a necessary connection should not obfuscate the role of the ECtHR as ultimate interpreter. Yet subsidiarity is also found at this (supranational) level when the ECtHR allocates a margin of appreciation and leaves it to the "better placed" state to decide. Therefore, in order to capture the practice fully, the interaction between the two levels needs to be precisely debunked.

Regrettably, however, the practice of the ECtHR has so far been neglected in the normative theorizing of human rights. This is not to say that the ECHR "system" has never been subjected to normative theorizing. George Letsas has argued for a liberal defence of the interpretation of ECHR rights based on a Rawlsian framework with a view to revising the ECtHR's use of the margin of appreciation in respect of Articles 8 to 11.[78] This is an internal debate as to how the ECtHR allocates the right to rule to States Parties in interpreting pan-European morality on sensible moral matters. As we shall see in Chapter 8, irrespective of the clarifications provided by Letsas and his fine analysis of the margin of appreciation doctrine in the case law of the ECtHR, much is needed to support the idea that the ECtHR should apply moral standards identical to those we could expect from richer conceptions of liberal justice within the state.

The other body of literature concentrates on the normative legitimacy of judicial review by the ECtHR. The argument is not new and has been raised in the constitutional context. Waldron and others have raised the concern that judicial review – in the case of the nation state primarily – conflicts in several ways with the morality of democracy and majoritarian voting.[79] It is difficult, however, to *a priori* identify the function of a (supranational) court as a constraint on internal democracy without an assessment of the localized reasons that the ECtHR gives for enlarging or restricting the scope of an ECHR right. Indeed, recent attempts to reactivate this argument do not reconstruct the reasoning of the ECtHR in great detail.[80] The ECtHR is particularly concerned with democracy since "democratic necessity" is involved in its formal review of the arguments given by States Parties to justify the limitation of Articles 8 to 11, as we shall see in greater length in Chapter 8.

More importantly for us, there has been no attempt to place the practice of the ECtHR in human rights theory. Despite the proliferation of historical works on

---

77 Besson, "The Human Right to Democracy – A Moral Defence with a Legal Nuance", 17.
78 Letsas, *A Theory of Interpretation of the European Convention on Human Rights*, Chapters 4 and 5.
79 Waldron, "A Right-Based Critique of Constitutional Rights"; see also Waldron, "The Core of the Case Against Judicial Review".
80 See, in particular, Wheatley, "On the Legitimate Authority of International Human Rights Bodies".

Introduction 21

the ECHR – with their emphasis on how "the ECHR drastically improved on the limited declarative purpose of UN instruments"[81] and the assumption that "a muscular rights regime first emerged"[82] in Europe – the implications of this practice for the ethical/political debate remain insufficiently studied. Besson suggests the following explanation:

> One explanation for the legal neglect in human rights may lie in a fundamental distinction made in all or most human rights theories: the opposition between concrete practice of human rights and the abstract standards of human rights. In fact, most human rights theorists identify that opposition as central to their account and situate the legal question in that opposition. They usually claim that they are (also) about human rights as legal and political practice and not (only) about human rights as abstract moral standards.[83]

The driving thought here is that the legal and judicial practice of human rights asks for a novel balancing between the political and the moral conceptions as philosophical resources for the normative theorizing of human rights. On the one hand, if human rights are *rights*, and not just interests or values, they have a dynamic character found in the judicial context where their duties are recognized, specified and allocated. I therefore assume that their conceptual structure *qua* rights should help us in distinguishing the practice of ECHR rights. In this sense, I follow the premise of Raz and Besson that "for a right to be recognized, a sufficient threshold must be established and weighed against other interests and other considerations with which it might conflict in a particular social context".[84] On the other hand, I use the concept of rights as the intermediary between interest and duty as a *heuristic device* only – that is, to distinguish the practice of ECHR rights among other forms of normative practice. True, the ECtHR uses the language of interests and duties in its routine of review. Yet I do not believe that such concepts can account for the normative breadth of ECHR rights in their legal and judicial specification when it comes to the quest of moral justification in the constructivist sense. As Edmundson puts it, an interest theory "does not, by itself, identify or distinguish among interests. It does not tell us what interests are, or whether all are important enough to generate correlative duties".[85] When the ECtHR addresses the claims of litigants, identifies and specifies the interest(s) correlative to the right, it specifies the normative content of those highly abstract

---

81 Cohen, "The Holocaust and the 'Human Rights Revolution': A Reassessment", 63. See also the contributions in Christoffersen and Madsen (eds), *The European Court of Human Rights between Law and Politics*.

82 Mazower, *No Enchanted Palace: The End of Empire and the Ideological Origins of the United Nations*, 8.

83 Besson, "Human Rights: Ethical, Political . . . or Legal? First Steps in a Legal Theory of Human Rights", 215.

84 Besson, "The Human Right to Democracy – A Moral Defence with a Legal Nuance", 8. For the seminal account, see Raz, "Legal Rights"; see also Raz, "On the Nature of Rights", 194.

85 Edmundson, *An Introduction to Rights*, 98.

22 *Introduction*

and indeterminate rights. Adjudication supposes an elaboration, in justificatory terms, of the reasons why such a right should be protected. In other words, examining the adjudication of the ECtHR opens the door for a characterization of the practice in non-functional terms.

1.5 The ECHR: ethical and political?

In abstracto, the ECHR "system" is no exception to the norm: ECHR rights play the typical role of standards of assessment and criticism of domestic institutions. This is the case when the ECtHR authoritatively interprets an ECHR right and when the respondent State Party executes the judgment, or when individuals invoke ECHR rights in national judicial proceedings. The ECtHR is a *subsidiary* instrument for the protection of basic civil and political rights enshrined in national constitutions. As a result, one could approach the ECHR via the resources of the political conception founded on the practical role that ECHR rights play: ECHR rights are entitlements against public institutions more generally (national, regional and international).[86] One difference, of course, is that here human rights are *rights*: the ECtHR recognizes, specifies and allocates their corresponding duties that States Parties fulfil.

Again, however, the normativity of the ECHR cannot be reduced to a functional account, albeit legal. Human rights are irremediably indeterminate and their concretization in the case law implies that the ECtHR addresses and specifies their underlying interests in substantive terms. Judicial law specifies the normative content of human rights. As a result, the normative basis that serves the role that ECHR rights play is already within the practice as a form of justificatory reasoning *qua* judicial reasoning. This is where we need another resource to account for the practice of ECHR rights – the ethical one – but it will have to be *legislated*, as the constructivists put it, by the standards found within the practice. As a result, the practice of ECHR rights leaves us with enough space to employ both the ethical and the political conceptions of human rights taken as philosophical resources. In other words, an institution is not just a system of assigned offices and roles. As Waldron puts it:

> An institution is not just a sociological construct; it is a human entity that confronts pleas, human claims, human proposals, and human petitions. And in that confrontation there is room for respect and dignity, for degradation and insult, and neither of these may be ignored in our theoretical assessment of the institutions we have . . .: we need a sophisticated philosophical understanding of the layers of values that are implicated in the assessment of our political institutions.[87]

Again, it does not follow that the conceptions of human rights we have do not have the basic conceptual and normative resources to account for the legal and

---

86 Besson, "The Egalitarian Dimension of Human Rights", 37–8.
87 Waldron, "Political Political Theory: An Inaugural Lecture", 13.

Introduction 23

judicial ECHR rights. Rather, we need to specify how those resources may be used to capture the legal and judicial practice of human rights before engaging with normative theorizing. I therefore fully agree with Besson that:

> not paying sufficient attention to the legal nature of human rights and by conflating the law of human rights with their politics and practice, current human rights theories miss on a central component of the normative practice of human rights. Worse, they deprive themselves from essential theoretical insights about the nature of normative practices and, hence, of resources in their effort to bridge the gap between human rights as critical moral standards and the political practice of human rights.[88]

1.6 The justificatory deficit of human rights *qua* law

Human rights today, no one will argue, are in good shape. They are the "lingua franca"[89] of an increasingly interconnected political, legal and cultural era. They increasingly serve as a guiding set of norms not only for the proper conduct of political societies, but also as standards for monitoring the behaviour of transnational companies, global institutions, and the like. In various contexts, they serve as an "aspirational and motivational resource".[90] In the ECHR "system", they authoritatively define the limits of what states can do to their subjects in 47 European legal and political orders. Beitz is correct in his view that human rights give reasons for different actions, but he does not circumscribe the post-national order(s) in which the legal and judicial dimensions of human rights prevail. This legal and judicial practice stands in urgent need of legitimacy. The ECHR "system" presupposes institutions, national and international, and those institutions together shape the lives of millions of persons by virtue of the authority devoted to ECHR rights in national legal orders. The need for justification is therefore inextricably connected with issues of legal adjudication as a result. As Buchanan puts it:

> The rationale for avoiding the issue of justification is no longer cogent. The very success of the institutionalization of human rights makes the issue of legitimacy and hence of justification inescapable. The more seriously the international legal system takes the protection of human rights and the more teeth this commitment is, the more problematic the lack of a credible public justification for human-rights norms becomes.[91]

To recall, the principled normative task is that "discovering the conditions of legitimacy is traditionally conceived as finding a way to justify a political system

---

88 Besson, "Human Rights: Ethical, Political . . . or Legal? First Steps in a Legal Theory of Human Rights", 217.
89 Tasioulas, "The Moral Reality of Human Rights", 75.
90 Baynes, "Discourse Ethics and the Political Conception of Human Rights", 17.
91 Buchanan, "Human Rights and the Legitimacy of the International Order", 41.

24   *Introduction*

to everyone who is required to live under it".[92] Rawls wrote something similar about his "basic structure" of society: "the basic structure of society and its public policies are to be justifiable to all citizens, as the principle of political legitimacy requires".[93] We should strive to find the best reasons, if any, to support and justify the institutional structures in which individuals find themselves to live. In my view, this forms the core of the exercise of normative political theory inherited from Rawls as it can apply to the ECHR: to reconcile our freedoms with the post-national institutional structures in which we find ourselves embedded. In taking the perspective of moral agents, the enterprise of justification is therefore an inherently *liberal* project that has to be assumed from the onset. Valentini put it as follows:

> Liberals are committed to public justification; the requirement of public justification prompts us to design our normative theories on the basis of the values already implicit in our shared practices; but the move from the values underpinning our practices to the principles that should govern them requires first-order moral reasoning.[94]

This may explain why rights theorists like Raz tend to favour a political conception of human rights. Their limited objective of the conceptual analysis of human rights as the intermediary between interests and duties is foreign to the sense of justification endorsed by constructivists. As Raz explains in a past article, moral interests differ from rights:

> There is no right to be loved, and none of the virtues can be understood in terms of rights. So, concern for the interests of individuals does not translate itself into principles of rights. At least it cannot be exhausted by them.[95]

It will be important therefore to specify the sense of *justification* implied in Rawlsian constructivism along the way.

To conclude, there is no good reason to think that the legal and judicial dimension of human rights practice should be an exception to the burden of justification. As Buchanan emphasizes, "human rights are understood as requiring justification, and the justification appeals to basic human interests, to the idea that these basic interests ought to be protected, to assumptions about what threatens these interests . . .".[96] Because the concept of human rights is also specified within legal and judicial frameworks, the task of normative theorists is to find a way to render their normative basis responsive to the political and legal practice

---

92 Nagel, *Equality and Partiality*, 33.
93 Rawls, *Political Liberalism*, 224.
94 Valentini, "In What Sense Are Human Rights Political?", 187.
95 Raz, "Rights and Politics", 31. On the Razian concept, see also Raz, "On the Nature of Rights". See also Raz, "Legal Rights".
96 Buchanan, "Equality and Human Rights", 74.

that modern human rights have generated, and thereby realize the ideal of reconciliation just outlined.

1.7 The plan of the book

The book is divided into nine chapters (including this introductory chapter). In Chapter 2 ("Ethical theories of human rights and their practice-independence"), I explore in more depth the moral/political debate in normative human rights theory, starting by reconstructing James Griffin's account of personhood. By defining human rights theorizing as the identification of rights-holders' interests, Griffin maintains what I call the *practice-independent* approach to human rights. I then survey a second ethical account, namely that of Rainer Forst. Both Griffin and Forst aim to preserve an independent moral basis ("the right to justification" and "human dignity", respectively). I take this point as distinctive of the moral conception for my further investigation of the ECHR.

In Chapter 3 ("Political theories and their practice-dependence"), I turn to the political conception of human rights and analyze specifically Charles Beitz's account. I also address Joseph Raz's conception in a second wave, but since Raz's account is limited to two articles and overlaps with that of Beitz, I only shed light on how Raz differs from Beitz and how both relate to Rawls' original account. In harsh contrast to Griffin, Beitz argues that a deeper layer of morality is not necessary to construct the idea of human rights. I show that this argument is contingent upon the kind of practice selected by Beitz. Beitz can eliminate the need for moral reasoning only by concentrating on the political dimension of human rights. The end result of Chapters 2 and 3 is a *mutual exclusion* pertaining to the status of facts and practices in the theorizing of human rights. The project of reconciliation through law is premised on this exclusion.

In Chapter 4 ("Theorizing human rights: a constructivist proposal"), I show how a constructivist approach to moral and political norms can reconcile the Beitzian specification of human rights as tied to the international state system, while preserving the core idea of Griffin shared by Forst that human rights are grounded in a layer of moral reasoning. On the one hand, Rawlsian constructivism takes institutions as the primary objects of justification. As such, it can account for the political and legal practice of human rights (hence their international dimension *pace* Beitz). On the other hand, constructivism can account for their special status as important moral rights through the public basis of justification that it is striving to find. I finally lay down three central methodological steps associated with the constructivist enterprise so construed and outline their application to human rights law.

In Chapter 5 ("The ECHR in historical perspective"), I turn to the ECHR and the ECtHR specifically and introduce this legal institution in historical terms. For the sake of concision, I divide the chapter into four major historical segments. First, I examine the burgeoning social and political process in the late 1940s to the ECtHR's operational establishment in 1959. Second, I review more specifically the development of the ECtHR (1959–69) as a judicial institution. The jurisdiction

26   *Introduction*

of the ECtHR was confirmed in 1958 with the necessary eight acceptances. The third segment, from the mid-1970s to the early 1990s, reveals the growing role of the ECHR in the legal and political life of the States Parties together with the increasing judicial autonomy of the ECtHR. Fourth, I examine the explosion of applications and the need for structural reform (from the early 1990s to date) partially addressed in the last protocols to the ECHR.

In Chapter 6 ("The normativity of ECHR law"), I turn to the legal normativity of the ECHR. To capture this normativity, I first introduce human rights law *qua* international law – that is, how this body of law is understood within the broader conceptual and terminological field of international law. I empha-size the discontinuum of human rights law from the classical understanding of public international law. Second, I introduce the special normativity of the ECHR *qua* international treaty in the legal orders of States Parties by captur-ing their legal status in domestic law. The crucial point is that most of its 47 States Parties have given direct effect to ECHR rights and the judgments of the ECtHR in their respective legal orders. In doing so, I present how the rela-tionship between the ECtHR and national courts articulates. Third, I address the limited judicial powers of the ECtHR as an international judicial organ, and finally I address the widely expressed claim that the role of the ECtHR amounts to that of a constitutional court.

In Chapter 7 ("Interpretation at the ECtHR: setting the stage"), I approach the adjudication process of the ECtHR more closely through the canons of inter-pretation it has developed over the years. If the ECtHR is clearly dismissive of conventional doctrines of interpretation, it does not have a uniform methodol-ogy for making explicit the meaning of contested terms, but rather what I call *interpretative poles* in which the *teleological* and the *evolutive* prevail. In terms of balancing, the ECtHR has not made explicit the standard that can outweigh the ECHR right under scrutiny. The application of a formal three-pronged test to justify interference is fuzzy. Moreover, the conditions for the use of the margin of appreciation do not add to clarity. In other words, the set of formal rules, routinely applied by the ECtHR by reference to the wording of the restriction clauses, falls short of informing us of the reasons for protecting the rights and the reasons for their restrictions. As a result, we need to conduct a right-based and case-based analysis, to which I turn in the next chapter.

In Chapter 8 ("Balancing and justification at the ECtHR: the pivotal concept of 'democratic necessity'"), I turn to the balancing of the ECtHR in respect of a specific range of provisions (Articles 8 to 11). If the *formal* design of the balanc-ing is opaque, there is enough, I show, in the substantive reasoning of the ECtHR in the case law to capture a form of *practical reason* – a set of powerful reasons by which the actions of states and individuals are judged – that may be subject to normative exploration. More precisely, I show that the third step of "demo-cratic society" plays a crucial normative role in informing the balancing. First, "democratic society" helps the ECtHR to identify the rights-holders whose con-tribution to the realization of that society is particularly central. This prominence leads the ECtHR to review their claim(s) with a particular scrutiny and rigour.

Introduction 27

Conversely, it identifies rights-holders who do not play such a crucial role and who do not qualify for such treatment. Second, and correlatively, the more the alleged interference of the respondent State Party endangers the core interests that form the conception, the more the ECtHR restricts the margin of appreciation devoted to States Parties. Third, the practical reason helps in striking a balance in that prominent rights outweigh other rights in the event of conflict with other ECHR rights.

In Chapter 9 ("Conclusion: constructing the normative foundations of the ECHR"), I show how the "practical reason" of the ECtHR can be justified by the standards of democratic theory and therefore reconcile the apparent mutual exclusion of the ethical and political conceptions defined in Chapters 2 and 3. Three analytical steps are distinguished in the reconciliation process. First, I reconstruct the role of the ECHR as it results from the examination of the authority of its rights and the judgments of the ECtHR in domestic legal orders. Second, I turn to the "deeper layer of reasons" that operates in the balancing of the ECtHR. Relying on Thomas Christiano's egalitarian argument for democracy, I argue that the reasoning of the ECtHR can be illuminated and justified in the constructivist sense by a unifying moral conception of democracy *qua* internal sovereignty. I distinguish two aspects of this conception: *equality in deliberation* and *equality in representation*. Finally, I establish my core argument by bridging the two aspects of ECHR rights *qua* international human rights (with special reference to Articles 8 to 11 and Article 3 of Protocol 1), consolidating democracy *qua* internal sovereignty and, by the same token, reinforcing the commitment to our status of political equals in the legal and political orders of the States Parties.

2 Ethical theories of human rights and their practice-independence

In Chapter 1, I articulated a distinction between ethical and political conceptions of human rights by stressing the role of facts and practices in theorizing the structure and content of those rights. I qualified James Griffin's theory as *practice-independent* and Charles Beitz's theory as *practice-dependent*. This distinction is approximate and needs to be examined in greater detail. While Chapter 3 addresses the political conception, I reconstruct in this chapter the moral conception – also sometimes termed "orthodox", "humanist", "traditional", or even "naturalistic". I concentrate on James Griffin's account of "personhood" and also survey Rainer Forst's account. Griffin's account is privileged for two reasons. On the one hand, his account has been seminal in the field of normative human rights theory in the past decade. His book initiated a significant debate among moral and political legal philosophers.[1] I aim to work from within this ongoing debate. On the other hand, Griffin's account most clearly exemplifies the practice-independent dimension of human rights theorizing that I seek to preserve.

In my close examination of Griffin's account of personhood, I first explain that despite Griffin's commitment to consider various aspects of human rights practice, the diagnosis of indeterminacy and the articulation of personhood as a remedying notion obtain at the level of ordinary moral reasoning only. This *modality* of reasoning is necessary and central to the enterprise of human rights theorizing because, in his view, human rights refer to a distinctive moral category. As a result, the role of normative facts and practices is confined to that of a test case. This is particularly the case with the legal and judicial dimensions of human rights practice. I aim to show, however, that such modality is independent of the substantive claim that personhood obtains irrespective of social, political or legal relations (the inherence view). I stress this distinction in order to query whether one could apply Griffin's practice-independent modality of reasoning to the normative role of human rights independently captured – that is, whether the reconstruction of political or legal practices could inform, but not determine, the nature, structure and content of those rights.

---

1 See the contributions in *Ethics* 120 (2010).

Ethical theories and practice-independence 29

Second, I turn to the three main critiques of Griffin's account in the recent literature: the *internal*, the *external*, and the *right-based*. The internal critique, owed to Raz, targets the difficulty of personhood to account fully for the most basic human rights such as the right not to be tortured. The external critique, owed to Beitz, targets the practical role of (international) human rights that Griffin's account does not address. The right-based critique, owed to Tasioulas and Raz, concerns the distinction between *values* or *interests* on the one hand and *rights* on the other. As Tasioulas puts it, Griffin takes "rights out of human rights".[2] Then I further suggest how one could preserve Griffin's independent moral reasoning while taking into account and specifying the external and right-based critiques by reference to the legal and judicial dimension of human rights.

Finally, I turn to Rainer Forst's account of human rights and critically identify his contribution to the field. Forst's distinctive contribution is an attempt to avoid the substantive content of Griffin while preserving an independent moral basis by introducing another deontological threshold, that of *mutual justifiability*. By contrast to Griffin, Forst's account is informed by the long practice of rights starting with the liberal revolutions of the seventeenth and eighteenth centuries. As such, Forst's reconstruction paves the way for a third, *practice-responsive* approach to human rights theorizing in that the reconstruction is conditioned, but not determined, by legal and political practice – a constructivist approach I develop in more detail in Chapter 4.

2.1 Griffin's moral conception

Let us now concentrate on Griffin's seminal contribution to normative human rights theory. In his book, *On Human Rights*, Griffin starts by emphasizing the long decline of the theological tradition of natural law: "there was continued secularization of the doctrine of natural law and natural rights, following the expanding role of human reason. There was the closely related abandonment of much in the way of metaphysical and epistemological background for them".[3] Modern human rights theorists still aim to *derive* their account of human rights from more basic principles. However, this is neither a *metaphysical* nor a *logical* derivation. As Hume, Kant and G.H. Moore have shown, a metaphysical derivation from the descriptive to the normative (from an "is" to an "ought") is fallacious (the "naturalistic fallacy"). If at all, the derivation takes place entirely within the normative realm. As Griffin explains, "my notions of human nature and human agent are already within the normative circle, and there is no obvious fallacy involved in deriving rights from notions as evaluatively rich as they are".[4] Therefore, it is because we *value* some aspect of human life and

---

2 Tasioulas, "Taking Rights out of Human Rights".
3 Griffin, *On Human Rights*, 11.
4 Ibid., 35.

30 Ethical theories and practice-independence

activity that we want to protect it by generating right claims, as Griffin does with the personhood account: "because we attach such high value to our individual personhood, we see its domain of exercise as privileged and protected".[5] In other words, he uses normative derivation as a "proposal based on a hunch that this way of remedying the indeterminacy of the term will best suit its role in ethics".[6]

2.1.1 Griffin's diagnosis of indeterminacy

Chapter 2 ("First Steps in an Account of Human Rights") further develops the claim that the concept of human rights we have today is strikingly similar to that of the Enlightenment:

> The notion of human rights that emerged by the end of the Enlightenment – what can reasonably be called the Enlightenment notion – is the notion we have today. There has been no theoretical development of the idea itself since then.[7]

Therefore, Griffin partly uses the history of moral and political ideas to make the diagnosis of indeterminacy: "the idea is still that of a right we have simply in virtue of being human, with no further explanation of what 'human' means here".[8] As Tasioulas explains, Griffin "starts not from a prior commitment to an off-the-shelf general moral theory but from the rich and complex discourse of human rights that originates in the late medieval period. And it strives for only as much higher-level explanation as that subject matter can plausibly sustain".[9]

However, this historical standpoint is clearly not sufficient to fully make the diagnosis of indeterminacy. Griffin repeatedly refers to current discourses on the notion across disciplines and domains and points to some underlying disagreement that reinforces the need for a more determinate concept. He takes the example of the UN Secretary-General claiming that "the opportunity to decide the number and spacing of their children is a basic human right" of parents. Griffin argues that we lack a ruling standard if we were to disagree over the meaning of the utterance "human rights": "we agree that human rights are derived from 'human standing', or 'human nature', but have virtually no agreement about the relevant sense of these two criteria-providing terms".[10] Otherwise put, the core concept remains, but its content is largely left unexplained.

---

5 Ibid., 33.
6 Ibid., 39.
7 Ibid., 13.
8 Ibid.
9 Tasioulas, "Taking Rights out of Human Rights", 649.
10 Griffin, *On Human Rights*, 16.

Ethical theories and practice-independence 31

At the level of rights theory, the need for determinacy is further reinforced in Griffin's view by the pre-eminence of *structural* theories of rights such as Feinberg's rights as *claims*, Dworkin's rights as *trumps* or Nozick's rights as *side-constraints*. If those accounts imply non-functional elements – such as the *separability of persons* in Nozick's case – they are insufficient to respond to the justificatory deficit of human rights. As Griffin puts it, "the largely structural and legal-functional accounts are short on explanatory power".[11] Later in the chapter, Griffin also draws on Raz's interest theory of rights and on *exclusionary reasons* for grounding a duty corresponding with a right. Here, too, Griffin emphasizes that the criterion for human rights is that it fails to provide a "sufficient condition for the existence of a right".[12]

2.1.2 Griffin's practice-independent account

Later in Chapter 2, Griffin presents the basis of his remedying notion of personhood as protecting our status of normative agents. Again, Griffin claims that he does not want to start with "an overarching principle, or principles, or an authoritative decision procedure"[13] to build his normative account of human rights. Interestingly, he wants to favour a "bottom-up approach" and suggests that "we need not treat the use of the term in present social life as beyond revision, but we need some understanding of what human rights are said to be derivable, and their social use is the most likely source".[14] Yet, the initial articulation of personhood seems to require nothing more than a form of independent ordinary moral reasoning:

> We human beings have a conception of ourselves and of our past and our future. We reflect and assess. We form pictures of what a good life would be – often, it is true, only on a small scale but occasionally also on a large scale. And we try to realize those pictures. This is what we mean by a distinctively human existence – distinctive so far as we know.[15]

Not only does Griffin identify those distinctive characteristics of human beings, he also claims that we *value* them to a very high extent: ". . . and we value our status as human beings especially high, often more highly than even our happiness. This status centers on our being agents – deliberating, assessing, choosing, and acting to make what we see as a good life for ourselves".[16] This formulation of the human person is the foundational basis of Griffin's *substantive* account of

11 Ibid., 21.
12 Ibid., 56.
13 Ibid., 29.
14 Ibid., 29.
15 Ibid., 32.
16 Ibid.

32 *Ethical theories and practice-independence*

human rights for those rights "can be seen as protections of our human standing or, as I shall put it, our personhood".[17]

Having identified the core notion of personhood, Griffin decomposes it into three main components.

- first, an *autonomy* condition: one must "choose one's path through life – that is, not be dominated or controlled by someone else".[18]
- second, a *minimum provision condition*: one must "at least have a certain minimum education and information. And, having chosen one's path, one must be then able to act; that is, one must have at least the minimum provision of resources and capabilities that it takes".[19]
- third, a *liberty condition*: "others must also not forcibly stop one from pursuing what one sees as a worthwhile life".[20]

If those three conditions are met, the value of personhood is realized.

Now this conception of the human person under the personhood account is sufficient, in Griffin's view, to derive the rights enshrined in "most of the conventional lists of human rights":[21] life, torture, security of person, political decision, free expression, assembly, free press, worship, education and minimum provision. The "generative capacities"[22] of personhood are therefore the *substantive* basis of Griffin's moral account. Moreover, personhood is also able to distinguish human rights from richer concepts such as human *good* or human *flourishing*. If we were trying to ground those richer concepts, we would not use the language of rights. While they may overlap, Griffin argues that personhood "imposes an obvious constraint on their content".[23] Human rights refer to what is necessary for the exercise of normative agency, but not beyond.

Later in the chapter (pp. 44–8), Griffin further specifies his conception of agency. Most importantly, being a normative agent involves the capacity of all human beings to "choose and to pursue our conception of a worthwhile life" and this is *distinctive* of human agents:

> Anyone who has the capacity to identify the good, whatever the extent of the capacity and whatever its sources, has what I mean by "a conception of a worthwhile life"; they have ideas, some of them reliable, about what makes a life better or worse.[24]

---

17 Ibid., 33.
18 Ibid.
19 Ibid.
20 Ibid.
21 Ibid.
22 Ibid.
23 Ibid., 34.
24 Ibid., 46.

Ethical theories and practice-independence 33

It is important to note that it is the *capacity* for normative agency that is foundational, not the rationality, quality or quantity of ideas and reasoning processed. However, the capacity itself, clearly, is not sufficient for its fruitful exercise. As Griffin emphasizes, "the value behind human rights is not just the dignity of being able to be this sort of agent but also of being one".[25] With the supplementary value of *liberty*, agents should be able to realize their self-defined life, and *minimum provision*, which makes sure we can exercise our capacity for normative agency. The link between minimal provision and liberty is clearly instrumental.

In Chapter 8 ("Autonomy") and Chapter 9 ("Liberty"), Griffin specifies *autonomy* and *liberty*. To better understand autonomy, Griffin contrasts his account with the kind of "patient autonomy" that equals autonomy with consent, on the one hand, and with the kind of Kantian autonomy that requires a pure and unflawed inferential reasoning with no alternation from feeling or attitude, on the other. However, Griffin maintains that *rational reasoning* is an essential component of the exercise of autonomy: "rationality enters importantly into the identification of human ends and interests, that judgments about them are subject to standards of correctness and incorrectness".[26] In other words, the foundational basis of the personhood account – that is, the interest in a self-authored life – is an *objective* statement in that it can be subject to standards of *correctness* and *incorrectness*.

In order to better understand liberty, Griffin argues that negative liberty (following Mill's principle) does not suffice to honour the value of personhood. Yet liberty does not require the *realization* of the worthwhile life either, but only its *pursuit*:

> What the *pursuit* of a conception of a worthwhile life largely requires, and what a society might sometimes have an obligation to help provide, are the all-purpose means to pursue any plausible conception of a worthwhile life . . . . To what level of all-purpose means? To the level needed to live as a normative agent.[27]

This implies, most importantly, that liberty can be unequally distributed if it fulfils the conditions of a normative agent:

> In general, we must accept, and build our lives from, our range of options with which fortune has endowed it. Society cannot do much to alter it, and the life of a normative agent does not require more than this.[28]

25 Ibid., 47.
26 Ibid., 154.
27 Ibid., 162.
28 Ibid., 163.

34 *Ethical theories and practice-independence*

As a result, there is clearly a *material constraint* on the abstract right to liberty that personhood entails. Griffin also identifies a *formal constraint* on the right to equality, which requires that "each of us has a right to liberty compatible with equality for all".[29]

2.1.3 Practicalities

The second step in Griffin's account is to incorporate what he calls "social manageability": "more than just determinateness of sense is likely also to be necessary for human rights to be manageable claims on others".[30] Griffin acknowledges that his personhood concept "is often not up to fixing anything approaching a determinate enough line for practice".[31] Later in the chapter, Griffin makes clear that the universality of human rights is grasped at the highest level of abstraction – that is, the values attached to agency – and that it asks for specification in local contexts: "it's a status we have independently of society".[32] "Practicalities" is the requirement of a good understanding of how individuals may have their personhood endangered under specific circumstances. Those practicalities are not only time- and context-sensitive, but also human-sensitive, that is, relative to the "limits of human understanding and motivation".[33] As Tasioulas puts it, practicalities "become relevant in the process of concretizing pre-given human rights in particular circumstances".[34] In Chapter 5 ("My Rights: But Whose Duties"), Griffin exemplifies this process by identifying the universal terms by which the right to health translated into the more particular form of the right of AIDS sufferers to anti-retroviral drugs.[35] Again, the specification of the personhood rights will be context-sensitive, but such sensitivity does not modify the normative basis of personhood that aims to remedy the justificatory deficit of human rights. As Nickel and Reidy put it, "Griffin's argument for rights proceeds from conjoining that good with timeless and universal practicalities regarding human nature and human societies and then reasoning to more determinate applications in local, contingent conditions".[36]

2.1.4 Equality

The third step for Griffin is to examine *equality* as a foundation for human rights: "it is obvious that on one interpretation of 'equality' – namely, equal respect – and

29 Ibid., 160.
30 Ibid., 38.
31 Ibid., 37.
32 Ibid., 50.
33 Ibid., 38.
34 Tasioulas, "Human Rights, Universality and the Values of Personhood: Retracing Griffin's Steps", 86.
35 Griffin, *On Human Rights*, 108–9.
36 Nickel and Reidy, "Philosophy", 56.

on one interpretation of 'grounds', equality is indeed a ground for human rights".[37] However, equality is clearly insufficient, Griffin argues, to derive a list of human rights. Equality "must be somewhere"[38] but it does not by itself help us to distinguish the specific grounding value of human rights. As Griffin argues, "my point is that the domains of human rights and fairness overlap but are not congruent".[39] Griffin goes through a couple of examples, such as free-riding and cheating at cards, in which some form of *fairness*, but not human rights, is at stake.

The only requirement of equality distinctive of human rights is internal to personhood as an equally distributed capacity: "a person is a bearer of human rights in virtue of being a normative agent, and women and men are equal in normative agency".[40] Note that in Chapter 5 ("Human Rights: Discrepancies Between Philosophy and International Law"), and on other occasions, Griffin reiterates his commitment to a minimal account of equality as a requirement of human rights in explaining that a wider notion of equality as fairness – which Griffin ascribes to defenders of a richer conception of "dignity" – would conflate human rights with other categories of morality such as fairness and distributive justice. One may therefore fall back on a richer idea of Kantian equal respect: "if we adopt this understanding, human rights would expand to fill that whole domain, which is so counter-intuitive a consequence that we must avoid it".[41]

2.1.5 Personhood and normative ethics

The last central aspect of the personhood account that Griffin develops in Chapter 3 ("When Human Rights Conflict") is how personhood fits into broader debates on normative ethics. Griffin assumes that "we cannot understand much about human rights until we know a fair amount about moral norms in general".[42] Griffin distinguishes clearly between *right–right* conflicts on the one hand and *rights–welfare* conflicts on the other. In the first case, personhood inevitably leads to concrete conflicts between interests that are both justified in abstract by it. As such, human rights are not absolute rights. The value of personhood in these conflicts – that is, the extent to which the interests affect our status of normative agents – should give us the guidance we need for arbitration: "virtually everyone would agree that an important part of their resolution comes by determining the degree of the values constitutive of personhood at stake".[43]

As for the rights *versus* welfare conflicts, Griffin holds that we should not strive to find the right answer "when the competing value *just* exceeds the right".[44]

---

37 Griffin, *On Human Rights*, 40.
38 Ibid.
39 Ibid., 41.
40 Ibid.
41 Ibid., 201.
42 Ibid., 73.
43 Ibid., 68.
44 Ibid., 76.

36   *Ethical theories and practice-independence*

Rather, he thinks we have to rely on a common sense notion of "quality of life" to arbitrate those conflicts:

> We have no choice but to take a highly practical turn in ethics, not just to ensure that our abstract principles are adequate to our practice, but also to accommodate the ways in which our practice – our human nature with all its limitations and the needs of our actual societies – determines the content of our principles.[45]

As such, Griffin's personhood account is *teleological* in that personhood identifies a cardinal value that is inherently worth pursuing (though specified by "practicalities") but that is not entirely resistant to trade-offs if the overall quality of life is seriously endangered. This teleological dimension distinguishes personhood from "complete" theories of morality such as consequentialism and utilitarianism in that it does not mirror what Griffin calls "moral mathematics",[46] that is, empirical calculations striving to find a threshold for moral action. Deontologism is confined to some formal "universalizability" test involving highly idealized agents, whereas utilitarianism is confined to some calculus going beyond human moral motivation: "although utilitarianism and consequentialism are forms of teleology, they restrict the test of rights and wrong to the production of as much good as rationality requires . . . . Teleology allows yet other ways of basing the right and the good".[47] In other words, there is a cardinal value, personhood, that all human rights serve and that should guide our ordinary moral choices, but which neither helps us in theorizing the good nor settle the dispute between deontologism and utilitarianism.

2.2 Griffin's normative scope

Having reconstructed the basis of the personhood account, I leave aside the chronological structure of Griffin's book and turn to what I take to be the most important implications of his account. I focus on two interrelated implications that reveal the scope of Griffin's substantive account. First, I specify how Griffin understands the role of *duties* that correlate with human rights (in Chapter 4, "My Rights: But Whose Duties"). Second, I explain how Griffin relates personhood

---

45 Ibid., 75. It must be noticed that this conception echoes Griffin's broader framework of ethical thinking that he develops in several earlier contributions – the seminal contribution being *Value Judgement: Improving Our Ethical Beliefs.* In this book, Griffin distances himself from the models of moral theory such as deontologism and utilitarianism. As Tasioulas explains, "Griffin has an alternative understanding of what justification in ethics amounts to that is more compelling and more modest. He seeks a grounding for ethical thinking in prudential and moral beliefs of 'highly reliability', beliefs which are not themselves inferred from anything non-evaluative, through their normative implications are shaped by facts about human capacities and social organization": Tasioulas, "Human Rights, Universality and the Values of Personhood: Retracing Griffin's Steps", 81.
46 Griffin, *On Human Rights*, 79.
47 Ibid., 80.

Ethical theories and practice-independence   37

to international law (in Chapter 11, "Human Rights: Discrepancies Between Philosophy and International Law").

As to the duties, Griffin makes it clear that personhood alone can determine not only the list of human rights we have, but also the duties correlative to those rights. The continuum from rights to duties is explained by the moral stringency of personhood and specified in context by practicalities. As Griffin explains in the case of the right to health, "our main project in the case of the right to health is to specify what is needed – some sort of basic kit of capacities – for life as an agent".[48] The scope of the duties is co-extensive to the scope of the right – personhood will tell us, in more or less determinate terms, what they are. There is no limiting factor other than practicalities for identifying duties. As we shall see later, this is highly problematic for *interest-based* theories of rights for which placing other under duties is a necessary condition for rights. As we shall see, Tasioulas argues that Griffin takes "rights out of human rights". As Besson also suggests, "because he does not conceive of human rights as rights that generate duties, the legal questions that usually arise out of conflicts of rights (and duties) and their claimability do not appear in Griffin's account".[49]

Griffin himself acknowledges that "it is characteristic of the work in identifying duty-owners that it, too, can be long, hard, and contentious".[50] It seems that Griffin is now taking a rather modest turn in identifying duty-bearers. This is another consequence of the exclusive reliance on personhood: "we know that there is a moral burden, without yet knowing who should shoulder it".[51] He acknowledges that the normative weight of personhood is demanding to the extent that there may be cases where the identification of the duty-bearer will be circumstantial and/or arbitrary. His emphasis on "ability" to help the needy, such as in the case of Bill Gates, reflects this rather unstable identification process: "all I wish to claim is that mere ability is one consideration in fixing where to place the duty to help".[52] Beitz rightly puts the point:

> Thus Griffin . . . holds that the obligation to help satisfy welfare rights rests on a general obligation (perhaps a natural duty) to help those in distress, combined with pragmatic considerations such as proximity and capacity . . . . From some perspectives this might be a precarious obligation to respect and promote human rights, and conceivably a naturalistic theory could say more.[53]

Clearly, in Griffin's view, duty-bearer identification is not necessary for the existence conditions of human rights: "perhaps the strongest claim that should be made is that for the great majority of rights with positive duties, institutions are

48 Ibid., 101.
49 Besson, "Human Rights: Ethical, Political . . . or Legal? First Steps in a Legal Theory of Human Rights", 220.
50 Griffin, *On Human Rights*, 103.
51 Ibid.
52 Ibid.
53 Beitz, *The Idea of Human Rights*, 66.

38   *Ethical theories and practice-independence*

necessary for claimability".[54] Against those who think either that claimability[55] is necessary for the existence conditions of human rights, or those who hold that enforcement is necessary for their existence[56] – human rights exist only when there is reliable access to the object that the right protects – Griffin claims that "the mode of reasoning then proceeds from interests to rights to duties".[57] In confining the content of human rights to the right-holders' interests, Griffin precisely maintains the continuum that I take as distinctive of the practice-independent approach. As we have already seen, this commitment raises strong scepticism towards the general normative structure of Griffin's account of *rights*.

2.2.1 Personhood and international law

The relation of personhood to international human rights law[58] also reflects the far-reaching scope of Griffin's normative account. Griffin reiterates at the beginning of Chapter 11 that from personhood "we should be able to derive all human rights".[59] The rights to life, to security of person, and the right not to be tortured are derived from the autonomy condition. The right to worship, to enjoy ourselves, to form personal relations, to create art, and to inform others what we believe are derived from the liberty condition. Some rights, Griffin argues, cut across the three conditions (autonomy, liberty, minimum provision), such as the right to privacy and the right to asylum. In Chapter 13 ("Privacy"), Griffin specifies the scope of the right to privacy to "informational" privacy). Indeed, this approximate listing – Griffin repeatedly asserts that there are more rights – serves as the basis for the criticism of conventional lists of human rights. The normative force of personhood therefore remains constant from the moral to the legal dimension of those rights; if we set aside the "practicalities", which are circumstantial specifications of the rights to personhood. As Besson puts it:

> Griffin locates the law exclusively in the practice of human rights, and he sees that practice as having to be aligned with the best philosophical account of human rights. This explains why he devotes a single chapter to the legal question, and a chapter that is situated at the end of the book, once his philosophical account of human rights has been spelled out.[60]

---

54 Griffin, *On Human Rights*, 108.
55 For the claimability view, see O'Neill, "The Dark Side of Human Rights".
56 For the enforcement view, see Geuss, *History and Illusion in Politics*, 143–6. Geuss's famous formulation is that "there is or there is not a mechanism for enforcing human rights. If there is not, it would seem that calling them 'rights' simply means that we think it would (morally) be a good idea if they were enforced . . . . Human rights is a vacuous conception, and to speak of 'human rights' is a kind of puffery or white magic".: ibid., 144. For a position that is fairly close to the "ought implies can" of Geuss, see Raz, "Human Rights in the Emerging World Order".
57 Griffin, *On Human Rights*, 108.
58 See also Griffin's early article on this issue: Griffin, "Discrepancies between the Best Philosophical Account of Human Rights and the International Law of Human Rights", 6–28.
59 Griffin, *On Human Rights*, 192.
60 Besson, "Human Rights: Ethical, Political . . . or Legal? First Steps in a Legal Theory of Human Rights", 220.

Ethical theories and practice-independence 39

We should note here that what Griffin understands by legal practice is merely the lists of rights in international treaties and one may doubt that this list only is in any sense "practical". Griffin is irremediably short in interpreting the legal dimension of human rights. Surely, most of the rights in the UDHR, Griffin argues, are entirely justified. However, Griffin is able to find some rights that cannot be justified, or are just partially justified with the resources of the personhood account. Some rights are just discarded, such as the right to inherit (Article 5 ICERD) and the right of protection against attacks on one's honour and reputation (Article 12 UDHR), while some rights, such as freedom of movement and residence within the borders of our own country (Article 13.1 UDHR), may be justified in some cases where the circumstances affect one of the three fundamental components of personhood. Griffin takes the example of the Greek worker forced to migrate to Germany where hostile conditions result in his not having an effective voice in political decisions – which would then violate the liberty condition.

More problematic are those rights that Griffin puts under the umbrella of "equality before the law" (e.g. Articles 7–11 UDHR, Article 14 ICCPR) that specify "second-order human rights to remedy of our human rights".[61] As explained earlier, it is central for Griffin that no consideration of equality except those of personhood can provide resources for justifying human rights. As a result, some of those equality rights will be human rights, some will not. Once again, there is for Griffin a rather strict division of labour between the equality of human rights *qua* protection of human rights and the equality derived from theories of *fairness* and *distributive justice*: "there is no inference from something's being a matter of justice to its being a matter of human rights".[62] While the rights not to be subjected to arbitrary arrest, detention or exile can clearly be found in personhood, the rights to be informed of the charge against one promptly and in detail, to have adequate time to prepare one's defence, and not be compelled to testify against oneself cannot be found in personhood – this will be possible, Griffin argues, only at the cost of enlarging the notion of *personhood* to some richer notion of *dignity*.

Similarly, Griffin applies the same "cleaning" process to the lists of social, economic and cultural rights. Not surprisingly, some rights are deemed unacceptable, such as the right of every worker to promotion of upward mobility in his employment (Article 7(c) of the Additional Protocol to the American Convention), while some are discarded after a more thorough discussion, such as the right to work (Article 23.1 UDHR) and the right to the "highest attainable standard of physical and mental health" (Article 12.1 UDHR). As discussed earlier, the scope of the right to health will be proportionate to that required by the status of agents as normative agents – in the exact same way as the right to welfare that Griffin elaborates in Chapter 10 ("Welfare"). Similarly, the right to equal pay for equal work (Article 23.1 UDHR, Article 7 ICESCR, Article 15 African Charter) cannot be generated by the equality of personhood, but by a standard of fairness largely independent of Griffin's foundational and criterial value.

---

61 Griffin, *On Human Rights*, 197.
62 Ibid., 198.

40   *Ethical theories and practice-independence*

2.2.2 The external critique

Let us now turn to the critical assessment of Griffin's seminal account. The first and main worry raised by Griffin's critics is whether personhood can illuminate the legal and political practices that we routinely associate with human rights. As shown above, Griffin relies exclusively on ordinary moral reasoning to construct the personhood account. Not only does the normative basis of personhood determine the list of human rights we have, but it also pervades the very structure of rights in determining the correlated duties. It serves as a standard of criticism to "clean" the conventional lists of human rights in international law. In his thorough critique of Griffin, Beitz argues in this sense: "naturalistic conceptions regard human rights as having a character and basis that can be fully comprehended without their embodiment and role in any public doctrine".[63] The normative content is attained through ordinary moral reasoning and this modality is distinctive of the practice-independent approach: the core content and structure of human rights is apprehended just by reflecting on the distinctively valuable aspects of human beings. The personhood account is a "superimposition of a philosophical theory that locates the authority of human rights in a received conception of human status or human flourishing".[64]

There are at least two ways in which the lack of practice-responsiveness may be articulated. Beitz contends that the personhood account is not equipped to illuminate the distinctive *political* role of human rights as triggering international concern. As we shall see in the next chapter, Beitz rightly identifies a set of paradigms of implementation that have come to constitute the core of the emergent practice of global human rights (accountability, inducement, assistance, domestic contestation and engagement, compulsion and external adaptation[65]). What is distinctive of human rights is the heterogeneity of actions for which they give reasons, but there is also a *legal* way in which one can question the practice-responsiveness of personhood. Human rights were first recognized in international law. From a legal standpoint, it is difficult to hold that human rights *qua* international norms do not depend for their very existence on any prior norm. Human rights have justified the signing, ratifying and amending of international law treaties by sovereign states. They have justified creating a number of institutional arrangements (national and supranational) in charge of examining human rights records (UN treaty bodies, national commissions, regional courts, etc.). They have also justified a range of external interventions (from military attack against the state to the imposition of sanctions upon that state). The institution of international law, together with the post-1945 international state system, therefore remains a central premise. While some aspects of this practice are mentioned in Griffin's inquiry, they do not arrive at the core structure and content of those rights. In fact, they do not even

63 Beitz, *The Idea of Human Rights*, 50.
64 Ibid., 67–8.
65 Ibid., 33–44.

Ethical theories and practice-independence 41

inform the philosophical examination. In confining his investigation to some exercise of independent moral reasoning, Griffin suggests that human rights capture a fundamental category that transcends the limited role(s) that human rights have been playing in (international) political and legal life and against which those roles and practices should be judged.

2.2.3 The internal critique

The second, internal problem of personhood concerns the range of rights that may be justified by personhood. As such, it is an internal critique. Raz argues that despite Griffin's specification of human rights via "practicalities", it fails to achieve what it was initially aimed at, that is, a standard by which we could circumscribe the domain of human rights. We may distinguish two levels in this critique. On the one hand, it appears that the standard of normative agency can be met in rather bare conditions – such as that of a slave: "just by being alive (and non-comatose) we have some knowledge, resources, and opportunities".[66] As such, normative agency may be realized and yet have the most basic human rights listed in disrespected international conventions. Similarly, the right against torture, for instance, seems not to be grounded only and primarily in our interest in normative agency, but rather in our interest in avoiding pain. As Tasioulas explains, "for the agency theorist, the pain of torture can only bear indirectly on the justification of that right, i.e. insofar as it impacts adversely on our personhood . . .".[67]

On the other hand, it seems that the satisfaction of normative agency may require more than what Griffin assumes. As we have seen, personhood requires for its exercise a list of goods to which the agent must have access (such as education, information, minimal opportunities and minimum provision) in order to fully exercise his capacity of normative agency. Raz argues that the list may well become exponential: "is it not so rich as to include all the conditions of the good life which one person can secure for another?"[68] In other words, personhood is too ample to justify only the goods that Griffin identifies as sufficient for the capacity of normative agency to be operative. Griffin "suggests a general standard. But then we lack criteria to determine what it should be. My fear is that this lacuna cannot be filled. There is no principled ground for fixing on one standard rather than another".[69] Surely, personhood goods are important universal moral goods, but Raz is sceptical that they are distinctive of the personhood goods rather than the conditions for a good life.

Both the *internal* critique of Raz and the *external* critique of Beitz converge on one point: why should we rely entirely on the single concept of personhood? As Raz puts it:

66 Raz, "Human Rights Without Foundations", 326.
67 Tasioulas, "The Moral Reality of Human Rights", 45.
68 Raz, "Human Rights Without Foundations", 326.
69 Ibid.

42 *Ethical theories and practice-independence*

> There is nothing wrong in singling out the capacity for normative agency, or more broadly the capacities which constitute personhood, as of special moral significance .... The problem is the absence of a convincing argument as to why human rights practice should conform to their theories.[70]

Now, although Griffin has not directly replied to Beitz, he has directly replied to Raz on the internal critique. As he explains, "Raz' point is that traditionalists, once they become more generous, have no way to stop becoming still more so".[71] His response is merely a reassertion of the sufficient conditions for being a normative agent cracked down to its two major components, autonomy and liberty: "human rights, I propose, are rights to what allows one to act merely as a normative agent, not as a normative agent with a good chance of getting what one aims at".[72] Griffin then re-emphasizes the formal and material constraints on personhood. If not success in life, Griffin still thinks we can clearly identify the sufficiency threshold for agents to have "a sense of what is or is not worth pursuing and the ability to build a worthwhile life".[73] Literacy, for instance, is below the threshold of the autonomy condition, while getting a university degree is not:

> If one cannot become a university professor, there are other careers in the fairly well-off society we are imagining in which one can have a thoroughly valuable life. That is, there are alternative worthwhile lives that society may reasonably leave one to get on with.[74]

2.2.4 The rights-based critique

I have so far emphasized two weaknesses of the personhood account as a distinctively *foundational* account. Most importantly, it appears that the external and internal critiques apply irrespective of human rights being *rights*. They may apply to human rights *qua* moral values, goods, aspirations and interests. Moral values and the interests that may be derived from them, in Griffin's view, straightforwardly justify the establishment of rights. His conception of rights is reduced to "an entitlement that a person possesses to control or claim something".[75] This limited perspective has yielded the scepticism of rights theorists. In the recent literature, Raz and Tasioulas focus on this aspect. Similarly, Raz argues:

> So much of that discussion focuses on the value of the putative rights or its object to the right-holder, as if this is sufficient to establish that there is such right. So often there is little concern to show why others are subject to duties in regard to the putative right or its object.[76]

---

70 Ibid., 328–9.
71 Griffin, "Human Rights and the Autonomy of International Law", 347.
72 Ibid., 348.
73 Ibid.
74 Ibid., 349.
75 Griffin, *On Human Rights*, 30.
76 Raz, "Human Rights in the Emerging World Order", 37.

Ethical theories and practice-independence 43

In insisting on duties, Tasioulas relies heavily on Raz's concept of *rights* as having a distinctive structure and normative force. Most importantly, rights, according to Raz, give a special kind of reason, *categorical* – that is, independent of the duty-bearer's balance of reasons – and *exclusionary* – that is, they exclude some of the duty-bearer's reasons.[77] This is how Raz and others identify the distinctive reasons-giving force of human rights:

> Just as rights generally being reasons for taking measures against their violators do not normally give reason for all measures, so human rights set some limit to sovereignty, but do not necessarily constitute reasons for all measures, against violators. Similarly, they may sanction action in some forum, but not in others.[78]

If those premises hold, then duties are conceptually prior to the establishment of a right. Interests, the formula goes, generate rights only when they possess the kind of importance necessary for others to be under a duty. This is again owed to Raz: "X has a right if and only if X can have rights, and other things being equal, an aspect of X's well-being (his interest) is a sufficient reason to holding some other persons(s) under such a duty".[79] As such, human rights become *rights* depending on their normative force beyond the right-holder: "individuals have them only when the conditions are appropriate for governments to have the duties to protect the interests which the rights protect".[80] In other words, the interest of the right-holder is not sufficient: "hence, while the right to education is an individual moral right, the considerations which establish it are complex and not all relate to the interest of the right-holder".[81] In his later article, Raz talks of *synchronic univer-sality*: "theories which opt for synchronic universality accept that different people can have different human rights, for they accept that factors others than being human determine which human rights one has".[82] We can therefore distinguish between the *recognition* of the interest (say, in freedom of expression), which crystallizes its moral dimension, from its *existence* as a right.

It is correct to point out that Griffin "takes rights out of human rights", as Tasioulas puts it. This is an indirect consequence of the practice-independent approach to human rights. If personhood fully determines the duties correlative to human rights, then the Razian condition of being able to place others under duties

---

77 Raz, "On the Nature of Rights".
78 Raz, "Human Rights Without Foundations", 334.
79 Raz, *The Morality of Freedom*, 166.
80 Raz, "Human Rights Without Foundations", 335.
81 Ibid., 336.
82 Raz, "Human Rights in the Emerging World Order", 42. It must be noticed here that Raz has slightly changed his view in his last article on this issue. Now legal recognition and enforcement are necessary conditions for human rights to exist: "if enforcement – fair, efficient, and reliable enforcement – is impossible, we should recognize that the right is not a human right, and refrain from calling for its enforcement": ibid., 43–7. For an analysis of this new position, see Besson, "Human Rights: Ethical, Political . . . or Legal? First Steps in a Legal Theory of Human Rights", 224–6.

44 *Ethical theories and practice-independence*

as necessary for a right to exist is not necessary. As for the Beitzian critique of Griffin, the Razian critique provided by Tasioulas does not imply, however, that the interests sufficient to generate duties cannot be moral, as Raz himself argues, or that they may not be justified by moral values. Irrespective of their structure, *rights* may be *justified* by values – such as in the case of personhood – without themselves being values. In other words, one may imagine capturing the existence conditions of human rights *qua* rights, and still ask those rights to be justified by values. This approach forms the basis of my constructivist alternative detailed in Chapter 3.

2.3 Forst's ethical variant

Let me finally survey another predominant ethical account of human rights, that of Rainer Forst. Forst's account is both a revision and a continuation of the ethical project initiated by Griffin. Most importantly, Forst seeks to avoid the substantive basis of Griffin's account: "what these ethical justifications of human rights share, however, is their focus on substantive notions of well-being or the 'good life' and their view of human rights as means to guaranteeing essential minimal conditions for such forms of human life".[83] The consequence of Griffin's account is that only some interests can qualify as human rights and, as we have seen, several problems, both internal and external to personhood, arise.

By contrast, Forst's distinctive account relies on an attempt to avoid any substantive basis while preserving an independent normative basis: "I believe that a conception of human rights needs to have an independent and sufficient moral substance and justification, though not one of an ethical kind that relies on a conception of the good".[84] More precisely, Forst aims to avoid the teleological and substantive layer of Griffin.[85] Instead, Forst introduces another deontological threshold, that of *mutual justifiability*:

> The moral basis for human rights, as I reconstruct it, is the respect for the human person as an autonomous agent who possesses a right to justification, that is, a right, to be recognized as an agent who can demand acceptable reasons for any action that claims to be morally justified and for any social or political structure or law that claims to be binding upon him or her. Human rights secure the equal standing of persons in the political and social world, based on a fundamental moral demand of respect.[86]

---

83 Forst, "The Justification of Human Rights and the Basic Right to Justification: A Reflexive Approach", 713.

84 Ibid., 718.

85 As Forst puts it, "a teleological view such as Griffin's identifies basic interests of persons in pursuing the good and transforms them into rights claims in accordance with their weight or value, while other interests (such as being loved, to employ that example again) do not qualify": ibid.

86 Ibid., 719.

Ethical theories and practice-independence   45

It appears that Forst endorses the status-based premise of normative agency. However, the standard of *mutual justifiability* and *the right to justification* are informed by a *historical* interpretation of the practice of rights. By contrast to Griffin, Forst refers primarily to the emancipatory movements that initiated the liberal revolutions of the seventeenth and eighteenth centuries:

> The language of these rights was a socially and politically emancipatory language, directed against a feudal social order and against an absolute monarchy that claimed "divine" rights for itself. That is a truism, yet an important one, for many of the views mentioned above, even some of those labelled as "political," tend to neglect the essential political message of human rights.[87]

By contrast to Griffin, whose personhood account fails to illuminate this historical continuum,[88] Forst ingenuously forges a thin moral concept that illuminates the long practice of (human) rights. Neither practice-dependent nor practice-independent, Forst is able to account for the underlying moral basis of human rights without falling prey to the *parochial* argument – between "their normative core as protecting basic human interests, their role in international law and political practice, and their claim to be universally justifiable across cultures and ethical ways of life".[89]

I retain two important points about Forst's practice-responsiveness. First, Forst's account shares Griffin's premise about humans as *agents of reasons*. To identify mutual justifiability requires taking an independent standpoint. However, human rights do not serve in Forst's account the particular value – personhood – that Griffin ascribes to them. Whereas Griffin privileges a *teleological* account, Forst defends a *deontological* account: rights derive from the status of humans *qua* agents of justification:

> This is a notion of respecting an other's autonomy which is neither attached to a reasonably contestable notion of the good nor requires a translation of a prudential ethical value "for me" to a moral reason "for all." The basic claim in that context is one of the active status as a justificatory equal, not of ethical interests and their importance in pursuit of the good.[90]

It is crucial to repeat, however, that Forst's normative basis is derived from a distinctively historical interpretation of the role of rights.

---

87 Ibid., 717.

88 As we have explained earlier, Griffin takes history to be important only as reinforcing the need for a more determinate account of human rights. Forst, by contrast, assigns history a more normative role: "I agree with the claim that the 'Enlightenment notion' of human rights is in need of an explicit philosophical justification, yet I think that the fact that the idea of natural rights was a polemical one directed against religious-political doctrines of the legitimacy of feudal social structures and absolute monarchy conveys a different and more determinate message than the one Griffin extracts from the historical account": ibid., 721.

89 Ibid., 716.

90 Ibid., 724.

46 *Ethical theories and practice-independence*

Second, Forst fully endorses a central tenet of the political conception of human rights, that is, the state-directedness of human rights: "that is a political notion of dignity as a relational concept, referring to the social and political standing of human beings as agents of justification who are equal to one another".[91] Echoing Rawls, Beitz and other promoters of the political conception, Forst believes that human rights are constitutively directed to political authorities. In this vein, the intrinsic connection between human rights and political legitimacy through the right to justification calls for the existence of a *right to democratic participation*. Rights are not taken primarily as an instrument for leading an autonomously chosen life but to "put an end to political oppression and the imposition of a social status that deprives one of one's freedom and of access to the social means necessary to being a person of equal standing".[92] "Dignity", Forst argues, is precisely the recognition of human beings as deserving reasons for political actions that have implications for them. Because human rights are decisive for the legitimacy of political authority, human rights must be legally binding. The law concretizes those fundamental moral rights grounded in the underlying right to justification.

Before turning to the political conception of human rights in the next chapter, I want to make a final remark about Forst's account. If Forst's specifically *constructivist* framework is not evident in the article in *Ethics* examined above, it is clearer in an earlier article written before the ethical/political debate emerged.[93] More precisely, Forst distinguishes *moral* from *political* constructivism and pleads for a complementary approach:

> The main reason why moral constructivism must be accompanied by and integrated with political constructivism is that, since moral constructivism can only lead to a very general list of rights for which we can assume that no normatively acceptable reasons count against their own validity, these rights can only be *concretely* justified, interpreted, institutionalized, and *realized* in social contexts, that it to say, only within a legally constituted political" order.[94]

In this sense, Forst differs from Griffin in that the foundations of human rights cannot be apprehended *just* by reflecting, through ordinary moral reasoning, on the distinctively valuable aspects of human beings. In this sense, he suggests that one could apply a form of independent moral reasoning from within particular and institutional relations. I further develop this constructivist approach in Chapter 4.

---

91 Ibid., 721.
92 Ibid., 725.
93 Forst, "The Basic Right to Justification: Towards a Constructivist Conception of Human Rights", 35–60.
94 Ibid., 48.

3 Political theories and their practice-dependence

In this chapter, I turn to the political conception of human rights and analyze specifically Charles Beitz' account in *The Idea of Human Rights*.[1] As we have seen, Griffin suggests that independent moral reasoning is sufficient to determine the grounding value of human rights, the list of rights and their correlative duties. In contrast, Beitz's approach to the practice of human rights excludes the appeal to such reasoning. Beitz certainly intervenes in selecting the practices, in unifying them and in abstracting from them conceptually but does not appeal to a deeper layer of moral reasoning to build his model of human rights. It is therefore crucial to explain what justifies the adoption of this quite radical approach.

There are three main steps in this explanation. First, I explain why Beitz's attachment to reconstructing the practice justifies viewing human rights as political rather than legal in nature. However, despite the fact that Beitz aims to build the most comprehensive account of human rights practice, some limitations must be noted. Most importantly, Beitz does not examine the judicial dimension of human rights practices in detail. This applies, for instance, to interpretative practices of UN treaty bodies, to the ECtHR and, more importantly, to the relation of those supranational organs to national adjudication and implementation of those rights.

Second, I reconstruct Beitz's inductive process from the identification of "global political practice" to his three-pronged concept of human rights (*urgent individual interests*, *state-directedness*, *international concern*) from which it is an abstraction. This not only allows us to clearly identify Beitz's practice-dependent modality of theorizing (in particular, the use of *empirical generalizations* and *probabilities*) but also to better show that Beitz's thin normative content adduced is contingent upon the kind of practice examined. The connection between the practical approach and the resulting normative content is therefore unnecessary.

Third, I examine rival political conceptions and, in particular, that of Joseph Raz. However, since Raz's account is (for now) limited to two articles and overlaps with that of Beitz, I explain only how Raz differs from Beitz in that Raz ascribes to human rights a universal moral basis while still making their very existence contingent upon considerations beyond the right-holder (fulfilment of duties).

---

1 Beitz, *The Idea of Human Rights*.

48 *Political theories and practice-dependence*

Finally, I explain how both relate to the seminal political conception of human rights in modern political theory, namely that of John Rawls.

I conclude that the ethical and the political conceptions exclude each other when it comes to including normative facts and practices in theorizing human rights. While Griffin navigates from the moral to the legal dimension of human rights with the same independent notion of personhood, Beitz's practice-dependent continuum develops from the descriptive and analytical to the normative levels of argument. I then briefly suggest how one could preserve Beitz's attention to practices while adopting the practice-independent standpoint cherished by Griffin and Forst.

3.1 The global perspective

It appears clearly from Chapters 2 ("The Practice") and 5 ("Normativity") of the book that Beitz adopts a *global* perspective on the doctrine and the practice of human rights. The historical *précis* by which he introduces the practice, the doctrinal content of human rights exposed, as well as the various accountability mechanisms in place clearly indicate that Beitz is referring primarily to the UDHR and the major UN human rights treaties. Adopting this perspective leads Beitz to articulate a few important preliminary claims. Most importantly, Beitz emphasizes the fact that the UDHR does not address the philosophical foundations of human dignity:

> Relatedly, it should be observed that the preamble does not seek to locate the universality or significance of the value of equal human dignity in further considerations of human nature or divine gift; it is simply asserted in its own right . . . . The drafters represented not only different countries, but also different religious and philosophical traditions and political positions; although there was a shared commitment to the idea of human rights, there was no shared philosophical view.[2]

The absence of a deeper layer of moral reasoning is not only distinctive of today's practice, it is "indispensable to the proper appreciation of its historical uniqueness".[3]

Second, adopting this global standpoint leads Beitz to conceive human rights as a set of common standards of aspiration, not as a set of legally enforceable claims. Indeed, Beitz quickly points out that the legal and judicial instruments developed at the global level "embody in various forms the reporting and monitoring elements of the original working group's implementation scheme. But there are no provisions for independent investigation of complaints, no system of sanctions for non-compliance, and, of course, no human rights court".[4] Those points are

2 Ibid., 20.
3 Ibid., 21.
4 Ibid., 24–5.

Political theories and practice-dependence   49

correct, but incomplete. It is one thing to notice that the practice of international human rights lacks anything close to a central enforcement mechanism or even a supranational judicial review mechanism. Yet it does not follow that human rights stand in a legal and judicial vacuum. True, Beitz notices that current mechanisms are limited to processes of "consultation, reporting, and public censure",[5] but he fails to account for the nature and scope of this practice such as the interpretative practices of UN treaty bodies.[6]

Indeed, the correlative indicator of the human rights expansion over the last three decades is the creation and development of international legal instruments, most importantly under the UN umbrella, dedicated to the "monitoring" of international human rights. The main responsibility for monitoring is entrusted to the international human rights treaty bodies,[7] established by the major international human rights treaties. They are the "creatures" of their respective treaties, most importantly the ICERD, the ICESCR and ICCPR, the CEDAW and the CAT. Those treaties have attracted a growing number of ratifications since they were formally adopted.[8] It is important to note that the two most important covenants – the ICCPR and the ICESCR, which together with the UDHR comprise what is referred to as the International Bill of Rights – were finalized in 1966, two decades after the UDHR. As we shall see in Chapter 5, this timing is related to the *late* explosion of international human rights.[9]

The five aforementioned treaties now have a monitoring body which may consider individual complaints.[10] The ICCPR, for instance, optionally allows for an individual right of complaint which is recognized in a separate covenant, the Treaty of the Optional Protocol to the International Covenant on Civil and Political Rights. The ICESCR lacked a protocol to establish an optional enforcement mechanism until 2008 when the UN General Assembly adopted an optional protocol that gives the treaty body jurisdiction to hear individual complaints, although not enough states have yet accepted this competence. The term *monitoring* is itself revealing of the role of the treaty bodies *qua* quasi-judicial organs: they *supervise* the states' implementation of human rights norms. Concretely, their role is to examine reports from States Parties on their fulfilment of human rights obligations established by the treaties. States are required to report initially one year after acceding to the Covenant and thereafter when requested by the Committee (usually every four years). Treaty bodies adopt General Comments,

---

5 Ibid., 32.
6 For a recent overview of this interpretative practice, see Schlütter, "Aspects of Human Rights Interpretation by the UN Treaty Bodies".
7 For a recent overview of the nature and scope of UN treaty bodies, see the contributions in Keller and Ulfstein (eds), *UN Human Rights Treaty Bodies: Law and Legitimacy*.
8 For updated information on state ratification, see UN Treaty Collection, available at http://treaties.un.org.
9 See, in particular, Moyn, *The Last Utopia: Human Rights in History*.
10 For an updated introduction and analysis of the individual complaint mechanisms of UN treaty bodies and their legal effects, see Van Alebeek and Nollkaemper, "The Legal Status of Decisions by Human Rights Treaty Bodies in National Law".

50 *Political theories and practice-dependence*

which are authoritative interpretations of human rights norms. They have adopted a large number of decisions and recommendations in the form of Concluding Observations and, most importantly, Views in response to individual complaints. They can also ask for the amendment or repeal of legislation, reopening of national proceedings, release of prisoners, commutation of sentence, investigation to establish the facts, bringing perpetrators to justice and making restitution for property, etc.

Those functions imply that UN treaty bodies have an important judicial dimension[11] although the processes do not amount to supranational judicial review *stricto sensu*. The UN "system" lacks anything close to a central, authoritative judicial organ for adjudicating disagreements through proper judicial proceedings and applying sanctions to non-compliant states similar to those found in constitutional regimes or regional human rights regimes. In addition, the treaty body decisions are non-binding as a matter of international law:

> The general perceptions of states that Views do not impose legal obligations on them has a substantial impact on decisions not to implement them . . . . Even states that have proved generally respectful of the work of the treaty bodies do at times insist on their discretion to either implement or reject the outcome of individual communication procedures.[12]

The ICCPR and the ICESCR remain the most important treaties that emerged initially from under the UN umbrella. In addition, the Human Rights Commission – since 2008 the Human Rights Council (HRC) – has established its own mechanism for responding to gross human rights violations and has developed Special Procedures consisting of independent rapporteurs and working groups that aim to address specific human rights violations. The HRC has also developed complaints procedures to address serious or systematic human rights violations. Most recently, the HRC implemented the Universal Periodic Review (UPR), a state-driven mechanism that involves a review of human rights violations in respect of 192 UN Member States once every four years. In addition, the Office of the High Commissioner for Human Rights (OHCHR), which essentially coordinates the administrative process for UN human rights bodies, may be mentioned, although it does not have authority to deal with human rights abuses. Their effects are contingent upon the discretion of national courts. As a result, it is the absence of *effects* of the views and recommendations of UN treaty bodies in national legal orders that Beitz in fact targets.[13]

---

11 As Nollkaemper and Van Alebeek explain, "treaty bodies are the principal interpreters of the UN human rights treaties": ibid., 358. For an overview of the interpretative practice of UN treaty bodies (HRC, CAT and ICERD), see Schlütter, "Aspects of Human Rights Interpretation by the UN Treaty Bodies".
12 Van Alebeek and Nollkaemper, "The Legal Status of Decisions by Human Rights Treaty Bodies in National Law", 372.
13 For a recent analysis of the effects of the decisions of UN treaty bodies, see Van Alebeek and Nollkaemper, ibid.

Political theories and practice-dependence 51

In Beitz's view, conceiving the normativity of human rights in the absence of a global legal system of sanctions and/or judicial review naturally leads to concern for their status as rights. This concern has been widely advanced in the literature. As O'Neill also argues, for instance:

> There is no effective rule of law without law enforcement, and law enforcement needs law enforcers who are assigned specific tasks, there is no effective accountability without institutions that allocate the tasks and responsibilities and hold specific office-holders to account.[14]

From this standpoint, global human rights may well be just "claims", "goals", "aspirations" or "needs", or if they are *rights*, they are *manifesto rights*. As Feinberg and Narveson put it in a seminal article, "if we persist, nevertheless, in speaking of these needs as constituting rights and not merely claims, we are committed to the conception of a right as entitlement to some good, but not a valid claim *against* any particular individual".[15] As Beitz also explains in an earlier article, "unlike, say, the financial or trade regime, human rights policy doesn't aim only to institutionalize and regulate existing interactions; it seeks to propagate ideals and motivate political change. Human rights stand for a certain ambition about how the world might be".[16]

The aspirational character of the global human rights doctrine is reinforced by the broad normative reach of those rights, which encompasses "the conditions of modern life".[17] This has to do with the proper content of human rights enshrined in the provisions of the ICCPR and the ICESCR. Global human rights indeed do not require much more than that posited by contemporary conceptions of social justice theories. As Beitz explains:

> International human rights seek not only to protect against threats to personal security and liberty and to guarantee some recourse against the arbitrary use of state power, but also to protect against various social and economic dangers and to guarantee some degree of participation in political and cultural life.[18]

This is certainly the case with economic, social and cultural rights, which many voices consider to be "virtual rights" compared with the first generation of civil and political rights. Article 12(1) ICESRC is often put forward: "the right of everyone to the enjoyment of the highest attainable standard of physical and mental health". It is difficult to conceive a maximal duty correlative to a human right. As Letsas rightly explains, "a legal right to something does not entail an

---

14 O'Neill, "The Dark Side of Human Rights", 428.
15 Feinberg and Narveson, "The Nature and Value of Rights".
16 Beitz, "What Human Rights Mean", 40.
17 Beitz, *The Idea of Human Rights*, 31.
18 Ibid., 30.

52 *Political theories and practice-dependence*

entitlement to the maximization of the value that right serves".[19] Beitz also notices the *heterogeneity* of duties listed in the treaties. Some rights prescribe specific policy guidelines while others remain vague. Similarly, some are described as urgent while others suppose a level of economic resources that many states will not be able to afford in the near future.

As we shall see later in the chapter, the distinctively political and heterogeneous normativity of human rights in global politics is the main reason for Beitz not to qualify the practice as a "regime", as this label depends upon the existence of institutional capacities for dispute resolution and sanction. As Beitz puts it, "the human rights system is notable for the weakness and unevenness of its capacities for adjudication and enforcement".[20] Although some aspect of the global human rights practice indeed displays a "juridical" character, Beitz concludes that:

> no analysis of human rights that did not capture this aspirational aspect would be faithful to the hopes and framers of modern human rights doctrine and to the roles that human rights have come to play in the discourse of global politics today.[21]

3.2 The emerging global practice of human rights

In the face of an absent supranational judicial organ or appellate review of findings, Beitz identifies a set of paradigms of implementation that form the core of the emerging global practice of human rights. This inventory is crucial to Beitz's selective account as it will form the basis of the normative model elaborated in Chapters 5 and 6. Yet the very act of selecting those patterns is central to capturing the limits of Beitz's account of the practice. This is my core critical claim: the selection of the *factual* premises is itself an interpretation of what counts as the relevant aspects of the practice. Let me first expose those descriptive claims before examining Beitz's analytical and normative claims:

1   *Accountability* refers to the process of reporting and auditing conducted by UN human rights treaty bodies – on the basis of human rights treaties – about human rights compliance in which NGOs play a crucial role as providers of independent information. Beitz rightly notices that the only sanctions that may result from this process are "naming and shaming".[22] True, global human rights also operate as goals of political change for increasingly professionalized NGOs and, more generally, civil society movements. In this context, global human rights provide a set of incentives to respect human rights that are driven by *soft* political action – "from the technique of shaming governments in exposing their human rights abuses to seeking ways to influence policies

19 Letsas, *A Theory of Interpretation of the European Convention on Human Rights*, 24.
20 Beitz, *The Idea of Human Rights*, 43.
21 Ibid., 44.
22 Ibid., 33.

of international organizations, to seeking new parts of the civil society for support, to assist UN peace-keeping operations and lobby activities within governments for purposes of communication and public advocacy".[23]

2   *Inducement*, by contrast, refers to the threat of non-coercive sanctions available to national governments such as "offers of diplomatic incentives, manipulation of access to economic, social, and cultural resources, preferential treatment in economic relations, and the attachment of conditions to bilateral assistance".[24] These are global human rights in their role of instruments of foreign policy. Beitz rightly notes the use of human rights compliance as a criterion for international financial institutions to enter into lending agreements or structural adjustment assistance.

3   *Assistance* refers to the aid given by outside agents to states and societies that lack the economic and institutional resources to sustain themselves autonomously in their human rights compliance efforts. As Beitz explains, "such measures, although not readily classified under the familiar headings of compulsion and inducement, plainly belong in any inventory of the means available to outside agents to improve protection of human rights".[25]

4   *Domestic contestation and engagement* refers to the mobilization and support of outside agents towards domestic actors "in bringing pressure on governments for changes in law and policy or to bring about changes in belief and practice within this society".[26] Beitz rightly argues that those normative roles are political or social, respectively. The social role of human rights is the idea that they have also become standards to which oppressed people may appeal in order to promote their cause and gain political visibility. Risse and Sikkink put the point clearly: "some domestic groups, however, recognizing that human rights claims have more international support and legitimacy, may take up the human rights banner because it is an easier way to criticize the government rather than because they profoundly believe in human rights principles".[27]

5   *Compulsion* refers to the use of coercive means of implementation of global human rights. As Beitz rightly explains, the spectrum of coercive intervention goes from "a change in behaviour of standing government to forcing a change in the regime itself".[28] At one end of the spectrum, we find the humanitarian interventions in Bosnia, Haiti, Somalia, Kosovo, East Timor, Iraq and, more recently, Libya. Beitz rightly explains that "the permissibility of humanitarian intervention in international law is disputed but its acceptability as a means of policy has been increasingly widely acknowledged".[29]

---

23 Beitz, *The Idea of Human Rights*, 31–44.
24 Ibid., 35.
25 Ibid., 36–7.
26 Ibid., 37.
27 Risse and Sikkink, "The Socialization of International Human Rights Norms into Domestic Practices: Introduction", 26.
28 Beitz, *The Idea of Human Rights*, 39.
29 Ibid.

54   *Political theories and practice-dependence*

6   Finally, *external adaptation* refers to the external obstacles that a state may face in its human rights compliance efforts. Beitz rightly cites the trade policies that "discriminate against agricultural products or intellectual property rules enforced in international law that increase the costs of pharmaceuticals".[30] This is just another reason for human rights to enter the stage as a form of justification to counter those policies.

3.3 Beitz's analytical account

This typology allows Beitz to articulate a first important analytical claim about the emerging global practice of human rights. Although enshrined in international treaties in origin, the reasons human rights give for action today are *political* in nature rather than *legal*: "neither the charter based nor the treaty based component of the UN human rights system have evolved effective mechanisms for the appellate review of findings or for the juridical application of sanctions".[31] It is true that the accountability function of global human rights carried out by public bodies established by international treaties comes close to what he terms "the juridical paradigm". However, Beitz captures the practice as having coercive intervention not at its core but rather at one end of its spectrum:

> It should be repeated that coercive intervention is the limiting, not the modal, case of "interference" and that some of the common forms of action for which agents claim to find justification in considerations about human rights can be counted as "interference" only in a capacious sense of the term.[32]

Beitz also identifies the political character of the agents that compose the background to the practice: "states acting individually or in coalitions, international organizations which are not part of the system constituted by the human rights treaties, and local and transnational nongovernmental actors".[33] In other words, despite their original legal recognition, human rights have acquired a normativity of their own to the extent that their immanent roles have multiplied in the transnational political arena – as Besson puts it in her review of Beitz's account, it is a "*sui generis*"[34] normative practice.

3.3.1 The limits of the global standpoint

It is crucial to note that the global standpoint results from a deliberate attempt to capture the most salient regularities associated with human rights on a global

30   Ibid., 40.
31   Ibid.
32   Ibid., 41.
33   Ibid.
34   Besson, "Human Rights *qua* Normative Practice: *Sui Generis* or Legal?", 127–33.

Political theories and practice-dependence 55

scale. As Beitz himself explains at the end of his typology, with regard to the nature and structure of human rights from the practice itself:

> The guiding ambition is to frame a reasonably clear and realistic conception of the practice as it presents itself in the range of source materials at hand. These include the major international texts and the reporting and monitoring mechanisms established by them; observations of critical public discourse, particularly when it occurs in practical contexts involving justification and appraisal; evidence of the public culture of international human rights found in its history and in contemporary public expression; and prominent examples of political action justified and reasonably regarded as efforts to defend or protect human rights, such as those which are subjects of historical and ethnographic studies.[35]

The processes that Beitz examines are inherently *political* in nature and *global* in reach. The horizon of theorizing is contingent on a complex ideal-typology of the main agents and processes on a global scale. The normative theorist is therefore incentivized to reflect upon those ideal-typical patterns associated with the global regime of human rights: "we want to understand how these objects called 'human rights' operate in the normative discourse of global political life".[36] This is not to say, however, that such selective standpoint involves evaluative claims. It concerns the selection of the relevant practices and the inherent limits of the global standpoint. The cost of the global standpoint is that some pattern(s) may be lost in the course of observation and analysis.

3.3.2 Beitz's practical inferences

We are now in a better position to understand the structure of Beitz's approach. The descriptive premises and the first analytical claims that Beitz articulates are fully contingent upon the global standpoint. Beitz infers that the reason-giving force of human rights is multifaceted and goes from coercive intervention to soft forms of criticism and assistance. In most of these instances, the normativity of human rights displays a highly *political* character.

Beitz needs now to abstract from the empirical and interpretative levels of argument: "what is needed is a facially reasonable conception of the practice's aim formulated so as to make sense of as many of the central normative elements as possible within the familiar interpretative constraints, coherence, and simplicity".[37] Beitz could have focused on only one pattern (Beitz uses the word "overlap"[38]). If that were the case, he could have investigated the internal views of those actors only, but that would then deviate from the global standpoint aimed at

---

35 Beitz, *The Idea of Human Rights*, 103.
36 Ibid., 105.
37 Ibid., 108.
38 Ibid., 40.

56 *Political theories and practice-dependence*

comprehensiveness. The epistemic limits of the global standpoint are salient: the three major elements identified are just those that survive the global standpoint.[39] First (1), human rights protect *urgent individual interests* (personal security and liberty, adequate nutrition, arbitrary use of state power) against standards threats in the modern world order composed of states. Second (2), human rights apply *in the first instance to institutions of the state*, which may carry out several types of action. Third (3), only when the state fails to do so, human rights trigger an *international concern*: "a government's failure to carry out its first-level responsibilities may be a reason for action for appropriately placed and capable 'second-order' agents outside the states".[40] Beitz rightly distinguishes between two levels in the overall model. (1) and (2) refer to the right-holder and duty-holder, while (3) refers to the reasons for action that human rights generate (international concern). The triggering is achieved by a set of second-order agents (states and non-state agents) and through a variety of actions (*accountability* mechanisms, *assistance* mechanisms and *interference* mechanisms).

Now it is crucial to note that the concepts of "urgency" and "standard threat" are given content not by normative reasoning but by generalizing from the practice itself. As Beitz puts it, "a model can draw attention to the relevant considerations but cannot settle the judgments".[41] Beitz is now equipped to articulate a first approximation of the concept of global human rights[42] in which the practice-dependence is salient. In particular, the use of *empirical generalizations* and *probabilities* are central: human rights protect interests that are "reasonable to recognize across a wide range of possible lives"; in the absence of protected rights there is "significant probability" that domestic institutions may endanger those rights; "the interest would be less likely to be endangered" if international means of action would be triggered. By contrast to Griffin, Tasioulas and Forst, at no point does Beitz use an independent evaluative standpoint to attain the core structure of this account.

Similarly, Beitz infers from this analysis a number of responses to broader normative questions about the implementation of human rights. In particular, he infers that human rights should not be enacted in state-level constitutional laws for this does not fit with the heterogeneous character of the practice: "the question of the desirability and importance of constitutional protection can be seen as one of contingent judgment rather than conceptual necessity".[43] Also, Beitz mentions but does not develop the normative claim that human rights are primarily duties addressed to states rather than individuals.[44] In those cases, too, the power of normative fact is decisive. It filters the possible answers to a range of normative questions about human rights. The conclusion of the *pro tanto* rather than

39 Ibid., 109.
40 Ibid.
41 Ibid., 110.
42 Ibid., 112.
43 Ibid., 114.
44 Ibid., 114–15.

Political theories and practice-dependence 57

conclusory nature of the reasons is also very illustrative of the practice-dependent character of theorizing. Once again, it is the global standpoint of Beitz that leads to his claim that "if we seek a model capable of representing the normative breadth of contemporary human rights doctrine",[45] then human rights give *pro tanto* rather than *conclusory* actions to act. Since this fact contradicts an essential component of our intuitive idea of a right – that is, its special stringent status – then we should definitely conceive global human rights as aspirational rights: "if we must retain the second of these conditions to be faithful to practice as we observe it, then we should let go the first and settle for an 'aspirational' view of human rights".[46]

3.4 Beitz's normative model

In Chapter 6 ("Normativity"), Beitz further specifies his two-level model and gives it its full normative force. Beitz's construction of the normative model suggests that the heterogeneity of interests protected by human rights justifies the model's poor evaluative content. Consequently, it is not the practice-based approach itself that leads to the normative model Beitz develops, but the very practices that survive the global standpoint selected to capture the phenomenon. In other words, the connection between the practice and the resulting normative conception is *contingent* rather than *necessary*. Since the model is rich empirically and conceptually, I concentrate on three major aspects. First and foremost, Beitz assesses once and for all the normative breadth of human rights. Unsurprisingly, the heterogeneous but distinctively political character of global human rights implies that such rights "do not appear as a fundamental moral category . . . . Human rights operate at a middle level of practical reasoning, serving to organize these further considerations and bring them to bear on a certain range of choices".[47] Here, again, the global standpoint is at play. It must make sense of a variety of normative patterns. The content of global human rights cannot derive from:

> a single, more basic value or interests such as those of human dignity, personhood, or membership. The reasons we have to care about them vary with the content of the right in question . . . . Human rights protect a plurality of interests and require different kinds and degrees of commitment of different agents.[48]

Second, Beitz breaks down its normative model into its three components and specifies how each of them constrains any plausible global human right. We should think of them as three cumulative and necessary conditions. The first concerns the *interest* protected by global human rights. It must be "sufficiently important when reasonably regarded from the perspective of those protected that

45 Ibid., 117.
46 Ibid., 120.
47 Ibid., 127–8.
48 Ibid., 128.

58 *Political theories and practice-dependence*

would be reasonable to consider its protection to be a political priority".[49] The model must accommodate the importance of the interest in such a way that it can "be recognized even by those who do not share it (such as 'being able to follow one's religion')". As a result, "it does not seem necessary to identify a list of relatively specific interests or values to serve as the grounds or subject-matters of human rights".[50] The second component concerns the advantageous protector of the interest – that is, the state. As mentioned earlier, this element is derived from "more-or-less substantial empirical generalizations about human social behaviour and the capacities and dynamics of social institutions".[51] Third, any plausible human rights "must be suitable objects of international concern".[52] This is the second level of normativity outlined earlier. This third condition further constrains the set of possible interests that may be global human rights: "whatever its importance regarded from the perspective of potential beneficiaries and however appropriate it would be as a requirement for domestic institutions, a protection cannot count as a human right of it fails to satisfy a requirement of this kind".[53]

3.4.1 The Rawlsian roots of practice-dependence

What transpires from this hopefully fair reconstruction of Beitz's account is a continuum from the descriptive to the normative level of argument. In sharp contrast to Griffin, the normative argument is reached just by interpreting and abstracting from the relevant political facts and practices of human rights on a global scale:

> We attend to the practical inferences that would be drawn by competent participants in the practice from what they regard as valid claims of human rights. An inventory of these inferences generates a view of the discursive function of human rights and this informs an account of the meaning of the concept.[54]

In the critiques addressed to Griffin's analysis surveyed in the last chapter, I distinguished between an *internal* and an *external* critique of the personhood account. Beitz focuses heavily on the latter. While the internal critique mainly concerns the capacity of personhood to generate the rights for which it claims to account, the external critique concerned the lack of practice-responsiveness. In particular, Beitz contends that the "naturalistic" conception of Griffin cannot illuminate the third standard of his normative model – human rights triggering international concern – that Beitz considers as distinctive of human rights in global political

---

49 Ibid., 137.
50 Ibid., 138–9.
51 Ibid., 139.
52 Ibid., 140.
53 Ibid.
54 Ibid., 103.

Political theories and practice-dependence 59

practice. This limitation (what Beitz calls "beneficiary centeredness") makes the personhood account inappropriate to account for the fact that human rights trigger, on the "supply side", some form of international concern. As Beitz explains, "these questions would be obvious if the discursive function of human rights as triggers were taken seriously".[55] More specifically, Beitz rightly points out the advantageous protector of the interest protected by human rights – that is, the institutional resources of the state. It is only when state institutions fail to protect those rights that some form of international action will be taken. As mentioned earlier, this normative feature is derived from "more-or-less substantial empirical generalizations about human social behavior and the capacities and dynamics of social institutions".[56]

3.4.2 The Rawlsian basis in Beitz and Raz

Before Beitz's book came out, Raz had already developed the argument about the lack of practice-responsiveness, although from a slightly different angle. As we have seen in the internal critique of Griffin, Raz focuses on the absence of a distinction between moral values and interests on the one hand, and rights and duties on the other. For Raz, human rights are moral rights, but their existence as rights is contingent upon considerations beyond those of the rights-holder: "individuals have them only when the conditions are appropriate for governments to have the duties to protect the interests which the rights protect".[57] The status of human rights *qua* rights resides "in not being grounded in a fundamental moral concern but depending on the contingencies of the current system of international relations".[58] This illustrates Raz's theory of rights as interests that are sufficiently important to hold others under a duty.

Now there is a strong overlap between Beitz and Raz in their appeal to the normative facts and practices of human rights as informing the existence conditions of those rights. However, while Beitz distinguishes this factual basis as multifaceted – from assistance to coercive intervention – Raz focuses exclusively on one pattern, that of sovereignty violation: "the dominant trend in human rights practice is to take the fact that a right is a human right as a defeasibly sufficient ground for taking action against violators in the international arena".[59] Whereas Raz preserves a moral basis, Beitz eliminates it from his normative model. To recall, global human rights "do not appear as a fundamental moral category . . . . Rights operate at a middle level of practical reasoning, serving to organize these further considerations and bring them to bear on a certain range of choices".[60] Beitz further argues that:

---

55 Ibid., 65.
56 Ibid., 139.
57 Raz, "Human Rights Without Foundations", 335.
58 Ibid., 336.
59 Ibid., 324.
60 Beitz, *The Idea of Human Rights*, 127–8.

60   *Political theories and practice-dependence*

there is no assumption of a prior or independent layer of fundamental rights whose nature and content can be discovered independently of a consideration of the place of human rights in the international realm and its normative discourse and then used to interpret and criticize international doctrine.[61]

This is what Besson[62] has termed the "*sui generis*" approach.

In a nutshell, Raz takes "international intervention" as distinguishing human rights in the class of moral rights. Beitz holds "international concern" as a necessary condition but without ascribing those rights a universal moral basis. There is, as a result, a broad meta-theoretical assumption about the task of the philosopher – that is, to start with the articulation of a normative notion's immanent employment in a given context. This consensus is precisely where the Rawlsian roots of practice-dependence are most salient. In the *Law of Peoples*, Rawls distinguishes a special class of urgent rights whose violation is condemned by both *liberal* and *decent hierarchical* peoples. To recall, the *Law of Peoples* is an international extension of Rawls' theory of domestic justice. The thought experiment of the veil of ignorance is conducted upon slightly different premises, however. Most importantly, the deliberators represent peoples and not individuals. Normative individualism – that is, the design of normative principles designed in accordance with the interests of individuals – is rejected in the international case. As Pogge explains:

> Representation is selectively granted only to peoples who are well-ordered by having either a liberal or a decent domestic institutional order, while the remainder ("outlaw states", "burdened societies", and "benevolent absolutisms") are not accepted as equals and thus denied equal respect and tolerance.[63]

In addition, the parties are not required to find general abstract principles that could help in assessing and reforming the global order but are only "charged with agreeing on a set of rules of good conduct that cooperating peoples should (expect one another to) obey".[64] The normative desideratum is therefore modest. By contrast to the domestic case, where the parties strive to find a set of guiding normative principles in the assessment and reform of state institutions, "in the international case, the parties are asked to endorse particular international rules directly".[65]

More precisely, Pogge distinguishes between Rawls' international rules as *interactional* and Rawls' domestic rules as *institutional*. The difference lies in the kind of task that deliberators have to achieve: international deliberators seek

---

61 Ibid., 102. In an earlier article, Beitz says essentially the same: there is no "independent layer of fundamental values whose nature and content can be discovered independently of reflection about the international realm and then used to interpret and criticize the international doctrine": Beitz, "Human Rights and the Law of Peoples", 6.
62 Besson, "Human Rights *qua* Normative Practice: *Sui Generis* or Legal?".
63 Pogge, "The Incoherence Between Rawls' Theories of Justice", 1740.
64 Ibid.
65 Ibid., 1746.

Political theories and practice-dependence 61

a mere set of rules of international conduct, whereas domestic deliberators are designing the basic principles of justice for their society:

> By conceiving his international theory *interactionally,* as seeking rules of good conduct, Rawls sidelines what he correctly identifies, within the domestic context, as the most important moral topic: the design of the institutional order, which crucially shapes the character of the relevant actors as well as the options and incentives they face.[66]

Several authors have criticized the absence of distributive justice principles in this construction.[67] Without addressing Rawls' theory of international justice specifically, I want to emphasize the continuum between Beitz, Raz and Rawls. One important premise is the normative weight of state autonomy that constrains the task assigned to international deliberators. This premise, supposedly derived from international practice, therefore constrains the normative desideratum of human rights. As Raz puts it, "the moral importance of state autonomy was fully appreciated by Rawls, and is a reason for his insistence that his doctrine of the justice of the basic structure (of the state) cannot be simply extended to the international arena".[68]

The asymmetry between the domestic and the international is salient in the minimal content of those international rules. To recall, international liberal and decent peoples together comprise a "Society of Peoples" whose actions are regulated by the "Law of Peoples". This law defines a shared basis, a "public reason" for taking action in the international arena. Abstractly conceived, the public reason refers to a normative commitment to take action when those rules are infringed. Human rights are just those rights that justify intervention. They also define the very conditions of political legitimacy *tout court*: "necessary conditions of any system of social cooperation. When they are regularly violated, we have command by force, a slave system, and no cooperation at all".[69] Now the content of the Rawlsian international public reason is what Rawls terms "decency". Human rights lie at the core of this threshold of decency. They are the right to life (to the means of subsistence and security); to liberty (to freedom from slavery, serfdom, and forced occupation, and to a sufficient measure of liberty of conscience to ensure freedom of religion and thought); to property (personal property) and to formal equality as expressed by the rules of natural justice (similar cases be treated similarly).[70]

---

66 Ibid., 1751.
67 As Valentini puts it, "although Rawls is a fervent advocate of domestic distributive justice, his outlook on international morality has no room for such distributive principles. Internationally, he defends the sovereign equality, territorial integrity and self-determination of nation-states, and affirms a duty of humanitarian assistance between them, ensuring that each community possesses the minimum level of resources to sustain its social and political life. For Rawls, international morality is a matter of mutual respect and assistance between different political communities": Valentini, "Global Justice and Practice-Dependence: Conventionalism, Institutionalism, Functionalism", 401.
68 Raz, "Human Rights Without Foundations", 331.
69 Rawls, *The Law of Peoples: With "The Idea of Public Reason Revisited"*, 68.
70 Ibid., 79–80.

62 *Political theories and practice-dependence*

Those minimal rights are necessary for a people to be respected as a member of the Society of Peoples and their respect is "sufficient to exclude justified forceful intervention by other peoples".[71] Whereas Rawls restricts international concern to forceful, military intervention, Raz defends a broader concept of intervention based on any form of sovereignty-limiting action: "following Rawls I will take human rights to be rights which set limits to the sovereignty of states, in that their actually or anticipated violation is a (defeasible) reason for taking action in the international arena".[72]

This threshold defined, Raz believes that we can readily use it to clean the list of human rights in international law: "international law is at fault when it recognizes as a human right something which, morally speaking, is not one whose violation might justify international action against the state".[73] Beitz, we have seen, in turn adds a number of softer forms of transnational response such as the offers of assistance or adaptation, and deprives human rights of any moral significance: "Rawls' functional explanation of human rights leaves the contents of the individual rights unworkably obscure."[74] Again, Rawls is closer to Raz in preserving a moral basis as necessary but not sufficient for the existence conditions of human rights – although Raz specifies in a later article that what makes rights "human rights" is their legal recognition and enforcement. Yet the appeal to some form of *public reason* as being decisive to the normativity of human rights is present in both Raz and Beitz. To recall, Rawls stresses that we should not derive human rights from a "theological, philosophical, or moral conception of the nature of the human person".[75] Although human rights are moral rights, "there is no appeal to any independent philosophical conception of a human right in Rawls' account of the content or authority of the doctrine".[76] This is where the practice-dependent overlap between Rawls, Beitz and Raz can be located. It is necessary for the political conception to appeal to the normative fact of a public reason whose human rights compose a part.

3.5 The practice-based distinction

We are now in a better position to capture the fundamental divergence between Griffin's moral conception and Beitz's political conception in how they view the role of normative facts and practices in human rights theory. In confining the task of theorizing human rights to the identification of the interests of rights-holders by independent moral reasoning, Griffin precisely maintains the continuum I seek to

---

71 Ibid.
72 Raz, "Human Rights Without Foundations", 328. For a critique of Raz's notion of sovereignty, see Tasioulas, "Are Human Rights Essentially Triggers for Intervention?", 944.
73 Raz, "Human Rights Without Foundations", 329.
74 Griffin, "Human Rights and the Autonomy of International Law", 343.
75 Rawls, *The Law of Peoples: With "The Idea of Public Reason Revisited"*, 81.
76 Beitz, *The Idea of Human Rights*, 99.

Political theories and practice-dependence 63

emphasize as distinctive of the practice-independent approach. Griffin and Forst not only preserve a normative basis (the right to personhood and the right to justification, respectively). They also firmly believe, on the methodological level, that the philosopher's enterprise is to theorize a concept "without reference to the global legal-institutional phenomenon of human rights".[77] My central claim here is that it is the *modality* through which the core structure and content of human rights is attained, the first-person moral standpoint, that is distinctive of the practice-independent approach in the ethical accounts examined. It is an independent claim, however, whether such modality of reasoning and derivation leads to point out a normative basis – such as personhood in Griffin's case – that may stand independently of institutional relations. This is clear in Forst's account: the fact that human rights stand at the core of our institutional relations does not imply that we end up in a normative vacuum as in Beitz. Tasioulas, we have seen, adds a requirement that has to do with the very concept of *right*. Griffin's conception of rights, in contrast, is reduced to "an entitlement that a person possesses to control or claim something".[78]

By contrast, Beitz's practice-independence lies in a continuum from the descriptive and analytical to the normative levels of argument. From the description of the paradigms of implementation of human rights to the construction of his normative model, this continuum is not evaluated. Of course, Beitz abstracts from the descriptive statements and isolates the three-pronged conceptual structure. First, human rights imply the protection of urgent *individual interests* (personal security and liberty, adequate nutrition, arbitrary use of state power) against standard threats in the modern world order composed of states. Second, human rights apply in the first instance to the institutions of the state. Third, human rights imply an international concern. The resulting normative content is there but at no point does Beitz seek to derive human rights from a deeper layer of morality. Beitz suggests attending to:

> the practical inferences that would be drawn by competent participants in the practice from what they regard as valid claims of human rights. An inventory of these inferences generates a view of the discursive function of human rights and this informs an account of the meaning of the concept.[79]

Not surprisingly, Beitz describes his own enterprise of theorizing as "modelling" – that is, it abstracts "from the particulars to describe in general the roles played by human rights in the public normative discourse of global politics".[80] However, if the standpoint selected for theorizing is contingent, it remains to be seen if the normative content of human rights would change if the standpoint were different. This is the project I aim to develop within the context of the ECHR.

---

77 Buchanan, "The Egalitarianism of Human Rights", 680.
78 Griffin, *On Human Rights*, 30.
79 Beitz, *The Idea of Human Rights*, 103.
80 Ibid., 106.

4 Theorizing human rights

A constructivist proposal

At the end of the last chapter, I concluded that the ethical and political conceptions of human rights are mutually exclusive when it comes to the role of facts and practices of human rights in constructing a theory. In this chapter, I lay down the basis for a reconciliatory approach. I show how one can incorporate the Beitzian requirement of human rights as tied to the international state system and the Razian concept of *rights* while preserving the modality of Griffin shared by Forst – that is, that human rights theorizing implies appealing to an independent level of moral reasoning. My core argument is that constructivism in moral and political theory has the resources to fruitfully reconcile those claims by reference to the legal and judicial practice of the ECHR.

The argument is two-fold. First, constructivism can fully incorporate the premise that human rights are part of a political-legal construct of an international kind (*pace* Beitz). This is because for constructivists the justification of moral principles is an inherently practical enterprise – that is, to obtain a public basis of justification for the governing role of independent social norms. As James puts it, "its aim is not to characterize the meta-ethical status of justice but to justify specific principles as a reasonable basis for public agreement in particular areas of social life".[1] As such, constructivism can conceptualize the legal and judicial practice of human rights as an independent normative. What aspect of the practice should count as relevant for constructivism? I argue that the status of ECHR rights and ECtHR judgments in national jurisdictions instantiates the public role of human rights norms: States Parties routinely abide by the judgments of an international court and individuals may thereby invoke them before any public institution (legislative, judicial, executive). This is the practical and international dimension of the practice. The standard of rights is fully there too: the authoritative adjudication of the ECtHR implies that the duties correlative to human rights are recognized, specified and allocated in the case law. By contrast to the UN human rights treaties, an accomplished, well-respected and quasi-constitutional judicial organ shapes the content of the ECHR and thereby determines the content and scope of our basic freedoms within the state.

---

1 James, "Political Constructivism", 251–2.

Theorizing human rights 65

Second, constructivism can also account for the special status of human rights as anchored in a moral layer of reasoning (*pace* Griffin and Forst). This is because, again, the founding objective of constructivism requires providing subjects of public norms with an interpretation of those norms that make them reasonably acceptable to all. Constructivism requires the exercise of a form of substantive moral reasoning in determining the deeper and "objective" reasons for sharing the social norms that affect us. A fundamental assumption of constructivists is that "the normative question arises for humans insofar as they are capable of reflecting on themselves and considering their thoughts and desires from a detached perspective".[2] The legal and judicial practice of ECHR rights is therefore subjected to this moral demand simply because they play such an important normative role in the public life of all Europeans in their respective legal and political orders. As James puts it, "the goal is not simply a sociological description of what is already assumed in a practice; it is also to constructively propose a version of the assumed practice that we as theorists can endorse as reasonable".[3] The attention devoted to concrete legal and judicial practices comprises the deeper aim of reconciling free and rational individuals with the institutions that govern their social relations – to "actualize" our freedoms within a given institutional ordering. Because the adjudication of the ECtHR authoritatively supports the role that the ECHR plays in domestic legal orders, it forms the more precise object of normative evaluation in the constructivist sense.

In order not to put the cart before the horse, I first elaborate on the constructivist approach to *justification* before showing how it can generate a *method of justification* for human rights practice by incorporating the three dimensions identified in the human rights theories reviewed so far (the *international* dimension, the *rights* dimension and the *moral* dimension, respectively). While the former essentially pertains to the question of how normative propositions can be deemed to be "objective" and how they can (if at all) be justified, the latter lays down the main methodological steps of the constructivist approach and how it applies to legal and judicial practice. It must be noted, however, that I do not embark on a fine-grained analysis of the disputes between the various post-Rawlsian accounts of moral and political constructivism (in particular, those of Scanlon, Korsgaard, O'Neill, Street and James[4]), and especially as it regards

---

2 Bagnoli, "Constructivism in Metaethics".
3 James, "Political Constructivism", 251.
4 For T.M. Scanlon's interpersonal constructivism, see Scanlon, *What We Owe to Each Other*. For Christine Korsgaard's substantive constructivism, see Korsgaard, *The Sources of Normativity*. See also Korsgaard, "Realism and Constructivism in Twentieth-Century Moral Philosophy". For a review of Scanlon and Korsgaard, see James, "Constructivism, Moral". For Onora O'Neill's version of constructivism, see O'Neill, "Constructivism vs. Contractualism"; see also O'Neill, "Constructivism in Rawls and Kant", 347. For Sharon Street's, see Street, "What Is Constructivism in Ethics and Metaethics?".

66 *Theorizing human rights*

the constructivist meta-ethical neutrality within the realist/anti-realist debate about moral value.[5] Rather, I want to show how constructivism can overcome the antagonisms of the ethical and political conceptions.

4.1 Constructivism *qua* justification

4.1.1 The third way of constructivism

The meta-ethical claim of constructivism is best introduced by what it is not. Constructivism assumes that one is not forced to choose between moral *realism* (claiming the existence of independent moral facts grasped by cognition) and moral *scepticism* (such as *subjectivism* or *relativism* about the existence of moral facts). First, constructivism is not a realist position in that it assigns "no place or weight to distinctively moral facts or properties, whether nature or non-natural, that can be discovered or intuited and do not seek foundations for ethics in such facts".[6] Since for the realist there are some normative truths that can outrun one's practical standpoint, constructivism just will not do. This is clear in Rawls' rejection of *intuitionism*: "it prescribed a plurality of unranked principles, so it offers no way of setting moral disputes".[7] However, there are not just internal reasons for not endorsing intuitionism. Constructivists also argue that the appeal to a realm of independent moral facts is not necessary for the practical concern of justification in society: "the intuitionist's realm of independent facts need not be supposed to exist for us to make good sense of normative justification".[8] Second, constructivism is not a *sceptical* position towards the objectivity of moral propositions either in that it assumes that they may be true, objective and motivational in a practical sense without giving moral values the sort of metaphysical objectivity that realism assumes. As James puts it:

> We can reject subjectivism, conventionalism, cultural relativism and any other view that immunizes individuals or groups from error, but without thereby accepting Platonism, theological voluntarism, or any other view that allows values to be radically esoteric, and so not *values* in the ordinary sense.[9]

One may therefore view constructivism as paving the way for a third option: moral principles are those that agents would agree, accept and act upon if they were to engage in an "idealized process of rational deliberation"[10] from within

---

5 For an overview of this issue, see "The Meta-Ethical Status of Constructivism and Its Import" section in Bagnoli, "Constructivism in Metaethics". See also Street, "Constructivism About Reasons" and Street, "What Is Constructivism in Ethics and Metaethics?", 370–9.

6 O'Neill, "Constructivism vs. Contractualism", 320.

7 Ibid.

8 Lenman and Shemmer. "Introduction", 4.

9 James, "Constructing Protagorean Objectivity", 60.

10 Bagnoli, "Constructivism in Metaethics".

Theorizing human rights 67

their normative practices. Rawls' famous slogan, "political, not metaphysical" (applied to the concept of justice) is seminal here:

> What justifies a conception of justice is not its being true to an order antecedent to and given to us, but its congruence with our deeper understanding of ourselves and our aspirations, and our realization that, given our traditions and embedded in our public life, it is the most reasonable doctrine for us.[11]

The core aim is to "enable all members of society to make mutually acceptable to one another their shared institutions and basic arrangements, by citing what is publicly recognized as sufficient reasons, identified by that conception".[12] We therefore strive to find a mutually justifiable set of principles that plays a central social role in society just by appealing to a normative standpoint which could be endorsed by all the participants of the practice as free and equal agents. Street calls this limited scope of constructivism the "restricted view" of constructivism: "viewed in this way, restricted versions of constructivism fall squarely in the realm of normative ethics, presenting themselves as explorations of what normative conclusions follow from what normative premises".[13]

Correlatively, the final normative principles are not fixed once and for all but remain constantly fallible and subject to revision. Indeed, constructivists separate the issue of content from the issue of procedure: "when constructivists do not give substantial arguments to particular conclusions, they therefore must at least show that we have clear enough understanding of reasoning that leads to recognizably moral results".[14] Again, this does prevent constructivists from qualifying the output as objective. Rather, constructivism implies that values "have no reality independent of idealized practical reason".[15] Again, for the sake of concision, I do not enter into the subtle distinctions between the many forms and developments of constructivism in the philosophical literature. The core idea I retain is that the moral "ought" is *just* the reasons which the inter-subjective procedure finds acceptable. Constructivism is a constructive procedure *from* and *for* a normative standpoint.

4.1.2 Constructivism in Rawls

Having introduced the core claim of the constructivist approach to political morality, I want to briefly explain its origins in Rawls – in *A Theory of Justice* and *Political Liberalism* and, more importantly, in his seminal article "Kantian Constructivism in Moral Theory". The latter article is considered as the "Kantian phase" of Rawls in which the meta-ethical status of constructivism is explicitly

---

11 Rawls, "Kantian Constructivism in Moral Theory", 519.
12 Ibid., 517.
13 Street, "Constructivism About Reasons", 218.
14 James, "Constructivism, Moral", 1067.
15 Ibid., 1069.

68   *Theorizing human rights*

assumed, whereas Rawls does not yet use the word "constructivism" in *A Theory of Justice* or *Political Liberalism*. In fact, some argue that his views in those masterpieces are *contractarian* rather than constructivist.[16] Rawls' central definition of Kantian constructivism – in contrast to constructivism *tout court*, and which makes it distinctive as a moral and political theory – goes as follows:

> What distinguishes the Kantian form of constructivism is essentially this: it specifies a particular conception of the person as an element in a reasonable procedure of construction, the outcome of which determines the content of the first principles of justice.[17]

Rawls' conception of the person is a core premise of the procedure of justification outlined above. As such, Rawlsian constructivism has affinities with Kantian ethics:

> A Kantian doctrine joins the content of justice with a certain conception of the person; and this conception regards persons as both free and equals, as capable of acting reasonably and rationally, and therefore as capable of taking part in social cooperation among persons so conceived.[18]

Human persons are conceived as having two moral powers: they have both a sense of justice – "the capacity to understand, to apply and act from (and not merely in accordance with) the principles of justice"[19] – and a "capacity to form, to revise, and rationally to pursue a conception of the good".[20] In the context of justice, Rawls argues that this conception of the moral person itself justifies the list of primary *moral goods* for "developing and exercising the two moral powers and for effectively pursuing a conception of the good".[21]

The second central Kantian element of Rawls is the fundamental idea that moral truth and guidance can be available to us through the use of the moral reasoning in ordinary practical circumstances:

> In the Kantian constructivist view, then, it is a feature attributed to persons (for the purposes of a conception of social justice) that they can stand above and critically survey their own final ends by reference to a notion of the Reasonable and the Rational. In this sense, they are independent from and moved by considerations other than those given by their particular conceptions of the good.[22]

---

16 In *A Theory of Justice*, Rawls does not use "constructivism" but merely "constructive criteria". For an overview of the evolution of the Rawlsian position on this issue, see O'Neill, "Constructivism in Rawls and Kant".

17 Rawls, "Kantian Constructivism in Moral Theory", 516.

18 Ibid., 518. In *Political Liberalism*, Rawls defines being reasonable as "being willing to propose and honour fair terms of cooperation and to recognize the burdens of judgments and accept their consequences": Rawls, *Political Liberalism*, 309.

19 Rawls, "Kantian Constructivism in Moral Theory", 525.

20 Ibid. For the elaboration of the two moral powers, see ibid., 543–54.

21 Ibid., 525–6.

22 Ibid., 548–9.

Theorizing human rights   69

This is also true of constructivism today: "like Kant, contemporary constructivists assume that morality must be understood in terms of reasoning that is, at least in principle, 'available' to use given the methods of reasoning and observation we ordinarily use".[23] Although they do not endorse the formalism and universalism of the Categorical Imperative, the very possibility of normative ethics contingent upon the agent's autonomous reflective and deliberative capacities is Kantian: "in both cases what we are looking for is principles themselves, for we need reasons, ways of choosing and justifying our actions or our policies, and reasons are derived from principles".[24] In this sense, Kant and Rawls converge in that justification and motivation are possible without supposing antecedent moral facts and agreements.

However, it is also clear that the Rawlsian constructivist procedure is tied to a certain institutional context of justification – what Rawls calls a "well-ordered society", which in effect corresponds with the functioning liberal democratic order or the modern international state system. As James notes, "Rawls never clearly formulates his constructivism independently of the specific social contexts that interest him, the major institutions of modern constitutional democracies and modern international law and practice".[25] This implies for Rawls that the normative standpoint suitable for the constructivist procedure must be sufficiently developed to display an *implicit basis of agreement* among participants in the practice. Rawls explains that "conditions for justifying a conception of justice hold only when a basis is established for political reasoning and understanding within a public culture".[26] Its political form in *A Theory of Justice* and *Political Liberalism* is essentially the liberal democratic state – what Street calls the "target set of normative judgments"[27] of Rawls: the just distribution of rights, liberties, opportunities, income, wealth, and so on. As O'Neill also explains, "within a closed democratic society, reasonable citizens will indeed and unsurprisingly be willing to seek and abide by shared principles and standards for the fundamental arrangements of life when this is possible".[28] It is therefore important to note that Rawls refers to a relatively *closed* society:

> An on-going society, a self-sufficient association of human beings which, like a nation-state, controls a connected territory. Its members view their common polity as extending backwards and forwards in time over generations, and they strive to reproduce themselves and their cultural and social life, practically speaking . . .[29]

---

23 James, "Political Constructivism: Foundations and Novel Applications", available at: http://phil papers.org/rec/JAMPCF, 1.

24 Korsgaard, "Realism and Constructivism in Twentieth-Century Moral Philosophy", 320.

25 James, "Political Constructivism: Foundations and Novel Applications", 1.

26 Rawls, "Kantian Constructivism in Moral Theory", 517.

27 Street, "Constructivism About Reasons", 210.

28 O'Neill, "Political Liberalism and Public Reason: A Critical Notice of John Rawls, Political Liberalism", 421.

29 Rawls, "Kantian Constructivism in Moral Theory", 536.

70 *Theorizing human rights*

The basic social and political arrangements of the liberal democratic nation-state are therefore implicit in the premises of the constructivist procedure. As Simmons specifies, "Rawlsian justification is principally a justification of coercion offered to those who already accept the necessity of living in some kind of state".[30] Of course, this second assumption goes against the Kantian universalism of moral norms and practical reason. Kant assumes no prior context of justification as structured to reach only a limited audience: "we can start with a purely formal understanding of the attitude of valuing and demonstrate that recognizably moral values are entailed from within the standpoint of any valuer as such".[31] True, Kant proposes a method to identify normative principles for practical life, but he does not take practical reason itself as susceptible to justification. As O'Neill specifies, "Kant takes it that the capacity of principles and standards to be made public to all others without restriction is constitutive of their reasonableness".[32] This poses the question of the applicability of constructivism to other contexts of justification.

4.2 Constructivism *qua* method of justification

Although constructivism according to Rawls remains tied to the liberal democratic order of the modern state, moral theorists have more recently specified the procedure of justification that is central to constructivism and which may be applied to other contexts of justification. To present this more general approach to constructivism and apply it to legal and judicial practice, I rely here mainly on the recent contributions of James and Street. Three main steps may be distinguished.

First, following James, constructivism requires the capturing of a practical reason operating in an independent normative practice:

> Reasoning to such principles begins from an organized group's own common practical reason. A group's "common practical reason" includes generally (perhaps implicitly) affirmed "fundamental ideas," as they are interpreted and applied in practice, in light of shared general understandings of the kind of social practice being maintained (e.g., a society seen as a fair scheme of cooperation among equals over time), and despite larger differences in worldview.[33]

This first specification is conducted in non-evaluative terms, as the political conception of human rights precisely requires. Street talks of the "restricted set of

---

30 Simmons, "Justification and Legitimacy", 758.
31 Street, "What Is Constructivism in Ethics and Metaethics?", 369.
32 O'Neill, "Political Liberalism and Public Reason: A Critical Notice of John Rawls, Political Liberalism", 423.
33 James, "Political Constructivism", 252.

Theorizing human rights 71

judgments" or "target set of normative judgments"[34] as the more precise domain selected. In accordance with constructivism, this domain is limited to a set of prevailing normative claims; it "justifies, by a reasonable procedure, both *for* and *from* a contingent and independently established 'basis', which includes both 'shared institutions' and an associated 'political culture'".[35]

Once this restricted set of normative claims is identified, the justification process can then start via a reconstructive and interpretative step. In the words of James:

> Reasoning from such sources is to proceed by elaborating a version of the common social practice that each involved can find reasonably acceptable, from their respective standpoints. This "elaboration" mixes moral judgments with what has come to be called "constructivist interpretation" of assumed fundamental ideas.[36]

In Rawls, the outcome of this process is the two basic principles (liberty and equality) considered to be implicit within liberal-democratic practices – an "impasse of our political culture".[37] This second step also implies switching from an *interpretation* of a given normative practice in its original terminological and conceptual specificities to a *moralized interpretation* of that same practice. Street speaks of the "results of construction"[38] to designate the resulting normative content. Those are "the reasons that are the subject matter of the target set of normative judgments".[39] It must be clear that this step is just a reconstruction of the layer of reasons that prevail within the practical standpoint selected. Obviously, "greater abstraction comes at the potential cost of outstripping the basis of agreement that is actually there".[40]

The third and last step goes beyond the purpose of moralized reconstruction and interpretation. Given the moralized framework, we are in a better position to see whether some *further* normative claims may be endorsed by the practical standpoint. Street's version of this step is particularly useful. The correctness of any further normative judgment depends on whether it survives the web of normative judgments in one's practical standpoint: "the subject-matter of ethics is what follows from within the standpoint of the creatures who are already taking this, that, or the other thing to be valuable".[41] At this stage of the process, one may rely on the "interlocking web of normative judgments"[42] when we need further reasons to admit some normative judgment. Street's version of constructivism

---

34 Street, "Constructivism About Reasons", 210.
35 James, "Political Constructivism: Foundations and Novel Applications", 9.
36 Ibid., 3.
37 Rawls, "Kantian Constructivism in Moral Theory", 519.
38 Street, "Constructivism About Reasons", 210.
39 Ibid.
40 James, "Political Constructivism", 258.
41 Street, "What Is Constructivism in Ethics and Metaethics?", 367.
42 Street, "Constructivism About Reasons", 235.

72 *Theorizing human rights*

applies more specifically to *normative reasons* alone: the core claim is that the very fact of making a normative claim – to take a sufficient reason to act – itself sets standards by which other reasons for action may possibly be endorsed by the practical standpoint. As Street further explains:

> As soon as one takes anything whatsoever to be a reason, one thereby legislates standards according to which, by one's own lights as a valuing agent, one is making a mistake, whether one knows it or not, if one endorses other normative judgments".[43]

James is more flexible regarding the transition from the second to the third step:

> There need not be any bright line between substantive moral judgment and moralized interpretive attribution . . . . The key is that anything we say along these lines must be credible, where the standard of credibility and ultimate success involves both normative and interpretive perspicuity.[44]

The practical standpoint is clearly identified and its premises captured before the justification can operate. As Street explains, "it is a mistake to ask about the correctness of *any* normative judgments in the utter abstract, without making at least implicit references to a standpoint constituted by some further set of normative judgments".[45] Constructivism is therefore designed to avoid the risk of esoteric morality. As James puts it, "it is intended to block the possibility that ordinary moral thought is radically in error, that moral truth could be radically esoteric".[46] As explained earlier, constructivism does not only recommend starting the reconstruction process within a well-defined normative practice. It is founded on the view that "the only standards of correctness that exist are those set from the practical point of view itself".[47]

4.3 Theorizing human rights: a constructivist proposal

Having presented the constructivist approach to justification, I now return to the conclusion I reached at the end of the last chapter. I hope that one can now better explain the well-spread scepticism towards Griffin's lack of practice-responsiveness. Griffin does not specify and interpret either the context, the kind of practice or discourse in which the justificatory deficit of human rights is identified or the appropriateness of the personhood account. Despite that Griffin refers to discursive elements – for example, some rights claim in the UN Secretary General's statements – they do not inform the core structure and content of those

---

43 Ibid., 230.
44 James, "Political Constructivism: Foundations and Novel Applications", 19.
45 Street, "Constructivism About Reasons", 220.
46 James, "Constructivism, Moral", 1070.
47 Street, "Constructivism About Reasons", 220.

Theorizing human rights 73

rights. Beitz's account, by contrast, confines the task of human rights theorizing to an interpretation of the most salient global political practices and argues that such a practical conception does not require appealing to a deeper layer of moral reasoning.

Constructivism suggests, I argue, a third, reconciliatory approach. On the one hand, constructivism as a general method of justification can account for the fact that, as Beitz argues, human rights are a political, legal and institutional construct with a normative role of their own. This is because, as explained above, constructivism *qua* political morality assumes that it is not necessary to engage in the debate about ultimate moral truth for the sake of institutional and practical evaluation. As Freeman puts it, "moral statements correspond to no antecedent moral facts or to a realm of values that are prior and independent of practical reasoning".[48] Normative correctness therefore inheres and remains confined within the reach of some practical standpoint. While this will not allow us to understand what *value* itself is, it does give us a sense of the *attitude of valuing*. As Street explains, "to speak metaphorically, the standards of correctness and incorrectness of normative judgments are thought to be given 'from within', or 'legislated by', some further practical standpoint: to be correct is to withstand scrutiny from that standpoint".[49] As we have seen, this means that the normative content is fully constituted by the outcome of the constructivist procedure: "what is distinctive of constructivist views is that they understand correctness to be *constituted* by emergence from a certain procedure and not merely *coincident* with it".[50]

Concretely, the constructivist method starts with a process of identification and interpretation of a relevant practical standpoint. This first step should be achieved in uncontroversial and non-evaluative terms – as the political conception of human rights precisely requires. As James puts it:

> We single out an object of social interpretation and moral evaluation, at first in relatively uncontroversial terms, with references to various interpretive "data points" or "source materials" that any further conception of the practice should take into account and explain (or "explain away").[51]

In the context of the ECHR, this step requires adopting the specifically legal and judicial framework in which the practice is confined. The ECHR together with the ECtHR are distinctively legal creatures of an international kind. International law is therefore needed to specify the conditions that are required for legal norms to shape the ordinary life of individuals and constitute the "common social practice"[52] that constructivism aims to identify. To this end, we need to understand the normativity of international human rights law *within* the broader field of

---

48 Freeman, "The Burdens of Public Justification: Constructivism, Contractualism, and Publicity", 7.
49 Street, "Constructivism About Reasons", 209.
50 Ibid., 212.
51 James, "Political Constructivism", 257.
52 Ibid.

74   *Theorizing human rights*

international law. In Chapter 6, I specify this step in the ECHR context by pointing to the status of *direct effect* of ECHR rights and ECtHR judgments in national jurisdictions in contrast to the UN treaty bodies, for instance, whose judgments are weaker. *Direct effect* means, in concrete terms, that ECHR rights and ECtHR judgments are binding within national law and are invocable by individuals *vis-à-vis* all state institutions, whether legislative, executive or judicial. This standard is the most relevant as it applies to every single individual residing on European soil. Of course, one can file a case at the ECtHR *if and only if* one has exhausted internal remedies in the domestic jurisdiction. Note that this characterization of the practice is *functional*, following Beitzian standards. However, ECHR rights *qua* human rights are not, as Beitz argues, *pro tanto* reasons for action. Rather, in light of their authority in domestic legal orders, they are *conclusory* reasons for its subjects (public institutions) to take action. Nevertheless, the Beitzian standard of human rights as tied to the international realm remains, although it must be adjusted to the regional and legal nature of the ECHR.

However, as we have already seen, the practice of the ECHR cannot be reduced to its authority in national legal orders. In addition, one must fully address the adjudicatory function of the ECtHR as *direct effect* applies to judgments as well. Here, the objective in constructivist terms is to reconstruct the judicial powers of the ECtHR together with how it has interpreted and specified the content of ECHR rights in its case law. In so doing, the relevant practical standpoint is further specified. As far as the former is concerned, it is important to note that the ECtHR does not have the power of judicial review that constitutional courts have. As I explain in Chapter 6, the ECtHR is empowered to *declare* whether one or several ECHR rights have been violated in a single case. States Parties remain free to choose how to comply with the Strasbourg judgment (*remedial* subsidiarity). As far as the latter is concerned, adjudication plays a decisive role in specifying the thick and abstract nature of human rights. As I show in Chapter 8, the ECtHR not only has to specify the interest(s) protected by those abstract rights in light of the situation brought before the ECtHR; it also has to balance them against normative considerations put forward by the respondent State Party. It may generate positive duties or accord a margin of appreciation to respondent States Parties depending on the circumstances. This is how ECHR rights acquire their character of *rights*. Their correlative duties are recognized, specified and allocated. Here, the considerations are properly *substantive*: we identify the reasons why the ECtHR protects such and such rights. Here, again, adjudication operates with distinctively legal standards that need to be specified. For instance, the ECtHR has rejected most of the conventional approaches to interpretation that place the consent of states as the authoritative standard of international legal legitimacy. Rather, the ECtHR has addressed the substance of the rights in non-functional terms. There is enough, I shall argue, in the reasoning of the ECtHR to capture a *practical reason* – a set of powerful reasons by which the actions of states and individuals are judged – which governs the adjudication process and which can be subjected to the constructivist procedure presented above.

Theorizing human rights 75

On the other hand, constructivism is not just a sociological and descriptive enterprise. It can also account for the special status of human rights as important moral rights in order to avoid the mere maintenance of the status quo *à la* Beitz or Raz. Once the practical reason is captured, interpreted and moralized, we need to look for a justificatory basis that *serves* the role that human rights play in practice and that can be shown to be reasonably acceptable to all participants involved in the practice under scrutiny. As Rawls puts it in the justice context:

> Whenever a sufficient basis for agreement is not presently known, or recognized, the task of justifying a conception of justice becomes: how can people settle on a conception of justice, to serve this social role, that is (most) reasonable for them in virtue of how they conceive of their persons and construe the general feature of social cooperation among persons so conceived.[53]

This step is both interpretative and normative, following James and Street. We look for a public basis of justification that is implicit in the practice examined. This is where the justificatory dimension of the reasoning of the ECtHR becomes particularly important. We construct a basis for public justification that is derived from the web of normative judgments that the ECtHR has held in its case law over the years. This is the proper substantive step of the procedure: "we engage in substantive moral reasoning about what the various relevant reasons support, as framed and guided by the specified framing conception".[54]

How does this constructivist proposal differ from the ethical approach to human rights? To recall, the foundational value of personhood in Griffin captures what he takes to be essential in human beings as reflective normative agents – deliberating, assessing, choosing and acting to make what one thinks as valuable in life. This value applies irrespective of any procedural consideration. This is because personhood captures a fundamental moral category. In contrast, constructivists are more demanding towards the characterization of the practice or discourse of human rights than that assumed by Griffin. For constructivists, justification cannot operate irrespective of practical and discursive standards. This is where the distinction between the practice-dependence of the *content* of norms under consideration and the practice-independence of justification of the same normative content becomes central. That is, one may imagine applying an independent modality – requiring some substantive moral reasoning – from within the practice in the constructivist sense. This is how, I believe, the constructivist framework can unlock the dispute between the ethical and political conception of human rights with reference to the legal and judicial practice of the ECHR.

---

53 Rawls, "Kantian Constructivism in Moral Theory", 517.
54 James, "Political Constructivism", 258.

5　The ECHR in historical perspective

Having laid down the constructivist approach to justification and the main methodological steps associated with it in the last chapter, I now turn specifically to the object of investigation, the ECHR. In this chapter, I review, with the aid of seminal historical work, the original context in which the ECHR and the ECtHR came into being, their founding goals as well as their subsequent evolutions.

There are two major reasons for falling back on historical interpretation at this stage of the investigation. On the one hand, in the context of the ECHR the constructivist approach requires addressing the normativity of legal and judicial norms *specifically*. Here, historical analysis helps to introduce this particular institution and fix the object of normative elucidation before applying the three-pronged constructivist procedure. This historical introduction is therefore a first specification of the political conception of human rights in the context of the ECHR. On the other hand, addressing historical considerations has to do with the constant reference, in the adjudication of the ECtHR, to the founding goal(s) of the ECHR to determine the scope of conventional obligations. As I show in Chapters 7 and 8, the appeal to the "object and purpose" of the ECHR is perhaps the best example.

For the sake of concision, the historical review is based on five major segments. The first is the period from its burgeoning social and political process in the late 1940s to the operational establishment of the ECtHR in 1959. In this segment, I address the initial enthusiasm for the need to prevent the return of totalitarianism via a supranational judicial organ. The European Movement played a crucial role in the first steps towards the creation of the Council of Europe (CoE) in 1949.

Second, I address the reception of the proposed Convention at the intergovernmental and legislative level. When the proposal for the Convention reached the Committee of Ministers of the CoE, its reception was far from enthusiastic. In fact, the Committee ignored the invitation to grant permission to the Consultative Assembly to debate the proposed Convention. By contrast to human rights promoters and their quest for individual justice, governments are attached to the idea of an "alarm bell" system against the return of totalitarianism without any loss of sovereignty.

Third, I review the burgeoning practice of the ECtHR (1959–69). The ECHR entered into force in 1953 when the 10 ratifications were obtained. Individual petition was made effective in 1955 when the required six acceptances were

The ECHR in historical perspective 77

completed. The jurisdiction of the ECtHR was confirmed in 1958 with the necessary eight acceptances, although the ECtHR did not become operational until 1959. Other than the Federal Republic of Germany, the only states to support this burgeoning institution were minor states, the two grand absentees, of course, being France and the United Kingdom. Also, the ECtHR was entirely dormant between 1960 and 1965. This is in line with the initial reluctance of intrusive judicial mechanisms, their erratic burgeoning of human rights and their rather recent establishment as the *lingua franca* of international political discourse.

The fourth segment addresses the decade between 1985 and 1995 and the emerging "overload crisis". The two crucial structural conditions for the explosion of petitions – the right of individual petition and the compulsory jurisdiction of the ECtHR – were by that time widely accepted. The independent and autonomous judicial practice of the ECtHR was growing. In international politics, the "new demand" towards human rights was established and the international political climate clearly favourable – most clearly, after the fall of the Berlin Wall in 1989. These factors combined can explain the attractiveness of the system for potential applicants and resulted in a shortage of both institutional and human resources. It was in the early 1990s that the first structural measures were taken.

5.1 The "alarm bell" against totalitarianism

In the aftermath of the Second World War, the political project of institutionalizing the protection of international human rights at the supranational level in Europe was burgeoning. The creation of the ECHR and the ECtHR was continuous with the immediate post-war reflections on how to prevent the return of totalitarian regimes through an international/legal response. The debate dates back to the European Movement, an independent and cross-national formation whose most concrete achievement is the creation of the CoE.[1] The first proposals for a European Convention on Human Rights were made under the auspices of the European Movement. The first notable event took place in The Hague in May 1948 through the Congress of Europe, a congress of civil society movements and state representatives presided over by Winston Churchill. Through a network of thinkers, political leaders and militant associations from all over Europe, more than 700 delegates met to discuss the response to war and the modalities of an agreement on human rights.[2] In the "Message to Europeans", the transnational movement called not only for a "Charter of Human Rights guaranteeing liberty of thought, assembly, and expression" as well as a "Court of Justice with adequate sanctions for the implementation of this Charter".[3]

---

1 On 5 May 1949, representatives of Belgium, France, Luxembourg, the Netherlands and the UK, Denmark, Ireland, Italy, Norway and Sweden signed in London the statutes of the Council of Europe, which notably implements the Parliamentary Assembly, the first supranational assembly with democratically elected representatives of national parliaments.
2 For a detailed description of the notable people present at this congress, see Simpson, *Human Rights and the End of Empire*, 560–3.
3 European Movement, *European Movement and the Council of Europe*.

78   *The ECHR in historical perspective*

Clearly an exploratory project, this embryonic movement was nothing but the first transnational discussion that would eventually lead not only to the ECHR but also, through a different path, to the creation of the European Union (EU). At the time, the distinction between the project of a human rights convention and the federalist project of the EU was not clear:

> The mission of the Convention as proposed by the Assembly was therefore open to interpretation, but it evidently had the potential to become a type of European Bill of Rights for the European Union that some in the Assembly hoped was imminent.[4]

A year later, in July 1949 in The Hague, the European Movement produced a 32-page document entitled "European Convention on Human Rights". The text contained the first list of rights and an explicit reference to the need for a supranational judicial organ subject to the separate Draft Statute for a Proposed European Court of Human Rights. The project was aimed at "the creation among the European democracies of a system of collective security against tyranny and oppression" and established that "without delay, joint measures should be taken to halt the spread of totalitarianism and maintain an area of freedom".[5] The first draft of the Convention therefore targeted totalitarian practices specifically. As Bates explains, "the first ambition of the European Movement, then, was that there should be no step-by-step regression in human rights standards, as had occurred with Germany's slide into dictatorship in the 1930s".[6] If the text is still vague and its implications unclear, the essence of the ECHR we know today is there. The conservatism and minimalism of the ECHR are also considered as a key explanatory factor in Moyn's account of the ECHR:

> From the beginning this energy in the movement to defend and define human rights as the essence of European civilization in the European Convention came from conservatives – Churchill and his allies out of power, anxious about the spectre of socialism at home, and opposite number on the Continent worried about the impeding triumph of "materialism" over "spiritual" values.[7]

For the sake of concision, two more specific points about the European burgeoning human rights movement may be retained. From a substantive standpoint, the emphasis on democracy and, in particular, on the respect for the rights of political opposition, is recurrent. The reference to an area of protected basic civil and political freedoms that sustain democracy within states shapes both the letter and spirit of the proposed Convention. Although suppressed in the final version of the Convention, Article 2 required each state "faithfully to respect the fundamental

---

4 Bates, "The Birth of the European Convention on Human Rights", 25.
5 See European Movement, *European Movement and the Council of Europe*.
6 Bates, "The Birth of the European Convention on Human Rights", 21.
7 Moyn, *The Last Utopia: Human Rights in History*, 79.

The ECHR in historical perspective 79

principles of democracy" and to proscribe any action "which would interfere with the right of political criticism and the right to organise a political opposition".

From an institutional point of view, the burgeoning European human rights movement was also at the core of the debates pertaining to the necessity of going beyond mere intergovernmental levels of cooperation and, in terms of international law, to develop a supranational organ that would independently revise states' human rights records. Of course, its judicial powers were subject to a sustained discussion until the proposal for the ECtHR was formally adopted in 1950. The tension evidently turned on the potential loss of sovereignty if the newly created Court enjoyed compulsory jurisdiction. As a result, Article 7(b) of the proposed Convention included the setting-up of a European Human Rights Commission that would be empowered to select and "screen" cases from individuals and states. Moreover, Article 8 required that "any state that failed to comply with the judgment would be referred to the Council of Europe for appropriate action". The *executive* function was therefore left at the intergovernmental level. In other words, if the idea of a supranational court was there, the powers of the envisaged ECtHR did not pose any serious threat to the sovereign states of Europe. As Bates explains:

> As to the Court, it would be the conscience of the free Europe, acting like an "alarm bell" warning the other nations of democratic Europe that one of their number was going "totalitarian". At this stage, then, the human rights guarantee was minimalist in its ambition.[8]

5.2 The Convention proposal at the legislative and intergovernmental levels

If we stick to the institutional level of historical analysis, the programmatic distinction between the Convention for human rights and the project of European federalism was achieved when the Convention, in May 1949, reached the Consultative Assembly of the CoE – its legislative body, composed of democratically elected members of national parliaments. In fact, the newly created CoE did not emerge as a supranational entity or federation of any kind, but as a mere *intergovernmental organization* and it is best depicted as a Western intergovernmental forum operating in the context of the Cold War. As Moravcsik explains:

> Certainly many leading advocates of the Convention were European federalists and viewed the ECHR as a step towards European integration. Yet there is little evidence that a shared transnational discourse influenced the positions of parliamentary members of the assembly, let alone representatives of national governments.[9]

---

8 Bates, "The Birth of the European Convention on Human Rights", 21.
9 Moravcsik, "The Origins of Human Rights Regimes: Democratic Delegation in Postwar Europe", 235.

80   *The ECHR in historical perspective*

Moreover, when the proposal for the Convention reached the Committee of Ministers of the CoE, the reception was far from enthusiastic. In fact, the Committee ignored the invitation to grant permission to the Consultative Assembly to debate the proposed Convention. As Simpson explains, "the truth is that a majority of the governments in the Council of Europe were, whatever their pretensions in public, unenthusiastic at the prospect of international European human rights protection".[10] In his study of the UK's position towards the ECtHR, Simpson corroborates this argument:

> For Bevin and the majority of his officials some degree of integration, or the eventual formation, in appropriate circumstances, of a Western bloc, meant cooperation between sovereign states, either through international conventions, or through consensus achieved by inter-state negotiation. It did not mean the surrender of sovereignty to a supranational organization.[11]

As Moravcsik has shown, the motivation of states to protect human rights through supranational legal instruments is difficult to retrieve. On the one hand, a loss of sovereignty is in principle perceived as costly. On the other hand, it can secure the protection of fundamental rights and democracy in an unstable era such as the immediate post-war moment: "sovereignty costs are weighted against establishing human rights regimes, whereas greater political stability may be weighted in favour of it".[12] For Moravcsik, the motive of states to ratify the ECHR was to "lock in democratic governance" and was by no means "a conversion to moral altruism".[13]

In this vein, the Committee of Ministers questioned the project of a supranational court that involved the surrender of state sovereignty. Some voices claimed that it would be unnecessary in light of existing constitutional guarantees. As Stone Sweet and Keller explain, "in the 50s, the leaders of most States assumed that ratifying the Convention would not require any meaningful adjustment on their part, in that they considered that the level of national rights protection was more than adequate".[14] Some authors also argued at the time that a human rights court may rival other international courts already in formation, such as the International Court of Justice (ICJ). All in all,

> if there was one superseding theme of these negotiations it was that human rights were one and the same both too integrated into national law and politics to be entirely entrusted to a new European court and too important to the idea of European integration to remain a question of national politics and law.[15]

---

10 Simpson, *Human Rights and the End of Empire*, 667.
11 Ibid., 563.
12 Moravcsik, "The Origins of Human Rights Regimes: Democratic Delegation in Postwar Europe", 235.
13 Ibid., 247–8.
14 Stone Sweet and Keller, "The Reception of the ECHR in National Legal Orders", 27.
15 Madsen, "The Protracted Institutionalization of the Strasbourg Court", 45.

The Consultative Assembly was finally given a chance to debate the proposed Convention, and those debates would eventually form part of the *travaux préparatoires*. On 19 August 1949, Pierre-Henri Teitgen, another founding father of the ECHR and future judge of the ECtHR, delivered a speech which was very much focused on the immediate need for protecting, through the Convention and its Court, the foundations of democracy:

> A list of rights and fundamental freedoms, without which personal independence and a dignified way of life cannot be ensured; the fundamental principles of democratic regime, that is, the obligation to consult the nation and to govern with its support, and that all Governments be forbidden to interfere with free criticism and the natural and fundamental rights to opposition.[16]

The ECHR proposal was first reviewed by the Committee on Legal and Administrative Questions and then presented to the Assembly as the so-called Teitgen Report. Again, the emphasis is on the conditions for an effective democracy: "these rights and freedoms are the common denominator of our political institutions, the first triumph of democracy, but also the necessary condition under which it operates. That is why they must be subject to the collective guarantee".[17] The proposal was then debated, amended and voted on 9 September 1959 by the legislative organ, and eventually formally adopted in the so-called Recommendation 38. Recommendation 38 was by no means the final version of the ECHR as the final word was reserved for the Committee of Ministers of the CoE, which, on 5 November 1949, examined the Recommendation. Before its examination by the Ministers, a Committee of Legal Experts had been set up to address the feasibility of the Convention; this Committee then came up with the first proper drafts of the Convention. The ECHR as we know it started to take shape at a high-level conference in Strasbourg between 8 and 17 June 1950.

An interesting aspect of the latest debates at the intergovernmental level concerned the need to protect the *right to education* and the *right to property*. The need to include these rights in the final draft of the Convention was predicated on the experience of totalitarian regimes and their propensity to indoctrinate children at school and deprive their political opponents of their properties. As Bates explains:

> All agreed on the great value of those rights in principle, when seen in the context of their abuse during the war and on the other side of the Iron Curtain, but the problem came with the actual drafting; the fear that a loosely drafted text would hand too much power to international institutions.[18]

---

16 Council of Europe. *Collected Edition of the "Travaux Préparatoires" of the European Convention on Human Rights*, 272.
17 Teitgen, "Establishment of a Collective Guarantee of Essential Freedoms and Fundamental Rights".
18 Bates, "The Birth of the European Convention on Human Rights", 24.

82   *The ECHR in historical perspective*

The debates happened to be intractable and the two rights were left out of Recommendation 38, although they were eventually included in Protocol 1 to the Convention. More generally, the Ministers hardly went beyond what was initially agreed by the Consultative Assembly. They decided that the ECtHR would be optional so that states could opt out of the right of individual petition (Article 25). As a result, the only mandatory process of judicial control was through interstate disputes (Article 24). Moreover, the Commission was conceived as the pillar of the newly born institution and charged with the task of receiving and investigating petitions, and deciding whether a case should be declared admissible. The Commission did not enjoy independence from publicity, however, in that it was obliged to refer to the Committee of Ministers to deliver the decisions and judgments. More precisely, the Commission "would draw a report on the facts and state its *opinion* as to whether the facts disclose a breach by the State concerned of its obligations under the Convention" (Article 35), but the Committee of Ministers was by no means bound by the Commission's report.

The political character of the process is reinforced by the conciliatory modalities by which the cases were supposed to be handled. Not all admissible cases were examined by the full Commission: "as it was originally drafted, therefore, contentious matters only, that is, those not already resolved by way of friendly settlement, would receive the full attention of the full Commission".[19] In effect, the only cases that could be brought before the Court were by the Commission or the states themselves (Article 44). This lasted until 1994 when Protocol 9 was adopted and individual access was reformed (Article 44 and Article 48 as amended). The Commission was eventually abolished when Protocol 11 took effect in 1998 (Article 25 as amended). The quasi-judicial power of the ECtHR was to *declare* whether there was a breach of the ECHR, while the judgments would be eventually transmitted to the Committee of Ministers, which should supervise their execution (Article 54).

When the Ministers reconvened for their sixth session, on 4 November 1950 in Rome, the governments of Belgium, Denmark, France, Germany, Iceland, Ireland, Italy, Luxembourg, the Netherlands, Norway, Saar, Turkey, and the UK signed the Convention for the Protection of Human Rights and Fundamental Freedoms. In substance, the ECHR contained the basic civil and political rights: the right to life (Article 2); the right to be free from torture, and inhuman and degrading treatment (Article 3); the right not to be held in slavery or servitude (Article 4); the right to personal liberty and security (Article 5); the right to a fair trial (Article 6); the right not to be punished without legal process (Article 7); the right to respect for private and family life (Article 8); freedom of thought, conscience and religion (Article 9); freedom of expression (Article 10); freedom of assembly and association (Article 10); the right to marry (Article 12); the rights to an effective remedy (Article 13); and prohibition against discrimination (Article 14).

When it was opened for signature, the ECHR needed ten ratifications to enter into force. This was achieved on 3 September 1953 (Denmark, Germany, Greece,

19 Ibid., 35.

The ECHR in historical perspective   83

Iceland, Ireland, Luxembourg, Norway, the Saar, Sweden, and the UK). The Commission was then ready to receive petitions from both states and individuals, the latter being contingent on state acceptance of the right of individual petition. What was once contemplated as an independent and supranational judicial court, enjoying compulsory jurisdiction with the aim of protecting of individual rights and liberal democracy, was now a mere state-controlled organ that aimed mostly to control interstate disputes. As Besson puts it:

> The ECtHR started as an international court applying an international Convention in the framework of an international organisation. It is only gradually that the latter turned into a supranational court both through the supranational status of ECHR rights and the strengthening of its judicial review powers.[20]

In other words, if the initial political impetus for the ECHR is tied to the preservation of democracy through the supranational judicial protection of individual rights, the diplomatic impetus clearly limited the scope of the ECHR to an interstate complaint and optional quasi-judicial mechanism. As Greer explains, "those who designed the Convention agreed that its *modus operandi* should be complaints made to an independent judicial tribunal by states against each other (the 'interstate process'), and not those made by individuals against governments".[21] The ECtHR itself, which became operative only in 1959, reflected this political dimension. Lord Lester explains:

> The judges and the Commissioners were part-timers and included former agents of the governments which secured their appointment. The Secretary and the Registry has to do their best to uphold the integrity of the system. I remember a senior judge and former government legal adviser telling me that he saw it as his duty to uphold national interests![22]

5.3 The embryonic practice of the ECtHR

If the birth of the ECtHR idea is marked by the solid conviction of the need for a supranational mechanism against the horrors of totalitarianism – either through individual justice, as the early advocates thought, or through interstate justice, as the diplomatic circles thought – the system of human rights protection in Europe was certainly shaped by two other issues of international politics at the time: the prospect of a third world conflict between the East and the West, as well as the emerging independence movements from colonial power. Indeed, the history of the early ECtHR may be viewed through the prism of the Cold War and

---

20 Besson, "European Human Rights, Supranational Judicial Review and Democracy – Thinking Outside the Judicial Box", 120.
21 Greer, "What's Wrong with the European Convention on Human Rights", 681–2.
22 Lester, "The European Court of Human Rights after 50 Years", 102.

84 *The ECHR in historical perspective*

decolonization. As Madsen puts it, "what is striking about the nascent institution-alization of the Convention was how the interplay between national diplomatic interests and the entrepreneurship of the leading actors formed this institution and its initial practice".[23]

The absorption of the ECHR into Cold War politics was almost immediate. As Bates explains, "the first proposals for a Convention were dominated by the idea that Europe was in danger of being overturned by the communists".[24] Simpson talks of Churchill's perception of the ECHR as "a declaration of Western ideol-ogy; in a derogatory sense therefore its function was propagandist. It could also prescribe the conditions for membership of the United Europe".[25] Moyn is on a similar line: "from its vague introduction as some sort of social democracy, the idea of human rights had been redeemed only as a concrete Cold War position".[26] However, the Cold War conflict is seen retrospectively as having contributed to the further institutionalization of the ECHR. As Madsen explains:

> It was well known at the time, particularly in light of the way that the Universal Declaration (UDHR) had fallen victim to Cold War bipolarities, that if human rights were to be ensured at the European level, it required both institutionalization and juridification.[27]

The development of the ECHR (1959–69) was irreducibly slow, however. In short, the Convention entered into force in 1953 when the 10 ratifications were achieved, and individual petition was made effective in 1955 when the required six acceptances were completed. Only in 1958 were the necessary eight accep-tances of the jurisdiction of the ECtHR confirmed. At that time, Ireland was the only state with judicial protection of fundamental rights. As Stone Sweet explains, "the constitutions of Belgium, Luxembourg, the Netherlands, and the UK either did not contain such rights, or they denied the judiciary the authority to review the legality of statutes".[28] The ECtHR itself did not became operational until 1959. As mentioned above, other than the Federal Republic of Germany, the states that supported this burgeoning legal and judicial practice were minor states. The two grand absentees, of course, were the late imperialist countries of France and the UK.

We can now see more clearly that the ECHR's debut was very responsive to the ongoing polarization of international politics at the time. However, if the Cold War politics essentially reinforced the impetus for a European human rights regime, the same cannot be said of decolonization politics. The first cases to appear

---

23 Madsen, "From Cold War Instrument to Supreme European Court: The European Court of Human Rights at the Crossroads of International and National Law and Politics", 143.
24 Bates, "The Birth of the European Convention on Human Rights", 18.
25 Simpson, *Human Rights and the End of Empire*, 605.
26 Moyn, *The Last Utopia: Human Rights in History*, 79.
27 Bates, "The Birth of the European Convention on Human Rights", 45.
28 Stone Sweet, "On the Constitutionalisation of the Convention: The European Court of Human Rights as a Constitutional Court", 2.

The ECHR in historical perspective   85

before the Commission revealed that the emerging legal and judicial practice of international human rights protection in Europe could not remain impermeable to the nascent decolonization politics in Europe and the rest of the world. In Europe, the countries most exposed to this pressure were the UK and France. France did not ratify the Convention until 1974, as time was needed to distance the country from the traumas of the Algerian war, which ended in 1962. As Madsen puts it:

> The French stance toward the ECHR was generally structured around a latter-day imperialist balancing consisting of both securing that colonial matters remained an issue of national politics and, simultaneously, continuing a tradition of supplying "universals" to the international level.[29]

Greece had submitted, in 1956, the interstate complaint about British practices in Cyprus. Greece accused the British Crown of violating the ECHR when it responded militarily to the insurrection of the Greek militant group EKOA, who demanded self-determination and unification with Greece. The issue was eventually resolved through the traditional diplomatic channel. As Madsen explains, the UK all in all "contributed to a diplomatic approach to the institution in the sense of an understanding that sought to balance legal progress with a tolerance of country-specific interests".[30] The UK eventually accepted both the right of individual petition and the jurisdiction of the ECtHR in 1966.

This apparent weakness may be interpreted in light of the strategy of what Madsen calls "legal diplomacy" – that is, the long-term objective of states to accept the two clauses of the right of individual petition and the jurisdiction of the ECtHR. In other words, "the result was a very measured legal development over the first fifteen years where the objective of providing justice to individuals was carefully balanced with both national and geopolitical interests".[31] In legal terms, the ECtHR could not fulfil its judicial role without the recognition of the right of individual petition and the jurisdiction of the ECtHR in States Parties, as well as a favourable international political climate.

5.4 The 1970s: the slow establishment of a supranational judicial authority

The more expansive role acquired by the ECtHR was clearly contingent on the acceptance by the mid-1970s of the right of individual petition and the ECtHR's jurisdiction in most of the States Parties. If States Parties, following Article 53 of the ECHR, are expected to abide by the decisions and judgments of the ECtHR, then the conjunction between acceptance of the right of individual petition and

---

29 Madsen, "From Cold War Instrument to Supreme European Court: The European Court of Human Rights at the Crossroads of International and National Law and Politics", 145.
30 Ibid. For the specific relationship of the UK with the early ECtHR, see Simpson, *Human Rights and the End of Empire*.
31 Madsen, "The Protracted Institutionalization of the Strasbourg Court", 44.

86   The ECHR in historical perspective

acceptance of the ECtHR's jurisdiction triggers, in principle, the judicial authority of the ECtHR. However, as described in the preceding section, the transformation was irreducibly slow over the first two decades.

Moreover, in the first decade of its existence the ECtHR had delivered only 10 judgments, had found only a few violations of the ECHR, and was entirely dormant between 1960 and 1965. If the legal and judicial apparatus is in principle operative and the ECtHR equipped to develop its own case law, it does not follow that it has the political leverage to imprint an autonomous form of judicial practice. Moreover, "what is certain, is that the Commission utilized fully its pre-screening competence to reduce the case-load thereby developing a very important jurisprudence on the notion of 'manifestly ill-founded' claims".[32] Again, Madsen insists on the strategy of "legal diplomacy" and the need to bring major European states on board to explain this reluctance to challenge state claims despite having the power to do so.

It was not before the late 1960s that the ECHR and the ECtHR developed a novel form of judicial activism. This is also in line with Moyn's argument of the late renaissance of human rights generally. As Moyn puts it:

> It is one thing to record the evolution of supranational human rights mechanisms, for example at the United Nations and in the European region, but another to explain the startling pike in cultural prestige they began to enjoy after decades of irrelevance.[33]

The distinctive element in the ECHR case is the legal and judicial apparatus to accommodate this novel demand for human rights. As Madsen puts it:

> As a vitalization of the dormant but very considerable legal tools available in the Convention, the ECHR system began to step out of the cloudy smoke-screen of post-war political strategies and jump on the bandwagon of this new legal practice of human rights.[34]

Of course, we can always ask the question at the more sociological level. Moyn, for instance, explains that the genesis of the ECHR "was to be far more a cultural and ideological victory in a later era that determined their legal availability and plausibility even in the European zone".[35]

Yet if we stick to the legal level of historical interpretation, the correlation of this novel demand is clearly the acceptance of the two clauses of individual petition and the jurisdiction of the ECtHR. This marks the paradigmatic turn from "interstate justice" to "individual justice". The UK accepted these clauses in 1966.

---

32 Ibid., 51.
33 Moyn, *The Last Utopia: Human Rights in History*, 122.
34 Madsen, "From Cold War Instrument to Supreme European Court: The European Court of Human Rights at the Crossroads of International and National Law and Politics", 152.
35 Moyn, *The Last Utopia: Human Rights in History*, 81.

The ECHR in historical perspective 87

In 1968, the *Belgian Linguistic* case,[36] finding a breach of Article 14 ECHR in Belgian legislation on access to education, showed the first signs of the judicial autonomy of the ECtHR. In 1973, Italy and Switzerland also accepted the two clauses. The mid-1970s is a significant period in the development of interpretative concepts and methods, which became the essential tools of the ECtHR as we know it today. The legal and judicial practice of the ECtHR, through a more autonomous kind of legal reasoning, arose during that period. It was as a result of a set of cases in the late 1970s that today's key interpretative concepts of "living instrument" and "practical effective" appeared in the nascent case law of the ECtHR. In the 1970s, the Commission received an average of 16 applications per year.[37]

Most notable is *Golder v. United Kingdom*[38] in which Golder, a prison detainee, intended to contact a lawyer to sue a warder who had accused him of having taken part in a mutiny. The problem of interpretation focused on the right to have access to a court and its derivation from the right to a fair trial (Article 6). The ECtHR answered affirmatively and detailed the motives behind the decision. Not only did the ECtHR make the conceptual assertion that without access to a lawyer the "rule of law" could not be secured, but it also explicitly rejected, in methodological terms, the original view that the terms of the ECHR should be understood in terms of the intentions of the drafters in the 1950s.

Rather, ECHR rights were to be understood as dynamic and the determination of their content – the correlated duties of those rights – as responsive to the evolution of European societies. Moreover, in *Airey v. Ireland*,[39] where Mrs Airey was deprived of access to a lawyer, the ECtHR held that the ECHR was conceived to protect "not rights that are theoretical and illusory but rights that are practical and effective". As we shall see, this reference of "practical and effective" is now constant in the adjudication of the ECtHR. The idea of responsiveness to societal developments was even more salient in *Tyrer v. United Kingdom*.[40] The ECtHR had to decide if "three strokes of the birch" was within the scope of "degrading punishment" under Article 3. The ECtHR famously asserted that the ECHR is "a living instrument" and "must be interpreted in light of the present-day conditions", and thereby found a breach of the ECHR.

As we shall see in exploring the case law, these concepts were not only to become central concepts in the case law of the ECtHR; they were to lay down the foundations of a novel judicial methodology in human rights adjudication at the expense of a number of pillars of international law. The contrast is salient when we remind ourselves of the Committee's mandated Legal Experts and their

---

36 *Belgian Linguistic Case*, App. Nos. 1474/62, 1677/62, 1691/62, 1769/63, 1994/63, 2126/64, 23 July 1968.
37 Stone Sweet, "On the Constitutionalisation of the Convention: The European Court of Human Rights as a Constitutional Court", 4.
38 *Golder v. United Kingdom*, App. No. 4451/70, 21 February 1975.
39 *Airey v. Ireland*, App. No. 6289/73, 9 October 1979.
40 *Tyrer v. United Kingdom*, App. No. 5856/72, 25 April 1978.

88 *The ECHR in historical perspective*

advisory opinion, which required that the "jurisprudence of a European Court will never, therefore, introduce any new element or one contrary to existing international law".[41] We can now envision the importance, for our subsequent normative endeavours, of the emerging and judicial practice of ECHR rights *qua* rights.

5.5 The explosion of human rights and the need for structural reform

It has become common for today's ECHR lawyers and academics to argue about the need for structural reform of the ECHR system in the face of the ever-increasing number of petitions lodged with the ECtHR – currently approximately 50,000 each year. In fact, the first symptoms of the lack of structural reform to address the ever-increasing case load date back to the mid-1980s and, in particular, the repetitive cases pertaining to the same type of violation. At that time, the debate turned on the further judicialization of the ECtHR and the problematic role of the Committee of Ministers, which remained decisive until the early 1990s. Harmsen explains that the Swiss proposal at the 1985 European Ministerial Conference on Human Rights "may be seen to have launched formal deliberations over major institutional reform, squarely backed the option of a single, full-time Court".[42] Of course, the two crucial structural conditions for the explosion of petitions – the right of individual petitions and the compulsory jurisdiction of the ECtHR – were by then widely accepted. The independence of the ECtHR was growing. The "new demand" towards human rights was under way and the international political climate was receptive. These factors combined can explain the growing attractiveness of the system for potential applicants and resulted in a shortage of both institutional and human resources. The central question, of course, was whether the gained effectiveness of a full-time, single-tiered ECtHR could outweigh the transitional costs of reforming the existing organ.

It was in the early 1990s that structural measures were taken. The fall of the Berlin Wall was certainly congruent to the demand for structural reform. The former communist states raised the ECHR's States Parties to 46 by the end of the 1990s and extended access to the ECtHR to millions of potential applicants. Protocol 11, which entered into force in 1990, is taken as marking the "full judicialization"[43] of the ECtHR in response to those developments. Three major amendments of the ECHR are notable. First, the European Commission of Human Rights – and its competence to decide on the merits of cases – was abolished (Article 25 as amended); and the Committee was limited to the role of supervision of the ECtHR's judgments. Second, the ECtHR became a full-time judicial organ in charge of all tasks previously performed by the Commission. Third, both the right of individual petition and acceptance of the ECtHR's

---

41 Quoted in Bates, "The Birth of the European Convention on Human Rights", 39.
42 Harmsen, "The Reform of the Convention System", 122.
43 Ibid., 123.

The ECHR in historical perspective   89

jurisdiction became compulsory. Yet, by the end of the 1990s, all States Parties had voluntarily accepted the two clauses. As a result, the ECtHR's case law became applicable in all States Parties' jurisdictions. As I specify in the next chapter, this normativity is unique in international law. Some legal scholars make the constitutional qualification of the ECHR contingent on the adoption of Protocol 11. As Stone Sweet explains:

> With Protocol No. 11, the ECHR established a system of constitutional justice: a system that entrenches fundamental rights, and provides for the judicial protection of those rights, at the behest of individuals. The ECHR is, thus, constitutional in this more profound sense.[44]

However, by the 2000s, the structural measures of Protocol 11 appeared to be clearly insufficient in face of the post-communist enlargement, the extent of which was not anticipated. The 2000–10 decade epitomized the overload petitions crisis. Continuing the reform, the more modest and laboriously achieved Protocol 14,[45] which entered into force in 2010, sought both to shorten the admissibility process of the ECtHR and improve the effectiveness of its judgments in States Parties. Two amendments of the ECHR may be mentioned. First, Protocol 14 streamlines the preliminary screenings of petitions in order to reduce the time-consuming process of selecting the cases that pass the admissibility test. This is done by switching from the Committees (three judges advised by one judge rapporteur and one Registry lawyer) to a single-judge formation (one judge and one Registry rapporteur) – the "juge unique" or "judicial downsizing" (Article 27 and Article 24(2)).[46] At the core of this measure are the 90 per cent of inadmissible petitions lodged with the ECtHR. According to Philippe Boillat, head of legal services at the ECtHR:

> On peut déduire qu'il y a environ 3% des requêtes qui portent sur des affaires qui posent de véritables questions de pétition et d'interprétation de la Convention, des affaires dans lesquelles la Convention joue véritablement son rôle d'instrument constitutionnel de l'ordre public européen. Le vrai défi de toute réforme est donc de trouver des solutions qui permettront à la Cour de se concentrer sur ces dernières affaires.[47]

Second, Protocol 14 aims to increase the institutional links between the ECtHR and the Committee of Ministers – the executive organ of the CoE and officially

---

44 Stone Sweet, "On the Constitutionalisation of the Convention: The European Court of Human Rights as a Constitutional Court", 2.
45 For a first assessment of this reform, see the contributions in BENEFRI, *La Cour européenne des droits de l'homme après le Protocole 14: premier bilan et perspectives/The European Court of Human Rights after Protocol 14: Preliminary Assessment and Perspectives*.
46 For a recent analysis, see, in particular, Caflisch, "Le Juge Unique et Les Comités".
47 Boillat, "Le passé et l'avenir de la réforme", 18.

90   *The ECHR in historical perspective*

in charge of monitoring the judgments – by giving the Committee the right to bring infringement proceedings before the ECtHR when a State Party has failed to comply with its obligations (Article 46(4) and (5)). This measure is clearly directed to recalcitrant states that fail to comply with the ECHR and the repetitive cases lodged with the ECtHR (55 per cent of the cases concern repetitive cases). Between 1995 and 2000, Greer reports that 58 per cent of the violations concerned the right to a fair trial under Article 6 and 37 per cent concerned unreasonable delay in the administration of justice under Article 13.[48] Note that Protocol 14 also introduces a new admissibility criterion (Article 35(b)(3)),[49] which allows the ECtHR to declare inadmissible the petitions in which

> the applicant has not suffered a significant disadvantage, unless respect for human rights as defined in the Convention and the Protocols thereto requires an examination of the petition on the merits and provided that no case may be rejected on this ground which has not been duly considered by a domestic tribunal.

Finally, and in parallel with the Protocols, the ECtHR itself started to address the problem of structural violations by issuing "pilot judgments". These are ordinary judgments containing general directives on how to remedy structural problems in domestic law following repetitive cases. They imply general measures in the operative part of the judgment and are therefore part of the *decisional authority* of the judgment – that which binds the State Party to the judgment. It follows the ECtHR's assessment of the merits in the text of the case.[50] As Besson explains, "the consequence of pilot judgments is to freeze similar claims made consecutively until the problems are resolved in the Contracting State concerned".[51] In the same vein, the ECtHR has started to recommend individual measures in its own judgments by requiring the state to undertake specific actions in the domestic legal order: "ce faisant, la Cour se fonde sur la résolution 2004/3 du Comité des Ministres qui invite la Cour à identifier la raison structurelle de la violation, mais aussi la meilleure manière possible de remédier efficacement à cette violation".[52] Those recent developments ground the claim that the ECtHR is now exercising a *strong form* of judicial review – in contrast with the strict review of violations in a single case. Moreover, both forms of judicial activism, structural and individual, have been severely criticized by states – mostly Western, surprisingly, and mostly on democratic grounds – arguing that the ECtHR goes beyond its competence on

48 Greer, "What's Wrong with the European Convention on Human Rights", 690.
49 See e.g. Greer, "The New Admissibility Criterion".
50 For a recent example, see e.g. *Greens et M.T. v. Royaume-Uni*, App. Nos 60041/08, 60054/08, 23 November 2010, paras 116–22.
51 Besson, "European Human Rights, Supranational Judicial Review and Democracy – Thinking Outside the Judicial Box", 110.
52 Besson, "Les effets et l'éxécution des arrêts de la Cour européenne des droits de l'homme – le cas de la Suisse", 173.

the basis of Article 46. Indeed, as Flauss explains, "c'est dire que l'on assiste à une modification de la nature de l'obligation de l'Etat découlant de l'article 46 de la Convention: on passe sensiblement d'une obligation de résultat à une obligation de moyens".[53] I examine more thoroughly the judicial powers of the ECtHR in the next chapter.

---

53 Flauss, "L'effectivité des arrêts de la Cour européenne des droits de l'homme: du politique au juridique et vice-versa", 32.

6 The normativity of ECHR law

Having introduced the legal and judicial practice of the ECHR in historical terms, I turn in this chapter to the normativity of the ECHR *qua* international treaty. Here, again, I further specify the object of normative elucidation that will then be subject to the constructivist procedure. *Pro memoria*, I showed in Chapter 4 how a constructivist account of human rights can incorporate the Beitzian specification of human rights as tied to international society, the Razian concept of *rights* (also adopted by Tasioulas), while preserving the core idea of Griffin, shared by Forst, that the normative force of human rights is anchored in a layer of substantive moral reasoning.

My argument is that the normativity of the ECHR requires both the ethical and political conceptions of human rights. On the one hand, the ECHR has a strong international dimension, following Beitz, in that the ECtHR authoritatively adjudicates ECHR rights, which themselves enjoy *direct effect* in national legal orders. On the other hand, if human rights are *rights* and not just interests or values, their substantive content is found in the localized circumstances in which their duties are recognized, specified and allocated. The judicial arena is therefore crucial for the normativity of human rights and needs to be accounted for. As Besson puts it, "human rights, unlike EU law, are legal norms that need to be specified in a political context. Interpreting or justifying them *in abstracto* would contradict their nature, as a result".[1] Because ECtHR judgments enjoy *direct effect*, the normative and substantive standpoint that is privileged is the adjudication of the ECtHR. From an abstract standpoint, therefore, there is no *discontinuity* between the normative role of human rights (emphasized by Beitz and Raz), their nature as *rights* (emphasized by Raz and Tasioulas) and the layer of reasons that concretizes and justifies them (privileged by Griffin and Forst) in the case law. This leaves room for a proper philosophical refinement – in the constructivist sense – that bridges the gap between practice and theory.

A *caveat* is in order here. Since constructivists assign priority to the practical role of public norms, I suggest focusing on the legal status of ECHR rights in national legal orders to capture this role. However, the normative basis that serves the role

---

1 Besson, "The 'Erga Omnes' Effect of the European Court of Human Rights", 172.

The normativity of ECHR law 93

in the practice is located in the adjudication of the ECtHR. The consequence here is that the two dimensions constitute the basis for normative exploration if the objective is to address and justify the practice in the first place. I leave this second dimension for Chapters 8 and 9, where I specifically examine the adjudication of the ECtHR on a case basis.

In this chapter, I reconstruct the normative role that ECHR rights play in national legal orders. In doing so, I further specify Beitz's international dimension of human rights in that human rights generate some form of international concern. It is important to bear in mind that the ECHR is an international law treaty. Its mere existence *qua* international treaty does not imply any role to play in the ordinary legal and political life of States Parties. As a result, what is needed is an account of the conditions for an international treaty to shape the ordinary life of individuals. The ECHR is a legal construct and involves standards not only for its normative existence, but also for its normativity in States Parties. This specification is conducted in non-evaluative terms as the political conception of human rights requires.

To capture this practice, I adopt a three-pronged approach. First, I introduce human rights law *qua* international law – that is, how to understand the distinctive concept of international human rights *within* the broader concept of international law. I also address the implications of the concept of human rights for the traditional view of the legitimacy of international law grounded in the analogy between states and individuals and the underlying idea of free and rational agents entering into a contract.

Second, I introduce the special normativity of the ECHR *qua* international treaty in the legal orders of States Parties. In this respect, the crucial point is that most of its 47 States Parties have given *direct effect* to ECHR rights and ECtHR judgments in their respective legal orders. Direct effect implies that ECHR rights and ECtHR judgments are immediately binding within national law and may be invoked by individuals against all state institutions, whether legislative, executive or judicial, without any legislative step. It contrasts with the UN covenants and their treaty bodies, for instance, respect for the rights and judgments of which is weaker.

Third, I address the ECtHR's distinctive judicial powers *qua* international judicial organ. We saw in the last chapter that the *compulsory jurisdiction* of the ECtHR is a central premise to the normative role of the ECHR and remains unique in international law. By the end of the 1990s, acceptance of the jurisdiction of the ECtHR became compulsory for new States Parties. As Ress puts it, "this is a rather revolutionary development in the field of international law, which has always been a field quite resistant to any form of compulsory international adjudication".[2] On this point, it is important to note that the ECtHR does not have the power of judicial review that constitutional courts have and cannot invalidate

---

2 Ress, "The Effect of Decisions and Judgments of the European Court of Human Rights in the Domestic Legal Order", 362.

94 *The normativity of ECHR law*

national legal norms that are deemed incompatible with the ECHR, or ask the state to reopen the procedure and revise the judgment in the domestic proceedings. The ECtHR is empowered primarily to *declare* whether one or several ECHR rights are violated in a single case. The limits of the review are therefore significant and should be accounted for in the overall balance.

6.1 Normativity and authority

In this chapter, I privilege the concept of *normativity* to that of *authority*, although the theoretical literature often refers to the *authority* of ECHR law or international law more generally.[3] The intuitive idea of authority implies the existence of a duty of obedience to its subjects. The various understandings of this concept in legal and political theory require distinguishing the *moral* and the *instrumentalist* senses. The moral sense of authority pertains to coercion of its subjects being morally justified. The reasons given by the authority for obeying the duties survive one's balance of reasons. This implies engaging the subjects of authority as moral persons and the presence of content-dependent reasons for subjects to obey. This is precisely the search for justification implied in the constructivist project of liberal reconciliation detailed in Chapter 6: the constructivist search for a public basis of justification in providing individuals with norms that they can find reasonably acceptable and with which they can regularly comply for genuinely moral reasons. By contrast, the *instrumentalist* sense of authority is independent of one's balance of reasons. The "Normal Justification Thesis" of Raz[4] – according to which a directive has authority when the subject is more likely to comply by virtue of the reasons that already apply to that subject if he or she accepts the directive than by assessing the moral merits of the directive – is the predominant view. Authority here is still *normative*, but content-independent.[5] We should notice here that the "Service Conception" assumes that the subject bound by the directive is autonomous "as this is the only way that its freedom to choose from a range of options can be furthered by an authoritative directive".[6]

In this chapter, I do not aim to provide the subjects of ECHR law with reasons to obey its duties – I leave these tasks for Chapters 7 and 8. In this sense, I use normativity and authority *co-extensively* as long as I refer to them *descriptively* as giving reasons for action to States Parties. In doing so, I stick to the *functional* characterization of the practice as Beitz encourages us to. In addressing the binding nature of the ECtHR later in the chapter, I first distinguish the *legal authority of* the ECHR as limited to the duty of States Parties to execute the decisional content of the ECtHR judgment, as specified by Article 46, from the *moral* or *persuasive* authority of the ECtHR. The legal authority or legal obligation refers

---

3 See e.g. Besson, "The Authority of International Law – Lifting the State Veil".
4 See Raz, *The Morality of Freedom*. See also Raz, "The Problem of Authority: Revisiting the Service Conception".
5 For an overview of those conceptions, see Christiano, "Authority" .
6 Besson, "Sovereignty, International Law and Democracy", 377–8.

The normativity of ECHR law 95

to that to which the subjects of ECHR law are *bound* to conform. As Green puts it, "an obligatory act or omission is something that law renders non-optional. Since people can *plainly* violate their legal obligations, 'non-optional' does not mean that they are physically compelled to perform, nor even that law leaves them without any eligible alternatives".[7]

However, if ECHR law makes an inherent claim to *legitimate* authority by virtue of the standards of legal validity that it proclaims, it does not follow that it has or can have such authority. This is where we need to turn to the question whether ECHR law *can* create duties to obey on the part of its subjects and, therefore, to the reasons it gives for action. The same is true of the States Parties subject to ECHR law. By ratifying the ECHR and/or its additional protocols, States Parties are bound by Article 46 according to which "the High Contracting Parties undertake to abide by the final judgment of the ECtHR in any case to which they are parties". As we shall see, the legal obligation in this context implies the *decisional* content of the ECtHR's judgment – that is, the content that binds the law's subjects to its authority by virtue of international law. In principle, the decision of an international judicial organ binds the parties to an interstate dispute (the *inter partes* effect). Of course, as the above quotes make clear, States Parties may fail to comply with their legal obligations. This is the empirical question of *effective compliance* with the legal duties of States Parties by virtue of ECHR law. By contrast, States Parties may abide by the *jurisprudential* or *interpretative* authority of ECtHR judgments. This dimension of authority is *moral* or *persuasive* as it is not included in the decisional content of the judgment to which States Parties are bound, which corresponds with the content of the individual decision recognizing the violation of the ECHR right (*res judicata*). The jurisprudential authority concerns the interpretative content (*res interpretata*) of the judgment.

Further, the ECHR may have authority in the sense that States Parties recognize the rights of individuals outside the territorial boundaries of the state and therefore outside their jurisdiction. This is because, following Besson, the concept of *jurisdiction* as it applies to the ECHR is not territorial but *functional* as it determines the relationship between a subject and an authority.[8] The extraterritoriality of the ECHR is therefore another facet of its authority and is co-extensive with the concept of *de facto* authority.[9] Such authority is not necessarily justified, as we have seen. It is an effective form of power which makes an inherent claim to authority. As such, it includes "a normative dimension by reference to the imposition of reasons for action on its subjects and the corresponding appeal to compliance (e.g. though giving instructions . . .)".[10] It requires the institutional structures to enforce those rights and identify their corresponding duties. For the sake of concision, I focus only on those two dimensions of the authority of the ECHR

---

7 Green, "Legal Obligation and Authority".
8 Besson, "The Extraterritoriality of the European Convention on Human Rights: Why Human Rights Depend on Jurisdiction and What Jurisdiction Amounts To", 863.
9 Ibid., 864–6.
10 Ibid., 865.

96   *The normativity of ECHR law*

throughout this chapter – *interpretative authority* and *direct effect* – as they best inform us of the scope of the normativity of the ECHR. The case law that pertains to extraterritoriality is indeed case-specific in the duties generated by the ECtHR and therefore less informative.[11]

6.2 Human rights norms *qua* international legal norms

Let us first distinguish in general terms the singularity of human rights law within international law. A conventional distinction is between the *vertical* model of international human rights law and the *horizontal* model of public international law. As a past president of the ECtHR puts it:

> There is an infinite variety of international agreements, from bilateral to multilateral treaties, from military alliances to trade agreements, from double taxation to the Charter of the United Nations, from the moon treaty to treaties for the prevention of transfrontier pollution. However, compared with most international agreements, human rights treaties have a unique character. They are not concerned with mutual relations and exchange of benefits between sovereign States. Instead, they proclaim the solemn principle of the human treatment of inhabitants of the participating States.[12]

In making individuals right-bearers of international norms, human rights norms change the commonly found structure between right-bearers and duty-bearers in public international law. Public international law establishes a horizontal network of relationships between equal sovereign states that recognize mutually binding principles. As Weiler explains:

> Historically, transactional international law was the predominant command mode. It is still a large and important part of the overall universe of international law. In its purest form, it is dyadic and represented best by the bilateral transactional treaty. It is premised on an understanding of the world order composed of equally sovereign states pursuing their respective national interest through an enlightened use of law to guarantee bargains struck.[13]

International human rights are *vertical* in the sense that states engage, by consent, on how to treat their own subjects within their own jurisdiction. The right-bearers, therefore, are not parties to the treaty although their interests are the object of protection. As Besson puts it, "unlike ordinary international treaties, international human rights treaties, such as the ECHR, generate general, non-reciprocal and objective obligations among States Parties".[14]

---

11 Ibid., 883.
12 Bernardt, "Thoughts on the Interpretation of Human Rights Treaties", quoted in Mowbray, "The Creativity of the European Court of Human Rights", 60.
13 Weiler, "The Geology of International Law – Governance, Democracy and Legitimacy", 553.
14 Besson, "The 'Erga Omnes' Effect of the European Court of Human Rights", 152.

The normativity of ECHR law   97

However, the mere existence of an international treaty such as the ECHR is not sufficient for the treaty to play any normative role in domestic legal orders. The status of an international human rights treaty is determined by the inherent freedom of sovereign States Parties to determine the rank, validity and effect of those norms in the national legal order. This concerns both the provisions of the treaty and the judgments of the judicial organ. This is the case, for instance, with reception of the case law of the UN treaty bodies:

> The general perceptions of states that Views do not impose legal obligations on them has a substantial impact on decisions not to implement them . . . . Even states that have proved generally respectful of the work of the treaty bodies do at times insist on their discretion to either implement or reject the outcome of individual communication procedures.[15]

International human rights until now have lacked anything close to a supranational judicial mechanism of protection *stricto sensu* – that is, a single judicial organ for settling disputes and applying sanctions to non-compliant states similar to the type we have in constitutional regimes or regional human rights regimes. This is not just a fact, but also a line of criticism towards international human rights law *qua* law. The existence of a court with general and compulsory jurisdiction involving an authoritative judicial review is considered to be a necessary condition for a legal system. If there is no judicial organ at the international level with universal jurisdiction, there cannot be an independent and authoritative review of the implementation of international human rights norms by States Parties such as that carried out by the constitutional court in the national sphere. As Besson and Tasioulas put it, "the absence of a centralized enforcement system, and in particular of a sanctions system or at least a courts system with universal and compulsory jurisdictions"[16] is used to ground the claim that international law *qua* law remains a *primitive* system of law. However correct as a normative claim, it is a descriptive point that I emphasize here: the vertical dimension of international human rights is still shaped by the broader horizontal structure of equal sovereign states with no world legislature, executive or judiciary.

In the case of the ECHR, which has given rise to a supranational organ with compulsory jurisdiction, the horizontal dimension remains salient in the *subsidiary* role devoted to the ECtHR through the principle of *exhaustion of domestic remedies* – what Besson calls "jurisdictional subsidiarity".[17] This comes together with Article 13, which requires States Parties to provide victims with an "effective remedy before the national authority". Although subsidiarity certainly serves the interests of individuals and applicants,[18] it also sheds light on the profound prevalence

---

15 Van Alebeek and Nollkaemper, "The Legal Status of Decisions by Human Rights Treaty Bodies in National Law", 372.

16 Besson and Tasioulas, "The Emergence of the Philosophy of International Law", 11.

17 Besson, "The 'Erga Omnes' Effect of the European Court of Human Rights", 152.

18 As Stone Sweet and Keller explain, "Article 13 covers virtually every aspect of how national legal systems are organized and function. Applicants routinely invoke Article 13, leading the Court

98   *The normativity of ECHR law*

of states as the irreducible makers and subjects of international human rights law. As Shaw puts it, "it is a method of permitting states to solve their own internal problems in accordance with their own constitutional procedures before accepted international mechanism can be invoked . . .".[19] Subsidiarity has more than one dimension: *remedial* subsidiarity is also central to the ECtHR's function. As we shall see, in principle the judgment of the ECtHR is *declaratory* and leaves the state to choose the appropriate measure to comply with the judgment. Subsidiarity is also central to the adjudication of the ECtHR, as we shall see in Chapter 10. For some ECHR rights – most importantly, those contained in Articles 8 to 15 – the ECtHR leaves more freedom to the State Parties to define the scope of the correlative duties through the margin of appreciation doctrine. This the *substantive* use of subsidiarity.

It is therefore the conjunction of the *jurisdictional, remedial* and *substantive* forms of subsidiarity that reveals the prevalence of states in ECHR law. Of course, subsidiarity is not necessarily a defect of international human rights law from a democratic perspective. It precisely permits the democratic reception of international norms. As Besson argues, "it is precisely the democratic process of reception that requires respecting the States' margin of appreciation".[20] I come back to this point in the next chapters.

6.2.1 The normative legitimacy of international law

As explained above, the core structure of the international state system of equal sovereign states has not been altered by the recognition of international human rights. As Shaw puts it:

> The *raison d'être* of international law and the determining factor in its composition remains the needs and characteristics of the international political system . . . .[21] Units of formal independence benefiting from equal sovereignty in law and equal possession of the basic attributes of statehood have succeeded in creating a system enshrining such values.[22]

The conventional view is that international law aims to foster the national interest(s) through contractual freedom – often called "voluntarism" and "consensualism" in international legal theory. As Shaw specifies, "states form the irreducible units of the international community and, given the absence of

---

     to review how national systems of justice operate at the deep structural level": Stone Sweet and Keller, "The Reception of the ECHR in National Legal Orders", 32.

19 Shaw, *International Law*, 273. As Birgit Schlütter puts it, "the subsidiarity principle reflects this fact: international human rights law review as a form of 'secondary', 'constitutional', or 'appellate' review can only continue the national review of human rights obligation": Schlütter, "Aspects of Human Rights Interpretation by the UN Treaty Bodies", 309.

20 Besson, "European Human Rights, Supranational Judicial Review and Democracy – Thinking Outside the Judicial Box", note 111.

21 Shaw, *International Law*, 44.

22 Ibid., 45.

The normativity of ECHR law   99

a system of organic representation, the idea of such community is nothing but other than the sum total of these states".[23] What makes international human rights norms interesting, therefore, is how their normativity is shaped by both the deep structure of the international political and legal systems of sovereign state unities with no world executive, legislature or judiciary *and* their special *telos* of protecting individual interests within and against states.

It is crucial to examine how the conventional conception of international law – as a *descriptive* claim – generates a conception of *normative legitimacy* of international legal norms.[24] True, as *de facto* authority, international law makes an inherent claim to *legitimate* authority. However, as I indicated earlier, it is *legitimate* or *justified* if, and only if, it has the right to rule – that is, whether it can create duties to obey on the part of its subjects. As Besson explains:

> Of course, as domestic law, international law usually benefits from *de facto* authority by the mere fact of exercising power over its subjects and/or being effectively complied with in practice . . . . By virtue of its legal validity, international law also lays a claim to legitimate authority . . . . The fact that international law inherently makes a claim to legitimate authority does not, however, entail that it actually possesses it, or even that it is capable of possessing it under realistic conditions.[25]

This distinction between authority in the sociological and normative senses applies to the foundations of international legal norms. *Consent* and *reciprocity* of states are viewed as the necessary and sufficient conditions for their legitimacy of international law – usually captured with the general principle of international law, *pacta sunt servanda*. International law treaties are conceived as "consensual arrangements instituting, through the medium of legal rights and duties, a reciprocal exchange of goods or benefits".[26] The analogy with contracts in municipal law is not far off: states are bound only by what they have consented to in the same way in which individuals enter into subjective contractual promises. As Buchanan puts it:

> The attraction of this view lies in an analogy with individual consent: if you and I consent to a certain arrangement as to how we shall treat each other, then surely that arrangement is legitimate. Similarly, it is said, if States consent to a certain arrangement for how their interactions are to be regulated, then it is legitimate.[27]

23 Tasioulas, "In Defence of Relative Normativity: Communitarian Values and the Nicaragua Case", 116.
24 As Besson explains, "the popularity of consent in accounts of the legitimacy of international law may partly be explained by the widespread failure to distinguish between the normative and sociological senses of legitimacy: at least on the basis of an individual analogy, there seems to be some empirical connection between believing that a norm is binding and having previously consented to it. In normative terms, however, as we have seen before, consent fails to provide independent authoritative reasons to obey the law": Besson, "The Authority of International Law – Lifting the State Veil", 371.
25 Ibid., 345.
26 Craven, "Legal Differentiation and the Concept of the Human Rights Treaty in International Law", 500.
27 Buchanan, "The Legitimacy of International Law", 91.

100   *The normativity of ECHR law*

The conventional conception of the legitimacy of international legal norms grounded in the analogy between states and individuals in contractual relationships is challenged by a number of legal theorists. The *post-ontological* turn in the philosophy of international law – which, instead of focusing on the nature of international law *qua* law, questions the normative legitimacy of international law – "certainly had a liberating effect – international legal scholars could turn to questions of justice, and identify or in some cases negate the values sustaining international law without having to fight back skeptical views about its legal nature".[28] Those critical views challenge the core standard of *state consent*. First, it is certainly unrealistic to assume that state consent is *effectively* obtained. This remains open to empirical confirmation. It is a matter of historical evidence that stronger states may "make the costs of their not consenting prohibitive".[29] As a result, if it is certainly true that consent helps in strengthening the legitimacy of international legal norms, it remains clearly *insufficient*. Moreover, some international legal norms cannot be drawn back to consent in the process of lawmaking and, as Besson puts it, "they can actually bind other international subjects than states consenting to them and a consent-based justification would leave a large part of international law unaccounted for".[30]

Second, the analogy between states and individuals entering into contracts is largely inaccurate since states are both the *subjects* and *makers* of international law – at least in traditional lawmaking processes such as treaties and customary law – in ways that individuals are not.[31] Following Waldron, this structure implies that states are international law's *officials* by contrast to individuals within the state: "it depends on states for the making, but also for the enforcement of its provisions. Governments are the officials or officers of the international legal system".[32] Moreover, it is hard to take state autonomy as having an ultimate normative value when one acknowledges that state autonomy "can only be explained in terms of the autonomy of individuals constituting it".[33] This gives the analogy of states and individuals very limited heuristic value.

6.2.2 The normative legitimacy of international human rights

If the limits of the conventional conception of legitimacy can be independently established, they become even more salient in light of recent developments in international law. As Besson explains, "with respect to its objects, international law no longer pertains only to interstate relations, but also to intra-state relations and

---

28 Besson, "The Authority of International Law – Lifting the State Veil", 347.
29 Buchanan, "The Legitimacy of International Law", 91.
30 Besson, "Sovereignty, International Law and Democracy", 377.
31 Waldron, "The Rule of International Law", 23–5.
32 Besson, "The Authority of International Law – Lifting the State Veil", 361.
33 Ibid., 364. Besson further extends the argument to the concept of *sovereignty*: "considered in both its internal and external dimensions, a state's sovereign autonomy is a purely legal construct, not something which value is to be assumed as a first principle of normative analysis": ibid., 373. See also Besson, "Sovereignty, International Law and Democracy".

The normativity of ECHR law 101

therefore, regulates the life of individuals alongside domestic law".[34] International law has not only expanded in the number of its norms. It has also diversified and new areas of international legal regulation have emerged: most notably, international trade law, environmental protection and human rights. The *fragmentation* of international law is now recognized to such an extent that it can no longer be envisaged as the exclusive domain of states and their apparatus as the relevant makers and subjects.

It does not follow, however, that the ways in which international legal relations are established (treaties, conventions, etc.) have changed. As Shaw explains, "the international system is composed increasingly of co-operative and competing elements participating in cross-boundary activities, but the essential normative and structural nature of international law remains".[35] States remain the primary lawmakers and subjects of international legal norms. In the case of human rights norms, states hold the primary responsibility for implementing those rights and incorporating their provisions into their constitutions and laws. It is rather the *normative* legitimacy of its newly developed relations that is questioned: the analogy between states at the international level and individuals at the domestic level, identified by the concept of consent as the ultimate normative principle, cannot survive the recent development of international legal relations. In addition, the consent-based argument certainly cannot account for peremptory norms (*jus cogens*) we find in international law, such as prohibiting war, crimes against humanity, slavery, torture, etc., which are considered legally binding even against the will of states.

Clearly, the limitations of the consent-based argument – now widely considered as "old positivism" – are even more salient for international human rights, which require taking the perspective of the right-bearers and their interests. As Besson explains, "most accounts of the legitimacy of international law do not look at it from the perspective of individual legal subjects".[36] This is clear in the case law of the ECtHR, as we shall see in the next chapters. As already mentioned, human rights *qua* international legal norms are undoubtedly distinctive in the interests they protect. Rather than merely creating reciprocal duties between states, human rights treaties protect specific interests of individuals within states. If human rights norms make individuals subjects of international law, the classical state consent argument for the legitimacy of international legal norms is inevitably doomed to fail. Buchanan puts the point clearly: "given that states often do not represent their citizens and do not act with their consent, how could the fact that states consent to international legal norms show that their enforcement on other collectivities and individuals is morally justified?"[37]

This allows me to connect the constructivist view of justification with the current state of international law. As explained in Chapter 4, the role of institutions

---

34 Besson, "The Authority of International Law – Lifting the State Veil", 349.
35 Shaw, *International Law*, 67.
36 Besson, "The Authority of International Law – Lifting the State Veil", 350.
37 Buchanan, *Justice, Legitimacy, and Self-Determination: Moral Foundations for International Law*, 309.

102   *The normativity of ECHR law*

is predicated on their enormous practical significance for individuals in their ordinary life and life prospects. As Besson puts it, "the potential moral effect of the law on people is in need of justification".[38] In this chapter, we have observed that human rights law within international law overlaps with this quest in the way in which it challenges the conventional conception of legitimacy in international law. As Besson explains, "*qua* international human rights treaty, the ECHR is formally an international treaty, but its content is materially of a constitutional kind".[39] As we shall see in the next chapters, the case law reveals how state consent is not only in principle limited, but is inoperative to a significant extent in the adjudication of the ECtHR.

6.3 The ECHR *qua* international human rights treaty

The ECHR *qua* international human rights law treaty has individuals and their interests as rights-bearers (material content), but it also has states as lawmakers and duty bearers (conventional origin). Now if we follow the conventional rationale of international legal legitimacy just outlined, we cannot but notice that:

> Each of these understandings, however, works against each other: human rights treaties cannot be simply "constitutional" insofar as they are constructed in the form of agreements between states (they do not in that sense precede those agreements, and exist only in relation to them) . . . By the same token, human rights cannot be simply "ordinary treaties", as they seem to be premised upon the idea that the rights pre-exist not only the treaties themselves.[40]

The tension between the right-holder and the quasi-constitutional content of the ECHR rights, on the one hand, and the lawmaker of international norms, on the other, is salient even in the most recent studies of UN treaty bodies.[41] Which of the two should prevail? Pulled to an extreme, the international law argument is that the ECHR is not really "law" as we know it in the municipal sphere. As Letsas puts it, "being an international treaty – the objection goes – the ECHR lacks the attribute of legality, as we know it in municipal law".[42] By the same token, it is the whole function of the ECtHR to review the ways in which states use coercion towards individuals that is questioned. As Besson puts it, "the question is therefore in which of those boxes to place the ECtHR".[43] If the ECHR is viewed through the international law lens, the principles that should govern the

---

38 Besson, "The Authority of International Law – Lifting the State Veil", 360.
39 Besson, "The 'Erga Omnes' Effect of the European Court of Human Rights", 128.
40 Craven, "Legal Differentiation and the Concept of the Human Rights Treaty in International Law", 493.
41 "The legitimacy of treaty bodies therefore depends, on the one hand, on their respect for relevant principles of treaty interpretation. On the other hand, it is also a function of their ability to effectively promote the protection of human rights": Keller and Ulfstein. "Introduction", 9.
42 Letsas, *A Theory of Interpretation of the European Convention on Human Rights*, 31.
43 Besson, "The 'Erga Omnes' Effect of the European Court of Human Rights", 152.

The normativity of ECHR law   103

adjudication of the ECHR should thereby be those codified in the conventional doctrines of international interpretation. As we shall see, the ECtHR has a rather non-conventional relationship with the principles of the Vienna Convention on the Law of Treaties (VCLT).[44] If the ECHR is viewed through the constitutional law lens, then the interpretation tends to focus more on the material content of those rights and the interests they protect – what Letsas, through the Dworkinian prism, calls the "moral reading" of ECHR rights.[45]

6.3.1 Monism and dualism

We have seen above that the conventional conception of legitimacy of international law implies that the normativity of the ECHR is determined by the broader horizontal structure of the international state system, grounded in the contractual freedom of states as irreducible units of international lawmaking. Independently of its material constitutional content, the normativity remains subject to the freedom of states to incorporate ECHR rights and execute ECtHR judgments. As Krisch explains, "from its inception, the Strasbourg organs were dependent on a positive stance by national authorities; with no enforcement tools at their disposal, compliance had to be essentially voluntary".[46]

If the state enjoys full contractual freedom, then it does not only have the freedom to sign and ratify an international law treaty; it also has the freedom to determine the status of international legal norms in the national legal order. The distinction between *monism* and *dualism* may be used here as a first landmark. In a nutshell, *dualism* conceives international law and domestic law as two firmly distinct bodies of law: as Besson puts it, "pour les tenants de cette doctrine, le droit international et le droit national constituent deux ordres juridiques égaux, indépendant et totalement séparés l'un de l'autre".[47] This applies to the object (within/outside the state), source (sovereignty of the state/international community) and subjects (individuals/states).

By contrast, *monism* assumes that international and national law form the same legal system:

> Les tenants de la doctrine moniste affirment l'unité fondamentale de l'ordre juridique international et de l'ordre juridique interne. Pour la théorie moniste, il s'agit de deux systèmes juridiques de même nature qui ne forment une fois unis qu'un seul ordre juridique interne.[48]

The practical implication of this distinction is that in monist states, the provisions of an international treaty may be applied by courts immediately: "ainsi, un traité

---

44 Vienna Convention on the Law of Treaties (entered into force 27 January 1980) 1155 UNTS 331.
45 Cf. Letsas, "Strasbourg's Interpretive Ethic: Lessons for the International Lawyer".
46 Krisch, *Beyond Constitutionalism: The Pluralist Structure of Postnational Law*, 139.
47 Besson, *Droit international public: abrégé de cours et résumés de jurisprudence*, 260.
48 Ibid., 259.

104 *The normativity of ECHR law*

conclu par un Etat fait partie intégrante de son ordre interne dès son entrée en vigueur".[49] Dualist states, by contrast, must "transform" or "adopt" those provisions to become applicable in domestic law: "aucune règle de droit n'est valide dans un Etat avant d'avoir été transformée en règle de droit interne et d'avoir ainsi acquis le rang d'une loi".[50]

The distinction between monism and dualism is abstract. Countries such as Germany and Italy are described as "moderately dualistic",[51] whereas monism may just mean that international law has *direct effect* in domestic law or that it holds a specific rank in the internal legal hierarchy (statutory level, above-statutory level, constitutional level, etc.). As a result, the *object*, *subject* and *sources* of international law are confined to a self-contained legal system. From a practical point of view, another distinction is whether the state has to *incorporate* (via a constitutional provision) or *transform* (via a translation of the international norm into a new norm) the international legal norm, which implies legislative adoption. As Keller and Stone Sweet sum up:

> In summary, there is no necessary causal linkage between ex ante monism or dualism, on the one hand, and the reception of the ECHR on the other. Put differently, the manner in which the ECHR is incorporated is an outcome of the reception process which will, in turn, impinge on reception ex post.[52]

Indeed, irrespective of whether a state has a monist or dualist tradition:

> A parliamentary act is usually required to give direct effect to the Convention's provisions. This act can be either the act of ratification, i.e. the law approving the treaty and authorizing the deposit of an instrument of ratification in Strasbourg, or a separate enabling act, as it is particularly the case in countries with a common law tradition.[53]

As a result, the monist/dualist distinction does not allow us to account for the normativity of international legal norms such as the ECHR in national legal orders. Most importantly for our normative endeavours, the distinction does not say anything about the *invocability* of ECHR rights by individuals, since they may be invocable in dualist states and not in monist states, or vice-versa.

6.3.2 Effect, validity and rank

The more informative distinction is between the *effect*, *validity* and *rank* of international legal norms. The question of *direct effect* (or "direct applicability") has

49 Ibid.
50 Ibid., 262.
51 Wildhaber, "The European Convention on Human Rights and International Law", 218.
52 Keller and Stone Sweet, "Assessing the Impact of the ECHR in National Legal Systems", 686.
53 Polakiewicz, "The Status of the Convention in National Law", 32.

The normativity of ECHR law   105

to do with the *invocability* of international legal norms by individuals before national courts. As Besson explains:

> Cela implique qu'elle fait directement naître, dans l'ordre juridique interne d'un Etat, des droits ou obligations à l'intention des personnes privées physiques ou morales, sans qu'il y ait besoin d'une concrétisation de la norme par le droit interne.[54]

It is primarily states that decide whether international legal norms enjoy direct effect (only in some cases, international law itself decides) but the conditions remain controversial.[55] As a result, the ratification of the ECHR does not itself entail a legal obligation to render its provisions internally applicable as invocable norms. As far as the ECHR is concerned, the only legal obligation stems from Article 13, which requires an effective internal remedy within the national orders. As Polakiewicz explains:

> According to the Court, instead of imposing an obligation to give direct effect to the substantive provisions of the Convention, article 13 of the ECHR only guarantees the availability at the national level of an effective remedy to enforce the substance of the Convention rights and freedoms in whatever form they might happen to be secured.[56]

The standard of direct effect allows us to capture the distinctive normative role of the ECHR in national jurisdictions. In contrast to the vast majority of international legal norms and their *indirect effect* – requiring a domestication of the norm in national law and therefore a legislative step – ECHR rights (and ECtHR judgments) have been given *direct effect* before national courts in almost all domestic orders of States Parties. As Nollkaemper explains, "what is meant by direct effect is that enforcement, whether by courts or executive branch, of an international obligation is not dependent on subsequent legislation that makes that particular obligation part of domestic law".[57] Although direct effect may be granted norm by norm, the ECHR as a single treaty has been granted direct effect before the national courts of most States Parties. We should also note here that the ECHR can be relevant in national judicial proceedings even if the norm in question does not enjoy direct effect: for instance, ratification may lead to giving the ECHR the status of an interpretative aid for judges. This is the case in the UK where the ECHR was raised in any judgment pertaining to human rights even though the ECHR lacked direct effect.[58]

More importantly, the standard of direct effect is independent of the question of the *validity* of international legal norms, which determines *if* and *how* the international

---

54 Besson, *Droit international public: abrégé de cours et résumés de jurisprudence*, 263.
55 Ibid., 265. See also Nollkaemper, *National Courts and the International Rule of Law*, Chapter 6.
56 Polakiewicz, "The Status of the Convention in National Law", 33.
57 Nollkaemper, *National Courts and the International Rule of Law*, 118.
58 Besson, "The Reception Process in Ireland and the United Kingdom", 47–50.

106   *The normativity of ECHR law*

norm needs to be incorporated via a specific provision in the national legal hierarchy. In other words, the answer to the question of validity is the function of the monism/dualism distinction. As Besson explains:

> La validité est un autre nom pour le monisme, soit le fait qu'une norme de droit international puisse s'appliquer en droit interne. Elle se distingue donc clairement de l'effet direct et se détermine indépendamment de celui-ci: peu importe que l'invocabilité directe soit reconnue ou non à une norme de droit international public, cette norme peut être immédiatement valide en droit interne dans un système moniste.[59]

If the state in question is monist, international legal norms are immediately valid in the national legal order, whereas in dualist states they necessitate a constitutional provision to establish the validity – that is, the incorporation of the new provisions into the national legal system. This is the case in traditionally dualist states such as Belgium, and states that have traditionally denied the direct applicability of treaty law, such as Austria. Both states have given ECHR rights a constitutional or quasi-constitutional status. In the UK, treaties may be ratified without the approval of Parliament, but they may not be invoked by individuals and therefore are not applied by national courts. As a result, "prior to incorporation, the ECHR remained an international convention without immediate validity in domestic law, and its status was, at best, a distant standard of interpretation for judges, whose rank in the legal order did not matter as a result".[60] The fact that international legal norms are valid only after incorporation through parliamentary enactment gave rise to the 1998 Human Rights Act.

Finally, the question of direct effect is also independent of the question of *rank*, which pertains to the *primacy* of international law – despite its principled superiority – over national law *and* its exact position *vis-à-vis* the sources of national law. The sub-constitutional rank pre-empts neither the supremacy of the parliament nor the constitution from prevailing over the ECHR. The question of rank is *practical*: it arises when a national legal norm and an international legal norm conflict with each other. As a result of state freedom, we may observe a striking variety of mechanisms of co-ordination in incorporating the ECHR into the domestic hierarchy – what Helfer calls "diffuse embeddedness";[61] some states (such as the Netherlands, Austria and San Marino) have incorporated the treaty into domestic law by granting it constitutional or quasi-constitutional status, while others fulfil their conventional obligations by giving effect to specific judgments of the ECtHR (by the introduction of legislative amendments, the reopening of national judicial proceedings, the granting of administrative remedies, or by paying monetary damages to individuals). This is particularly the case in the vast

---

59 Besson, *Droit international public: abrégé de cours et résumés de jurisprudence*, 266.
60 Besson, "The Reception Process in Ireland and United Kingdom", 48.
61 Helfer, "Redesigning the European Court of Human Rights: Embeddedness as a Deep Structural Principle of the European Human Rights Regime".

The normativity of ECHR law 107

majority of States Parties in Central and Eastern Europe where the ECHR is applicable at an above-statutory level but inferior to the constitution.[62]

From the standpoint of normative individualism, the concept that matters primarily is that of *direct effect* and therefore the idea of *direct invocability* in national legal orders of States Parties. Direct effect is central to the role of the ECHR since it implies not only the *justiciability* of the norm and, as such, a specification of the *content* of rights, their *right-holders* as well as their *duty-holders*, but it also implies that State Parties have made the ECHR an immediate source of individual rights before all national authorities. As Gardbaum further explains:

> Unlike EU law, in which direct effect is one of its central constitutional principles, the ECHR does not formally require that its provisions themselves are invocable in, and penetrate, the national legal system – only individuals whose rights have been violated "shall have an effective remedy before a national authority".[63]

From the perspective of normative individualism, the consequence is decisive: individuals may invoke ECHR rights before all national authorities independently of the right to individual petition before the ECtHR. This allows us to foresee the limits of Beitz's *functional* argument about the normativity of human rights in general and their legal dimension in particular. Beitz's claim that "the human rights system is notable for the weakness and unevenness of its capacities for adjudication and enforcement"[64] is not only contingent and incomplete on a global scale but also misguiding in the case of the ECtHR. The functional concept of direct effect allows us to capture the scope of the normativity of the ECHR for individuals within the state. As Letsas puts it:

> The ECHR is treated by the relevant actors (i.e. States Parties, applicants, and judges) as enshrining rights that states have a primary obligation to respect when deploying coercive force, as opposed to a *secondary* obligation to compensate victims should they be found to be in breach of the Convention by the European Court of Human Rights.[65]

The *contingent* normative role of the ECHR in national legal orders remains unique in both international law and international human rights law and requires a willing act from the State Parties. As Nollkaemper puts it, "in the absence of any rules that require direct effect, the decision whether to allow courts to give direct effect to international law – as well as the decision of courts to grant direct effect – is primarily a political and normative choice, both for state and its courts".[66]

---

62 Wildhaber, "The European Convention on Human Rights and International Law", 218–19.
63 Gardbaum, "Human Rights as International Constitutional Rights", 760.
64 Beitz, *The Idea of Human Rights*, 43.
65 Letsas, *A Theory of Interpretation of the European Convention on Human Rights*, 9.
66 Nollkaemper, *National Courts and the International Rule of Law*, 126.

108   *The normativity of ECHR law*

6.3.3 The constitutionalist argument

What transpires from the three-pronged analysis is the difficulty, in legal scholarship, to depict the legal status of the ECHR in light of its normativity in States Parties. The status of the ECHR *qua* international law treaty, together with the underlying conception of international legal legitimacy – envisioning states by analogy with individuals enjoying contractual freedom – reinforces this reading. The jurisdictional and remedial subsidiarity as forms of weak judicial review also reflect the original objectives of the ECHR in its burgeoning years. As Helfer explains, "the result, in short, is that ECtHR judgments are persuasive authority. They are highly persuasive, to be sure. But they retain their status as interpretations of international law until they have been domesticated by national courts".[67] The quasi-judicial supervision of the execution of ECtHR judgments is also clearly confined within the traditional *inter partes* regime in international law. Moreover, as we shall see in the next chapter, this international law prism goes all the way down to the interpretation and the originalist methods it may use – as well as the role of substantive subsidiarity through the *margin of appreciation* doctrine. From this standpoint, the normativity of the ECHR is in principle determined by the inherent freedom of sovereign states to conceive the status of international legal norms within the national legal order, and this applies both to the ECHR and the case law of the ECtHR even though they have accepted the ECtHR's jurisdiction. As Stone Sweet puts it, "for the Convention to make a difference, domestically, national officials must take decisions that give agency to the Court's jurisprudence". [68]

In this regard, the normativity of the ECHR (comprising the ECHR, its protocols and the ECtHR judgments) in national legal orders remains unique both in international law and international human rights law – to the extent that some, at the other extreme of the spectrum, recognize it as the constitution of Europe. This is where the constitutional law lens operates. As Stone Sweet nicely puts it, "if a duck-like creature looks, walks and quacks like a duck, then it might just be a duck".[69] Beyond the explicit contention of the ECtHR that the ECHR has become the "constitutional instrument of European public order",[70] and despite the material content of ECHR rights, it is the *direct effect* of these rights and the ECtHR's judgments in the national legal order that ground the constitutional status that many legal scholars attribute to the ECtHR. The compulsory jurisdiction introduced by Protocol 11 has played a crucial role in this process. As Stone Sweet explains, the ECHR has been "constitutionalised by the combined effects of the entry into force of Protocol No. 11, and the incorporation of the Convention into national legal orders".[71]

---

67 Helfer, "Redesigning the European Court of Human Rights: Embeddedness as a Deep Structural Principle of the European Human Rights Regime", 137.
68 Stone Sweet, "On the Constitutionalisation of the Convention: The European Court of Human Rights as a Constitutional Court", 4.
69 Ibid., 5.
70 *Loizidou v. Turkey*, App. No. 15318/89, 18 December 1996, para. 75.
71 Stone Sweet, "On the Constitutionalisation of the Convention: The European Court of Human Rights as a Constitutional Court", 2.

The normativity of ECHR law 109

However, a number of points about the constitutionalist argument need to be qualified. The first relates to the role of the ECHR *in abstracto*. Given the material content of ECHR rights, the ECtHR certainly plays the role that is conferred upon the constitution within states – that is, it determines the limits of what states can do to individuals in the pursuit of public and political objectives. As Gardbaum explains:

> There is inherently something constitutional in the very nature and subject-matter of international human rights law, in that one of its primary functions is to specify the limits on what governments can lawfully do to people within their jurisdictions. This is a central constitutional function.[72]

Clearly, this function is not reserved to the ECHR. It is the principled role of international human rights in general in the international legal system. As a result, the point is valid only if we set aside the various ways in which a State Party incorporates and applies, or fails to apply, ECHR rights and ECtHR judgments in its legal order – as well as supervision of the execution of the ECtHR's judgments by the Committee of Ministers. As a result, it is the *direct effect* attributed to ECHR rights and ECtHR judgments – making ECHR rights binding within national law and invocable by individuals *vis-à-vis* all state institutions, whether legislative, executive or judicial – which best reinforces the constitutionalist argument. Direct effect implies, among other things, that the norms are clear enough to be directly enforced in national courts. This is a definitional character of constitutions. As Elster explains, "the constitutions must have precise, enforceable behavioral implications. Those implications must be enforced, and the enforcement of those implications must be causally linked with the existence of the constitution".[73]

In addition, the constitutionalization of the ECHR in the national hierarchy – that is, the constitutional rank attributed to the ECHR – is another important argument for the constitutionalist position. As Stone Sweet explains:

> Modes of incorporation are capable of altering the constitutional precepts of any legal order and, especially, doctrines associated with separation of powers and parliamentary sovereignty . . . . In most states, the incorporation of the Convention has had greater consequences for the exercise of public authority than has any formal act of constitutional revision.[74]

Moreover, incorporation takes the role of supplementing the State Party's judicially enforceable bill of rights – be it the constitution or some other basic provision. In filling certain gaps of other constitutional provisions and by enabling

72 Gardbaum, "Human Rights as International Constitutional Rights", 752.
73 Elster, "Constitutional Bootstrapping in Philadephia and Paris", 63.
74 Stone Sweet, "On the Constitutionalisation of the Convention: The European Court of Human Rights as a Constitutional Court", 9.

110   *The normativity of ECHR law*

courts to review the compatibility of any legislative act of any public authority, the ECHR is constitutionally active within the national legal order.

There are strong arguments against the constitutionalist reading, too. Founding states have ratified a convention, not a constitution. Prior to the most significant legal developments of the ECHR – and, in particular, Protocol 11 – the constitutionalist argument hardly held as the remedial authority of the ECtHR was not mandatory. The objections do not necessarily contest the constitutional character and function of the ECHR outlined above. They rather question whether those attributes are *sufficient* to qualify the ECtHR as fully constitutional. First, the ECtHR does not have the power of judicial review that constitutional courts have and it cannot invalidate national legal norms that are deemed incompatible with the ECHR, or ask the state to reopen the procedure and revise the judgment in the domestic proceedings. The ECtHR is empowered primarily to *declare* whether one or several ECHR rights have been violated in a single case. As a result, and despite the quasi-constitutional content of ECHR rights, it is important to recall the specific role of the "external minimal guarantee" and therefore the *complementarity* rather than the identity of ECHR rights and constitutional rights. Again, there is no necessary connection between international human rights law and supranational adjudication. As Besson explains, "international human rights institutions should not aim at replacing domestic judicial authorities, but should on the contrary situate themselves in a relationship of cooperation with them".[75] This argument clearly pleads for a *disanalogy* between the ECtHR and a constitutional court.

Second, we have explained how the inherent freedom of the States Parties to determine the effect, validity and rank of ECHR rights and ECtHR judgments inevitably gives rise to a diversity of modes of incorporation and effects of the ECHR in national legal orders. Krisch, for instance, characterizes the ECHR as "pluralist" rather than "constitutional". In his thorough study of the Spanish and French cases, he shows that we cannot identify one overarching rule that would typify the relationship as to how national orders "treat" the ECHR: "while the domestic and European human rights law have indeed become increasingly linked and Strasbourg decisions are regularly followed by national courts, this does not indicate the emergence of a unified, hierarchically ordered system along constitutionalist lines".[76] Krisch therefore emphasizes the *heterarchical* rather than *hierarchical* order in that "the relationship between the two levels is then determined not by one overarching rule, but by an oversupply of competing rules, among which solutions can only be found through political negotiations, often in the form of judicial politics".[77]

It is hardly practicable, given the specificities of each national legal order, for states to converge on a hierarchically unified set of norms that would fit within the constitutionalist model that Krisch has in mind. Moreover, the points to which

75 Besson, "The 'Erga Omnes' Effect of the European Court of Human Rights", 155.
76 Krisch, *Beyond Constitutionalism*, 151.
77 Ibid., 127.

The normativity of ECHR law 111

Krisch directs are essentially of an empirical character. As a result, Stone Sweet's response merely consists of envisioning the possible future: "the more any State has incorporated the ECHR into the national legal order, as judicially enforceable text, and the more that State has conferred upon the Convention supra-legislative status, the less important is the objection".[78]

6.4 The ECtHR *qua* international judicial organ

However central it is from the perspective of individuals, the normativity of the ECHR cannot be reduced to its domestication in national legal orders. If that were the case, then there would be no difference between the ECHR and other international human rights norms that enjoy direct effect. As Besson puts it:

> There is no necessary connection, however, between supranational law (e.g. human rights) and supranational adjudication. Human rights law of supra-national origin ought to be interpreted, specified and applied by domestic institutions and in particular by domestic courts in priority, without necessarily benefiting from the aid of a supranational court reviewing national law.[79]

In ratifying the ECHR, states do not only engage in respecting a list of rights within their jurisdictions, but also abiding by the judgments of the judicial organ created by the same convention (Article 46). The ECtHR is empowered to give "the final authoritative interpretation of the rights and freedoms" (Article 32). In ratifying Protocol 11, States Parties have made the ECtHR a permanent and inde-pendent court with compulsory jurisdiction (effective since November 1998). It correlated with the abolition of the European Commission of Human Rights, and resulted in the qualification of the ECtHR as constitutional or quasi-constitutional, as we shall see later. Most importantly, Protocol 11 made obligatory state accep-tance of the individual petition procedure and the compulsory jurisdiction of the ECtHR. As Stone Sweet puts it, "in doing so, States have transferred authority to 'complete' or 'construct' Convention rights, rendering them more determinate over time for all members, despite, national diversity".[80]

Of course, as we have already seen, the ECtHR remains a *remedial* organ. *Remedial subsidiarity* implies that national judges play a primary role in the adju-dication of the ECHR and that the ECtHR finds itself in a constant dialogue with the domestically defined relationship of national courts and their laws with the ECHR. Despite the authoritative power conferred upon the ECtHR by Article 19, subsidiarity implies that the ECtHR has to address domestic law and the inter-pretation provided by national courts. It transpires from the case law that the

---

78 Stone Sweet, "On the Constitutionalisation of the Convention: The European Court of Human Rights as a Constitutional Court", 16.
79 Besson, "European Human Rights, Supranational Judicial Review and Democracy – Thinking Outside the Judicial Box", 103.
80 Stone Sweet, "On the Constitutionalisation of the Convention: The European Court of Human Rights as a Constitutional Court", 4.

112 *The normativity of ECHR law*

judicial dialogue is intense. As Besson explains, "the Court does not have exclusive jurisdiction on the interpretation of the ECHR. Its jurisdiction is grounded in the principle of jurisdictional subsidiarity".[81] This dialogue, we shall see later, counts against the qualification of the ECtHR as a constitutional court.[82] More generally, Neuman notes that the interpretation by international tribunals taking into account the interpretation of national courts is also "a deliberate strategy of conflict avoidance or it may produce dissonance-reducing effects as a by-product of other purposes".[83]

The ECtHR is therefore a *supranational* judicial organ only when there is a conjunction between its compulsory jurisdiction – as enshrined in the ECHR itself (Article 46) – and the direct effect given to its judgments. As Besson explains, "there is supranational review when supranational courts' decisions that review the incompatibility between national law and supranational law are (i) binding within national law and (ii) directly invocable by individuals (direct effect) (iii) vis-à-vis Contracting States' institutions".[84] The compulsory jurisdiction of the ECtHR is therefore central to its role as final arbiter of state–individual conflicts as well as crucial from the perspective of individuals.[85] As Ress puts it:

> The process of globalization of international human rights has found a solid procedural foundation in the shape of the Court. This is a rather revolutionary development in the field of international law, which has always been a field quite resistant to any form of compulsory international adjudication.[86]

As a result, it is the right of individual petition that plays the triggering role between the domestically defined relationship with the ECHR and the ECtHR as final arbiter – provided that internal remedies have been exhausted (what Besson calls "jurisdictional subsidiarity"[87]). Following the recent accession to the CoE of Central and Eastern Europe, the right of individual petition now extends to more than 800 million people in 47 European states. The centrality of the right of individual petition is also made clear by historical analysis. As explained in the last chapter, this right was perceived as a significant advancement towards the "post-alarm bell idea" role of the ECHR. As Bates explains, "acceptance of the right to individual petition was important for the Convention to evolve beyond a limited

---

81 Besson, "The 'Erga Omnes' Effect of the European Court of Human Rights", 152.
82 Krisch, *Beyond Constitutionalism*.
83 Neuman, "Human Rights and Constitutional Rights: Harmony and Dissonance", 1881.
84 Besson, "The 'Erga Omnes' Effect of the European Court of Human Rights", 103.
85 It must be noticed here that the ECtHR's jurisdiction equals the area over which states claim to have jurisdiction, which may go beyond the state's territorial area – its extraterritorial effects. As Ress explains, "the Court has held that it has jurisdiction over the territory of the Contracting States in relation to all acts and omissions of the state and also with respect to acts and omissions of the state outside this territorial area if a Contracting State has territorial control in that specific area": Ress, "The Effect of Decisions and Judgments of the European Court of Human Rights in the Domestic Legal Order", 364.
86 Ibid., 362.
87 Besson, "The 'Erga Omnes' Effect of the European Court of Human Rights", 152.

The normativity of ECHR law   113

conceptualization of it as an interstate, democratic "alarm bell for" Europe".[88] The rate of formal petitions began to rise precisely when the mechanism was made compulsory by the late 2000s – reaching over 40,000 petitions a year – over 30 times the annual average of the first 30 years of existence of the ECHR. Legal scholars correctly take the right of individual petition as the distinctive characteristic of the ECHR among human rights protection systems. As Helfer and Slaughter explain, "commentators have stressed the importance of this individual access right as crucial to the success of the Convention in altering the domestic landscape".[89] This mechanism is certainly at the heart of the development of European human rights law in general and, in particular, the compliance of States Parties with the judgments of the ECtHR.

As a result, this intricate mechanism of enforcement of ECtHR judgments is of decisive importance for the normativity of the ECHR. In addition to their right to invoke ECHR rights before national authorities on the basis of direct effect, individuals may submit their case to an independent, permanent and authoritative supranational court, which will evaluate whether their ECHR rights have been violated on individual merit. Moreover, the mechanism grounds the constitutional qualification of the ECHR: Gardbaum's analysis in terms of "constitutionalization as federalization" is a based on this argument: "the ECHR operates within the member states' legal orders as an invocable and supreme law and, accordingly, can be understood as a federalized and constitutionalized regional human rights system".[90]

6.4.1 The execution of judgments

Having captured the legal status of the ECHR in States Parties and the limited judicial powers of the ECtHR, I turn to the question of the *execution* of the ECtHR's judgments. What does occur, in legal terms, if the ECtHR finds a breach of one or more ECHR rights? There is no obligation stemming from the judgment for the respondent State Party to execute it. As Stone Sweet puts it, States Parties "may decide to ignore the Court's interpretation of the Convention, even on the point, and even where Convention rights have been domesticated through incorporation".[91] Moreover, if the state decides to execute the judgment, *remedial subsidiarity* implies that the state will choose the appropriate measures to respond to the judgment. The *declaratory* nature of the judgments implies that the ECtHR, in principle, does not recommend specific or general measures to the respondent state. As Besson explains, "elle ne peut ordonner ni recommander les mesures individuelles ou générales d'exécution de ses arrêts".[92]

88 Bates, "The Birth of the European Convention on Human Rights", 36.
89 Helfer and Slaughter, "Toward a Theory of Effective Supranational Adjudication", 294.
90 Gardbaum, "Human Rights as International Constitutional Rights", 760.
91 Stone Sweet, "On the Constitutionalisation of the Convention: The European Court of Human Rights as a Constitutional Court", 4.
92 Besson, "Les effets et l'exécution des arrêts de la Cour européenne des droits de l'homme – le cas de la Suisse", 170.

114 *The normativity of ECHR law*

In other words, the *responsibility* of the state is limited to putting an end to the violation and repairing the victim's position to what it was prior to the violation – subsumed under the principle of *restitutio in integrum*. As Flauss explains:

> Le contentieux devant la Cour européenne étant un contentieux de respon-sabilité internationale, le respect effectif de la chose jugée se mesure à l'aune de deux paramètres classiques: d'une part, le principe de *restitutio in integrum*, d'autre part l'obligation de la cessation de l'illicite.[93]

It is the principle of *restitutio in integrum* that implies the adoption of individual measures, while putting an end to the violation generally implies the adoption of general measures by the respondent State Party.

In the cases where the ECtHR finds a breach of ECHR rights but where full reparation in the form of *restitutio in integrum* is impossible, the ECtHR has the competence to award just satisfaction "if necessary" (Article 41). In fact, the ECtHR enjoys some latitude in determining "necessity". If it decides to make a monetary award, it requires the respondent State Party to pay the applicant within three months of delivery of the judgment. As Lambert Abdelgawad notes, in such a case "l'arrêt acquiert ainsi la valeur de jugement prestatoire, par opposition au jugement déclaratoire qu'il est de façon classique".[94] Typically, it awards just satisfaction when the nature of the breach for the injured party precludes *restitutio in integrum*. It may also exercise this competence when *restitutio in integrum* is impossible or where the state is unable or unwilling to grant satisfaction. The application of the principle *restitutio in integrum*, which stems from customary international law,[95] may imply the reopening of legal proceedings: "l'effet le plus spectaculaire qu'un jugement international puisse produire".[96] However, as White and Ovey note, "the need for such a measure arises primarily in respect of criminal proceedings, since problems with civil proceedings can frequently be remedied through financial compensation".[97] Lambert Abdelgawad specifies that "la réouverture de la procédure en matière pénale a pu entraîner l'acquitement de l'individu et l'effacement de sa condam-nation du casier judiciaire ou, plus rarement, la confirmation de sa culpabilité et éventuellement de sa peine".[98]

The organ in charge of supervising the execution of ECtHR judgments is the Committee of Ministers of the CoE (Article 46(2)),[99] an intergovernmental organ

---

93 Flauss, "L'effectivité des arrêts de la Cour européenne des droits de l'homme: du politique au juridique et vice-versa", 29.

94 Lambert Abdelgawad, *L'exécution des arrêts de la Cour européenne des droits de l'homme*, 13.

95 See Besson, *Droit international public: abrégé de cours et résumés de jurisprudence*, 310. See also Brownlie, *Principles of Public International Law*, 463–4.

96 Lambert Abdelgawad, *L'exécution des arrêts de la Cour européenne des droits de l'homme*, 18.

97 White, Ovey and Jacobs, *The European Convention on Human Rights*, 57.

98 Lambert Abdelgawad, *L'exécution des arrêts de la Cour européenne des droits de l'homme*, 20.

99 For an overview of this issue, see ibid.

The normativity of ECHR law   115

that can be traced back to the early "alarm bell" conception of the role of the ECtHR. The political character of the executory organ is a sensitive issue.[100] In principle, the Committee does not have the competence to review the means by which states enforce ECtHR judgments, but it does have, by contrast to the ECtHR, the power to sanction non-compliant states – the most coercive sanctions being suspension of the state's voting rights in the Committee (in which each State Party has a representative) or the expulsion of States Parties from the CoE.[101]

From a historical angle, this political character of the Committee pertains to the original role and powers of the ECHR. As explained in the last chapter, the diplomatic impetus clearly confined the role of the ECHR to an interstate optional and quasi-judicial mechanism of complaint – the Commission on Human Rights. The persistence of the political character of the Committee of Ministers until today reflects this legacy. As Flauss explains:

> Les rédacteurs du Protocole 11 n'ont pas sérieusement envisageé de modifier radicalement l'office du comité des ministres en la matière, et encore moins à le supprimer. Les auteurs du Protocole 14 n'ont même pas envisagé de s'y intéresser. Le contrôle par le Comité des Ministres était en effet censé présenter un avantage pour les Etats: en tant qu'auto-contrôle exercé par les pairs il apparait comme plus malléable que celui qui serait confié à une juridiction indépendante.[102]

The supervision of the execution of the judgments of the ECtHR is therefore essentially a matter of negotiation with the respondent State Party, governed by the Rules of Procedure of the Committee of Ministers.[103] In practice, released judgments are referred to the Committee by the Directorate of Human Rights and Legal Affairs of the CoE. The Committee then schedules special human rights meetings, at which the respondent state is invited to inform the Committee about the measures it will take in response to the judgment, which include the provision of any just satisfaction awarded by the ECtHR. Not surprisingly, most of the deliberations of those meetings are still confidential.[104] If the respondent state is unable to provide this information, the case is automatically assigned to the next meeting, which occurs every six months. As Greer explains, "not surprisingly, the ECtHR's workload problems are also mirrored in the enforcement process with

---

100 On this issue, see Flauss, "L'effectivité des arrêts de la Cour européenne des droits de l'homme: du politique au juridique et vice-versa".
101 For an overview of the political pressures that the ECtHR and the CoE can exercise, see ibid., 39–58.
102 Ibid., 30.
103 For an overview of those measures and their recent evolution, see Lambert Abdelgawad, *L'exécution des arrêts de la Cour européenne des droits de l'homme.*
104 See Flauss, "L'effectivité des arrêts de la Cour européenne des droits de l'homme: du politique au juridique et vice-versa", 33–4.

116   *The normativity of ECHR law*

about three thousand cases scheduled for each session, only 30–40 of which are actually debated".[105] When it is provided that necessary measures are undertaken by the respondent State Party (possibly entailing compensation), the Committee publicly announces that it has fulfilled its duties of supervising the execution of the judgment. The evolving division of labour between the ECtHR and the Committee suggests that "le contrôle de conventionalité est désormais partagé entre la Cour et le Comité des Ministres".[106]

As we have already seen, Protocol 14 increases the institutional links between the ECtHR and the Committee of Ministers by giving the Committee the right to bring infringement proceedings before the ECtHR when a State Party has failed to comply with its obligations (Article 46(4) and (5)). This measure targets recalcitrant States Parties that fail to make the appropriate changes in their internal legal orders to conform with the ECHR and the resulting repetitive cases lodged with the ECtHR. Finally, and in parallel with the Protocols, the ECtHR itself has started to address the problem of structural violations by issuing "pilot judgments". These are ordinary judgments containing general directives on how to fix structural problems in domestic law following repetitive cases; they imply general measures in the operative part of the judgment and are therefore part of the decisional authority of the judgment – the part that binds the State Party affected by the judgment.

In the same vein, the ECtHR has started to recommend individual measures in its own judgments by requiring the state to undertake specific actions in the national legal order – for instance, to reopen domestic procedures. Those recent developments ground the claim that the ECtHR is now exercising a strong form of judicial review by contrast to the strict review of violations in single cases. As Flauss explains, "il l'est assurément s'agissant des mesures d'exécution dites individuelles dans la mesure où le Comité des ministres entend donner une pleine portée au principe de *restitutio in integrum*".[107] Both forms of judicial activism, structural and individual, have been severely criticized by states – mostly Western, surprisingly, and mostly on democratic grounds – arguing that the ECtHR goes beyond its competence on the basis of Article 46, what is known as *ultra vires* in international law. The ECtHR is empowered only to declare whether ECHR rights are violated, and *remedial subsidiarity* implies that the respondent State Party selects the appropriate measures in response to the judgment. Pilot judgments are therefore one case in which the ECtHR is going beyond its original mission. Indeed, as Flauss explains, "c'est dire que l'on assiste à une modification de la nature de l'obligation de l'Etat découlant de l'article 46 de la Convention: on passe sensiblement d'une obligation de résultat à une obligation de moyens".[108]

---

105 Greer, "Europe", 472.
106 Flauss, "L'effectivité des arrêts de la Cour européenne des droits de l'homme: du politique au juridique et vice-versa", 38.
107 Ibid., 31.
108 Ibid., 32.

The normativity of ECHR law   117

6.4.2 The binding force of judgments

The compulsory jurisdiction of the ECtHR and the direct effect of ECHR rights and ECtHR judgments in national legal orders imply that national courts diligently follow the interpretation of ECHR rights provided by the ECtHR. As Gardbaum explains:

> States Parties generally abide by that decision as required by Article 46 and, where necessary, amend or repeal their domestic laws and/or policies, including their constitutions. In this only slightly attenuated way in comparison with that of the EU, the ECHR operates with the States Parties' legal system as an invocable and supreme law.[109]

As such, the role of the ECtHR is remarkable among the international judicial organs that currently exist. Moreover, this articulation of the role of the ECtHR sheds light on the importance of its adjudication, examined in the next chapters. Article 19 grants the ECtHR final jurisdiction over "all matters concerning the interpretation and petition of the Convention" and gives the Court the competence to determine the limits of its own jurisdiction (*Kompetenz-Kompetenz*). According to Article 46, its judgments bind all national authorities (legislative, executive and judicial). However, the judgments do not have an *invalidating* effect, as we have seen; the nature of the judgment is *declaratory* and does not review how it *should* be enforced ("obligation de résultat" vs. "obligation de moyens"). As Helfer and Slaughter explain in a comparative study with the European Court of Justice (ECJ), "the ECHR does not have an Article 177 mechanism allowing it to communicate directly with national courts. The ECHR thus faces a different task of convincing national legislatures, at least in the first instance, to conform to its judgments".[110]

6.4.3 Decisional and jurisprudential authority

However respected in the States Parties' jurisdictions, the judgments of the ECtHR remain *declaratory*. The ECtHR is empowered to declare whether one or several ECHR rights have been violated in a single case, each case being assessed on its own merit. We have also seen that the ECtHR (and the Committee of Ministers) may go beyond this individualized and declaratory function. Along with the development of its case law, and in view of enhancing the subsidiarity of the ECHR system, the ECtHR has also come to recognize the *erga omnes* effect (EOE) of its judgments. Originally, it was one of the measures proposed by the

---

109 Gardbaum, "Human Rights as International Constitutional Rights", 759.
110 Helfer and Slaughter, "Toward a Theory of Effective Supranational Adjudication", 297. For an empirical study of the ECHR on policy changes of State Parties, see Helfer and Voeten, "International Courts as Agents of Legal Change: Evidence from LGBT Rights in Europe", 77–110.

118   *The normativity of ECHR law*

2010 Interlaken Action Plan,[111] but the qualification of the ECtHR's judgments and its discussion among legal scholars is not new.[112] The EOE is a jurisprudential creation and therefore an act of legal recognition. The term refers to the original status of the ECHR *qua* international law treaty. In principle, the decision of an international judicial organ binds the parties to an interstate dispute (the *inter partes* effect). The generalization of the content of the judgments to all States Parties to the treaty grounds their EOE – despite the ambiguity that most cases before the ECtHR are state–individual rather than state–state disputes. As Besson explains, "granting those decisions jurisprudential authority in all States Parties to the Convention amounts therefore to recognizing their erga omnes effect".[113]

Besson uses the distinction between the *decisional authority* and the *jurisprudential authority* to designate, respectively, the *inter partes* effect and the EOE of the judgments of the ECtHR. The *inter partes* effect *qua* decisional authority of an ECtHR judgment is the "authority of the operative part of a Court's judgment and comes on the top of the authority of the ECHR right at stake".[114] By contrast, the EOE effect *qua* jurisprudential authority is "the authority of the interpretation of a Convention right. Once released by the Court, that interpretation becomes an integral part of the authority of the ECHR right itself. As such, it binds all 47 States Parties to the Convention".[115] Jurisprudential authority does not imply an obligation to *execute* the judgment, however, as the State Party is required only to abide by the decisional authority of the judgment. The latter is the aspect that triggers the responsibility of the state. As Besson explains, "the violation of a judgment's decisional authority amounts to a non-execution of a Court's judgments and triggers one or all procedures described in Article 46 paragraph 2 to 4 ECHR".[116]

Besson uses another distinction to conceptualize the EOE of the ECtHR's judgment that pertains to the *content* of the judgment. The EOE *qua* jurisprudential authority corresponds to the interpretative content (*res interpretata*) of the judgment, whereas the *inter partes* effect *qua* decisional authority corresponds to the content of the individual decision, recognizing the violation of the ECHR right (*res judicata*). By contrast to the latter, the former "may only be found, as a result, in the grounds of the judgment and not in its operative provisions".[117] If the ECtHR has been rather equivocal regarding the concept of precedent – it is not formally bound by its own decisions – the EOE of the judgment operates in the same way as the precedent operates. The fact that a judgment binds all

---

111 Interlaken Declaration, High Level Conference on the Future of the European Court of Human Rights, 1 February 2010, available at www.echr.coe.int/Documents/2010_Interlaken_FinalDeclaration_ENG.pdf
112 Besson, "The 'Erga Omnes' Effect of the European Court of Human Rights", 144–9.
113 Ibid., 131.
114 Ibid., 129.
115 Ibid.
116 Ibid., 130.
117 Ibid., 131.

other States Parties conversely implies that the ECtHR respects the jurisprudential authority of this judgment in future cases: "since 1990, the Court has repeatedly regarded its case law as part of the sources of ECHR law".[118] *Qua* jurisprudential authority, the EOE has a wider scope *ratione temporis* and *ratione personae*: "elle concerne par conséquent toutes les autorités nationales de tout Etat partie qui pourraient voir se reproduire les circonstances dans lesquelles la Convention a été violée dans l'affaire en cause".[119]

---

118 Ibid., 138.
119 Besson, "Les effets et l'exécution des arrêts de la Cour européenne des droits de l'homme – le cas de la Suisse", 138. See also Besson, "The 'Erga Omnes' Effect of the European Court of Human Rights", 159–64.

7 Interpretation at the ECtHR

Setting the stage

In the last chapter, I addressed the normative status of ECHR rights and ECtHR judgments in national jurisdictions. This status is shaped by the particular judicial powers conferred upon the Court by the States Parties. Most importantly, I privileged the status of *direct effect* that ECHR rights and ECtHR judgments enjoy in almost all national legal orders. Chapter 6 therefore corresponded with the first step of the constructivist methodology attached to capturing the salient normative role of the ECHR from the standpoint of the individual. This preliminary identification was conducted in non-evaluative terms, as the political conception of human rights requires.

In addition, I have emphasized the *subsidiary* character of the Court – in its jurisdictional, remedial and substantive dimensions. I also noticed, however, that when a State Party executes a judgment of the ECtHR, it generally amends or strikes down the relevant legislation independently of the case-specific process of *restitutio in integrum*. Also, certain countries have implemented procedures for reopening the procedures to revise a judgment declared contrary to the ECHR. All in all, the complementary role of ECHR rights *vis-à-vis* constitutional rights and, more precisely, their role of external minimal guarantee is crucial to capture.

It is clear, however, that ECHR law cannot be reduced to this functional characterization for it misses the crucial step of the interpretation of its enshrined provisions. If the ECtHR is conferred with ultimate authority on matters of interpretation of the ECHR (by virtue of Article 46), the normativity of ECHR rights in States Parties depends on the adjudication of their content. In declaring the conformity of domestic laws with the ECHR, the ECtHR recognizes, specifies and allocates the duties correlative to ECHR rights. Therefore, there is no strict *discontinuity* between the practical (and international) role of human rights (emphasized by Beitz and Raz), their nature as *rights* (emphasized by Raz and Tasioulas) and the layer of reasons that justifies them (emphasized by Griffin and Forst).

In this chapter, I survey the adjudicative role of the ECtHR. First, I explain that the Court has been dismissive of conventional methods of adjudication such as intentionalism, textualism and literalism. Rather, the ECtHR has relied on the "object and purpose" of the ECHR and developed a *teleological* approach to interpretation. Second, I reconstruct the problematic role of consensualism as underlying the allocation by the ECtHR of the margin of appreciation. Finally,

Interpretation at the ECtHR 121

I critically examine one prominent theoretical account of the Court's adjudication, namely George Letsas's "moral reading" and show that a non-conventional and predominantly teleological approach does not necessarily amount to a quest for moral truths.

7.1 The semantic exercise

Abstractly conceived, the ECtHR arbitrates the laws of States Parties (and their application) against the ECHR rights held by the applicant. The applicant brings a body of facts before the Court establishing an alleged interference with one or more ECHR rights. This body of facts must establish an alleged interference with one or more ECHR rights. This basic proposition suggests that interpretation should be faithful to some original object there to be interpreted – the provisions in the treaty, the protocols or the Preamble. The common positivist view is that legal interpretation is a *deductive* inference the premises of which are the positivized norms. The legal norms comprise binding legal sources (legislation, judicial decisions and customs, principles) and various canons of interpretation.

When the ECtHR assesses whether the situation brought by the applicant falls within the scope of the ECHR right in question, the wording of the ECHR and the meaning of the relevant terms of a provision become crucial. The ECHR, together with its protocols, is a relatively short document. Using a Hartian formulation, Registrar Mahoney argues that "the open textured language of the Convention leaves the Court with significant opportunities for choice in interpretation; and particularly when faced with changed circumstances and attitudes in society, the Court makes new law".[1] How the Court selects and justifies its method of adjudication to resolve interpretative questions hence becomes decisive: "the key to the resolution of individual complaints ultimately lies in how the Court interprets the Convention's sparse text".[2]

This being said, the choice of the method of adjudication does not necessarily lead to reaching a decision. I rely here on the distinction by Gerards and Senden between the *definition* of the scope of the right(s) at hand, which addresses the claim made by the applicant, and the *justification* of the interference, which addresses the claim made by the respondent State Party.[3] The *definition* involves the enterprise of interpretation – that is, the imposition of a meaning on an object and therefore the ECtHR's determination of the conditions under which an utterance of a particular word is correct. By contrast, the *justification* involves the enterprise of balancing conflicting interests and providing reasons for selecting one over the other. The burden of proof switches from one to the other in the Court's process of review.[4] The ECtHR clearly considers itself an arbiter of

---

1 Mahoney, "Marvellous Richness of Diversity or Invidious Cultural Relativism", 2.
2 Greer, "What's Wrong with the European Convention on Human Rights", 696.
3 Gerards and Senden, "The Structure of Fundamental Rights and the European Court of Human Rights".
4 Ibid., 641–5.

122 *Interpretation at the ECtHR*

interests. The initial establishment was made in *Soering* (concerning Article 3 of the ECHR).[5] As we shall see in Chapter 8, the ECtHR has applied the "Soering mantra"[6] across a majority of ECHR rights. However, I leave the issue of balancing for Chapters 8 and 9.

Interpretation focuses primarily on how to fix the content and scope of a contested term in a provision. As Marmor puts it, "interpretation must be an exception to the standard instances of understanding expressions, as it requires the existence of a language which, and about which, the interpretation is stated".[7] The main task of this chapter, therefore, is to reconstruct how the ECtHR has envisaged facing the almost infinite number of cases that may arise under ECHR rights through the canons of interpretation it has itself established and developed. This has been achieved by the ECtHR in a set of seminal cases since its establishment, from which self-created labels of interpretation have emerged ("living instrument", "evolutive and dynamic", "autonomous concepts", "practical and effective"). The guiding rules of interpretation that today pervade the case law are, for the most part, *jurisprudential creations*.

Interpretation by the ECtHR is opaque. Lord Lester termed the interpretation of the ECHR "slippery and elusive as an eel".[8] One may say that the very enterprise of interpretation implies some vagueness. If interpretation in the law faces the same methodological issues as explanation does in the social sciences in general – in particular, if one is committed to retrieving the meaning of a term via an understanding of an internal point of view, the so-called *Verstehen* method – then interpretation may not deliver strong results. In addition, the opaqueness in this particular judicial context lies in the Court's indeterminate approach to interpretation. The widely held view is that although methodological options and methods are identifiable, "they fall in no particular order . . . . The process of interpretation is said to be governed by the application of a dozen principles. Some of these are explicit in the text, while others have been inferred by the Strasbourg institutions".[9] Dworkinian scholars have emphasized this erratic reasoning to point to the deep disagreement in the law: "no matter what judges do, they will still be exercising choice in the sense of privileging one conception of the ECHR over the other".[10] However, my objective here is not specifically one of legal theory. It is limited to a descriptive overview of the different *interpretative poles* that the ECtHR has distinguished and developed, which in turn will constrain the substantive reasoning in the balancing exercise (addressed in Chapter 8).

The Court's indeterminate approach echoes the difficulty in determining the legal regime of the ECHR mentioned at the end of the last chapter; if the ECHR

---

5 *Soering v. United Kingdom*, App. No. 14038/88, 7 July 1989, para. 89.
6 Mowbray, "A Study of the Principle of Fair Balance in the Jurisprudence of the European Court of Human Rights", 307.
7 Marmor, *Interpretation and Legal Theory*, 22.
8 Lord Lester of Herne Hill, "University Versus Subsidiarity: A Reply", 75.
9 Greer, "What's Wrong with the European Convention on Human Rights", 696.
10 Letsas, *A Theory of Interpretation of the European Convention on Human Rights*, 55.

Interpretation at the ECtHR 123

is viewed through the international law lens, the principles that govern the fixing of ECHR terms are codified in the conventional tools of international adjudication – the VCLT principles as well as the conventional doctrines of originalism, textualism or consensualism. The interpretative resources – the "fictitious author", as Marmor puts it[11] – here concentrate on the intentions, traditions and practices of states (past or present). In contrast, if the ECHR is viewed through the constitutional law lens, then the interpretation tends to focus on the material content of ECHR rights and the interests they protect – a broadly *teleological* methodology. As Schlütter puts it, "if human rights have a particular *lex specialis* nature that distinguish them from the rules of general international law, it is argued that interpretation must pay due regard to this special nature or even develop special rules".[12] As we shall see, Letsas in particular argues that:

> The Court's interpretive ethic became one of looking at the substance of the human right at issue and the moral value it serves in a democratic society, rather than engaging in linguistic exercises about the meaning of words or empirical searches about the intentions of the drafters.[13]

Also, if the ECHR is viewed through the constitutional law lens, then the reasoning tends towards a statement of principle rather than a mere *ad hoc* assessment of the alleged violation in an individual case.

Now, the quasi-constitutional *content* of ECHR rights partly explains why the ECtHR has been dismissive of the conventional approaches interpretation in international law. Such content can also explain why, for the most part, prevalent doctrines are jurisprudential creations and focus on the "object and purpose" of the ECHR, as we shall see. As White, Ovey and Jacobs explain, the ECtHR:

> has viewed the task of interpretation as a single complex operation, though reference to the object and purpose of the provision in the context of the Convention as a whole has been the most influential of the principles applied by the Court, and has been described as the "sheer anchor of the Convention's principles of interpretation".[14]

However, the claim that the prevalent doctrines concentrate on the "object and purpose" of the ECHR, or that the meaning of ECHR terms is "evolutive" or "dynamic", may not succeed if this object and purpose is not *a priori* specified and justified. The ECtHR could reconstruct the object and goal of the ECHR in light of the evolving and dynamic practices of the States Parties, for instance. As Letsas explains, "individuating the object and purpose of the treaty is by no means

---

11 Marmor, *Interpretation and Legal Theory*, 25.
12 Schlütter, "Aspects of Human Rights Interpretation by the UN Treaty Bodies", 263.
13 Letsas, "Strasbourg's Interpretive Ethic: Lessons for the International Lawyer", 513.
14 White, Ovey and Jacobs, *The European Convention on Human Rights*, 65.

124 *Interpretation at the ECtHR*

a mechanical exercise; it is itself an interpretive question".[15] When the ECtHR claims in *Golder* that the ideal of the rule of law is contained in the object and purpose of the ECHR, it does not specify and justify *a priori* what this object and purpose entails, as we shall see next.

7.2 From the VCLT principles to the quest for moral truths

If interpretation is opaque, there are landmark cases in which the ECtHR takes a principled stand on how it views its task of interpreter. As an international treaty, the starting point for the interpretation of the ECHR is the 1969 Vienna Convention on the Law of Treaties (VCLT). Whether the VCLT principles are meant to apply to all types of international law treaty – bilateral, multilateral, lawmaking, contractual, dispositive or constitutive – was the first methodological issue faced by the nascent ECtHR. It was in its eleventh (*Golder v. United Kingdom*) case that the Court took a clear stance on methodological matters when it stated that Articles 31 to 33 VCLT should be used as guides in the interpretation of the terms of ECHR rights:

> The Court is prepared to consider, as do the Government and the Commission, that it should be guided by Articles 31 to 33 of the Vienna Convention of 23 May 1969 on the Law of Treaties. That Convention has not yet entered into force and it specifies, at Article 4, that it will not be retroactive, but its Articles 31 to 33 enunciate in essence generally accepted principles of international law to which the Court has already referred on occasion.[16]

However, the case law has only scarcely referred to the VCLT and it is invoked mostly when it has to take into account other treaties or general principles of international law – citing Article 31(3) VCLT, according to which other subsequently agreed treaties or any relevant rules of international law should be taken into account.[17] This is a pervasive issue in the interpretation of human rights law generally. A recent analysis of the case law of the HRC shows that references to VCLT principles are similarly scarce although it considers itself bound by those rules.[18] It is widely argued that the ECtHR seldom refers, on its own initiative, to international law – only if it has to in a given case where other international sources are at stake. As Forowicz explains, "generally, they prefer to remain within the confines of the ECHR, which were clearly mandated by the contracting states . . . . This shows a lack of any initiative on the part of the Court or Commission to refer to international law".[19]

---

15 Letsas, "Strasbourg's Interpretive Ethic: Lessons for the International Lawyer", 533.

16 *Golder v. United Kingdom*, App. No. 4451/70, 21 February 1975, para. 29.

17 In his study, Letsas specifies that the VCLT "has been cited no more than sixty out of the more than ten thousand judgments which the ECtHR has delivered": Letsas, "Strasbourg's Interpretive Ethic: Lessons for the International Lawyer", note 10.

18 See Schlütter, "Aspects of Human Rights Interpretation by the UN Treaty Bodies".

19 Forowicz, *The Reception of International Law in the European Court of Human Rights*, 369–70.

The key question is, therefore, how the VCLT has nonetheless shaped the interpretative approach of the ECtHR in its burgeoning years. The key element here is to be found in Articles 31(1) and 32. Article 31(1) states that "a treaty shall be interpreted in good faith in accordance with the ordinary meaning to be given to the terms of the treaty in their context and in light of its object and purpose". More precisely, the "object" and "purpose" of the ECHR were subject to the teleological approach in the early case law. The later doctrines of "evolutive" and "dynamic" interpretation, which I address shortly, are congruent with this orientation. In this regard, Article 32 specifies that the Preamble may be used as a source of content: "preparatory work may be consulted, or the circumstances of its drafting consulted, where the meaning of the text itself is ambiguous or obscure, or where it would otherwise lead to a manifestly absurd or unreasonable result".

The reliance on the values and principles contained in the Preamble has become a landmark in the interpretative phase as well as in the balancing phase. In *Golder*, the ECtHR more specifically held that:

> The preamble is generally very useful for the determination of the 'object' and 'purpose' of the instrument to be construed. In the present case, the most significant passage in the Preamble to the European Convention is the signatory Governments declaring that they are 'resolved, as the Governments of European countries which are like-minded and have a common heritage of political traditions, ideals, freedom and the rule of law, to take the first steps for the collective enforcement of certain of the Rights stated in the Universal Declaration of 10 December 1948'.[20]

7.2.1 The rejection of intentionalism in Golder

As Marmor argues, interpretation is essentially a matter of attributing intentions to a fictitious author: "the characterization of 'the author' constitutes a certain framework of reference, as it were. It defines the parameters employed throughout the interpretation in question".[21] In rejecting intentionalism and later textualism, the ECtHR excluded some fictitious authors. What are the distinctive elements of *Golder*? Golder, a prison detainee, intended to contact a lawyer to sue a warder who had accused him of having taken part in a mutiny. The problem of interpretation turned on the question whether the right of access to a court may be derived from the right to a fair trial (Article 6). The ECtHR answered affirmatively by focusing on the "object and purpose" (Article 31(1) VCLT) of the ECHR on the basis of the Preamble (and also Article 3 ECHR), which refers to the "common heritage of the political traditions, ideals, freedom and the rule of law" of the States Parties – citing the Preamble. The typical connection between the VCLT principles, which point to the "object and purpose" of the treaty – which itself

---

20 *Golder v. United Kingdom*, para. 34.
21 Marmor, *Interpretation and Legal Theory*, 31.

126 *Interpretation at the ECtHR*

points to the Preamble and the notions of "political traditions, ideals, freedom and the rule of law" – are today central to the adjudication of the ECtHR. In *Golder*, the ECtHR held:

> Taking all the preceding considerations together, it follows that the right of access constitutes an element which is inherent in the right stated by Article 6 para. 1 (art. 6–1). This is not an extensive interpretation forcing new obligations on the Contracting States: it is based on the very terms of the first sentence of Article 6 para. 1 (art. 6–1) read in its context and having regard to the object and purpose of the Convention, a law-making treaty.[22]

As far as the VCLT is concerned, the first consequence of *Golder* was to prioritize the Preamble over other sources permitted by VCLT principles, such as the preparatory works mentioned in Article 32. The relegation of the preparatory works as an interpretative aid has been reinforced throughout subsequent case law. In *Sigurdur A. Sigurjonsson v. Iceland*, the ECtHR held:

> As to the question of the general scope of the right in issue, the Court notes, in the first place, that although the aforementioned judgment took account of the *travaux préparatoires*, it did not attach decisive importance to them; rather it used them as a working hypothesis.[23]

More generally, "the *travaux préparatoires* (Art. 32 of the Vienna Convention), referred to in abundance by the defendant government, were undertaken only as a second step and then only to reinforce the interpretation given by the Commission to the provision in question".[24] Forowicz confirms that "usually, the Court has applied Article 32 in a flexible manner and used its discretion to resort to the preparatory works when it felt to do so would contribute to the resolution of the case".[25]

The broader interpretative question that *Golder* points to is whether recourse to the VCLT principles, and in particular the driving reference to the object and purpose of the ECHR, is sufficient to construct a clear and consistent interpretative methodology. Former judge of the ECtHR, Franz Matscher, argues that the VCLT "gives no directions on the questions – questions more of legal polity than legal theory – of a static or historical as opposed to a dynamic or evolutive interpretation, and of narrow as opposed to a broad interpretation".[26] *Golder* is distinctive not so much in the Court's discovery of the appropriate methodology but in the harsh confrontation of the holders of human rights with the conventional approaches of international interpretation. Individual rights, as captured by the Dworkinian

---

22 *Golder v. United Kingdom*, para. 36.
23 *Sigurdur A. Sigurjonsson v. Iceland*, App. No. 16130/90, 30 June 1993, para. 35.
24 Ost, "The Original Canons of Interpretation of the European Court of Human Rights", 288.
25 Forowicz, *The Reception of International Law in the European Court of Human Rights*, 68.
26 Matscher, "The Methods of Interpretation of the Convention", 65.

Interpretation at the ECtHR 127

structure of 'trumps',[27] are inherently *anti-majoritarian*. The interpretation of rights cannot but be responsive to this structure. As Schlütter explains:

> It becomes evident that the ultimate task of interpretation is the definition of the material content and core of a human right. And it is perhaps due to the special nature of human rights interpretation; any interpretation would need to ensure that this core will be protected.[28]

In an ambitious article, Letsas argues that the fate of human rights courts is to develop a moral conception of what human rights protect. Although his argument is grounded in contestable meta-ethical assumptions, Letsas claims that "the purpose of human rights courts is to develop, through interpretation, a moral conception of what these fundamental rights are. It is to discover, over time and through persuasive moral argument, the moral truth about these fundamental rights".[29] I come back to Letsas's ambitious claim at the end of this section.

Surely, in opting for the teleological method of interpretation, the ECtHR is dismissing a number of alternatives approaches. In the *Golder* case, the ECtHR may have claimed, as the UK did in its response, that the absence of a right of access to court in the text of the ECHR speaks against its existence. It may have focused on the intentions of the drafters (back in the 1950s and 1960s) to support this interpretation. Instead, the ECtHR has confined its interpretative inquiry to an autonomous conceptual analysis of the "rule of law" as a foundational element of the ECHR. As Letsas puts it, the ECtHR "felt confident that the 'object and purpose' of the ECHR contains the ideal of the rule of law which leaves no ambiguity . . . as to whether it contains a right of access to court".[30] Indeed, *Golder* is landmark case in the *rejection* of intentionalism, a variant of the broader doctrine of originalism, famously debated in the United States.

In conclusion, there is today a large consensus that the "the VCLT has played a minor role in the interpretation of the ECHR".[31] The VCLT principles "provided a crucial foundation on which to build the Court's unique, autonomous, and specific methodology".[32] One may argue that the ECtHR simply addressed the material and quasi-constitutional content of ECHR rights. In fact, the ECtHR just rejected the idea that the meaning of ECHR terms is "frozen in time" in the intentions of the drafters. Originalism in its intentionalist variant requires the ECtHR to ask the drafters whether the ECHR term in question encompasses the situation brought before it. The rejection of intentionalism is a claim that the ECtHR explicitly made in *Matthews v. United Kingdom* when it held that "the mere fact that a body

---

27 Dworkin, *Taking Rights Seriously*, 91–2.
28 Schlütter, "Aspects of Human Rights Interpretation by the UN Treaty Bodies", 281.
29 Letsas, "Strasbourg's Interpretive Ethic: Lessons for the International Lawyer", 540.
30 Ibid., 517.
31 Ibid., 513.
32 Forowicz, *The Reception of International Law in the European Court of Human Rights*, 71.

128 *Interpretation at the ECtHR*

was not envisaged by the drafters of the Convention cannot prevent that body from falling within the scope of the Convention".[33] This allows us to foresee the implications of human rights for issues of interpretation in international law. As I explained in the last chapter, in making individuals right bearers of international norms, human rights norms change the commonly found structure between right bearers and duty bearers in public international law. The whole issue of interpretation is then affected.

7.2.2 The rejection of textualism in Engel

The rejection of intentionalism as a prevalent doctrine does necessarily lead to an autonomous form of interpretation. In *Golder*, the ECtHR may have chosen another alternative – that ECHR terms should be defined in light of the ordinary meaning of the terms of the legal culture of the State Party involved. As Letsas explains, "the rejection of the intentionalist presumption left another question open, namely whether the Court should define Convention terms by reference to the meaning they have in the domestic law of the respondent state".[34] In doing so, the ECtHR may have relied on the "ordinary meaning to be given to the terms" enshrined in Article 31(1) VCLT. In *Engel*, however, the ECtHR also rejected *textualism* as an interpretative doctrine. As Ost more generally argues, "the textual argument is either presented as decisive or secondary depending on whether it can be supported by other considerations based on the 'spirit' of the Convention and not its 'letter'. The textual argument alone is never decisive or sufficient".[35]

Engel is another important landmark case in the judicial history of the ECtHR. The interpretative issue here turned on the meaning and scope of the term "criminal charge" contained in Article 6 (fair trial). Mr Engel and four other conscript soldiers serving in the Dutch army claimed, among other things, that in the military sentences they received the military authorities had violated Article 5 (liberty and security) and Article 6 (fair trial) in the proceedings. The respondent State Party argued that military penalties do not constitute criminal offences and therefore do not fall within the scope of Article 6. The ECtHR accepted the distinction and recognized it as a long-standing practice of States Parties. Yet the Court did not take this practice to be decisive, stating that the meaning of the term "criminal charge" by a national court is only one factor to be taken into account in determining the scope of an article. The *nature* of the term "criminal charge" has a greater importance:

> The very nature of the offence is a factor of greater import. When a service-man finds himself accused of an act or omission allegedly contravening a

---

33 *Matthews v. United Kingdom*, App. No. 24833/94, 18 February 1999, para. 39.
34 Letsas, "Strasbourg's Interpretive Ethic: Lessons for the International Lawyer", 523.
35 Ost, "The Original Canons of Interpretation of the European Court of Human Rights", 286.

Interpretation at the ECtHR 129

legal rule governing the operation of the armed forces, the State may in principle employ against him disciplinary law rather than criminal law. In this respect, the Court expresses its agreement with the Government.[36]

In doing so, the ECtHR inaugurated the doctrine of "autonomous concepts", which has been applied to various central concepts of the ECHR, such as "possessions", "association" and "victim",[37] and which emphasizes the degree of interdependence of the domestic meaning with that of the ECtHR. As Letsas further explains, "emphasis is put on the fact that domestic use of that concept is a 'starting point'".[38]

If ECHR rights are not simply what the original drafters or national legal cultures take them to be, then it follows that their content can evolve over time. *Golder* and *Engel* paved the way for the development of the doctrines of *autonomous concepts* and *evolutive interpretation*, respectively, with the effect of replacing in the case law the generic VCLT references with the purpose and goal of the ECHR. As Forowicz puts it, "initially, the Court resorted to the VCLT in order to mould its own means of interpretation".[39] Those two labels are today central poles of interpretation.

However, what *Golder* and *Engel* did not teach is how, given those rejections, the ECtHR should capture the evolutive "object and purpose" of the ECHR. As Letsas forcefully explains:

> Saying that treaties must be interpreted according to their object and purpose does not commit one to using a single technique of interpretation (e.g., seeking to discover the intentions of the drafters or the ordinary meaning of terms) for all treaties; it simply makes interpretive methods relative to the object and purpose of each treaty.[40]

Many different methods of interpretation are compatible with this guiding idea. Ost also explains that "the way the Court sees the aim and purpose of the Convention leads it to adopt a wide interpretation of the rights it seeks to protect or at least to reject a narrow construction of them".[41] The teleological method of the ECtHR stands in need of specification. This is true of ECHR rights, and of human rights generally. Schlütter explains in his study of the UN treaty bodies that "the determination of what actually constitutes the object and purpose of a treaty can already be a contentious issue".[42]

---

36 *Engel and Others v. The Netherlands*, App. Nos 5100/71, 5101/71, 5102/71, 5354/72, 5370/72, 8 June 1976, para. 82.
37 Letsas, "Strasbourg's Interpretive Ethic: Lessons for the International Lawyer", 525.
38 Letsas, *A Theory of Interpretation of the European Convention on Human Rights*, 46.
39 Forowicz, *The Reception of International Law in the European Court of Human Rights*, 25.
40 Letsas, "Strasbourg's Interpretive Ethic: Lessons for the International Lawyer", 533.
41 Ost, "The Original Canons of Interpretation of the European Court of Human Rights", 293.
42 Schlütter, "Aspects of Human Rights Interpretation by the UN Treaty Bodies", 278.

130 *Interpretation at the ECtHR*

7.2.3 The ambivalent role of consensualism

Despite the rejection of intentionalism and textualism, the ECtHR may use another international doctrine that could help it to fix the meaning and scope of ECHR rights when it has to explain why a given situation falls within the scope of the right in question: that of *consensualism*. Consensualism in the context of the ECHR resonates with the Preamble to the extent that "the Governments of European Countries . . . are like-minded and have a common heritage of political traditions, ideals, freedom and the rule of law". It also has a residual basis in the "ordinary meaning" in Article 31(1) VCLT. The core idea is clear and simple: the meaning and scope of contested ECHR terms is established by investigating the current practices of States Parties. The method implies comparing the various national legislative enactments across Europe and inductively identifying the appropriate level of protection. In doing so, the ECtHR gives credence to the evolutive meaning of ECHR rights across Europe without bypassing the practices of States Parties. As Carozza explains, the evolution of ECHR "should be no less dependent on the developments within those on-going, vital constitutional traditions".[43]

As with the other methods examined earlier, consensualism is a response to the indeterminacy of the ECHR rights. As Toma explains :

> Le recours *à la* technique du droit comparé s'explique par l'utilité de son concours dans la matière des droits de l'homme, où les principes du droit international en général apportent peu d'éléments de nature à guider le juge vers la solution du problème soumis.[44]

As Helfer also explains, "the consensus methodology is one of the primary tools available for both the Court and the Commission to implement the Convention's object and purpose".[45] In terms of legitimacy, the use of the consensualist method certainly pertains to the subsidiary role of the ECtHR. Given that the ECtHR is not conceived as a "superstructure" above the States Parties, it is "because the European system is supposed to be derived from the national systems of the Member States that the comparative argument takes so much weight".[46] Since the execution of the judgment is conducted by the State Party in its own legal order, the consensualist argument allows the ECtHR to maintain its democratic legitimacy *qua* external sovereignty. As Carozza explains:

> Since all the details of the actual implementation of the Convention norms will thus be effected through national legal systems, the only way to

---

43 Carozza, "Uses and Misuses of Comparative Law in International Human Rights: Some Reflections on the Jurisprudence of the European Court of Human Rights", 1226.
44 Toma, *La réalité judiciaire de la Cour européenne des droits de l'homme*, 31.
45 Helfer, "Consensus, Coherence and the European Convention on Human Rights", 140.
46 Brems, "The Margin of Appreciation in the Case Law of the ECHR", 276–7.

Interpretation at the ECtHR 131

adequately assess the compliance of any one domestic order is by reference to other domestic legal systems.[47]

This method is certainly the least problematic according to conventional conceptions of the legitimacy of international law. It reflects *the will of the majority*. As Benvinisti further explains:

> From a theoretical point of view, this doctrine can draw its justification only from nineteenth century theories of State consent. Given the importance of state sovereignty, the only way to impose newly evolving duties on States Parties is by resorting to the notion of emerging custom, or "consensus".[48]

However, in light of the overall case law, it is far from clear what principled role consensualism plays when a new situation is brought before the Court – especially when the comparative references are associated with the use of other canons of interpretation. As Brems noted long ago, "like the margin analysis in general, the Court should elaborate a methodology for its consensus analysis, identify criteria that play a role, in order to increase the transparency and predictability of its approach".[49] The key standard is whether there is indeed some commonality found across the practices of the States Parties. The ECtHR uses the comparison of national legislations as a justificatory device in favour of the applicant only when there is *enough* commonality between States Parties. It is only when "the practices achieve a certain measure of uniformity, a 'European consensus' so to speak, the Court and the Commission raise the standards of rights protection to which all states must adhere".[50]

The ECtHR initially took issue with consensualism in *Tyrer v. United Kingdom*, which inaugurated the use of the *evolutive* and *dynamic* interpretation – the so-called "living instrument" doctrine. In this case, the question was whether judicial corporal punishment of juveniles amounts to a form of degrading treatment under Article 3 (torture). The ECtHR held that the scope of the correlative duties of ECHR rights are determined neither by the domestic definition of the State Party (the predominant moralistic views of the majority on the Isle of Man in this case), nor by the common practices across the CoE; the ECtHR held that:

> The Convention is a living instrument which, as the Commission rightly stressed, must be interpreted in light of present-day conditions. In the case now before it the Court cannot but be influenced by the developments and commonly accepted standards in the penal policy of the Member States of the Council of Europe.[51]

---

47 Carozza, "Uses and Misuses of Comparative Law in International Human Rights: Some Reflections on the Jurisprudence of the European Court of Human Rights", 1227.

48 Benvenisti, "Margin of Appreciation, Consensus, and Universal Standards", 852.

49 Brems, "The Margin of Appreciation in the Case Law of the ECHR", 285.

50 Helfer, "Consensus, Coherence and the European Convention on Human Rights", 134.

51 *Tyrer v. United Kingdom*, App. No. 5856/72, 25 April 1978, para. 84.

132   *Interpretation at the ECtHR*

The prevalence of the evolutive and dynamic interpretation doctrines reveals that interpretation as *retrieval of intentions* is not all there is to interpretation and this is because the reasons for selecting them are not static. As Raz argues:

> Since meaning is relative to a normative perspective, it can change as that perspective changes. Our concepts are rich enough to accommodate both ways of thinking about meaning: as timeless, from one and the same perspective, and as changing, with the change of the perspective.[52]

More specifically, *Tyrer* also revealed the internal deficiencies of the consensualist approach. The ECtHR did not bring *evidence* about the nature and scope of the alleged consensus among States Parties. Despite resorting to the comparative law approach, the ECtHR appealed *in fine* to the very nature of the act of punishment – a substantive justification:

> The very nature of the judicial corporal punishment is that it involves a human being inflicting violence on another human being. Furthermore, it is institutionalized violence that is in the present case violence permitted by the law, ordered by the judicial authorities of the State and carried out by the police authorities of the case.[53]

Moreover, as Helfer more generally shows, the ECtHR has not specified the nature of the consensus that is expected (a legal consensus, an expert consensus, a moral consensus, etc.). In *Sunday Times v. United Kingdom*, for instance, the ECtHR used the term "fairly substantial measure of common ground"[54] without referring to legal components. Nor has the ECtHR specified the sufficient amount of consensus to be attained. Consensualism certainly does not imply that an *overall* consensus from the states has to be found, but a *majoritarian* consensus. However, as Helfer explains, "the tribunals have yet to clarify the relative weight that they should be given in determining the presence or absence of an evolving European viewpoint".[55] In another famous case, *Marckx v. Belgium*,[56] the ECtHR, despite researching common standards in other international conventions, selected the "evolution of rules and attitudes" as the ultimate measure of the common ground. As Letsas puts it, "in Marckx, 'living instrument' meant, above all, keeping in pace with evolving European attitudes and beliefs rather than specific legislation to be found in the majority of member states".[57] Finally, the ECtHR has not specified the *scope* of the consensus. This is precisely the case when the Court supports its decisions by reference to other international conventions that go beyond the States Parties of the CoE.

---

52 Raz, "Interpretation Without Retrieval", 175.
53 *Tyrer v. United Kingdom*, para. 33.
54 *Sunday Times v. United Kingdom (No. 1)*, App. No. 6538/74, 26 April 1979, para. 59.
55 Helfer, "Consensus, Coherence and the European Convention on Human Rights", 140. See also Neuman, "Human Rights and Constitutional Rights: Harmony and Dissonance", 1884.
56 *Marckx v. Belgium*, App. No 6833/74, 13 June 1979.
57 Letsas, "Strasbourg's Interpretive Ethic: Lessons for the International Lawyer", 530.

Interpretation at the ECtHR 133

However, when "pan-European" commonality is not found, consensualism plays the role of restricting the scope of the ECHR rights and thereby hinders the very idea of "evolutive and dynamic interpretation". In the seminal case of *Rees v. United Kingdom*, for instance, in which the ECtHR had to deal with non-recognition of a post-operative transsexual's new sexual identity as an alleged violation of Article 8 (private life), the absence of consensus justified the use of the margin of appreciation doctrine:

> As the Court pointed out in its above-mentioned *Abdulaziz, Cabales* and *Balkandali* judgments the notion of "respect" is not clear-cut, especially as far as those positive obligations are concerned: having regard to the diversity of the practices followed and the situations obtaining in the Contracting States, the notion's requirements will vary considerably from case to case . . . . In other States, such an option does not – or does not yet – exist. It would there-fore be true to say that there is at present little common ground between the Contracting States in this area and that, generally speaking, the law appears to be in a transitional stage. Accordingly, this is an area in which the Contracting Parties enjoy a wide margin of appreciation.[58]

The ECtHR revisited the case on several occasions over the following years until 2002, when it reversed its case law in giving priority to the interests of the applicant in *Goodwin v. United Kingdom*.[59] By that time, consensus had become sufficient in the eyes of the Court to grant protection to the applicant and restrict the State Party's margin of appreciation. Gerards is therefore right in the view that the "living instrument" doctrine "would seem to adequately describe the Court's approach, rather than serve as a guiding principle that may help to choose between effective rights protection and respect for the different States Parties".[60] As a result, "inter-state comparison often provides the rhetorical key that opens the door to one or the other of these interpretive techniques".[61] In those cases, consensualism is therefore a method of *justification* rather than a method of *interpretation*. Its absence triggers the application of the margin of doctrine device and the State Party's interest is given priority. It is therefore not "a method that actually yields the meaning of a Convention's provision, but instead used to legitimate the Court's exercise of discretion".[62]

7.3 The "teleological" doctrine: a quest for moral truths?

In abstracto, interpretation by the ECtHR is best depicted by a set of poles at the Court's disposal, which fall in no logical order. Clearly, each pole cannot

---

58 *Rees v. United Kingdom*, App. No. 9532/81, 17 October 1986, paras 36–7.
59 *Goodwin v. United Kingdom*, App. No. 28957/95, 11 July 2002.
60 Gerards, "Judicial Deliberations in the European Court of Human Rights".
61 Carozza, "Uses and Misuses of Comparative Law in International Human Rights: Some Reflections on the Jurisprudence of the European Court of Human Rights", 1221.
62 Ibid., 1225.

134 *Interpretation at the ECtHR*

fully explain the Court's practice. Further, tensions obviously arise when two poles appear to be mutually exclusive. While the consensualist approach displays a strongly deferent character, "the unity and consistency of application sought through autonomous interpretation could be understood to preclude any margin of appreciation to the States Parties".[63] Similarly, "evolutive interpretation and the margin of appreciation represent diametrically opposed directions of judicial policy".[64] As Greer puts it, "it is, however, strange, that such an unstructured approach should be uncritically accepted because some of these principles are intimately more connected with the Convention's core purposes than others".[65] True, the choice of the methodological labels has always had to be replaced in a reflection of the subsidiary role of the ECtHR. The need for democratic legitimation of the ECHR certainly explains the ambivalent use of the consensualist approach. The ECHR is not "a superstructure imposed on the contracting states from above".[66] Again, however, the reliance on democratic legitimacy is itself insufficient to provide a method of interpretation or to illuminate what the ECtHR is currently doing.

More importantly, the prevalent teleological approach focusing on the object and purpose of the ECHR stands in need of specification. To use again Marmor's idea of a fictitious author, "the more abstract the characterization of the fictitious author, the greater the interpretation's tendency to become invention".[67] If the ECtHR famously held that the ECHR is "the constitutional instrument of European public order in the field of human rights",[68] the mere fact of acknowledging the prevalent class of interpretation – the *teleological* one – does not say anything about the normative content that should guide the reasoning. Interpretation, if it aims to play the role it says, should be about *what counts* as the object and purpose (on pain of infinite regress).

Letsas reveals the scope of the erratic reasoning of the ECtHR on this very point in a series of articles that culminated in his 2010 article in the *European Journal of International Law*.[69] Letsas is strongly attached to the issue of interpretation. In his 2007 monograph,[70] he examines the erratic methodology of the ECtHR to reveal the deep disagreement in legal reasoning and reaches the Dworkinian conclusion, according to which disagreement is the crucial component of law.[71] In his article, Letsas makes the case for the "moral reading" of ECHR rights by the ECtHR. His main claim is clear and simple:

---

63 Ibid., 1226.
64 Arai-Takahashi, *The Margin of Appreciation Doctrine and the Principle of Proportionality in the Jurisprudence of the ECHR*, 203.
65 Greer, "What's Wrong with the European Convention on Human Rights", 695.
66 Brems, "The Margin of Appreciation in the Case Law of the ECHR", 276.
67 Marmor, *Interpretation and Legal Theory*, 33.
68 *Ireland v. United Kingdom*, App. No. 5310/71, 18 January 1978, para. 239.
69 Letsas, "Strasbourg's Interpretive Ethic: Lessons for the International Lawyer".
70 Letsas, *A Theory of Interpretation of the European Convention on Human Rights*.
71 See, in particular, ibid., Chapter 2.

The Court's interpretive ethic became one of looking at the substance of the human right at issue and the moral value it serves in a democratic society, rather than engaging in linguistic exercises about the meaning of words or empirical searches about the intentions of the drafters.[72]

This is a specific claim about the ECtHR's reasoning. However, Letsas wants to make a general case for the interpretation of international human rights: "the purpose of human rights courts is to develop, through interpretation, a moral conception of what these fundamental rights are. It is to discover, over time and through persuasive moral argument, the moral truth about these fundamental rights".[73]

Letsas's article is certainly among the most thought-provoking written on the theory of interpretation of the ECtHR in the recent literature and it is worth being addressed at this specific point of the investigation. Letsas specifies very early in his article what he means by "interpretation" by the ECtHR: "any general normative propositions which the Court has systematically endorsed in its case law, in relation either to the nature of interpretation or the nature of human rights interpretation".[74] In other words, Letsas wants to reconstruct, on the basis of the case law, a theory of the normative judgment adopted by the ECtHR. In section 6 of his article, Letsas articulates a general argument about human rights interpretation and generalizes his findings about the ECtHR. In this section, we begin to see the philosophical assumptions that explain Letsas's emphasis on the moral. Most importantly, Letsas is relying on G.A. Cohen's view of the logical structure of the normative judgment, according to which,

> for every fact which the interpreter takes into account as relevant for determining the purpose of a treaty (such as the preamble, the treaty terms, dictionary definitions, the preparatory works, etc.), there must be a non-factual explanation of why this fact (and not some other fact) is relevant for so doing . . . . Facts by themselves cannot justify the relevance of other facts. Unless a non-factual explanation is given at some point, the attempt to provide a justification will go on forever.[75]

It clearly appears that Letsas identifies the nature of legal interpretation with the nature of moral judgment and justification. It is by an abrupt (but yet central to his argument) *excursus* on the nature of moral reasoning and the reference to the view of the subject of moral philosopher, G.A. Cohen,[76] that the ability to generalize the argument is obtained, not via an inductive reasoning based on the case law (from the ECtHR or from other international courts). Despite a close analysis of seminal

---

72 Letsas, "Strasbourg's Interpretive Ethic: Lessons for the International Lawyer", 520.
73 Ibid., 540.
74 Ibid., 511.
75 Ibid., 534.
76 Cohen, "Facts and Principles".

136   *Interpretation at the ECtHR*

cases brought before the ECtHR, Letsas does not provide such reasoning. As a result, if one wants to dispute the very distinctive content of the article, those very assumptions, again, must be addressed.

It is rather easy to follow Letsas in his thorough analysis of seminal ECtHR cases, his conclusive argument about its non-conventional relationship with the VCLT principles and its dismissive attitude towards most of the conventional interpretative tools in treaty interpretation – such as originalism, intentionalism or textualism. While I agree with Letsas upon this point, I disagree with the inference that the rejection of those doctrines implies in turn a "moral reading" of ECHR rights as he understands it, that is, in the Cohenite way. What is the textual basis brought by Letsas to support the "moral reading" thesis? In section 2 of his article, Letsas notably analyses *Golder v. United Kingdom.* As we saw above, the interpretative question in this case was whether the right to have access to a court – absent from the text of the ECHR – may be derived from the right to a fair trial (Article 6). The ECtHR answered affirmatively and explicitly rejected the originalist view. The Court instead focused on the "object and purpose" (Article 31(1) VCLT) of the ECHR on the basis of the Preamble (and also Article 3 ECHR), which refers to the "common heritage of the political traditions, ideals, freedom and the rule of law" of the States Parties. In section 4 of his article, Letsas analyses *Engel and Others v. The Netherlands*, in which the ECtHR rejected the textualist assumption that the meaning of terms should be assigned by the ordinary meaning within the legal traditions of States Parties.

In section 5 of his article, Letsas focuses on *Tyrer v. United Kingdom*, in which the question was whether judicial corporal punishment of juveniles amounted to a form of degrading treatment (Article 3). The ECtHR implied that the scope of the correlative duties of ECHR rights is determined neither by the domestic definition of the respondent state (the predominant moralistic views of the majority on the Isle of Man) nor by the common practices across the CoE – Letsas persuasively shows that the ECtHR often fails to explain how this "common practice" is to be found. Rather, the ECtHR appealed to the very *nature* of the act of punishment. Do those foundational cases suffice to infer that the ECtHR instantiates Cohen's conception of normative judgment? Well, it depends on how we understand Cohen.

First, it helps to say a few more things about Cohen's claim than is covered by Letsas. Despite the fact that he relies "heavily" on Cohen, the reference is just in a footnote.[77] In his famous article "Facts and Principles", G.A. Cohen persuasively develops a claim about the structure of the normative judgment. Cohen claims that "all principles that reflect facts reflect facts because they also reflect principles that do not reflect facts, and the latter principles form the ultimate foundation of all principles, fact-reflecting principles included".[78] In other words, "it is always a further principle that confers on a fact its principle-grounding power".[79] To clarify his claim, Cohen specifies what it is not. First, it is not a causal claim (why people

---

77   Letsas, "Strasbourg's Interpretive Ethic: Lessons for the International Lawyer", 534.
78   Cohen, "Facts and Principles", 231.
79   Ibid., 215.

Interpretation at the ECtHR 137

come to hold such and such normative principles). Second, it is not a psychological claim ("it is immune to psychological facts"[80] as Cohen puts it). Third, it is neutral to the main question of meta-ethics ("which principles we should adopt"). Fourth, it is independent of the claim that there are objective moral truths. As far as the last claim is concerned, Letsas is quick in arguing that the purpose of the ECtHR "is to discover, over time and through persuasive moral argument, the moral truth about these fundamental rights".[81] As far as the second claim is concerned, it is not necessary that the normative agents "realize" this logical point since Cohen specifies that "that person may not know that her endorsement is fact-based or not, and there may not be an answer to that question, since the person herself may be radically unclear".[82]

Second, what Letsas does not discuss is the meta-ethical position against which Cohen argues: moral and political constructivism, according to which normative principles we ought to follow are those that best survive a fact-dependent procedure – that of inter-subjective justifiability. Cohen takes this point as the distinctive element of Rawlsian constructivism and his "first principles of justice". As he explains, "first principles, in general, are a response to the facts of the human condition".[83] He refers to Rawls' principles of justice that are generated within the confined framework of the veil of ignorance. This framework is indeed fact-dependent. It is because the veil of ignorance constrains the information that individuals have (among other things) that some principles are generated. This factual knowledge is therefore inherent in the substantive principles that we ought to follow. Cohen certainly agrees with Rawls that facts are indispensable to the justification of normative principles but that those facts do not hold the grounding justificatory power: "facts cast normative light only by reflecting the light that first principles shone on them".[84]

Of course, as we saw in Chapter 6, constructivists are attached to inter-subjective justification because they assume meta-ethical agnosticism as an ontological position. As Ronzoni and Valentini explain:

> If we believe that there exist mind-independent normative facts, we will tend to think that such facts should be discovered or intuited; on the other hand, if we are doubtful or agnostic about the existence of such facts, we will be inclined to take the view that valid moral principles should be constructed through appropriate procedures.[85]

As a result, Cohen's claim may be defensible if, and only if, he engages with ontological questions – which he openly wishes to avoid. The conclusive point

---

80 Ibid., 233.
81 Letsas, "Strasbourg's Interpretive Ethic: Lessons for the International Lawyer", 540.
82 Cohen, "Facts and Principles", 233.
83 Ibid., 237.
84 Ibid., 242.
85 Ronzoni and Valentini, "On the Meta-ethical Status of Constructivism: Reflections on G.A. Cohen's 'Facts and Principles'", 415.

138   *Interpretation at the ECtHR*

made by Ronzoni and Valentini is therefore that "constructivists can accept the formal structure of Cohen's meta-ethical thesis, while rejecting the idea they ultimately have to rely on fact-insensitive, *substantive* normative principles".[86]

We are now in a better position to see that Letsas is drawing from different disciplinary literatures, which he does not discuss at the same level of detail despite the centrality of his own meta-ethical assumptions in his final argument. Letsas's assumption about the nature of normative justification is the key to his argument about treaty interpretation and international human rights adjudication:

> Normative truths permeate the process of individuating the project states choose to pursue and which means are appropriate and necessary in order to facilitate it . . . . In sum, the task of individuating the object and purpose of a treaty and of interpreting the treaty, is – from the beginning to the end – a thoroughly interpretive, not empirical, exercise.[87]

The terms "moral values", "moral truths" or "first-person moral reading" are directly inferred from his Cohenite meta-ethical assumptions. Finally, the conclusions of Letsas are contingent upon a meta-ethical view that needs to be more thoroughly illustrated in the case law. In addition, one may question the overemphasis on issues of interpretation as speaking of the deeper layer of reasons that operates in the case law. As I suggest in the next chapters, the balancing of the ECtHR is more informative.

---

86   Ibid., 414.
87   Letsas, "Strasbourg's Interpretive Ethic: Lessons for the International Lawyer", 535.

8 Balancing and justification at the ECtHR

The pivotal concept of "democratic necessity"

In the last chapter, I surveyed the role of the ECtHR *qua* legal interpreter. As we have seen, the ECtHR tends to privilege a *teleological* and *evolutive* interpretation of rights. This immersion alone allows us to envision that the terms of the dispute between ethical and political conception may need to be reconsidered. To recall, Beitz's central claim is that moral reasoning is unnecessary to account for the practices. Legal interpretation suggests the opposite: the process of legal interpretation specifies and concretizes, in non-functional terms, the core structure and content of human rights as protecting individual interests *vis-à-vis* States Parties. Needless to say, such process takes place within a specific legal and international institutional framework: the ECtHR captures the interests protected by an international treaty within the constraints of its judicial role specified in Chapter 6.

That being said, the interpretative methodology of the ECtHR is difficult to reconstruct *in abstracto*, as we have seen. If the Court is clearly dismissive of conventional doctrines of interpretation, it does not have a uniform approach for making explicit the meaning of contested ECHR terms, but rather the use of interpretative poles in which the *teleological* and the *evolutive* prevail. In this chapter, I turn to the balancing exercise carried out by the ECtHR and therefore to the Court's substantive reasoning on a specific range of provisions (Articles 8 to 11). While *interpretation* primarily applies to the terms of the treaty, *balancing* occurs when the ECtHR has acknowledged that there has been a violation and considers whether this violation was nevertheless necessary and hence justified. At this stage, the Court turns to the grounds advanced by the respondent State Party and develops an adversarial form of reasoning.

In this chapter, I reconstruct the Court's crucial phase of balancing and examine, in particular, Articles 8 to 11 (privacy, reunion and assembly, expression, thought and religion). In addition, I examine the right of free elections (Article 3 Protocol 1). In order to determine whether the respondent State Party "struck a fair balance" between the rights and some collective interest(s), the Court has to determine whether the interference found was nevertheless "necessary in a democratic society" and whether it responded to "a pressing social need". I argue that there is enough at this stage of the balancing exercise to capture a prevalent "practical reason" in the constructivist sense – a set of powerful reasons by which

140 *Balancing and justification at the ECtHR*

the actions of states and individuals are judged – that may be subject to moral exploration. Since "democratic society" is at least as indeterminate as the wording of the rights themselves, the Court has had to specify its normative content and explain how each of those rights (in Articles 8 to 11) fits within it. The premise here is that the limits adduced to the rights tell us much about what the rights (in terms of their nature and their role) are about.

There are three main stages at which the ECtHR constructs its "democratic reason". First, it identifies the right-holders whose contribution to "democratic society" is particularly central. This prominence leads the Court to review their claim(s) with particular scrutiny and rigour. Second, and correlatively, the more the interference in question endangers "democratic society", the more the ECtHR restricts the margin of appreciation given to States Parties. Conversely, there are ECHR rights the content of which is not specified and which lend themselves to a consensualist justification – that is, the absence of consensus justifies a wider margin of appreciation. Third, those favoured rights outweigh other rights in the event of conflict and the justificatory reasoning is continuous with the reasons advanced to justify the existence of the right in the first place. This is the case, for instance, with the conflict between the right to reputation under Article 8 and the right to freedom of expression under Article 10. However, before adopting a right-based approach, I want first to introduce in broader terms the structure of the balancing test.

8.1 The balancing test and the margin of appreciation doctrine

If the ECtHR has developed doctrines of interpretation to address an alleged interference with an ECHR right, this semantic specification often does not play the decisive role in the judgment. Rights are rights only when the interest they protect is specified and weighed in given circumstances. True, in some cases, the ECtHR incorporates the balancing exercise into the definition of the scope of the ECHR right at hand: "as a result, public interests in some cases play a role in defining the scope of the rights in question".[1] Moreover, the Court may also fail to address the justification provided by the respondent State Party for the interference at hand. When the ECtHR applies the consensualist doctrine and does not find any majoritarian consensus, the practice under scrutiny is said to fall "within the margin of appreciation" and there is no violation of the ECHR right in question. This was the case, most famously, in *Handyside v. United Kingdom*,[2] where the rationale for establishing limitations on freedom of expression was declared to be *subjective*, and since no European consensus was found, a wide margin of appreciation was accorded. If the consensus is found,

---

1 Gerards and Senden, "The Structure of Fundamental Rights and the European Court of Human Rights", 643.
2 *Handyside v. United Kingdom*, App. No. 5493/72, 7 December 1976.

Balancing and justification at the ECtHR 141

the margin is likely to be restricted. This was the case, most famously, in *Sunday Times v. United Kingdom*,[3] where the basis for restricting free expression was held to be *objective* and, since a European consensus was found, the margin of appreciation shrank and the applicant's view prevailed. In those cases, the choice of the method of *interpretation* combines with the method of *justification* of the interference.

However, in the vast majority of cases brought before it, the ECtHR balances the interests that the ECHR right protects with the argument(s) presented by the respondent State Party and assesses whether the national courts have "struck a fair balance" between them. In doing so, the ECtHR is switching from the assessment focused on the *terms* of the ECHR right in question in light of the facts brought by the applicant, to the assessment focused on the State Party's *reasons* for interfering with the ECHR. As Gerards and Senden explain, "even when the Court finds an interference with the so-called derogable Articles 8–11 (private life, religion, expression, peaceful assembly and association), a further examination is required to determine whether it survives the three-pronged test".[4] In doing so, the ECtHR specifies the normative weight of the interests at stake – or, as the ECtHR puts it, the "merits" of the case under scrutiny. As the ECtHR held in the seminal *Belgian Linguistic Case*, "the Convention therefore implies a just balance between the protection of the general interest of the Community and the respect due to fundamental human rights while attaching particular importance to the latter".[5]

The uniform application of the test originates in the almost identical structure and content of the second paragraph of Articles 8–11. This structure implies that the national law cannot redefine the clauses at will. The first step of the test reviews whether the interference under scrutiny has been "prescribed by law" or "in accordance with law".[6] This first standard is flexible: "la 'loi' est comprise de manière si souple par la Cour que le contrôle qui en résulte peut voir son utilité remise en cause".[7] A mere prison regulation can be considered as "law". In the Court's view the standard is two-pronged. First, the legal norm in question must be accessible to the individual – the *publicity* or *accessibility* of law.[8] This implies that the law in question has to be published.[9] Second, the legal norm must be formulated with precision as to its meaning and scope – the *foreseeability* of the law. As the ECtHR held in *Sunday Times v. United Kingdom*:

---

3 *Sunday Times v. United Kingdom (No. 1)*, App. No. 6538/74, 26 April 1979.
4 Gerards, "Judical Deliberations in the European Court of Human Rights", 15.
5 *Belgian Linguistic Case*, App. Nos. 1474/62, 1677/62, 1691/62, 1769/63, 1994/63, 2126/64, 23 July 1968, para. 5.
6 For a recent case, see e.g. *Boychev and Others v. Bulgaria*, App. No. 77185/01, 27 January 2011, paras 51–2.
7 Jacquemot, *Le standard européen de société démocratique*, 186.
8 See e.g. *Sunday Times v. United Kingdom*, para. 49, *Lithgow v. United Kingdom*, App. Nos. 9006/80, 9262/81, 9263/81, 9265/81, 9266/81, 9313/81, 9405/81, 8 July 1986, para. 110.
9 For a more recent case, see e.g. *Rotaru v. Romania*, App. No. 23753/02, 20 September 2007, para. 54.

142 *Balancing and justification at the ECtHR*

The law should be accessible to the persons concerned and formulated with sufficient precision to enable the citizen to regulate his conduct: he must be able to foresee – if need be, with appropriate advice – to foresee, to a degree that is reasonable in the circumstances, the consequences which a given action may entail.[10]

The second standard clearly leaves the ECtHR with a certain amount of discretion. It holds that the level of precision is contingent on "the context of the instrument considered, the field it is designed to cover and the number and status of those to whom it is addressed".[11]

The second step reviews whether the interference pursued a "legitimate aim", as specified in the second paragraph of Articles 8 to 11: the protection of public safety, public order, health or morals, or for the protection of the rights and freedoms of others, etc. This standard is ambiguous: its wording suggests that it incorporates a *justificatory* dimension, although the ECtHR treats it as an exercise in *classification*. As Jacquemot explains, "il en résulte que des buts poursuivis par les Etats, *in concreto*, sont insérés dans les buts légitimes mentionnés par la Convention par le biais d'une interprétation extensive".[12] The Court rarely finds a violation on this ground. This is explained by the recurrent conflation of the second step with the third, and far more important, step of "democratic necessity" – that is, whether the interference was "necessary in a democratic society" or whether there was a "pressing social need" for it – when the ECtHR turns to a proper assessment of the justificatory grounds provided by the State Party. The assessment of the legitimate aim can itself trigger the use of the margin of appreciation doctrine, such as in the case of *Vo v. France*[13] concerning the application of Article 2 (life) to a fetus. All in all, "le caractère aléatoire du contrôle du but lègitime poursuivi et le caractère laxiste du contrôle de légalité font qu'ils n'apportent pas de réponse édifiantes quant au contenu du standard".[14]

The third step is by far the most evaluative of the assessment process and is also the most controversial. The ECtHR has tautologically specified that "democratic necessity" implies that the interference is "relevant and sufficient"[15] and "convincingly established",[16] and that it must be "convincing and compelling"[17] with the

---

10 See e.g. *Sunday Times v. United Kingdom*, para. 51. For a recent case, see e.g. *Editorial Board of Pravoye Delo and Shtekel v. Ukraine*, App. No. 33014/05, 5 May 2011, paras 65–6.
11 See e.g. *Chorheer v. Austria*, App. No. 13308/87, 25 August 1983, para. 25.
12 Jacquemot, *Le standard européen de société démocratique*, 196.
13 See e.g. *Vo v. France*, App. No. 53924/00, 8 July 2004, para. 42.
14 Jacquemot, *Le standard européen de société démocratique*, 201.
15 *Handyside v. United Kingdom*, para. 50; *Dudgeon v. United Kingdom*, App. No. 7525/76, 22 October 1981, para. 54. *Sunday Times v. United Kingdom*, para. 63; *Özgur Gundem v. Turkey*, App. 23144/93, 16 March 2000, para. 57.
16 *Autronic AG v. Switzerland*, App. No. 12726/87, 22 May 1990, para. 61; *Weber v. Switzerland*, App. No. 11034/84, 22 May 1990, para. 47; *Société Colas Est v. France*, 14 April 2002, App. No. 37971/97, para. 47.
17 *Freedom and Democracy Party (ÖZDEP) v. Turkey*, App. No. 23885/94, 8 December 1999, para. 44.

Balancing and justification at the ECtHR 143

public interest "narrowly interpreted".[18] By "necessity", the ECtHR is deemed to assess, on an *ad hoc* basis, whether the collective interest is normatively sufficient to override the competing interest protected by the right. The relevant paragraph in the text of the case usually starts with the following sentence: "In exercising its supervisory jurisdiction, the Court must look at the interference in the light of the case as a whole, including the content of the impugned statements and the context in which they were made". In some cases the Court assesses whether another measure would have been less restrictive.

However, it is evident that the labels of proportionality and the margin of appreciation mask the normative choices made by the ECtHR on an *ad hoc* basis. As McHarg puts it, "there is radical indeterminacy both in the formulation of each element and in the way they related to one another".[19] It is highly questionable whether the assessment of "democratic necessity" or "proportionality", which all end up conflated with the "margin of appreciation" label, are the correct concepts to depict the Court's balancing exercise. The ECtHR is deemed to "solve" the normative conflict between, on the one hand, the protection of the deontological, right-as-trump-card conceived ECHR rights of the applicant and, on the other hand, the pursuit of collective, utilitarian-sensitive interests of the respondent State Party. When the ECtHR had to decide whether night flights at Heathrow airport in London amounted to a violation of the right to private life under Article 8,[20] it had to strike a balance between the individual interest in sleep against the interests of the community (airline operators, travellers, the economic interest of the country, etc.). The inevitability of such normative choices implies that the margin of appreciation as an analytical concept has no significant explanatory value to describe what the ECtHR actually does as arbiter and reasoner. As Letsas puts it, "the idea of the margin of appreciation in itself clearly lacks any normative force that can help us strike a balance between individual rights and public interests".[21]

8.1.1 The margin of appreciation doctrine

Let us therefore turn more specifically to the margin of appreciation doctrine. Although it appears in the European Movement proposal,[22] the doctrine is found neither in the ECHR and its Protocols nor in *the travaux préparatoires*. In his study of the concept in international law, Shany explains that "the authority of international courts and tribunals to grant states a margin of appreciation is rarely grounded on explicit treaty norms".[23] It is therefore a jurisprudential creation that

---

18 *Klass v. Germany*, App. No. 5029/71, 6 September 1978, para. 42; *Sunday Times v. United Kingdom*, para. 65.
19 McHarg, "Reconciling Human Rights and the Public Interest: Conceptual Problems and Doctrinal Uncertainty in the Jurisprudence of the European Court of Human Rights", 686.
20 *Hatton and Others v. United Kingdom*, App. No. 36022/97, 8 July 2003.
21 Letsas, "Two Concepts of the Margin of Appreciation", 711.
22 Simpson, *Human Rights and the End of Empire*, 676–7.
23 Shany, "Toward a General Margin of Appreciation Doctrine in International Law?", 911.

144   *Balancing and justification at the ECtHR*

takes us to the core of the reasoning practised by the ECtHR in its role of arbiter of interests. As Arai-Takahashi puts it, "if placed in the spectrum from purely descriptive to purely evaluative, it is geared towards the evaluative pole".[24] Indeed, since the doctrine is "l'instrument de mesure d'une atteinte portée à un droit fondamental au regard de l'objectif que poursuit cette restriction",[25] the objective pursued by the State Party cannot be known and assessed *a priori* by the ECtHR.

In fact, the doctrine appeared for the first time in the report of the Human Rights Commission in the interstate case of *Greece v. United Kingdom*,[26] in which the Commission asserted that the UK authorities "should be able to exercise a certain measure of discretion in assessing the extent strictly required by the exigencies of the situation". The ECtHR explicitly relied on the margin of appreciation in the very first case (interstate) brought before it – *Ireland v. United Kingdom*[27] – using the same notion of "discretion". The first definition of the margin of appreciation doctrine is found in *Lawless v. Ireland*, when the Commission asserted that the respondent state enjoys "a certain discretion – a certain margin of appreciation . . . in determining whether there exists a public emergency which threatens the life of the nation and which must be dealt with by exceptional measures derogating from its normal obligations under the Convention".[28]

If the doctrine of the margin of appreciation was initially restricted to derogation situations under Article 15, in which the collective state interest was an event threatening the life of the state (such as national security issues,[29] public order,[30] immigration control[31]), the doctrine has also been employed in cases involving interference with Article 6 (fair trial), Article 8 (private life), Article 9 (freedom of religion), Article 10 (freedom of expression), Article 11 (peaceful assembly and association), Article 1 of Protocol 1 (property), Article 3 of Protocol 1 (elections), Article 14 (non-discrimination) and Article 15 (derogation).[32] As Yourow explains:

---

24 Arai-Takahashi, "Disharmony in the Process of Harmonisation? – The Analytical Account of the Strasbourg Court's Variable Geometry Decision-Making Policy based on the Margin of Appreciation Doctrine", 97.

25 Ducoulombier, *Les conflits de droits fondamentaux devant la Cour européenne des droits de l'homme*, 636.

26 *Greece v. United Kingdom*, Yearbook II (1958–59), 14 December 1959.

27 *Ireland v. United Kingdom*, App. No. 5310/71, 18 January 1978.

28 *Lawless v. Ireland*, App. No. 332/5, 1 July 1961, para. 82.

29 *Klass v. Germany*, para. 49; *Arrowsmith v. United Kingdom*, App. No. 7050/75, 16 May 1977, paras 36–7; *Leander v. Sweden*, App. No. 9248/81, 26 March 1987, para. 59; *Purcell and Others v. United Kingdom*, App. No. 15404/89, 16 April 1991, paras 278–9.

30 *Rassemblement jurassien and unité jurassienne v. Switzerland*, App. No. 8191/78, 10 October 1979.

31 *Amuur v. France*, App. No. 19776/92, 25 June 1996, para. 41.

32 For an overview of the application of the doctrine to those articles, see Arai-Takahashi, *The Margin of Appreciation Doctrine and the Principle of Proportionality in the Jurisprudence of the ECHR*, Part II. For an analysis of the historical evolution of the doctrine, see also Yourow, *The Margin of Appreciation Doctrine in the Dynamics of European Human Rights Jurisprudence*.

The doctrine, originating as a state defense in extraordinary cases of national derogation from the Convention under Article 15, was effectively transposed as a standard for judging alleged state transgression in non-emergency situations in the "Personal Freedoms" domain, mostly under Articles 8–11.[33]

While Article 3 (torture) has very rarely been subject to the doctrine,[34] the ECtHR has applied it to Article 2 on the question whether a fetus has a right safeguarded by the article.[35] In all those instances, the ECtHR does not furnish a uniform standard of review or a clear account of the variability with which the margin is granted. This should not be a surprise. I have presumed that the ECtHR intentionally lacks an account of the conditions under which it applies the doctrine and what can consistently strike the balance between individuals on an *ad hoc* basis in order to deliver individual justice. In every case brought before it, the ECtHR "must look at the interference in the light of the case as a whole", including "the content of the impugned statements" and the "context in which they were made". As Greer puts it:

> The central problem with the "balance model" is that it suggests a weighing of rights and collective rights which does not only down-grade to interests, but requires judges – who are ill-equipped to decide what is in the public interest – constantly to defer to non-judicial determinations of how the balance between the two should be struck.[36]

To capture what lies behind the margin of appreciation heading in practice, Letsas forcefully distinguishes between the *substantive* concept of the doctrine, which addresses the relationship between individual and collective goals and which "resolves" the balancing of conflict interests, and the *structural* concept of the doctrine, which limits the assessment exercise performed by the ECtHR. In other words, Letsas rightly distinguishes between the "'limitability' or non-absoluteness of the Convention"[37] and the cases in which the ECtHR's "power to review decisions taken by domestic authorities should be more limited than the power of a national constitutional court or other national bodies that monitor or review compliance with an entrenched bill of rights".[38]

In the first case – of a *substantive* nature – the margin of appreciation is used to mask the Court's recognition of the collective interest that overrides the interest protected by the ECHR right. In the language of the ECtHR, if the interference is permissible, the State Party is said to act "within the margin of appreciation". The Court is driven by a substantive form of balancing, but fails to fully acknowledge

---

33 Yourow, ibid., 56.
34 *Soering v. United Kingdom*, App. No. 14038/88, 7 July 1989.
35 *Boso v. Italy*, App. No. 50490/99, 5 September 2002, para. 1; *Vo v. France*, para. 80.
36 Greer, "Constitutionalizing Adjudication under the European Convention on Human Rights", 412.
37 Letsas, "Two Concepts of the Margin of Appreciation", 711.
38 Ibid., 721.

146   *Balancing and justification at the ECtHR*

the interests involved and their proper balance. As De Schutter and Tulkens put it, "the 'national margin of appreciation' would be highly contestable if it really did what it says. But in most cases, it does not".[39] In referring to a sphere *within* the margin of appreciation, the ECtHR falsely asserts that is has a clear standard that can determine what the margin of appreciation covers. As Letsas puts it, "it conveys the misleading image that the logical space occupied by an authority's margin of appreciation is tantamount to all the acts (or omissions) that authority may undertake without violating any rights".[40]

In the second case – of a *structural* nature – the margin of appreciation is used to mask the Court's judicial restraint. By contrast to the first, it does not misname its reasoning; it just limits the intensity of review by virtue of its function *qua* supranational organ. As Ducoulombier also explains, "la Cour semble bien procéder à une balance entre les droits et interêts mais, en réalité, défère à la décision de l'Etat, en donnant à la solution qu'il a prise un brevet abstrait de conventionalité".[41] The ECtHR reviews the legality of the interference at stake, but *refrains* from balancing the interests at stake. As Letsas puts it:

> Under the structural concept of the doctrine, we may say that state authorities enjoy a margin of appreciation, in that the ECtHR will not scrutinize their decision. Their margin has to do with the relationship between the European Court of Human Rights and national authorities, rather than with the relationship between human rights and public interest.[42]

This is what the ECtHR has meant by the idea that national authorities are "better placed" than the international judges to decide a given case.

Moreover, Letsas persuasively explains that the "better placed" idea has two distinct uses. First, it implies that the there is no *consensus* among States Parties on some morally sensitive issues – "public morals" in the language of the ECtHR. As Arai-Takahashi further explains, "this doctrine has been regarded as the most appropriate means for protecting public morals under Articles 8–11, taking into account the particular cultural or traditional values as espoused by national societies",[43] insisting on the state's *direct access* to the knowledge of the particular morals. In that respect, *Handyside v. United Kingdom* (the "Little Red Schoolbook" case) was seminal. The ECtHR held that:

> It is not possible to find in the domestic law of the various Contracting States a uniform conception of morals . . . . By reason of their direct and continuous

---

39 De Schutter and Tulkens, "Rights in Conflicts: The European Court of Human Rights as a Pragmatic Institution", 200.
40 Letsas, "Two Concepts of the Margin of Appreciation", 713.
41 Ducoulombier, *Les conflits de droits fondamentaux devant la Cour européenne des droits de l'homme*, 614.
42 Letsas, "Two Concepts of the Margin of Appreciation", 721.
43 Arai-Takahashi, *The Margin of Appreciation Doctrine and the Principle of Proportionality in the Jurisprudence of the ECHR*, 206.

Balancing and justification at the ECtHR   147

contact with the vital forces of their countries, State authorities, in principle, are in a better position than the international judge to give an opinion on the exact content of those requirements as well as on the "necessity" of a "restriction" or "penalty" intended to meet them.[44]

Note that the ECtHR may review and balance the interest at stake, reject the justification given by the State Party and still apply the doctrine. In another seminal case, *Open Door*,[45] the ECtHR reviewed the case and rejected the State Party's argument, but eventually applied the doctrine.

Second, the structural concept implies that national authorities are "better placed" to decide sensitive issues. On those issues, the state "possesses a 'compelling interest' justification to offer to the international authorities, who manifest a sympathetic attitude to the arguments of state authorities in this regard".[46] The doctrine was first applied in the derogation cases under Article 15. Here, *Ireland v. United Kingdom* was seminal. The ECtHR held:

> By the reasons of direct and continuous contact with the pressing need of the moment, the national authorities are in principle in a better position than the international judge to decide on both the presence of such an emergency and on the nature and scope of the derogations necessary to avert it. In this matter article 15 paragraph 1 leaves the authorities a wide margin of appreciation.[47]

This argument is not clear, however. It seems that there is a crucial difference between saying, on the one hand, that the State Party is in a "better place" – and that given this better epistemic access it can deliver a better account of both the factual circumstances of the case and therefore better inform the balancing of the case – and saying, on the other hand and at the normative level of reasoning, that the alleged interference in question does or does not amount to a violation of the ECHR right in question. The fact that the national court "knows" better is a *prima facie* reason to claim that the ECtHR can "decide" better whether this particular interference amounts to a violation. This implies not only that national judges are better placed, but that they are simply better judges. As Ducoulombier explains:

> Cela semble illogique et injustifié. On ne comprend pas pourquoi la Cour serait, par définition, moins bien placée que les Etats pour trancher la question du rapport entre des droits dont elle a l'interprétation et la charge .... [Elle] "n'est pas limitée dans son contrôle par l'origine des actes contestée par le requérant".[48]

---

44 *Handyside v. United Kingdom*, para. 48. See *Otto-Preminger-Institut v. Austria*, App. No. 13470/87, 20 September 1994, para. 48.

45 *Open Door and Dublin Well Woman v. Ireland*, App. Nos. 14234/88, 14235/88, 29 October 1992.

46 Yourow, *The Margin of Appreciation Doctrine in the Dynamics of European Human Rights Jurisprudence*, 52.

47 *Ireland v. United Kingdom*, para. 207.

48 Ducoulombier, *Les conflits de droits fondamentaux devant la Cour européenne des droits de l'homme*, 616.

148 *Balancing and justification at the ECtHR*

8.1.2 The ad hoc *balancing*

Let us now turn to the Court's balancing exercise in context. Before addressing specific cases, a few preliminary remarks are in order about the conditions needed for the test of democratic necessity to play its central normative role. As outlined in the last chapter, the crucial stage is the exercise of balancing the specified ECHR right(s) with the conflicting collective interest(s) advanced by the State Party. Once specified, the ECHR right in question has to outweigh the respondent State Party's justification in light of the Court's definition and scope of the restriction clauses. The second stage of the assessment therefore switches the burden of proof onto the respondent State Party. As Gerards and Senden explain:

> When examining whether a set of facts comes within the scope of the freedom of expression, a court may apply the classical methods of interpretation (such as textual or structural interpretation), while it must apply the typical method of balancing in the context of scrutinizing the justification.[49]

It should be noticed that the ECtHR tends to address the balancing exercise from the perspective of the invoked right(s). "Preferential framing", as it is called, has been criticized in the literature as "the overemphasis on the right invoked causes the Court to decide the conflict in favor of the right to the detriment of the other neglected right".[50] This sheds light on the constructive character of the identification of the conflict of rights at the ECtHR.

The distinction between the two stages may be indistinguishable in the text of the case. An absence of consensus among States Parties over the scope of an ECHR right can trigger the margin of appreciation doctrine and be decisive for the case. True, the conflict may be an apparent one and not give rise to balancing; this may be as a result of the presentation of the case. In most situations, however, the ECtHR is confronted with a genuine conflict of interests. Whereas the Court has some latitude in determining the scope of ECHR rights, the balancing exercise implies a thorough examination of the justification given by the State Party for its interference. As Greer puts it:

> The central issue is not about how the meaning of a given right should be determined, but about whether a clearly defined right should be overridden by a competing collective goal, the pursuit of which is deemed more compelling in the circumstances.[51]

The text of the ECHR does not specify how its rights are placed in hierarchical order and balanced. The reasoning of the ECtHR therefore pertains to an *ad hoc* balancing. As we have already seen, each case brought before the

---

49 Gerards and Senden, "The Structure of Fundamental Rights and the European Court of Human Rights", 625.
50 Smet, "Freedom of Expression and the Right to Reputation: Human Rights in Conflict", 185.
51 Greer, *The European Convention on Human Rights: Achievements, Problems and Prospects*, 212.

Balancing and justification at the ECtHR 149

Court is assessed "on its own merit", addressing the grounds of the litigants and the respondent State Party. This "casuistic" and "empirical" approach *pro et contra* prevents one from clearly distinguishing general and systematic claims endorsed by the ECtHR on the stringency of the collective interest at stake for the interference to be deemed legitimate – despite recourse to the margin of appreciation as an alleged balancing tool. As Gerards and Senden explain, "a definitive conclusion about the alleged violation can be reached only when the soundness of the justification adduced by the government has been scrutinized".[52]

It has long been acknowledged that ECHR rights do not give rise to the same degree of balancing. The so-called "non-derogable" rights in Article 3 (torture, inhuman and degrading treatment), Article (4) (slavery and servitude), Article 4 (2) (forced labour) and, to a lesser extent, Article 4(3) (liberty and security), Article 6 (fair trial), Article 7(1) (criminal offence), Article 2(2) (use of lethal force) and Article 15 (derogation clauses) are applied with what Greer refers to as a strong "priority to rights" principle, according to which the ECtHR "systematically accords rights a greater weight than collective goods".[53] For those rights, if the Court considers that the breach is salient, there is no need to assess the justifications of the State Party through the fine-grained identification of a conflicting collective interest. Of course, the ECtHR will ground its decisions and cite its own and other most recent case law but the identification of the conflicting interests at stake is not salient in the text of the judgment. Yet the active justificatory reasoning remains relatively low. The more the ECtHR elaborates on its own reasoning, the more it ascertains the normative grounds of the ECHR right in question.

As we have seen, the active role of the ECtHR *qua* reasoner and arbiter is most salient where the Court applies what has come to be called the "fair-balance test",[54] a self-created procedure that is applied in accordance with a three-pronged test ("prescribed by law", "legitimate" and "necessary in a democratic society" contained in the second paragraph of Articles 8 to 11 and in Article 2(3) of Protocol 4). This test may apply to all ECHR rights allegedly breached, but the test is systematically applied to Articles 8 to 11 (privacy, expression, religion, association and peaceful assembly), where the ECtHR can more frequently grant a margin of appreciation to the respondent State Party in its interference – "a particularly fertile source of conflict".[55] It is now acknowledged that the restriction clauses in those articles may be enlarged to all ECHR rights. De Schutter and Tulkens explain:

---

52 Gerards and Senden, "The Structure of Fundamental Rights and the European Court of Human Rights", 623.

53 Greer, "Constitutionalizing Adjudication under the European Convention on Human Rights", 413.

54 For an overview, see Mowbray, "A Study of the Principle of Fair Balance in the Jurisprudence of the European Court of Human Rights". For a more detailed and recent study, see Ducoulombier, *Les conflits de droits fondamentaux devant la Cour européenne des droits de L'homme.*

55 Greer, "Balancing and the European Court of Human Rights: A Contribution to the Habermas-Alexy Debate", 424.

150 *Balancing and justification at the ECtHR*

The case law of the European Court of Human Rights has extended this approach to certain rights and freedoms whose formulation in the Convention does not follow this two-tiered structure, progressively developing what may be called a general theory of restrictions to the guarantees of the European Convention of Human Rights.[56]

If the interest of the State Party passes the three-pronged test, then there is no violation of the ECHR right in question, despite the alleged interference. The three-pronged test "presents two significant advantages; it dispenses the Court from explicitly acknowledging the existence of a conflict; and it ensures that the conflict will be addressed by reliance on a well-established technique which both the Court and the commentators are familiar with".[57]

It is true that the application of the test tends to focus on the third step – "democratic necessity" – when the ECtHR assesses whether the respondent State Party struck a fair balance between the interests at stake. As Arai-Takahashi explains, "the Strasbourg organ may prefer to focus their scrutiny on the third standard, finding it unnecessary to ascertain compliance with the first and second standard".[58] This implies that the parties acknowledge that there was indeed an interference with an ECHR right and may recognize the existence of a conflict of interest. The remainder consists in discussing whether the interference was "necessary in a democratic society" by assessing the existence of a "pressing social need" as required by the clauses in Articles 8 to 11. This is where the ECtHR tends to fully address and list the "fundamental principles" of its case law on the given provision. This is also where the margin of appreciation may be granted, and the ECtHR usually specifies before the discussion that States Parties "have a certain margin of appreciation in assessing whether such a need exists, but it goes hand in hand with European supervision, embracing both the legislation and the decisions applying it, even those given by an independent court".

Moreover, except in cases of an absence of "consensus" and grounds for derogation where the ECtHR claims that States Parties are "better placed", it is widely agreed that this step is nothing but an *ad hoc* balancing exercise between the deontologically conceived rights of the applicant against the utilitarian-friendly interest of the respondent State Party, when the ECtHR assesses whether the interference amounts to a "pressing social need" – such as the "rights of others", "public interest", "public order", "national security", "state emergency", "prevention of crime", "protection of health or morals". The *ad hoc* character of the reasoning has been well captured in the legal literature. As McHarg explains, "the fluidity and imprecision of the 'democratic necessity' test is such that the

---

56 De Schutter and Tulkens, "Rights in Conflicts: The European Court of Human Rights as a Pragmatic Institution", 188.

57 Ibid., 189–90.

58 Arai-Takahashi, *The Margin of Appreciation Doctrine and the Principle of Proportionality in the Jurisprudence of the ECHR*, 9.

Balancing and justification at the ECtHR 151

Court and the Commission appear to have no clear understanding of the proper relationship between rights and their exceptions".[59] This does not mean that the Court's resolution of complaints can be reduced to ECHR rights being valid until a certain collective interest is sufficiently important to interfere with them in some given circumstances. This framework is of limited explanatory value as I explain in the next chapter.

8.1.3 The pivotal concept of "democratic society"

Bearing in mind the highly circumstantial balancing by the ECtHR, I now concentrate on a case-specific review of the ECtHR and on the third and decisive "democratic necessity" test, which involves the measurement of the proportionality of the interference with the "legitimate aim" pursued by the State Party (the second step of the test). We need to look at specific cases as the ECtHR does not have principally established a general collective standard that outweighs the ECHR right under scrutiny. The Court's reasoning may terminate with a factual inquiry into the state's act and circumstances with no evaluative weighing, explicit or implicit, of the competing interests. This is the case, for instance, with the margin of appreciation doctrine applied to issues of "public morals", in which the ECtHR claims that the national authorities are "better placed" to decide on given case. As Letsas puts it, "the notions of proportionality and deference . . . cannot by themselves provide any clear guidance since their content turns on which moral theory underlies human rights".[60]

In other words, the framing of the conflict between rights and the "necessity" test leads to prioritizing one right over the other, "which results in obfuscating the reality of the conflict itself" . . . . 'Balancing' may be closer to a slogan than to a methodology".[61] Otherwise put, the ECtHR does not have a clear idea of when the utilitarian argument strikes back against ECHR "trump cards". In a seminal case, *Young, James and Webster v. United Kingdom*, it implicitly rejected the theorizing of the public interest: "democracy does not simply mean that the views of the majority must always prevail. A balance must be achieved which ensures the fair and proper treatment of minorities and avoids any abuse of a dominant position".[62] As a result, "the balancing between the various conflicting interests takes place *ad hoc*, in the absence of a normative theory. This has naturally appeared arbitrary, particularly in view of the general requirement that courts must justify their decisions".[63] Former judges have justified this lack of clarity by insisting on its *subsidiary* function:

---

59 McHarg, "Reconciling Human Rights and the Public Interest", 673.
60 Letsas, "Two Concepts of the Margin of Appreciation", 731.
61 De Schutter and Tulkens, "Rights in Conflicts: The European Court of Human Rights as a Pragmatic Institution", 191.
62 *Young, James and Webster v. United Kingdom*, App. Nos. 7601/76, 7806/77, 18 October 1982, para. 63.
63 Letsas, "Two Concepts of the Margin of Appreciation", 715.

152 *Balancing and justification at the ECtHR*

> La Cour européenne n'a pas pour fonction de juger dans l'abstrait de la compatibilité ou de l'incompatibilité d'une loi, d'une jurisprudence établie ou d'une pratique administrative nationales avec les exigences de la Convention. Elle n'a pas à établir une "théorie générale", une phrase que l'on rencontre souvent dans ses arrêts.[64]

The margin of appreciation doctrine is also conceived by legal commentators as "la réponse juridique à un problème d'ordre politique, à savoir le rapport qui doit exister entre une juridiction internationale et les Etats parties au traité dont elle assure la défense".[65] As we have already seen, the ECHR is not considered as "a superstructure imposed on the contracting states from above".[66] I do not believe that such responses are satisfactory, however. If the "judicial politics" are so prevalent in the case law, then they may be just part of ECHR law *tout court*. The distinction holds only if there is an established theory of ECHR law.

True, the opaqueness is reinforced, as we have already seen, by the conflation of "democratic necessity" with proportionality and the margin of appreciation doctrine. From the above, the indeterminacy of the concept of "democratic necessity" renders the reasoning opaque and does not suit itself to a clear reconstruction. Ducoulombier also argues that:

> Some authors distinguish between the test enshrined in the second paragraph of Articles 8 to 11, principally based on proportionality, and a balancing test that should be favoured to solve conflicts of rights. But it remains unclear what the difference between the two methods is.[67]

There is no clear distinction between the assessment of proportionality and fair balance, and a restriction is deemed proportionate when a "fair balance between interests has been struck".

It is also clear that the use of the margin of appreciation may be allocated in light of democratic legitimation of ECtHR judgments in national legal orders using the consensualist-justificatory doctrine of interpretation. As Besson argues, "it is precisely the democratic process of reception that requires respecting States' margin of appreciation".[68] At the level of law application, it is clear that "national actors have superior law application capabilities to those of international courts".[69] For our normative endeavours, however, I retain that the balancing exercise gives

---

64 Matscher, "La Cour européenne des droits de l'homme, aujourd'hui et demain, au lendemain de son cinquantième anniversaire: regards d'un ancien juge de la Cour", 917.

65 Ducoulombier, *Les conflits de droits fondamentaux devant la Cour européenne des droits de l'homme*, 612.

66 Brems, "The Margin of Appreciation in the Case Law of the ECHR", 276.

67 Ducoulombier, "Conflicts between Fundamental Rights and the European Court of Human Rights", 227.

68 Besson, "European Human Rights, Supranational Judicial Review and Democracy – Thinking Outside the Judicial Box", note 111.

69 Shany, "Toward a General Margin of Appreciation Doctrine in International Law?", 918.

Balancing and justification at the ECtHR 153

us a privileged access to the practical reason of the ECtHR. As Ducoulombier explains, "c'est la nature de la balance elle-même qui impose que le juge déploie un argumentaire justificatif puisqu'il ne peut résoudre le litige par l'application syllogistique d'une règle de droit claire".[70]

8.1.4 The practical reason of the ECtHR

I have just indicated that the practical reason of the ECtHR is not found within the application of formal rules that the ECtHR applies at the stage of interpretation. If sometimes the standard of "democratic society" is employed to mask the prevalence of the collective interest overriding the right, in a majority of cases it allows the ECtHR to specify the normative content (the nature and role) of an ECHR right. The more abstract the right, the greater the space for the specification of its scope in the judicial arena. As Marshall puts it, "general terms like 'public safety' cannot be invoked for the imposition of restrictions on individual rights in an absolute and uncontrolled manner".[71]

Following the constructivist method outlined in Chapter 4, the task is to identify the "target set of normative judgments"[72] in which the practical reason of the ECtHR is most salient. Three instances of this practical reason are distinguished. First, the ECtHR identifies the right-holder(s) whose contribution to the realization of "democratic society" is particularly central, which leads the ECtHR to review their claim(s) with particular scrutiny and rigour. This is what has also been called "preferential framing" in the legal literature. Conversely, it identifies right-holders who do not play such a crucial role and do not qualify for such treatment. The task of normative evaluation consists of explaining the distinction.

Second, and correlatively, the more the state interference in question endangers "democratic society", the more the ECtHR restricts the margin of appreciation devoted to States Parties. Conversely, there are ECHR rights the content of which is not specified and which lend themselves to a consensualist justification – that is, that the absence of consensus justifies a wider margin of appreciation. It is clear in these cases that "the Court takes the moralistic preferences of the majority as being synonymous with 'public morals' and thus constituting a legitimate aim".[73] The ECtHR clearly argues in the case law that the nature of the aim of the restriction, as well as the nature of the actions involved, affect the scope of the margin of appreciation. Yet distinctions can be made among ECHR rights. Specialists in the subject have correctly noticed that "moral relativism must not be admitted in such a manner as to call into question the secular and pluralist premises of democracy".[74]

---

70 Ducoulombier, *Les conflits de droits fondamentaux devant la Cour européenne des droits de l'homme*, 576.
71 Marshall, *Personal Freedom through Human Rights Law*, 40.
72 Street, "Constructivism About Reasons", 3–4.
73 Letsas, *A Theory of Interpretation of the European Convention on Human Rights*, 121.
74 Arai-Takahashi, "Disharmony in the Process of Harmonisation? – The Analytical Account of the Strasbourg Court's Variable Geometry Decision-Making Policy based on the Margin of Appreciation Doctrine", 102.

154 *Balancing and justification at the ECtHR*

Third, those favoured rights are given the normative force to clearly outweigh other rights in the case of conflict and reasons given are continuous with the reasons advanced to justify the existence of the right in the first place. This is the case, for instance, with the conflict between the right to reputation under Article 8 and the right of freedom of expression under Article 10. It should finally be noted that those reasons may also be used to generate *positive duties* on the part of the state for the rights that best serve "democratic society". In those instances, the ECtHR is not only protecting the individuals from state interference – the classical requirement of state neutrality. It is openly *promoting* a conception of "democracy" and "democratic society". In the assessment of other ECHR rights, by contrast, the ECtHR refrains from generating positive duties on such reasons and it refrains from specifying the core interest protected. While the ECtHR also recognizes positive duties in rights that do not serve democratic society to the same extent, States Parties may enjoy a wider margin of appreciation on those positive duties as well.

8.2 "Democratic society" and the internal concept of sovereignty: Article 10 (expression)

Article 10 guarantees the right of freedom of expression. It clearly holds a prominent status in the pursuit of "democratic society" in the case law of the ECtHR. In the seminal *Handyside v. United Kingdom*, the ECtHR held that "freedom of expression constitutes one of the essential foundations of such a society, one of the basic conditions for its progress and for the development of every man".[75] The normative force of freedom of expression is therefore derived from a conception of democracy that permits the development of individuals. This is a point that the ECtHR recently confirmed in *Szima v. Hungary*, where it held that freedom of expression is "one of the basic conditions for its progress and for each individual's self-fulfilment".[76] How does democracy enhance the development of man? Is it just the interest to have one's opinion heard and its instrumental value in enhancing individual autonomy? Is freedom of expression justified only insofar as it allows individuals to express their views?

More importantly, the ECtHR has connected freedom of expression with the pluralism that *should* animate a democratic society. As the Court repeatedly asserts, "democracy thrives on freedom of expression".[77] The ECtHR here clearly aims to protect an individual interest, but that interest takes its normative force within the collective framework of "democracy" or "democratic society". In *Handyside v. United Kingdom*, in which the ECtHR reviews the role of the press, it emphasizes that such exercise of expression contributes to debates on political matters and issues of public interest. In other words, the normative force originates in the content of the views to be expressed – those views that pertain to an

---

75 *Handyside v. United Kingdom*, para. 49.
76 *Szima v. Hungary*, App. No. 29723/11, 9 October 2012, para. 25.
77 *Freedom and Democracy Party (ÖZDEP) v. Turkey*, para. 44.

Balancing and justification at the ECtHR 155

issue of public interest. The interest concerns the conditions for democracy – that is, the extent to which the interest serves to impart ideas and opinions on political matters and on other matters of public interest. Pluralism as a normative concept applies to those ideas and opinions in the first place.

It transpires from the case law on Article 10 that the ECtHR takes pluralism to be an inherent fact of modern societies and that the expression of pluralism on issues of public interest should be encouraged. For instance, a democratic society with a single party, although elected democratically, would not deserve that description. The ECtHR does not just require agents to be able to make their claim in public *fora*; it requires that in those *fora* the views heard should be plural and adversarial. As we shall see next, the degree of protection from the ECtHR depends on the nature of the views expressed – those that concern issues of public interest, which itself may determine the margin of appreciation left to States Parties. Also, as we shall see later in the chapter, the same is true for Articles 9 and 11, albeit with some specificities.

The concept of pluralism and its normative force in modern societies is therefore of paramount importance in the Court's justification of the *scope* of the right of freedom of expression. There is a clear *instrumental* connection between the former and the latter. In the search for pluralism, it is clearly freedom of expression that serves democracy as conceived and therefore justifies its extended scope and duties. As the ECtHR held in *Handyside v. United Kingdom*:

> It is applicable not only to "information" or "ideas" that are favourably received or regarded as inoffensive or as a matter of indifference, but also to those that offend, shock or disturb the State or any sector of the population. Such are the *demands* of that pluralism, tolerance and broadmindedness without which there is no "democratic society".[78]

The normative force of political pluralism here is salient. As Lécuyer puts it, "le lien est si étroit que l'on peut être tenté de condenser les trois valeurs – pluralisme, tolérance et esprit d'ouverture – et de les enchaîner à la liberté pour faire de cette dernière le *primus inter pares* de ces fondements".[79] Clearly, the normative force of political pluralism is about political ideas and opinions primarily. This has been a constant position of the ECtHR from the *Handyside* case in 1969 until today; in the *Porubova* case of 2010, for instance, the Court "reiterates in this connection that under Article 10 § (2) of the Convention very strong reasons are required to justify restrictions on political speech or debates on questions of public interest".[80] It is therefore crucial to note the emphasis on the *collective* and *societal* dimensions of Article 10 as concretized and specified through the seminal concepts of *political pluralism, tolerance* and *broadmindedness* governing the

---

78 *Handyside v. United Kingdom*, para. 49. See also *Jersild v. Denmark*, App. No. 15890/89, para. 37 (author's emphasis).
79 Lécuyer, *Les droits politiques dans la jurisprudence de la Cour européenne des droits de l'homme* 180.
80 *Porubova v. Russia*, App. No. 8237/03, 8 October 2009, para. 42.

156   *Balancing and justification at the ECtHR*

Court's reasoning. Those concepts govern the reasoning of the ECtHR not only in its assessment of Article 11, but also Articles 10, 9 and Article 3 Protocol 1, as we shall see next.

Clearly, the right of freedom of expression is the ECHR right that best serves the realization of this state of affairs. Every political party, group or individual should be granted the right to express its political opinions and ideas on issues of public interest in the public arena. The ECtHR has made explicit that the state is the "ultimate guarantor"[81] of this position. The emphasis on political pluralism was also salient in the seminal case of *Lingens v. Austria*, in which the ECtHR stated that "more generally, freedom of political debate is at the very core of the concept of a democratic society which prevails throughout the Convention".[82] In a model of formal democracy recording and counting the views of individuals is insufficient. In *Young, James and Webster v. United Kingdom*, the ECtHR held that "democracy does not simply mean that the views of a majority must always prevail: a balance must be achieved which ensures the fair and proper treatment of minorities and avoids any abuse of a dominant position".[83] The ECtHR is fostering a richer conception of democracy that is *deliberative* and *adversarial* in nature. I come back to this point at length later in the chapter.

8.2.1 Why pluralism?

Why is political pluralism important in the Court's view? Through its case law, the ECtHR has specified the reasons not only for protecting but also for actively promoting political pluralism. Most importantly, the ECtHR first specified the *object* to be protected: ideas and opinions on issues of public interest. Second, it specified conditions in which those ideas and opinions should be expressed: an arena of informed public and pluralist debate. The ECtHR makes explicit that one's views on issues of public interest should be *informed* by public, transparent and adversarial discussion of views on issues of public interest; this point was made explicit in *Piermont v. France*: "a person opposed to official ideas and positions must be able to find a place in the political arena".[84] In *Erdoğdu and İnce v. Turkey*, the ECtHR found a violation of Article 10 on the ground that interviewing a sociologist pertaining to the analysis of the political situation in south-east Turkey could not be conceived as exacerbating the Kurdish nationalist sentiment in the region: "domestic authorities in the instant case failed to have sufficient regard to the public's right to be informed of a different perspective on the situation in south-east Turkey, irrespective of how unpalatable that perspective may be

---

81 *Informationsverein Lentia and Others v. Austria*, App. Nos. 13914/88, 15041/89, 15717/89, 15779/89, 17207/90, 24 November 1983, para. 38.
82 *Lingens v. Austria*, App. No. 9815/82, 8 July 1986, para. 42.
83 *Young, James and Webster v. United Kingdom*, App. Nos. 7601/76, 7806/77, 13 August 1981, para. 68.
84 *Piermont v. France*, App. Nos. 15773/89, 15774/89, 24 July 1995, para. 76.

Balancing and justification at the ECtHR 157

for them".[85] A recent instance of this reasoning is found in *Çamyar and Berktaş v. Turkey*, in which the ECtHR assessed the content of a book that severely criticized the Turkish penitentiary system.[86]

In other words, not only the professional journalist but all those who seek to convey information on issues of public interest via the press or other printed media are prevalent right-holders. This was the case of a political scientist identified to a journalist in *Riolo v. Italy*:

> La Cour note d'emblée que le requérant n'exerce pas régulièrement la profession de journaliste, mais est un chercheur en sciences politiques à l'université de Palerme. Cependant, puisque l'intéressé a écrit un article destine à être publié dans le journal Narcomafie, et qui, de plus, a été repris par le quotidien national Il Manifesto (paragraphe 13 ci-dessus), ses propos, à l'instar de ceux de toute autre personne se trouvant dans une situation comparable, doivent être assimilés à ceux d'un journaliste et jouir de la même protection sous l'angle de l'article 10 de la Convention.[87]

The scope of "public interest" can apply to a fairly large number of issues, including when they *a priori* relate to a specialized audience. In *Azevedo v. Portugal*, the ECtHR extended the scope of expression to criticisms of literature on the history of a Portuguese city:

> Examinant le contexte de l'affaire et l'ensemble des circonstances dans lesquelles les expressions incriminées ont été proférées, la Cour considère en premier lieu que le débat en question peut être regardé comme relevant de l'intérêt général, même si la controverse, portant sur l'analyse historique et symbolique d'un monument important de la ville de Castelo Branco, a trait à un domaine assez spécialisé.[88]

Moreover, when a critical view on an issue of public interest is expressed, the extended right to freedom of expression must be accompanied with a right to reply from the person subject to such criticism; in *Melchynuk v. Ukraine*, which concerned the critique of books of a recognized Ukrainian author, the Commission held:

> The Court considers that the right of reply, as an important element of freedom of expression, falls within the scope of Article 10 of the Convention. This flows from the need not only to be able to contest untruthful information, but also to ensure a plurality of opinions, especially in matters of general interest such as literary and political debate.[89]

---

85 *Erdoğdu and İnce v. Turkey*, App. Nos. 25067/94, 25068/94, 8 July 1999, para. 51.
86 *Çamyar and Berktaş v. Turkey*, App. No. 41959/02, 15 February 2011, paras 37–8.
87 *Riolo v. Italy*, App. No. 42211/07, 17 July 2008, para. 63.
88 *Moreira de Azevedo v. Portugal*, App. No. 11296/84, 23 October 1990, para. 31.
89 *Melchynuk v. Ukraine*, App. No. 28743/03, 5 July 2005, p. 2.

158 *Balancing and justification at the ECtHR*

As a result, it is not just the interest to have one's opinion heard and its instrumental value to individual autonomy that matters. It is that views on issues of public interest should be informed and confronted in the public arena – with particular emphasis on the actions of elected governments. As the ECtHR held in *Yazar v. Turkey*, "in a democratic system the actions or omissions of the government must be subject to the close scrutiny not only of the legislative and judicial authorities but also of the press and public opinion".[90]

From political pluralism as the prevalent and wide definitional concept of "democratic society", which Article 10 serves best, the ECtHR draws some important implications that reveal both the nature and scope of its justificatory reasoning along those lines. Not only does the search for political pluralism help the ECtHR to develop and specify the content of the reasons that justify various ECHR rights, but this specification in turn determines the respective normative weight of other ECHR rights that serve "democratic society". Specific right-holders are designated and protected for their central contribution to "democratic society" so defined, such as the press in the case of Article 10 or political parties in the case of Article 11, which leads the ECtHR to scrutinize the content of the views expressed with a high degree of rigour. The same is true for the judiciary, in respect of which the ECtHR has held that "it is important that the courts have an opportunity to obtain feedback on how their acts and judicial decisions are understood and regarded by the public".[91]

Moreover, when the ECtHR has to examine an ECHR right that conflicts with Article 10 – such as the right to reputation under Article 8 – the Court clearly focuses its assessment on Article 10 and, despite *recognition* of the conflict of interests, the Court does not modify this scrutiny. It reasserts the normative breadth of the right of freedom of expression but does not specify the breadth of the conflicting right. As I indicated earlier in this chapter, the ECtHR is using a form of "preferential framing" in those cases. This is most clearly the case with defamation of politicians.

8.2.2 The normative basis

Let us now turn to the normative basis governing the practical reason on this provision. First, the ECtHR has repeatedly held that an interference with Article 10 cannot be justified if the aim pursued by the applicant falls within the ideal of a pluralist and informed debate on issues of public interest. As the Court held in *Dupuis v. France*:

> The promotion of free political debate is a fundamental feature of a democratic society. The Court attaches the highest importance to freedom of expression in the context of political debate and considers that very strong reasons are

---

90 *Yazar and Others v. Turkey*, App. Nos. 22723/93, 22724/93, 22725/93, 9 April 2002, para. 59.
91 *Semik-Orzech v. Poland*, App. No. 39900/06, 15 November 2011, para. 62.

Balancing and justification at the ECtHR 159

required to justify restrictions on political speech. Allowing broad restrictions on political speech in individual cases would undoubtedly affect respect for freedom of expression in general in the State concerned.[92]

The literature on the case law of the ECtHR has correctly noted this emphasis. As Lécuyer puts it, "la Cour hisse le débat public et politique au sommet de la hiérarchie des opinions couvertes par l'article 10 afin d'empêcher l'asthénie de la société démocratique et reconnaît une marge d'appréciation particulièrement étroite dans ce domaine".[93] If this principle holds, then any finding of it is *prima facie* legitimate. As the ECtHR firmly held in *United Communist Party of Turkey and Others v. Turkey*:

> From that point of view, there can be no justification for hindering a political group solely because it seeks to debate in public the situation of part of the State's population and to take part in the nation's political life in order to find, according to democratic rules, solutions capable of satisfying everyone concerned.[94]

More importantly, the more the interference endangers the pursuit of an informed political debate on issues of public interest, the more the State Party should *prima facie* refrain from interfering. In principle, the ECtHR asserts that freedom of expression is central to the normative conception of informed political debate to the extent that its restrictions "must, however, be construed strictly, and the need for any restrictions must be established convincingly".[95] This is a core and constant principle on which the ECtHR is extremely severe. As a result:

> In determining whether a necessity within the meaning of Article 11 § 2 exists, the Contracting States have only a limited margin of appreciation, which goes hand in hand with rigorous European supervision embracing both the law and the decisions applying it, including those given by independent courts.[96]

8.2.3 The prominent rights-holders of Article 10

Second, there are right-holders whose contribution to the realization of "democratic society" requires a slimmer margin of appreciation. This is one important instance of the practical reason of the ECtHR. The Court has identified that the *right-holder* most at risk from endangering the search for an informed political

---

92 *Dupuis and Others v. France*, App. No. 1914/02, 7 June 2007, para. 40.
93 Lécuyer, *Les droits politiques dans la jurisprudence de la Cour européenne des droits de l'homme*, 201.
94 *United Communist Party of Turkey and Others v. Turkey*, App. No. 29400/05, 19 June 2012, para. 57.
95 *Steel and Morris v. United Kingdom*, App. No. 68416/01, 15 February 2005, para. 87. See also *Pakdemirli v. Turkey*, App. No. 35839/97, 22 February 2005, para. 32.
96 *Socialist Party and Others v. Turkey*, App. No. 21237/93, 25 May 1998, para. 50.

160　*Balancing and justification at the ECtHR*

debate were state interference to be legitimate is the press. If public informed debate is crucial for an effective "democratic society", then freedom of the press comes first. The first case involving Article 10, in 1962, was interestingly about the freedom of the press.[97] Since the seminal cases of *Sunday Times v. United Kingdom* and *Lingens v. Austria*, the ECtHR has reiterated the reasons why the press holds such a prominent status among the right-holders under Article 10. More precisely, the freedom of the press is vital for an effective democracy in the role of transparently forming the opinions of individuals on issues of public interest. In *Özgur v. Turkey*, the ECtHR held the following:

> As these cases also concern measures against newspaper publications, they must equally be seen in the light of the essential role played by the press for ensuring the proper functioning of democracy . . . . While the press must not overstep the bounds set, inter alia, for the protection of the vital interests of the State, such as the protection of national security or territorial integrity against the threat of violence or the prevention of disorder or crime, it is nevertheless incumbent on the press to convey information and ideas on political issues, even divisive ones. Not only has the press the task of imparting such information and ideas; the public has a right to receive them. Freedom of the press affords the public one of the best means of discovering and forming an opinion of the ideas and attitudes of political leaders.[98]

Here, again, the interest in informed and pluralist debate on issues of political and public interest shapes the duties of the State Party not to infringe Article 10. The press plays the role of "public watchdog"[99] in a "democratic society" as conceived by the ECtHR: this is because its principles *serve* the search for informed and pluralist debate on issues of public interest. In *Jersild v. Denmark*, the ECtHR clearly inferred the centrality of the role of the press from the right of individuals to be informed. It held the following:

> It is nevertheless incumbent on it to impart information and ideas of public interest. Not only does the press have the task of imparting such information and ideas: the *public also has a right to receive them*. Were it otherwise, the press would be unable to play its vital role of "public watchdog". Although formulated primarily with regard to the print media, these principles doubtless apply also to the audio-visual media.[100]

97　*De Becker v. Belgium*, App. No. 214/56, 27 March 1962.
98　See also *Lingens v. Austria*, para. 41, and *Fressoz and Roire v. France*, App. No. 29183/95, 21 January 1999, para. 45.
99　*Handyside v. United Kingdom*, para. 65.
100　*Jersild v. Denmark*, para. 31 (author's emphasis). See also *Thorgeir Thorgeirson v. Iceland*, App. No. 13778/88, 25 June 1992, para. 63, and *Bladet Tromsø and Stensaas v. Norway*, App. No. 21980/93, 20 May 1999, para. 62.

Balancing and justification at the ECtHR 161

The right of the public to receive information is correlative to the clear recognition by the ECtHR of the press's "duty . . . to impart – in a manner consistent with its obligations and responsibilities – information and ideas on all matters of public interest".[101] The rationale is the same for other persons or entities performing the same basic role, such as audio-visual companies[102] and NGOs.[103] In other words, the search for an informed political debate on issues of public interest is not guaranteed by the press freely exercising its right to convey information; the press has a strong *duty* to serve this normative ideal in a democratic society. Moreover, the ECtHR makes clear that when fines are imposed on journalists, those fines should not be so high as to produce a "chilling effect" on the rest of the profession. Upon the finding of such an effect, the sanction is disproportionate – in conformity with the three-pronged test. As the ECtHR held in *Kasabova v. Bulgaria*:

> In any event, the Court finds that the overall sum which the applicant was required to pay was a far more important factor in terms of the potential chilling effect of the proceedings on her and other journalists. The four fines imposed on her came to a total of BGN 2,800, which, even taken alone, looks considerable when weighed against her salary.[104]

If press freedom is the vehicle for informed political or public debate on issues of public interest, then it implies that, within the formal reasoning of the ECtHR, the margin of appreciation left to States Parties should be significantly slim. By "political" or "public" it can mean post-electoral comments in *Lingens v. Austria*, political analysis in *Piermont v. France*, the status of past political figures in *Lehideux and Isorni v. France*,[105] non-political but public debates such as the issue of doping in sport as in the recent *Ressiot and Others v. France*[106] or the quality of public water in the recent *Šabanović v. Montenegro and Serbia*.[107]

The press as the guarantor of informed debate on issues of public interest is central in the ECtHR's view to the extent that the right of freedom of expression can override the offence of insulting a foreign head of state; in *Colombani v. France*, the ECtHR found a violation of Article 10 pertaining to the criticism, in the French newspaper *Le Monde*, of the involvement of the King of Morocco's entourage in drug trafficking.[108] In *Dalban v. Rumania*, the ECtHR held that "it would be unacceptable for a journalist to be debarred from expressing critical value judgments unless he or she could prove their truth".[109] Finally, the prevalence

---

101 *Radio France and Others v. France*, App. No. 53984/00, 30 March 2004, para. 30.
102 *Radio Twist A.S. v. Slovakia*, App. No. 62202/00, 19 December 2006, paras 57–8.
103 *Vides Aizsardzības Klubs v. Latvia*, App. No. 57829/00, 27 May 2004, para. 42.
104 *Kasabova v. Bulgaria*, App. No. 22385/03, 19 April 2011, para. 71.
105 *Lehideux and Isorni v. France*, App. No. 24662/94, 23 September 1998, para. 51.
106 *Ressiot and Others v. France*, App. Nos. 15054/07, 15066/07, 28 July 2012, para. 114.
107 *Šabanović v. Montenegro and Serbia*, App. No. 5995/06, 31 May 2011.
108 *Colombani v. France*, App. No. 51279/99, 25 June 2002, para. 41.
109 *Dalban v. Romania*, App. No. 28114/95, 28 September 1999, para. 49.

162   *Balancing and justification at the ECtHR*

of a free press can, in some cases, precede the imperative of the search for national security provided by the respondent State Party.[110]

Moreover, if the connection between the views expressed in the press and the normative ideal of informed public debate is foundational to the ECtHR, and if the views and opinions that contribute to this ideal should freely circulate in the public space, then those views do not need factual verification; it promotes a journalistic ethic in requiring that journalists act with "an obligation to provide a sufficient factual basis for their assertions"[111] and "provide accurate and reliable information".[112] One of the few cases in which the ECtHR did not protect freedom of expression was where the views held in a book "failed to respect the fundamental rules of historical method"[113] or when the views expressed may affect the core interest in the right to reputation under Article 8.[114] In principle, the ECtHR firmly distinguishes between *information* and *value judgment* on the ground that the latter cannot be subject to the same factual assessment:

> In the Court's view, a careful distinction needs to be made between facts and value-judgments on this issue. The existence of facts can be demonstrated, whereas the truth of value-judgments is not susceptible of proof. The Court notes in this connection that the facts on which Mr Lingens founded his value-judgment were undisputed, as was also his good faith.[115]

The factual basis supporting the criticism of politicians, for instance, may justify the Court's extended tolerance to what may appear to be *insulting* – especially if the contentious issue is of public interest. In *Lopes Gomes da Silva v. Portugal*, which involved a provocative article about the fascist ideas of a candidate for the city council of Lisbon, the ECtHR held that "admittedly, the applicant's article and, in particular, the expressions used could be considered to be polemical. They do not, however, convey a gratuitous personal attack because the author supports them with an objective explanation".[116] In *Dyuldin v. Russia*, the weaker requirement of factual support was decisive for the finding of a violation by the ECtHR precisely because of the political context in which those views were held:

> The Court would in any event observe that the distinction between statements of fact and value judgments is of less significance in a case such as the present one, where the impugned statement was made in the course of a lively political

---

110 See *Observer and Guardian v. United Kingdom*, App. No. 13585/88, 26 November 1991, and *Sunday Times v. United Kingdom*.
111 *Cumpănă and Mazăre v. Romania*, App. No. 33348/96, 17 December 2004, para. 101.
112 *Bladet Tromsø and Stensaas v. Norway*, para. 65.
113 *Chauvy and Others v. France*, App. No. 64915/01, 29 June 2004, para. 231.
114 *Kasabova v. Bulgaria*, para. 63.
115 *Lingens v. Austria*, para. 42.
116 *Lopes Gomes da Silva v. Portugal*, App. No. 37698/97, 28 September 2000, para. 29.

Balancing and justification at the ECtHR   163

debate at local level and where elected officials and journalists should enjoy a wide freedom to criticise the actions of a local authority, even where the statements made may lack a clear basis in fact.[117]

As the ECtHR makes clear, the scrutiny of the reasons for an interference can be further modified. The relatively weak demand for factual support is also salient in the classical conflict of Article 10 with the right to reputation under Article 8. *Flux v. Moldova* involved the conviction of journalists for having accused the communist party of having accepted bribes from large fuel importers; although it was not proved that the fuel company had indeed received money, the ECtHR found a violation of Article 10.

> [It] considers that, with the passage of time, not only does it become more difficult for the media to prove the facts on which they may have relied, but also the damage to the person allegedly defamed by the relevant material is bound to fade away.[118]

It seems that the need to convey information to the public without factual proof can outweigh the interest in the protection of reputation – especially if there is a public interest at stake. Finally, the central role of the press goes together with the protection of *journalistic sources*. As the ECtHR held in *Goodwin v. United Kingdom*:

> Without such protection, sources may be deterred from assisting the press in informing the public on matters of public interest. As a result the vital public-watchdog role of the press may be undermined and the ability of the press to provide accurate and reliable information may be adversely affected.[119]

Correlatively, if the press plays a crucial role in the search for informed public debate, then the ECtHR must protect the *diffusion* of information and opinion accordingly. This further implication is principally stated in *Muller v. Switzerland*.[120] The claim was reasserted and broadened in the recent case of *Kılıç and Eren v. Turkey* in which the ECtHR held that "Article 10 protects not only the substance of the ideas and information expressed, but also the form in which they are conveyed".[121]

The other right-holder under close scrutiny as far as political informed debate under Article 10 is concerned is the *elected representative* and the electorate, as well as the *political party* as a whole. First, elected representatives play a crucial role in informing the electorate about issues of public interest. This role is obviously central throughout the pre-electoral period in which the candidates

---

117 *Dyuldin v. Russia*, App. No. 25968/02, 31 July 2007, para. 49.
118 *Flux v. Moldova*, App. No. 28702/03, 21 November 2007, para. 32.
119 *Goodwin v. United Kingdom*, App. No. 17488/90, 27 March 1996, para. 39.
120 Seminal elements are found in *Handyside v. United Kingdom*, para. 49.
121 *Kılıç and Eren v. Turkey*, App. No. 43807/07, 29 November 2011, para. 28.

164 *Balancing and justification at the ECtHR*

compete for the election. This role in turn makes justification of the role of the press in organizing the confrontation of ideas even stricter. In *Lingens v. Austria* the ECtHR asserted that "freedom of the press affords the public one of the best means of discovering and forming an opinion of the ideas and attitudes of political leaders".[122] Independently of the election period, the press as a vehicle for the views of politicians is salient as, for instance in *Castells v. Spain*, in which the freedom of the press "gives politicians the opportunity to reflect and comment on the preoccupations of public opinion; it thus enables everyone to participate in the free political debate which is at the very core of the concept of a democratic society".[123] Miguel Castells was a Spanish senator of the (then) Batasuna political party; he openly questioned Spain's responsibility in a series of assassinations in Pamplona, which led to the withdrawal of his parliamentary immunity. In the recent case of *Otegi Mondragon v. Spain*, the ECtHR confirmed:

> There is little scope under Article 10 § 2 for restrictions on freedom of expression in the area of political speech or debate – where freedom of expression is of the utmost importance – or in matters of public interest. While freedom of expression is important for everybody, it is especially so for an elected representative of the people. He represents his electorate, draws attention to their preoccupations and defends their interests.[124]

Furthermore, the ECtHR made explicit in this case that government officials should be subject to more intrusive scrutiny in comparison with a politician *tout court*:

> The limits of permissible criticism are wider with regard to the Government than in relation to a private citizen, or even a politician. In a democratic system the actions or omissions of the Government must be subject to the close scrutiny not only of the legislative and judicial authorities but also of the press and public opinion.[125]

Of course, the premise to the role of politicians' ideas being mediated is the interdependence of Article 10 with Article 3 of Protocol 1, which protects the right to regular, free and fair elections, and on which I elaborate later. The continuum between Article 10 and Article 11 is another facet of the practical reason of the ECtHR, which has defended this interdependence as a single normative claim as, for instance, in *Bowman v. United Kingdom*:

> The two rights are inter-related and operate to reinforce each other: for example, as the Court has observed in the past, freedom of expression is one of the "conditions" necessary to ensure the free expression of the opinion of the

---

122 *Lingens v. Austria*, para. 42.
123 *Castells v. Spain*, App. No. 11798/85, 23 April 1992, para. 43.
124 *Otegi Mondragon v. Spain*, App. No. 2034/07, 15 March 2011, para. 50.
125 Ibid., para. 46.

Balancing and justification at the ECtHR 165

people in the choice of the legislature. For this reason, it is particularly important in the period preceding an election that opinions and information of all kinds are permitted to circulate freely.[126]

The claim was confirmed in a recent case, *Şükran Aydın and Others v. Turkey*, in which the ECtHR held that "free elections are inconceivable without the free circulation of political opinions and information".[127] As Lécuyer explains, "sans que l'on puisse très bien mesurer l'impact de ces émissions, le but est de garantir une égalité des chances devant les suffrages par un nivellement de la pénétration médiatique des candidats et de leur opinions".[128] In the same vein, the ECtHR pays special attention to the protection of *legislative immunity* granted to parliamentarians by most of the States Parties. Not only does the ECtHR justify its prevalence on the same normative basis, but it also specifies that the views must be expressed within the prevalent arena of politics, that is, the parliament. The *Cordova* cases are in this sense particularly informative.[129]

Conversely, the ECtHR has extended the protection of Article 10 to criticism of elected representatives. In the Court's view, this is simply the counterpart of their own extended right to freedom of expression. However, this relationship is again to be mediated by the prevalence of the interest in representation. This is best seen in the way the ECtHR understands Article 10 and the right to reputation of politicians subject to criticism. The Court reflected on the limits of acceptable criticism in *Oberschlik v. Austria (No. 2)* in which the applicant was convicted and fined for having used the term "idiot" as a reaction to a speech by Austrian politician, Jörg Haider:

> As to the limits of acceptable criticism, they are wider with regard to a politician acting in his public capacity than in relation to a private individual. A politician inevitably and knowingly lays himself open to close scrutiny of his every word and deed by both journalists and the public at large, and he must display a greater degree of tolerance, especially when he himself makes public statements that are susceptible to criticism. He is certainly entitled to have his reputation protected, even when he is not acting in his private capacity, but the requirements of that protection have to be weighed against the interests of open discussion of political issues, since exceptions to freedom of expression must be interpreted narrowly.[130]

Note here that in its reasoning the ECtHR relied heavily on the fact that the term "idiot" was used in the context of a distinctively *political* debate – that is, it

---

126 *Bowman v. United Kingdom*, App. No. 24839/94, 19 February 1998, para. 42.
127 *Şükran Aydın and Others v. Turkey*, App. Nos. 49197/06, 14871/09, 23196/07, 50242/08, 60912/08, 22 January 2013, para. 55.
128 Lécuyer, *Les droits politiques dans la jurisprudence de la Cour européenne des droits de l'homme*, 207.
129 *Cordova v. Italy (No. 1)*, App. No. 40877/98, 30 January 2003; *Cordova v. Italy (No. 2)*, App. No. 45649/99, 30 January 2003.
130 *Oberschlik v. Austria*, App. No. 20834/92, 1 July 1997, para. 29.

166 *Balancing and justification at the ECtHR*

concerned the standing of an elected politician. This implies an evidently heavier weight ascribed to Article 10 when it conflicts with the right to reputation under Article 8. Moreover, the emphasis on the right to political criticism pertains not so much to the confrontation of views on issues of public interest as to the ethics of the relationship between the elected politician and the electorate. In *Melnytchenko v. Ukraine*, the ECtHR held:

> By obliging them to put themselves forward publicly, in a full and frank manner, the electorate can assess the candidate's personal qualifications and ability to best represent its interests in parliament. Such requirements clearly correspond to the interests of a democratic society.[131]

I return in more detail to the specifics of this relationship in my analysis of the interdependence between Article 10 and Article 11, which best explains the extended right to freedom of expression to criticism of politicians – and, in particular, government officials – compared with other individuals.

Second, the ECtHR has developed firm case law on the normative role of political parties in a "democratic society" and the conditions for their dissolution. Political parties are interesting right-holders in the case law in that they do not figure in the text of the ECHR. Here, again, the ECtHR has *constructed* the normative role of political parties through the prism of political pluralism. They hold a special status in the search for political pluralism and informed political debate on issues of public interest. The most illustrative set of cases is perhaps the Islamist political parties in Turkey, on which the ECtHR has reflected on several occasions. Although the cases also involve alleged violations of freedom of religion (Article 9), the ECtHR has focused its assessment on the political dimension of the cases. In *Refah Partisi and Others v. Turkey*, the Ankara Constitutional Court qualified the Islamist party Refah Partisi as *anti-secularist*. This was not sufficient for the ECtHR to ban a political party given the central role of political parties in the search for informed and pluralist political debate on issues of public interest. As the ECtHR held:

> It is in the nature of the role they play that political parties, the only bodies which can come to power, also have the capacity to influence the whole of the regime in their countries. By the proposals for an overall societal model which they put before the electorate and by their capacity to implement those proposals once they come to power, political parties differ from other organisations which intervene in the political arena.[132]

Again, the ECtHR has verified that the views expressed by those political parties are counterbalanced in the public arena, as it specified in *Gündüz v. Turkey*:

---

131 *Melnytchenko v. Ukraine*, App. No. 17707/02, 19 October 2004, para. 58.
132 *Refah Partisi and Others (The Welfare Party) v. Turkey*, App. Nos. 41340/98, 41342/98, 41343/98, 41344/98, 13 February 2003, para. 87.

Balancing and justification at the ECtHR 167

The applicant's extremist views were already known and had been discussed in the public arena and, in particular, were counterbalanced by the intervention of the other participants in the programme; and lastly, they were expressed in the course of a pluralistic debate in which the applicant was actively taking part.[133]

8.2.4 The limits of Article 10

Third, the ECtHR has clarified the limits of Article 10. As I explained above, the Court is particularly tolerant when the views expressed fall within the scope of an informed debate on issues of public interest – including insulting terms towards elected politicians. The general limit is extended when the free speech takes places within the contexts of election campaigns and the elections themselves. A recent example is *Lepojić v. Serbia*:

> The Court has also repeatedly upheld the right to impart, in good faith, information on matters of public interest, even where this involved damaging statements about private individuals . . . and has emphasised that the limits of acceptable criticism are still wider where the target is a politician . . . . While precious for all, freedom of expression is particularly important for political parties and their active members . . ., as well as during election campaigns when opinions and information of all kinds should be permitted to circulate freely.[134]

The emphasis on public debate of views, ideas and opinions on issues of public interest is stringent to the extent that both exaggeration and even provocation are allowed – what the ECtHR calls "immoderation". The same is true where the views are held in a live broadcast – even in a press conference where there is less time for reflection. As the ECtHR held in *Otegi Mondragon v. Spain*:

> Turning to the expressions themselves, the Court accepts that the language used by the applicant could have been considered provocative. However, while any individual who takes part in a public debate of general concern – like the applicant in the instant case – must not overstep certain limits, particularly with regard to respect for the reputation and the rights of others, a degree of exaggeration, or even provocation, is permitted, in other words, a degree of immoderation is allowed . . . . The Court observes that, while some of the remarks made in the applicant's speech portrayed the institution embodied by the King in a very negative light, with a hostile connotation, they did not advocate the use of violence, nor did they amount to hate speech, which in the Court's view is the essential element to be taken into account . . . .

---

133 *Gündüz v. Turkey*, App. No. 35071/97, 4 December 2003, para. 51.
134 *Lepojić v. Serbia*, App. No. 13909/05, 6 November 2007, para. 74.

168 Balancing and justification at the ECtHR

The Court further takes account of the fact that the remarks were made orally during a press conference, so that the applicant had no possibility of reformulating, refining or retracting them before they were made public.[135]

In the same vein, debate on issues of public interest matter to the extent that individuals should not be prevented from participating in debate on grounds of linguistic inabilities – especially during pre-electoral periods. As the ECtHR held in *Şükran Aydın and Others v. Turkey*:

> Turning to the facts of the present cases, the Court finds that they are distinguishable from the cases cited above because they do not concern the use of an unofficial language in the context of communications with public authorities or before official institutions. Rather, the cases concern a linguistic restriction imposed on persons in their relations with other private individuals, albeit in the context of public meetings during election campaigns. In this connection, the Court reiterates that Article 10 encompasses the freedom to receive and impart information and ideas in any language that allows persons to participate in the public exchange of all varieties of cultural, political and social information and ideas.[136]

Also, the ideal of informed debate on issues of public interest is such that the ECtHR uses it when it reviews the balancing of national courts – that is, in addition to its own preferential framing. This was the case in *Romanenko v. Russia*, in which the ECtHR held:

> However, there is no evidence in the domestic judgments that the courts performed a balancing exercise between the need to protect the plaintiffs' reputation and the right of the members of the press to impart information on issues of general interest.[137]

In this context, and when it conflicts with the right to reputation under Article 8, the prohibition of the use of the terms "nazi", "insane", or "neofascist" cannot justify an interference when the views expressed concern an issue of public interest. A recent instance of this reasoning can be found in *Cornelia Popa v. Romania*:

> Dans ce contexte, les expressions utilisées par la requérante dans son article à l'égard de la juge C.C. ne sauraient passer aux yeux de la Cour pour des allégations délibérément diffamatoires, mais pour le pendant d'une liberté journalistique qui comprend aussi le recours possible à une certaine dose d'exagération, voire même de provocation.[138]

---

135 *Otegi Mondragon v. Spain*, para. 54.
136 *Şükran Aydın and Others v. Turkey*, para. 52.
137 *Romanenko and Others v. Russia*, App. No. 11751/03, 8 October 2009, para. 42.
138 *Cornelia Popa v. Romania*, App. No. 17437/03, 29 March 2011, para. 40.

Balancing and justification at the ECtHR 169

The same is true when the expression involved concerns the President of the French Republic, as in the recent *Eon v. France*.[139] Yet the ECtHR has in some cases established limits. One is when despite the need for exaggeration and provocation in "democratic society", a significant *distortion of facts* can strike the balance, as in *Kania and Kittel v. Poland*:

> It is true that, when taking part in a public debate on a matter of general concern – like the applicants in the present case – an individual is allowed to have recourse to a degree of exaggeration or even provocation, or in other words to make somewhat immoderate statements . . . . However, the Court considers that there is a difference between acceptable exaggeration or provocation, or somewhat immoderate statements, and the distortion of facts known to the journalists at the time of publication.[140]

Similarly, in *Lindon, Otchakovsky-Laurens and July v. France*, the ECtHR held that the terms "executioner" and "chief of a gang of killers" exceeded the limits of the right to freedom of expression.[141] The case involved a series of criminal convictions related to the publication of a book on French politician and former head of the *Front National* party, Jean-Marie Le Pen, which raised Le Pen's responsibility in the party's violent action. Note here that the prohibition concerned the publication of a journal article relating to the content of the book rather than the book itself. Yet this is a case in which defamation and reputation outweighed expression.

There are other limits to the exercise of Article 10. For instance, the private life of Princess Caroline of Monaco does not fall within the domain of issues of public interest. The ECtHR circumscribes the domain of "public interest" in a radical tone:

> The Court considers that a fundamental distinction needs to be made between reporting facts – even controversial ones – capable of contributing to a debate in a democratic society relating to politicians in the exercise of their functions, for example, and reporting details of the private life of an individual who, moreover, as in this case, does not exercise official functions. While in the former case the press exercises its vital role of "watchdog" in a democracy by contributing to "impart[ing] information and ideas on matters of public interest . . .", it does not do so in the latter case.[142]

Is the scope of expression specified thereby unlimited? For instance, a press article on police brutality is certainly a matter of public interest, but is not of a political nature in the eyes of the ECtHR. As the Court explained in *Thorgeir Thorgeirson v. Iceland*:

---

139 *Eon v. France*, App. No. 26118/10, 14 March 2013, para. 60.
140 *Kania and Kittel v. Poland*, App. No. 35105/04, 21 June 2010, para. 47.
141 *Lindon, Otchakovsky-Laurens and July v. France*, App. Nos. 21279/02, 36448/02, 22 October 2007.
142 *Von Hannover v. Germany*, App. No. 59320/00, 24 June 2004, para. 63.

170   Balancing and justification at the ECtHR

The Court's Lingens v. Austria judgment of 8 July 1986 (Series A no. 103), Barfod v. Denmark judgment of 22 February 1989 (Series A no. 149) and Oberschlick v. Austria judgment of 23 May 1991 (Series A no. 204) showed that the wide limits of acceptable criticism in political discussion did not apply to the same extent in the discussion of other matters of public interest. The issues of public interest raised by the applicant's articles could not be included in the category of political discussion, which denoted direct or indirect participation by citizens in the decision-making process in a democratic society.[143]

Is the right to freedom of expression as specified by the ECtHR thereby absolute? Of course it is not. In *Lehideux and Isorni v. France*, which involved the publication of article depicting the career of Marshal Pétain in a positive fashion, the ECtHR did not find a violation of Article 10 – arguing that "that forms part of the efforts that every country must make to debate its own history openly and dispassionately".[144]

This view was confirmed in the recent case of *Gündüz v. Turkey*. The ECtHR famously held that the mere fact of defending the implementation of Sharia law in the public arena falls within the scope of Article 10. True, the ECtHR recognizes that:

> It was difficult to declare one's respect for democracy and human rights while at the same time supporting a regime based on sharia. It considered that sharia, which faithfully reflected the dogmas and divine rules laid down by religion, was stable and invariable and clearly diverged from Convention values.[145]

Yet the ECtHR, relying clearly on political pluralism, did not find it sufficient to follow the State Party's restriction:

> The applicant's extremist views were already known and had been discussed in the public arena and, in particular, were counterbalanced by the intervention of the other participants in the programme; and lastly, they were expressed in the course of a pluralistic debate in which the applicant was actively taking part. Accordingly, the Court considers that in the instant case the need for the restriction in issue has not been established convincingly.[146]

In principle, the ECtHR recognizes that such a political project, based on the party's discourses, is incompatible with the values of the ECHR. However, the mere fact of defending such a project in the public arena remains within the bounds of

---

143   *Thorgeir Thorgeirson v. Iceland*, para. 61.
144   *Lehideux and Isorni v. France*, para. 51.
145   *Gündüz v. Turkey*, para. 51.
146   Ibid.

Balancing and justification at the ECtHR 171

legality because it contributes to an informed and pluralist political debate. In *United Communist Party of Turkey and Others v. Turkey*:

> It cannot be ruled out that a party's political programme may conceal objectives and intentions different from the ones it proclaims. To verify that it does not, the content of the programme must be compared with the party's actions and the positions it defends. In the present case, the TBKP's programme could hardly have been belied by any practical action it took, since it was dissolved immediately after being formed and accordingly did not even have time to take any action. It was thus penalised for conduct relating solely to the exercise of freedom of expression.[147]

The expression of separatist views similarly falls within the scope of Article 10. In *Stankov and the United Macedonian Organisation Ilinden v. Bulgaria*, the ECtHR held that "demanding territorial changes in speeches and demonstrations does not automatically amount to a threat to the country's territorial integrity and national security".[148] "The Court finds, therefore, that the probability that separatist declarations would be made at meetings organised by Ilinden could not justify a ban on such meetings".[149] Defending Sharia law or separatism falls within the scope of Article 10. The threshold, in the ECtHR's eyes, lies not in the *expression* of anti-democratic or separatist views, but whether the political project deemed detrimental to the values of the ECHR has a chance of being realized in the near future. This was the ground given by the ECtHR in not finding a violation of Article 10 in *Refah Partisi v. Turkey*, which had been dissolved by the Constitutional Court of Ankara:

> The Court accordingly considers that at the time of its dissolution Refah had the real potential to seize political power without being restricted by the compromises inherent in a coalition. If Refah had proposed a programme contrary to democratic principles, its monopoly of political power would have enabled it to establish the model of society envisaged in that programme.[150]

In the expression of political views, any political party or group may promote an alternative "societal model"[151] through constitutional change. However, two conditions apply to the expression and promotion of such a project. First, constitutional change must be conducted through democratic rules. The right to free elections contained in Article 3 Protocol 1 is certainly implied here. Second, the content of the reforms threatens the basic requirements of a "democratic society" – again

---

147 *United Communist Party of Turkey and Others v. Turkey*, para. 58.
148 *Stankov and the United Macedonian Organisation Ilinden v. Bulgaria*, App. Nos. 29221/95, 29225/95, 2 October 2001, para. 97.
149 Ibid., para. 98.
150 *Refah Partisi (The Welfare Party) and Others v. Turkey*, para. 108.
151 Ibid., para. 87.

172 *Balancing and justification at the ECtHR*

identified as political pluralism and informed political debate. Banning pluralism implies, in the eyes of the ECtHR, destroying the very core of such society. More importantly, incitement to violence for promoting a political project, or the use of violence once in power, cannot fall within the scope of Article 10 and opens the door to the application of the margin of appreciation doctrine, as in *Fatih Taş v. Turkey*:

> Enfin, là où les propos litigieux incitent à l'usage de la violence à l'égard d'un individu, d'un représentant de l'Etat ou d'une partie de la population, les autorités nationales jouissent d'une marge d'appréciation plus large dans leur examen de la nécessité d'une ingérence dans l'exercice de la liberté d'expression.[152]

The ECtHR makes a special effort in documenting whether the incitement to violence is found in the writings of Kurdish militants[153] or the Basque political party, Eusko Abertzale Ekintza, in its relationship with Batasuna and ETA.[154] Perhaps the clearest and most widely cited account of the conditions for interfering with Article 10 are stated in *Refah Partisi v. Turkey*:

> The Court considers that a political party may promote a change in the law or the legal and constitutional structures of the State on two conditions: the means used to that end must be legal and democratic; secondly, the change proposed must itself be compatible with fundamental democratic principles. It necessarily follows that a political party whose leaders incite to violence or put forward a policy which fails to respect democracy or which is aimed at the destruction of democracy and the flouting of the rights and freedoms recognised in a democracy cannot lay claim to the Convention's protection against penalties imposed on those grounds.[155]

The right to free elections, protected in Article 3 Protocol 1, is clearly implied. As the ECtHR held in *Socialist Party and Others v. Turkey*:

> The Court finds nothing in them that can be considered a call for the use of violence, an uprising or any other form of rejection of democratic principles. On the contrary, he stressed on a number of occasions the need to achieve the proposed political reform in accordance with democratic rules, through the ballot box and by holding referenda.[156]

---

152 *Fatih Taş v. Turkey*, App. No. 36635/08, 5 April 2011, para. 29.
153 *Belek v. Turkey*, App. Nos. 36827/06, 36828/06, 36829/06, 20 November 2011, para. 28.
154 *Eusko Abertzale Ekintza – Acción Nacionalista Vasca (EAE-ANV) v. Spain*, App. No. 40959/09, 15 January 2013, para. 71.
155 *Refah Partisi (The Welfare Party) and Others v. Turkey*, para. 98.
156 *Socialist Party and Others v. Turkey*, para. 46.

The ECtHR therefore found a violation of Article 10. The principle itself is now clearly recurrent in the case law: in *Halis Dogan v. Turkey*, "de fait, dans l'ensemble, la teneur des articles peut passer pour inciter à l'usage de la violence, à la résistance armée, ou au soulèvement; c'est là, aux yeux de la Cour, un élément essentiel à prendre en considération".[157] To improve its assessment of this point, the ECtHR thoroughly compares parties' programmes with parties' discourses held by party leaders – which the Court takes to be the views of the whole party – and makes sure that both cannot be *interpreted* as an incitement to violence. In *Erdoğdu and İnce v. Turkey*, the ECtHR held:

> It would appear to the Court that the domestic authorities in the instant case failed to have sufficient regard to the public's right to be informed of a different perspective on the situation in south-east Turkey, irrespective of how unpalatable that perspective may be for them. As noted previously, the views expressed in the interview cannot be read as an incitement to violence; nor could they be construed as liable to incite to violence.[158]

In *Zana v. Turkey*, for instance, regarding incitement to violence in the words of an activist involved in the Kurdish cause, the ECtHR held:

> Those words could be interpreted in several ways but, at all events, they are both contradictory and ambiguous. They are contradictory because it would seem difficult simultaneously to support the PKK, a terrorist organisation which resorts to violence to achieve its ends, and to declare oneself opposed to massacres; they are ambiguous because whilst Mr Zana disapproves of the massacres of women and children, he at the same time describes them as "mistakes" that anybody could make.[159]

Also, the ECtHR may review all this material for the simple reason that a political party may hide some political ideas that are incompatible with the ECHR. In *Linkov v. Czech Republic*, the ECtHR held:

> On ne saurait exclure que le programme politique d'un parti cache des objectifs et intentions différents de ceux qu'il affiche publiquement. Pour en savoir plus, il faut comparer le contenu de ce programme avec les actes et prises de positions des membres et dirigeants du parti en cause. Or, en l'espèce, le programme du PL, tel que précisé par son comité préparatoire au cours de la procédure devant les autorités nationales, n'aurait guère pu se voir démenti par de quelconques actions concrètes car, sa demande d'enregistrement ayant été rejetée, le parti n'a pas même eu le temps d'en mener.[160]

---

157 *Halis Dogan v. Turkey (No. 3)*, App. No. 4119/02, 10 October 2006, para. 34.
158 *Erdoğdu and İnce v. Turkey*, para. 52.
159 *Zana v. Turkey*, App. No. 18954/91, 25 November 1997, para. 56.
160 *Linkov v. Czech Republic*, App. No.10504/03, 7 December 2012, para. 44.

174 *Balancing and justification at the ECtHR*

8.3 Article 11 (assembly and association)

Let us now turn to Article 11. First, the Article clearly lacks an independent normative basis in the case law. In terms of justification, it is to a significant extent reduced to the reasons specified for Article 10. A clear instance of this absence can be seen when the applicant claims that both Articles have been violated and the ECtHR assesses the merits of the claims under Article 10 only. This was the case, for instance, in *Steel and Others v. United Kingdom*: "the Court does not find that this complaint raises any issues not already examined in the context of Article 10. For this reason it is unnecessary to consider it".[161] In *Vogt v. Germany*, the ECtHR specified that "the protection of personal opinions, secured by Article 10 (art. 10), is one of the objectives of the freedoms of assembly and association as enshrined in Article 11 (art. 11)".[162] Such reasoning shows how the "democratic society" of the ECtHR transpires from the practical reason across several ECHR rights. When the Court makes explicit the distinctive role of each right, the continuum is salient. In a nutshell, the ECtHR clearly takes association to be a collective form of expression. The *leitmotif* of the ECtHR is the following:

> The Court reiterates that notwithstanding its autonomous role and particular sphere of application, Article 11 must also be considered in the light of Article 10. The protection of opinions and the freedom to express them is one of the objectives of the freedoms of assembly and association as enshrined in Article 11. That applies all the more in relation to political parties in view of their essential role in ensuring pluralism and the proper functioning of democracy. As the Court has said many times, there can be no democracy without pluralism. It is for that reason that freedom of expression as enshrined in Article 10 is applicable, subject to paragraph 2, not only to "information" or "ideas" that are favourably received or regarded as inoffensive or as a matter of indifference, but also to those that offend, shock or disturb. The fact that their activities form part of a collective exercise of freedom of expression in itself entitles political parties to seek the protection of Articles 10 and 11 of the Convention.[163]

Moreover, in the more recent case of *Vellutini and Michel v. France*, the ECtHR formally established the instrumental relationship between the two provisions and the primacy of Article 10: "la Cour rappelle que le droit à la liberté d'expression garanti par l'article 10 constitue l'un des principaux moyens permettant d'assurer la jouissance effective du droit à la liberté de réunion et d'association consacré par l'article 11".[164]

---

161 *Steel and Others v. United Kingdom*, App. No. 24838/94, 23 September 1998, para. 113.
162 *Vogt v. Germany*, App. No. 17851/91, 26 September 1995, para. 64.
163 *Stankov and United Macedonian Organisation Ilinden and Others v. Bulgaria*, para. 27.
164 *Vellutini and Michel v. France*, App. No. 32820/09, 6 October 2011, para. 32.

Balancing and justification at the ECtHR 175

Once the essentially political purpose of Article 11 is established, the ECtHR enlarges the scope of application to the political forms of association – those associations the aim of which is to express views on issues of public interest. Still, in *Stankov and the United Macedonian Organisation Ilinden v. Bulgaria*, in which the ECtHR reviewed the activities of an organization that fostered the recognition of the Macedonian minority in Bulgaria, the Court specified the stringent interest behind the freedom of association and the link to freedom of expression: "such a link is particularly relevant where – as here – the authorities' intervention against an assembly or an association was, at least in part, in reaction to views held or statements made by participants or members".[165] An interesting recent case in this respect is the Court's assessment in *Alekseyev v. Russia* of the prohibition of the gay parade in Russia. The ECtHR made clear that while the issue of sexual minorities may still be subject to the consensualist-justificatory approach, the very fact of exercising the right to campaign for their right cannot be, which plainly falls within the scope of the provision. The granting of the margin of appreciation must incorporate this distinction:

> In any event, the absence of a European consensus on these questions is of no relevance to the present case because conferring substantive rights on homosexual persons is fundamentally different from recognising their right to campaign for such rights. There is no ambiguity about the other member States' recognition of the right of individuals to openly identify themselves as gay, lesbian or any other sexual minority, and to promote their rights and freedoms, in particular by exercising their freedom of peaceful assembly. As the Government rightly pointed out, demonstrations similar to the ones banned in the present case are commonplace in most European countries . . . . The Court is therefore unable to accept the Government's claim to a wide margin of appreciation in the present case.[166]

8.3.1 The normative basis restated

Second, if the wording of Article 11 protects both *private* and *public* forms of association, the intention of right-holders to defend an opinion on an issue of public interest takes precedence and enjoys a wider scope of protection as well as more rigorous scrutiny of the alleged interference by the ECtHR. The normative basis, founded on the paramount importance of the expression of views and opinions on issues of public interest, is restated. This is most clearly seen when the ECtHR reviews the public counter-demonstration against a private form of association. In *Ollinger v. Austria*, the ECtHR reviewed the Austrian measure of prohibiting the counter-protest of a commemoration ceremony held by a former group of SS held in parallel:

---

165 *Stankov and United Macedonian Organisation Ilinden and Others v. Bulgaria*, para. 85.
166 *Alekseyev v. Russia*, App. Nos. 4916/07, 25924/08, 14599/09, 21 October 2010, paras 84–5.

176 *Balancing and justification at the ECtHR*

The Court therefore finds that they gave too little weight to the applicant's interest in holding the intended assembly and expressing his protest against the meeting of Comradeship IV, while giving too much weight to the interest of cemetery-goers in being protected against some rather limited disturbances.[167]

It had stated earlier in the case:

In the Court's view, the unconditional prohibition of a counter-demonstration is a very far-reaching measure which would require particular justification, all the more so as the applicant, being a member of parliament, essentially wished to protest against the gathering of Comradeship IV and, thus, to express an opinion on an issue of public interest.[168]

In others words, given the over-determination of Article 11 by Article 10 in the interest it protects, the ECtHR tends to enlarge the scope of application of the latter to an extent similar to the former – that which is determined by the normative conception of pluralism and the free circulation of ideas on issues of public interest. In *Güneri and Others v. Turkey*, the ECtHR brought the instrumental link between Article 11 and democracy to a closer degree – without, however, making explicit the claim that freedom of assembly is *derived* from the normative conception of democracy:

La Cour rappelle que la liberté de réunion et le droit d'exprimer ses vues à travers cette liberté font partie des valeurs fondamentales d'une société démocratique. L'essence de la démocratie tient à sa capacité à résoudre des problèmes par un débat ouvert. Des mesures radicales de nature préventive visant à supprimer la liberté de réunion et d'expression en dehors des cas d'incitation à la violence ou de rejet des principes démocratiques – aussi choquants et inacceptables que peuvent sembler certains points de vue ou termes utilisés aux yeux des autorités, et aussi illégitimes les exigences en question puissent-elles être – desservent la démocratie, voire, souvent, la mettent en péril.[169]

In *Cetinkaya v. Turkey*, the ECtHR insisted on the need for specifically political ideas to be expressed through freedom of assembly:

A cet égard, elle rappelle que dans une société démocratique fondée sur la prééminence du droit, les idées politiques qui contestent l'ordre établi et dont la réalisation est défendue par des moyens pacifiques doivent se voir offrir une possibilité convenable de s'exprimer à travers l'exercice de la liberté de réunion ainsi que par d'autres moyens légaux . . . . La liberté de participer à

167 *Ollinger v. Austria*, App. No. 76900/01, 29 June 2006, para. 49.
168 Ibid., para. 44.
169 *Güneri and Others v. Turkey*, App. Nos. 42853/98, 43609/98, 44291/98, 12 July 2005, para. 76.

Balancing and justification at the ECtHR   177

une réunion pacifique revêt ainsi une telle importance qu'elle ne peut subir une quelconque limitation, dans la mesure où l'intéressé ne commet pas lui-même, à cette occasion, un acte répréhensible.[170]

8.3.2 The prominent rights-holders of Article 11

Third, the case law distinguishes Article 10 from Article 11 mostly by emphasizing the collective dimension of Article 11, but the core interests protected imply a similar set of duties: the protection of collective expression and the circulation of political ideas and opinions through the formation of political groups. The case law on freedom of association reveals a broader continuum of this kind; NGOs, for instance, have been given a significant role in the search for informed political debate on issues of public interest. Pluralism and the need for counter-power are clearly present in the practical reason of the ECtHR on freedom of association. This is the case, for instance, in *Vides Aizsardzības Klubs v. Latvia*, where the ECtHR clearly identified the role of NGOs in relation to the press in the search for transparent information on issues of public interest, such as the protection of the environment:

> En tant qu'organisation non gouvernementale spécialisée en la matière, la requérante a donc exercé son rôle de "chien de garde" conferé par la loi sur la protection de l'environnement. Une telle participation d'une association étant essentielle pour une société démocratique, la Cour estime qu'elle est similaire au rôle de la presse tel que défini par sa jurisprudence constante . . . . Par conséquent, pour mener sa tâche à bien, une association doit pouvoir divulguer des faits de nature à intéresser le public, à leur donner une appréciation et contribuer ainsi à la transparence des activités des autorités publiques.[171]

In *Grande Oriente d'Italia v. Italy*, in which the ECtHR reviewed an Italian norm requiring candidates for public office to reveal their membership, it held:

> Freedom of association is of such importance that it cannot be restricted in any way, even in respect of a candidate for public office, so long as the person concerned does not himself commit any reprehensible act by reason of his membership of the association. It is also clear that the association will suffer the consequences of its members' decisions. In short, the prohibition complained of, however minimal it might be for the applicant association, does not appear "necessary in a democratic society".[172]

The rationale of political pluralism is also particularly relevant in the protection of freedom of assembly of political parties, national and ethnic minorities. In *United Communist Party of Turkey and Others v. Turkey*, the ECtHR applied the

---

170 *Cetinkaya v. Turkey*, App. No. 75569/01, 27 June 2006, para. 27.
171 *Vides Aizsardzības Klubs v. Latvia*, para. 42.
172 *Grande Oriente d'Italia v. Italy*, App. No. 35972/97, 2 August 2001, para. 26.

178   *Balancing and justification at the ECtHR*

basis of Article 11 to Article 10 and thereby inferred that "the exceptions set out in Article 11 are, where political parties are concerned, to be construed strictly; only convincing and compelling reasons can justify restrictions on such parties' freedom of association".[173] The protection of national and ethnic minorities who express political ideas and opinions, in the search for political pluralism, is also salient in the review by the ECtHR – although, as we shall see later in the chapter, it draws a red line when it comes to the demands of self-determination. In *Gorzelik and Others v. Poland*, the ECtHR held:

> The implementation of the principle of pluralism is impossible without an association being able to express freely its ideas and opinions, the Court has also recognised that the protection of opinions and the freedom of expression within the meaning of Article 10 of the Convention is one of the objectives of the freedom of association.[174]

As the Court held in *Stankov and the United Macedonian Organisation Ilinden v. Bulgaria*:

> It may have been true that the majority of the Bulgarian population considered that there was no Macedonian minority in their country and that the demonstration of the applicants' ideas could shock and appear offensive to that majority. It was however essential, in a pluralist democratic society, to allow the free expression of minority ideas and it was the duty of the authorities to guarantee the applicants the right to demonstrate peacefully.[175]

8.3.3 The limits of Article 11

The ECtHR has identified the limits of Article 11. The prominence of certain right-holders leads the Court to review their claims with particular scrutiny and rigour. Conversely, it identifies right-holders that do not play such a crucial role and do not qualify for such treatment. As the ECtHR held in *Christian Democratic People's Party v. Moldova*:

> Freedom of association and political debate is not absolute, however, and it must be accepted that where an association, through its activities or the intentions it has expressly or by implication declared in its programme, jeopardises the State's institutions or the rights and freedoms of others, Article 11 does not deprive the State of the power to protect those institutions and persons. It is for the Court to give a final ruling on the compatibility of such measures with the freedom of expression enshrined in Article 10.[176]

---

173 *United Communist Party of Turkey and Others v. Turkey*, para. 46.
174 *Gorzelik and Others v. Poland*, App. No. 44158/98, 17 February 2004, para. 91.
175 *Stankov and the United Macedonian Organisation Ilinden v. Bulgaria*, para. 64.
176 *Christian Democratic People's Party v. Moldova*, App. No. 28793/02, 14 February 2006, para. 69.

Balancing and justification at the ECtHR   179

The case of trade unions is certainly illustrative here. While the ECtHR protects the right of individuals to join or not to join a trade union as well as the right of trade unions to defend the interests of workers, the freedom to form a trade union is not inherent in Article 11 and therefore the Court does not grant the same level of protection. As the ECtHR held in *Syndicat national de la police belge v. Belgium*:

> La Cour relève que l'article 11 par. 1 (art. 11–1) présente la liberté syndicale comme une forme ou un aspect particulier de la liberté d'association; il ne garantit pas aux syndicats, ni à leurs membres, un traitement précis de la part de l'État et notamment le droit d'être consultés par lui. Non seulement ce dernier droit ne se trouve pas mentionné à l'article 11 par. 1 (art. 11–1), mais on ne saurait affirmer que les État contractants le consacrent tous en principe dans leur législation et leur pratique internes, ni qu'il soit indispensable à l'exercice efficace de la liberté syndicale. Partant, il ne constitue pas un élément nécessairement inhérent à un droit garanti par la Convention.[177]

Similarly, the ECtHR does not recognize the right to collective negotiation for trade unions.[178] On the other hand, the protection of political parties plainly falls within the scope of Article 11 in the Court's view despite the fact that they do not figure in the wording of Article 10. The ECtHR has formally recognized that political parties are prominent right-holders of freedom of association, as it held in *United Communist Party of Turkey and Others v. Turkey*:

> However, even more persuasive than the wording of Article 11, in the Court's view, is the fact that political parties are a form of association essential to the proper functioning of democracy. In view of the importance of democracy in the Convention system (see paragraph 45 below), there can be no doubt that political parties come within the scope of Article 11.[179]

In the same case, the Commission derived the right to pursue political activities freely from Article 11: "the Commission took the view that freedom of association not only concerned the right to form a political party but also guaranteed the right of such a party, once formed, to carry on its political activities freely".[180] In the same case, the ECtHR elaborated on the prevalent role of association for political parties:

> Such expression is inconceivable without the participation of a plurality of political parties representing the different shades of opinion to be found within a country's population. By relaying this range of opinion, not only within political institutions but also – with the help of the media – at all levels

---

177 *Syndicat national de la police belge v. Belgium*, App. No. 4464/70, 27 October 1975, para. 38.
178 *Schmidt and Dahlström v. Sweden*, App. No. 5589/72, 6 February 1976.
179 *United Communist Party of Turkey and Others v. Turkey*, para. 25.
180 Ibid., para. 33.

180   *Balancing and justification at the ECtHR*

of social life, political parties make an irreplaceable contribution to political debate, which is at the very core of the concept of a democratic society.[181]

The subject matter is essentially the creation and dissolution of political parties in view of democratic elections. In *Presidential Party of Mordovia v. Russia*, the ECtHR emphasized how the interference with Article 11 prevented the political party from running for elections:

> The Court accepts that the measure in question must have affected the applicant party, as claimed, since it was unable to function for a substantial period of time and could not participate in regional elections. Furthermore, the damage appears irreparable given that, under current legislation, the party cannot be reconstituted in its original concept.[182]

In other words, the review by the ECtHR is particularly scrupulous when the formed association intends to submit its ideas and political project to the public and run for elections. The continuum is reinforced by the provision in the ECHR dedicated to this issue, to which I turn next.

8.4 Article 3 Protocol 1 (free elections)

Article 3 Protocol 1 provides for the right to regular, free and fair elections. It is intuitively obvious that this Article is normatively central to the pursuit of "democratic society" and "democracy". However, the more subtle question is how the ECtHR articulates the specific role of elections within the conception of democracy outlined above. Clearly, this Article leads the ECtHR to further its specification of "democratic society" in nature and scope. As I have argued above, the substantive and normative conception that transpires from Articles 10 and 11 is founded on the expression of views and opinions on issues of public interest. I now identify the role that Article 3 Protocol 1 plays in this practical reason in light of the nature and scope attributed to its correlative duties. Does the right to regular, free and fair elections imply that the regional parliament within the state should run elections? Do foreigners have to participate in elections? Does the right to elections imply a right to a referendum?

The abstract and indeterminate wording of Article 3 Protocol 1 implies that the ECtHR had to specify its object and scope in the very first case brought before it. In the seminal case of *Mathieu-Mohin v. Belgium*, the ECtHR held: "since the Court is being asked to determine complaints under Article 3 of Protocol No. 1 (P1-3) for the first time, it deems it necessary to indicate the meaning it ascribes to that Article (P1-3) in the context of the instant case".[183] The centrality of Article 3 (Protocol 1) to "democratic society" and "democracy" was stated immediately:

181 Ibid., para. 44.
182 *Presidential Party of Mordovia v. Russia*, App. No. 65659/01, 5 October 2004, para. 31.
183 *Mathieu-Mohin and Clerfayt v. Belgium*, App. No. 9267/81, 2 March 1987, para. 46.

According to the Preamble to the Convention, fundamental human rights and freedoms are best maintained by "an effective political democracy". Since it enshrines a characteristic principle of democracy, Article 3 of Protocol No. 1 (P1-3) is accordingly of prime importance in the Convention system.[184]

This became a general principle of the ECtHR until the most recent cases, such as *Yumak and Sadak v. Turkey*.[185] In *X v. United Kingdom*, the former Commission had already specified that:

La "libre expression de l'opinion du peuple" signifie essentiellement que les élections ne sauraient comporter une quelconque pression sur le choix d'un ou plusieurs candidats et que, dans ce choix, l'électeur ne soit pas indûment incité à voter pour un parti ou pour un autre.[186]

In other words, the right to election implies the right to a *secret ballot* by universal suffrage.

8.4.1 The specification of "legislative body"

In the same *Mathieu-Mohin* case, the ECtHR approved the Commission's specification: the right to free election implies the "right to vote", "the right to stand for election for the legislature" and "universal suffrage".[187] The ECtHR has also distinguished the right to vote and the right to run for election in their passive/ active aspects, as in *Etxeberria and Others v. Spain*:

La Cour distingue entre le droit de vote, dans l'aspect « actif » des droits garantis par l'article 3 du Protocole no 1 et le droit de se présenter aux élections, qui en constitue son aspect « passif » entre le droit de vote, dans l'aspect « actif » des droits garantis par l'article 3 du Protocole no 1 et le droit de se présenter aux élections, qui en constitue son aspect "passif".[188]

The rationale is now established:

The Court points out that implicit in Article 3 of Protocol No. 1, which provides for "free" elections at "reasonable intervals" "by secret ballot" and "under conditions which will ensure the free expression of the opinion of the people", are the subjective rights to vote and to stand for election.[189]

---

184 Ibid., para. 47.
185 *Yumak and Sadak v. Turkey*, App. No. 10226/03, 8 July 2008, para. 105.
186 *X v. United Kingdom*, App. No. 7140/75, 6 October 1976, p. 99.
187 *X v. Federal Republic of Germany*, App. No. 2728/66, 6 October 1967, p. 38.
188 *Etxeberria and Others v. Spain*, App. Nos. 35579/03, 35613/03, 35626/03, 35634/03, 11 December 2007, para. 50.
189 *Labita v. Italy*, App. No. 26772/95, 6 April 2000, para. 201.

182 Balancing and justification at the ECtHR

This has been a constant reasoning, as in the recent case of *Sitaropoulos and Giakoumopoulos v. Greece*.[190] However, the lack of determination remains: what is a legislative body? Some important developments are found in early cases reviewed by the Commission in the early 1980s. For instance, in *Moureaux and Others v. France*, the Commission specified that a legislative body must issue provisions that must have "the force of law" and "in matters expressly assigned to it".[191] In doing so, the ECtHR prevents *consultative bodies* from falling within the scope of the Article. In *Booth-Clibborn v. United Kingdom*, which related to the qualification of metropolitan county councils, the former Commission held that the mere power to initiate laws does not fall within the scope of the notion: "they do not possess an inherent primary rule-making power and those powers which have been delegated to them are qualified by the parliament of the United Kingdom and exercised subject to that Parliament's ultimate control".[192] In *X v. The Netherlands*, the Commission also ruled out the right to vote for *professional associations* despite the fact that the association in question has a legislative function.[193]

Interestingly, the ECtHR waited until 1999 to specify "legislative body" in face of the developing EU – in particular, in light of the Maastricht Treaty in 1999 – and the qualification of its Parliament as a supranational representative organ in *Matthews v. United Kingdom*, to which the Court answered affirmatively. Most importantly, the ECtHR held that the body should be "a means of providing for electoral representation"[194] with "a decisive role to play in the legislative process".[195] Moreover, the legislative body must exercise control over the executive body, as the ECtHR noted in the case of the Council of the European Union: "it is not open to the Council to pass measures against the will of the European Parliament".[196] It has previously made explicit that the right to vote does not apply to executive bodies[197] and that it does not imply the right to a referendum.[198] Those early jurisprudential developments clearly suggest that the Court's supervision focuses on the election of the national parliament, but not exclusively. As the ECtHR held in *Py v. France*, "the Court reiterates at the outset that the word 'legislature' does not necessarily mean the national parliament; it has to be interpreted in the light of the constitutional structure of the State in question".[199] When significant powers are transferred to regional parliaments, as is the case in federalized states, the Commission and the ECtHR have recognized the applicability of Article 3

---

190 *Sitaropoulos and Giakoumopoulos v. Greece*, App. No. 42202/07, 15 March 2012, para. 59.
191 *Moureaux v. France*, App. No. 9267/81, 12 July 1983, para. 61.
192 *Booth-Clibborn and Others v. United Kingdom*, App. No. 11391/85, 5 July 1985, p. 248.
193 *X v. The Netherlands*, App. No. 2290/64, 6 February 1967, p. 248.
194 *Matthews v. United Kingdom*, App. No. 24833/94, 18 February 1999, para. 42.
195 Ibid., para. 50.
196 Ibid., para. 51.
197 *Habsburg-Lothringen v. Austria*, App. No. 15344/89, 14 December 1989.
198 *Bader v. Austria*, App. No. 26633/95, 15 May 1996.
199 *Py v. France*, App. No. 66289/01, 11 January 2005, para. 36.

Balancing and justification at the ECtHR 183

Protocol 1. This is the case, for instance, with Austrian[200] and German *Länder*[201] as well as Spanish regions.[202]

8.4.2 The interest protected

By contrast to the vast majority of ECHR rights, the wording of Article 3 Protocol 1 does not establish individual rights and freedoms, but requires States Parties to comply with the requirement of democratic elections. As the ECtHR explained in *Zdanoka v. Latvia*:

> Article 3 of Protocol No. 1 differs from other rights guaranteed by the Convention and its Protocols as it is phrased in terms of the obligation of the High Contracting Party to hold elections which ensure the free expression of the opinion of the people rather than in terms of a particular right or freedom.[203]

As a result, it is through legal reasoning that the ECtHR came to identify the individual interest protected by the provision. For instance, a set of important implications pertains to the *protection of the mandate* of elected politicians. Here, again, the ECtHR is recognizing, specifying and allocating the duties of the right in question. In doing so, the Court ascertains the normative reach of the ECHR right in question. More precisely, the fulfilment of the right to have free, fair and regular elections itself – that is, whether the election is effectively realized – is not sufficient for the value it protects, the representation of the electorate; it is crucial that the elected parliamentarian actually can hold office. In *Sadak and Others v. Turkey*, "the Court, like the Commission, considers that this Article guarantees the individual's right to stand for election and, once elected, to sit as a member of parliament".[204] The ECtHR went on to rely on the principle of *legitimate expectation*, according to which the elected parliamentarian should serve the representation of his or her constituents. In *Lykourezos v. Greece*, which involved the disqualification by the Special Supreme Court of a Greek parliamentarian for exercising a profession, the ECtHR found a violation:

> In those circumstances, the Court concludes that, by considering the applicant's election under the new Article 57 of the Constitution without taking into account that he had been elected in 2000 in full accordance with the law, the Special Supreme Court had caused him to forfeit his seat and had deprived

---

200 *X v. Austria*, App. No. 7008/75, 12 July 1976.
201 *Timke v. Germany*, App. No. 27311/95, 11 September 1995.
202 *Federacion nacionalista Canaria v. Spain*, App. No. 56618/00, 7 June 2001.
203 *Zdanoka v. Latvia*, App. No. 58278/00, 16 March 2006, para. 102.
204 *Sadak and Others v. Turkey (No. 2)*, App. Nos. 25144/94, 26149/95, 26150/95, 26151/95, 26152/95, 26153/95, 26154/95, 27100/95, 27101/95, 11 June 2002, para. 33.

184 *Balancing and justification at the ECtHR*

his constituents of the candidate whom they had chosen freely and democratically to represent them for four years in Parliament, in breach of the principle of legitimate expectation.[205]

The ECtHR places great weight on the citizen's interest in effective representation after the election has taken place. In *Kavakçı v. Turkey*, it created a rule:

> Il lui faut s'assurer que les conditions auxquelles sont subordonnés les droits de vote ou de se porter candidat à des élections ne réduisent pas les droits dont il s'agit au point de les atteindre dans leur substance même et de les priver de leur effectivité . . . . De même, une fois le choix du peuple librement et démocratiquement exprimé, aucune modification ultérieure dans l'organisation du système électoral ne saurait remettre en cause ce choix, sauf en présence de motifs impérieux pour l'ordre démocratique.[206]

The interest of citizens in being effectively represented by their elected politicians is clearly driving the reasoning of the ECtHR, as it held in *Ahmed and Others v. United Kingdom*:

> Members of the public also have a right to expect that the members whom they voted into office will discharge their mandate in accordance with the commitments they made during an electoral campaign and that the pursuit of that mandate will not flounder on the political opposition of their members' own advisers.[207]

The interest captured by the ECtHR is also salient when the ECtHR specifies what a "regular election" implies. Why is the regularity of free and fair elections important? In *Timke v. Germany*, the Commission explicitly tackled the justification of this clause:

> The Commission finds that the question whether elections held at reasonable intervals must be determined by the reference to the purpose of parliamentary elections. That purpose is to ensure that fundamental changes in prevailing public opinion are reflected in the opinions of the representatives of the people. Parliaments must in principle be in a position to develop and execute its legislative intentions – including longer term legislative plans. Too short an interval between elections may impede political planning for the implementation of the will of the electorate. Too long an interval can lead to the petrification of political groupings in Parliament which may no longer bear any resemblance to the prevailing will of the electorate.[208]

---

205 *Lykourezos v. Greece*, App. No. 33554/03, 15 June 2006, para. 57.
206 *Kavakçı v. Turkey*, App. No. 71907/01, 5 April 2007, para. 41.
207 *Ahmed and Others v. United Kingdom*, App. No. 22954/93, 2 September 1998, para. 53.
208 *Timke v. Germany*, p. 160.

Balancing and justification at the ECtHR 185

Clearly, the ECtHR is protecting the expression of the opinion of the electorate through the right to free, fair and regular elections. There must be a regular *test* of representation between the opinions of the represented electorate and the representative legislative body which enacts laws. This emphasis on the protection of "prevailing public opinion" also allows one to capture the normative interdependence, in the Court's view, of Article 3 Protocol 1 with Article 10 (freedom of expression) and Article 11 (freedom of association) through the overarching conception of democracy they serve. In the recent *Lesquen du Plessis-Casso v. France*, the ECtHR makes clear that the same rationale applies for the elected member of the opposition under Article 10 (freedom of expression):

> La Cour rappelle également que, précieuse pour chacun, la liberté d'expression l'est tout particulièrement pour les partis politiques et leurs membres actifs. En effet, des ingérences dans la liberté d'expression d'un membre de l'opposition, qui représente ses électeurs, signale leurs préoccupations et défend leurs intérêts, commandent à la Cour de se livrer à un contrôle des plus stricts.[209]

Of course, if they form part of a continuum, they do not play the same specific role. Freedom of expression, we have seen, prevails during pre-electoral periods. In *Bowman v. United Kingdom*, the ECtHR held that "for this reason, it is particularly important in the period preceding an election that opinions and information of all kinds are permitted to circulate freely".[210] The role of the press and its special status in the practical reason of the ECtHR are also central to the quest for the electorate to be represented by the legislative body, as we have seen. In other words, in the Court's view, respect for Articles 10 and 11, as specified by the ECtHR, are necessary conditions for the expression of public opinion and its representation by the legislative body through Article 3 Protocol 1, and therefore precedes it.

Further, the ECtHR connects the right to elections with freedom of expression associated with the interest specified – that is, the protection of informed debate on issues of public interest. In *Bowman v. United Kingdom*, the ECtHR held the following:

> Free elections and freedom of expression, particularly freedom of political debate, together form the bedrock of any democratic system . . . . The two rights are inter-related and operate to reinforce each other: for example, as the Court has observed in the past, freedom of expression is one of the "conditions" necessary to "ensure the free expression of the opinion of the people in the choice of the legislature".[211]

---

209 *Lesquen du Plessis-Casso v. France*, App. No. 54216/09, 12 April 2012, para. 38.
210 *Bowman v. United Kingdom*, para. 42.
211 Ibid.

186 *Balancing and justification at the ECtHR*

The practical reason of the ECtHR is here fully deployed: not only does the Court recognize and allocate the correlative duties of ECHR rights; it also clearly determines their respective role in the pursuit of "democratic society".

8.4.3 The limits of Article 3 Protocol 1

Should all candidates be equally equipped to run for elections? Should all constituencies have the same representation in the parliament irrespective of their population? Does the right to free elections imply the right to a referendum? These are some of the questions on which the ECtHR reveals the limits of its supervision and, consequently, the limited duties correlative to the right in question. As I have explained earlier, the structure of the practical reason of the ECtHR is such that it enlarges or restricts the margin of appreciation shown to States Parties depending on how the right in question serves the normative conception pursued. This specification in turn determines the respective normative weight of other ECHR rights and the correlative duties that serve the ideal. The interdependence of Articles 10 and 11 and Article 3 Protocol 1 is particularly salient. The interest protected by Article 3 Protocol 1 and specified by the ECtHR also implies that the correlative duties are limited to the core of the interest – especially when an enlarged set of duties would imply significant changes in the constitutional arrangements of States Parties.

The prevalent interest protected by Article 3 Protocol 1 is the expression of the opinion of the electorate in the legislative body. Conditions for elections "must reflect, or not run counter to, the concern to maintain the integrity and effectiveness of an electoral procedure aimed at identifying the will of the people through universal suffrage".[212] The ECtHR generates positives duties for States Parties to meet this threshold. As it reiterated in the recent case of *Yumak and Sadak v. Turkey*: "The State is under an obligation to adopt positive measures to 'organise' democratic elections 'under conditions which will ensure the free expression of the opinion of the people in the choice of the legislature'".[213] This implies, most importantly, the absence of pressure on the voters, as the ECtHR held in the same case:

> The words "free expression of the opinion of the people" mean that elections cannot be conducted under any form of pressure in the choice of one or more candidates, and that in this choice the elector must not be unduly induced to vote for one party or another.[214]

However, the ECtHR does not require States Parties to conform to a specific system of elections and representation and the type of ballot designed (proportional, majority, etc.) as long as this core interest is effectively protected, as the ECtHR held in the seminal *Mathieu-Mohin v. Belgium*:

---

212 *Lykourezos v. Greece*, para. 52.
213 *Yumak and Sadak v. Turkey*, para. 106.
214 Ibid., para. 108.

Balancing and justification at the ECtHR   187

Article 3 (P1-3) provides only for "free" elections "at reasonable intervals", "by secret ballot" and "under conditions which will ensure the free expression of the opinion of the people". Subject to that, it does not create any "obligation to introduce a specific system" . . . such as proportional representation or majority voting with one or two ballots. Here too the Court recognises that the Contracting States have a wide margin of appreciation, given that their legislation on the matter varies from place to place and from time to time.[215]

Furthermore, the ECtHR has made explicit that neither *equality of opportunity* for election nor *equality of the result* of the election fall within the scope of Article 3 Protocol 1:

It does not follow, however, that all votes must necessarily have equal weight as regards the outcome of the election or that all candidates must have equal chances of victory. Thus no electoral system can eliminate "wasted votes". For the purposes of Article 3 of Protocol No. 1 (P1-3), any electoral system must be assessed in the light of the political evolution of the country concerned; features that would be unacceptable in the context of one system may accordingly be justified in the context of another, at least so long as the chosen system provides for conditions which will ensure the "free expression of the opinion of the people in the choice of the legislature".[216]

A similarly limited supervisory role is reflected in *Bompard v. France*, in which the ECtHR had to assess whether population differences infringed the principle of equal suffrage of constituencies in France. In this decision, the ECtHR clearly confines its assessment to the core interest of the protected right:

In view of the foregoing, the Court considers that the introduction of such a system of electoral boundaries ensured that the right to vote was granted under conditions that reflected the need to ensure both citizen participation and knowledge of the particular situation of the region in question, fully in accordance with Article 3 of Protocol No. 1 . . . . In particular, those conditions could not in themselves have had the effect of impeding the "free expression of the opinion of the people in the choice of the legislature".[217]

In other words, discrepancies in representation do not affect the core interest on which the ECtHR focuses. Note that the Court here is referring to the *structural* use of the margin of appreciation outlined earlier in this chapter, according to which it *refrains* from balancing the interests at stake and does not specify the reasons for limiting the scope of ECHR rights. As I have argued, following Letsas, "the notions of proportionality and deference . . . cannot by themselves provide any

215 *Mathieu Mohin and Clerfayt v. Belgium*, para. 54.
216 Ibid.
217 *Bompard v. France*, App. No. 44081/02, 4 April 2006, p. 9.

188 *Balancing and justification at the ECtHR*

clear guidance since their content turns on which moral theory underlies human rights".[218] The same is true, for instance, for domestic legislation that imposes a minimum age for exercising the right to vote.[219]

Another illustrative subject area concerns right-holders who hold a position as a public official (civil servants, police officers, the judiciary, etc.) of the respondent State Party. In general, the ECtHR is reluctant to restrict this right given its centrality to the concept of democracy pursued.[220] However, absent from the text of the ECHR, the ECtHR has assessed the issue in light of the core interest protected – that is, the representation of the prevailing opinions of the electorate by the elected legislative body – for public officials may have a greater power of influence as candidates and may exercise pressure over voters as a result of their position. In *Gitonas v. Greece*, which concerned the right to run for election for deputy head of the Greek Prime Minister's private office, the ECtHR held:

> Such disqualification, for which equivalent provisions exist in several member States of the Council of Europe, serves a dual purpose that is essential for the proper functioning and upholding of democratic regimes, namely ensuring that candidates of different political persuasions enjoy equal means of influence (since holders of public office may on occasion have an unfair advantage over other candidates) and protecting the electorate from pressure from such officials who, because of their position, are called upon to take many – and sometimes important – decisions and enjoy substantial prestige in the eyes of the ordinary citizen, whose choice of candidate might be influenced.[221]

Note that the ECtHR held a similar view on the right of lawyers to run for elections.[222] However, the Court justifies its position on *consensualist*, rather than substantive grounds. As explained earlier in this chapter, the ECtHR uses the comparison of national legislation as a justificatory device in favour of the applicant only when there is *enough* commonality between States Parties – an inductive form of reasoning.

A final illustration of the practical reason of the ECtHR applies to the right to a referendum. *A priori*, why shouldn't the right to a referendum fall within the scope of the right to free, fair and regular elections? The only difference between the two is that the referendum does not address the candidate for parliamentary representation, but addresses a norm. The ECtHR has firmly rejected the right to a referendum on the ground that the Article protects the right to elect the legislative body only.[223] The Court's attachment to parliamentary and representative democracy – national, or regional in some special cases – as the domain of Article 3

218 Letsas, "Two Concepts of the Margin of Appreciation", 731.
219 *Hilbe v. Liechtenstein*, App. No. 31981/96, 7 September 1999.
220 *Kavakçı v. Turkey*, para. 45.
221 *Gitonas and Others v. Greece*, App. Nos. 18747/91, 19376/92, 19379/92, 28208/95, 27755/95, 1 July 1997, para. 40.
222 *Lykourezos v. Greece*, para. 57.
223 *Hilbe v. Liechtenstein*, p. 3.

is therefore salient. The same is true for the issue of bicameralism: the ECtHR has made explicit that the right to election applies "only to the election of the 'legislature', or at least of one of its chambers if it has two or more".[224] This has been constant in the reasoning of the Court, as in the recent case of *Sejdić and Finci v. Bosnia-Herzegovina.*[225]

8.5 "Democratic society" and the external concept of sovereignty: Article 9 (freedom of thought and religion)

The wording of the first paragraph of Article 9 proclaims freedom of thought, conscience and religion. The second paragraph largely replicates the formula used for balancing interests in the restriction clauses of Articles 8, 10 and 11. We may expect that the reasoning of the ECtHR is congruent with the "practical reason" developed in respect of Articles 10 and 11. Here, again, the ECtHR is recognizing, specifying and allocating the duties correlative to the right in question in a way that informs our quest for the normative foundations of ECHR rights. As with other Articles, the abstract wording of Article 9 required the Commission and the ECtHR to specify the interest that it protects. The "general principle" asserted by the ECtHR regarding the role of freedom of thought, conscience and religion in serving "democratic society" is found most clearly in *Kokkinakis v. Greece*:

> As enshrined in Article 9 (art. 9), freedom of thought, conscience and religion is one of the foundations of a "democratic society" within the meaning of the Convention. It is, in its religious dimension, one of the most vital elements that go to make up the identity of believers and their conception of life, but it is also a precious asset for atheists, agnostics, sceptics and the unconcerned. The pluralism indissociable from a democratic society, which has been dearly won over the centuries, depends on it.[226]

As for Articles 10 and 11, the notion of pluralism plays a core justificatory role; "democratic society", the ECtHR argues, cannot hold without a plurality of religious beliefs, as it cannot hold without a plurality of political ideas and opinions. Yet the case law of the ECtHR on Article 9 displays some intriguing peculiarities. It is congruent with the reasoning under Articles 10 and 11 and Article 3 Protocol 1 only to a limited extent. In the following sections, I show that the cases brought before the ECtHR and the interests protected do not receive similar scrutiny and are not resolved by the Court through the same justificatory grounds. This is salient in the loose definition of the core of the interests protected by the rights, the absence of positive duties generated as well as a wider margin of appreciation given to States Parties in a significant set of cases where the ECtHR assesses the conception of morals within the State Party in question.

---

224 *Mathieu-Mohin and Clerfayt v. Belgium*, para. 53.
225 *Sejdić and Finci v. Bosnia-Herzegovina*, App. Nos. 27996/06, 34836/06, 22 December 2009, para. 40.
226 *Kokkinakis v. Greece*, App. No. 14307/88, 25 May 1993, para. 31.

190 *Balancing and justification at the ECtHR*

This is not to say that the ECtHR does not protect Article 9 rights on independent grounds and that those grounds are salient in the case law. I do not hold that rights in general and ECHR rights in particular derive from a single normative foundation.[227] "Personal identity", "conception of life" or "dignity", as in the *Kokkinakis* case, are instances of those. In the absence of convincing argument by the respondent State Party, the ECtHR does not scrutinize whether the wearing of religious symbols, for instance, should be valued on grounds other than those. There are typical cases of violations of Article 9 in which the ECtHR finds violations just by discarding the list of possible restriction clauses one after the other.[228] The clearest case perhaps concerns the curtailing of access to places of worship and restricting the ability of adherent participants in religious observances.[229] Yet those arguments refer to the requirement of *state neutrality vis-à-vis* individuals rather than the accountability or responsiveness of the state in exercising public power. This was precisely the argument advanced by the respondent State Party in *Dahlab v. Switzerland*[230] and reiterated in the recent case of *Bayatyan v. Armenia*:

> The Court has frequently emphasised the State's role as the neutral and impartial organiser of the exercise of various religions, faiths and beliefs, and stated that this role is conducive to public order, religious harmony and tolerance in a democratic society. The State's duty of neutrality and impartiality is incompatible with any power on the State's part to assess the legitimacy of religious beliefs or the ways in which those beliefs are expressed.[231]

The idea that individual flourishing is served by the exercise of religious faith can operate without assuming any specific understanding of the representation of individuals in legislative bodies and their right to equal say in public debate. In other words, Article 9 serves an *individual* end in *itself*, while Articles 10 and 11 and Article 3 Protocol 1 serve an end that is *societal* and *political*, as their normative force lies in the normative legitimacy of the elected representatives. In other words, I show that we cannot explain such asymmetry – in terms of margin of appreciation and justificatory grounds – without emphasizing the respective normative weight of those rights in the search for a conception of "democratic society" as it transpires from Articles 10 and 11 and Article 3 Protocol 1. True, the emphasis of the ECtHR on pluralism, both in political ideas and religious faith, is anchored in the same justificatory pattern – it is deemed to be "foundational" to democratic society. The protection of pluralism in religious faiths is conducive to social cohesion in the Court's view, as it held in *Erçep v. Turkey*:

---

227 Waldron, *Dignity, Rank, and Rights*, 17.
228 *Ahmet Arslan and Others v. Turkey*, App. No. 41135/98, 23 February 2010, paras 46–52.
229 *Cyprus v. Turkey*, App. No. 25781/94, 10 May 2001.
230 *Dahlab v. Switzerland*, App. No. 30814/06, 18 March 2011.
231 *Bayatyan v. Armenia*, App. No. 23459/03, 7 July 2011, para. 120.

Ainsi, une situation où l'Etat respecte les convictions d'un groupe religieux minoritaire, comme celui auquel appartient le requérant, en donnant à ses membres la possibilité de servir la société conformément aux exigences de leur conscience, est de nature à assurer le pluralisme dans la cohésion et la stabilité et à promouvoir l'harmonie religieuse et la tolérance au sein de la société.[232]

However, those latter articles pertain to the free circulation and representation of political ideas and opinions on issues of public interest. By contrast, Article 9 remains tied to personal beliefs and conscience – in particular, those that have to do with religious faith. The ECtHR made the distinction between "opinions" or "ideas" and "beliefs" explicit in *Campbell and Cosans v. United Kingdom*:

> In its ordinary meaning the word "convictions", taken on its own, is not synonymous with the words "opinions" and "ideas", such as are utilised in Article 10 (art. 10) of the Convention, which guarantees freedom of expression; it is more akin to the term "beliefs" (in the French text: "convictions") appearing in Article 9 (art. 9) – which guarantees freedom of thought, conscience and religion – and denotes views that attain a certain level of cogency, seriousness, cohesion and importance.[233]

I will try to show that this distinction is of paramount importance in the articulation of the practical reason of the ECtHR. As I have argued above, the interdependence, in the Court's view, of Article 3 Protocol 1 with Article 10 (freedom of expression) and Article 11 (freedom of association) is significant. Moreover, I have argued that this interdependence is governed by the Court's "democratic society" that those rights each serve. Article 9 serves this normative conception too, but only to a limited extent – an extent that needs to be captured. When it does not serve the ideal, the stringency of the protection is limited – primarily via a more expansive use of the margin of appreciation doctrine.

Of course, the current limited standing of Article 9 in the case law is primarily because the Article *prima facie* embraces the same set of values and interests as its neighbouring guarantees in the text of the ECHR – especially with regard to Articles 10 and 11. The wording of the Article – in particular, the terms "thought, conscience and religion" in the first paragraph and "religion or beliefs" in the second – suggests interests that may be fully operative within the scope of Articles 10 and 11. Freedom of speech, for instance, is associated with certain foreseeable patterns of behaviour that clearly imply freedoms of thought, conscience and religion. The external dimension of freedom of thought – in particular, its manifestation in the public sphere – may be clearly interpreted in light of Article 10. As Marshall puts it, "the qualified part of Article 9, like Article 10, is perceived as concerned with external public manifestation, hence the more likely availability

---

232 *Erçep v. Turkey*, App. No. 43965/04, 22 November 2011, para. 62.
233 *Campbell and Cosans v. United Kingdom*, App. Nos. 7511/76, 7743/76, 22 February 1982, para. 36.

192 Balancing and justification at the ECtHR

of a range of intervening public interests, potentially limiting the limitations of rights".[234] Also, when Article 9 is invoked in its collective dimension – most clearly in instances of worship with others – then it is interpreted in light of Article 11. As a result, the ECtHR has made explicit that Article 9 does not guarantee the expression or act motivated by personal thought, conscience and belief in the public sphere. In *Van Den Dungen v. The Netherlands*, the Commission held:

> However, in protecting this personal sphere, Article 9 (Art. 9) of the Convention does not always guarantee the right to behave in the public sphere in a way which is dictated by such a belief. The Commission has constantly held that the term "practice" in Article 9 para. 1 (Art. 9-1) does not cover each act which is motivated or influenced by a religion or belief.[235]

As a result, the grounds invoked by applicants for an alleged violation of Article 9 may already be operative in an alleged violation of Article 10 or 11. The ECtHR has in many instances concluded that the issues raised by an application are better resolved by considering the applicability of Article 10[236] or Article 11.[237] Note that this a point about the scope of applicability of the Article, not a point about the justificatory grounds invoked by the ECtHR. True, freedom of thought, conscience and religion rarely serves the normative conception of "democratic society" in a way that is not already instantiated by the interests covered by Articles 10 and 11 and Article 3 Protocol 1. However, it remains to be seen where Article 9 operates, what are the prevalent interests protected and how those are weighed against competing collective interests in given circumstances. I show that the practical reason developed by the ECtHR in the distinctive cases under Article 9 contrasts with those Articles in the substantive reasons provided for grounding, enlarging or restricting the scope of these rights, and that we need to appeal to other rights to explain the differential treatment.

8.5.1 The interest protected

Protection of personal thought, conscience and belief clearly implies the right to hold and change those beliefs. For the statement to hold, there must be a manifestation of a personal thought, conscience or belief of some kind in the public or private sphere.[238] As a result, the freedom implies the right to manifest a belief[239] or not to manifest a belief[240] as well as the freedom not to disclose a belief to the state – if, however, the right-holder can prove that the religious belief and its

---

234 Marshall, *Personal Freedom through Human Rights Law?*, 141.
235 *Van Den Dungen v. The Netherlands*, App. No. 22838/93, 22 February 1995.
236 *Feldek v. Slovakia*, App. No. 29032/95, 12 July 2001, paras 91–2.
237 *Refah Partisi (The Welfare Party) and Others v. Turkey*, para. 137.
238 *Arrowsmith v. United Kingdom*, paras 71–2.
239 *Buscarini and Others v. San Marino*, App. No. 24645/94, 12 February 1999, para. 39.
240 *Kokkinakis v. Greece*, para. 31.

Balancing and justification at the ECtHR 193

implications are really his or her own.[241] In all those instances, the interest in *personal autonomy* and *flourishing* is fully operative: to have the right to those freedoms implies not only the development and refinement of autonomous beliefs but also and correlatively the duty to protect from state indoctrination. The Commission is explicit in *Van Den Dungen v. The Netherlands* when it uses the term *"forum internum"* as the sphere of personal autonomy to be protected:

> The Commission recalls that Article 9 (Art. 9) of the Convention primarily protects the sphere of personal beliefs and religious creeds, i.e. the area which is sometimes called the *forum internum*. In addition, it protects acts which are intimately linked to these attitudes, such as acts of worship or devotion which are aspects of the practice of a religion or belief in a generally recognised form.[242]

In *Kokkinakis v. Greece*, the ECtHR emphasized the crucial contribution of freedom of thought, conscience and religion in the making of one's identity and conception of life. The fundamental character of the *forum internum* to the formation of an autonomous life is salient:

> It is, in its religious dimension, one of the most vital elements that go to make up the identity of believers and their conception of life, but it is also a precious asset for atheists, agnostics, sceptics and the unconcerned. The pluralism indissociable from a democratic society, which has been dearly won over the centuries, depends on it.[243]

Up to this point, the reasons advanced by the ECtHR to justify freedom of thought, conscience, religion, expression, assembly and association are interdependent. The continuum is salient: whether in the expression of a political opinion on issues of public interest or the thought in which it originated, the same appeal to the notions of personal autonomy – the *forum internum* – is at stake. However, the reasoning of the ECtHR reveals a *discontinuity* between Article 9 and other Articles and therefore questions the interests that those rights respectively serve or may serve. While the Court had to deal with distinctively political beliefs (such as pacifism[244] or communism[245] and treated them as alleged violations of Articles 10 and 11), the vast majority of cases scrutinized by the ECtHR concerns the holding of religious beliefs and the limits to the manifestation of those beliefs. This is where the discontinuity occurs in the reasoning of the ECtHR, which needs to be specified and accounted for.

---

241 *Kosteski v. The Former Yugoslav Republic of Macedonia*, App. No. 55170/00, 13 April 2006, para. 39.
242 *Van Den Dungen v. The Netherlands.*
243 *Kokkinakis v. Greece*, para. 31.
244 *Arrowsmith v. United Kingdom.*
245 *Hazar, Hazar and Acik v. Turkey*, App. No. 31451/03, 13 January 2009.

194 *Balancing and justification at the ECtHR*

As indicated above, Article 9 does not protect any kind of belief or any kind of manifestation of the belief. It therefore can be said that it determines the scope of the rights without specifying the core interest that the right protects. In the seminal *Pretty v. United Kingdom*, which concerned the belief in assisted suicide, the ECtHR held:

> The Court does not doubt the firmness of the applicant's views concerning assisted suicide but would observe that not all opinions or convictions constitute beliefs in the sense protected by Article 9 § 1 of the Convention. Her claims do not involve a form of manifestation of a religion or belief, through worship, teaching, practice or observance as described in the second sentence of the first paragraph. As found by the Commission, the term "practice" as employed in Article 9 § 1 does not cover each act which is motivated or influenced by a religion or belief.[246]

In other words, although the terms contained in the Article are wide, the reasoning of the ECtHR indicates a narrow approach focused on the intensity and stringency of personal thoughts and beliefs – those typically associated with religious faith and worship. In the same vein, the ECtHR does not protect within the scope of Article 9 a group's cultural identity,[247] the disposal of human remains after death[248] or the distribution of anti-abortion material.[249] This is where the prevalent interest protected by Article 9 can be identified. Note that this not informative about how those rights should be balanced against competing considerations, to which I turn next. Personal beliefs, to fall within Article 9, must "attain a certain level of cogency, seriousness, cohesion and importance" and the belief must reflect a "weighty and substantial aspect of human life and behaviour".[250]

8.5.2 The limits of Article 9

Once the interest is specified, it remains to see how the ECtHR circumscribes it and balances it with competing interests. It is one thing to say that the reasoning of the ECtHR under Article 9 targets an aspect of human life that pertains to the cogency of personal beliefs and thought – in particular, those beliefs related to the *forum internum*; it is another to say that such rights deserve a special level of protection when they compete with a compelling justification advanced by the respondent State Party. Rights are "rights" only when the interest they protect is specified and weighed against a competing interest in given circumstances.

First, the specification of the interest may not be so successful as to draw a clear line between what is "cogent thought and belief" and what is not, or what is

---

246 *Pretty v. United Kingdom*, App. No. 2346/02, 29 April 2002, para. 82.
247 *Sidiropoulos v. Greece*, App. No. 26695/95, 10 July 1998.
248 *Belgian Linguistic Case*.
249 *Knudsen v. Norway*, App. No. 11045/84, 8 March 1985.
250 *Campbell and Cosans v. United Kingdom*, para. 36.

Balancing and justification at the ECtHR 195

a manifestation of that belief and what is not. As many scholars have noted, the ECtHR has not specified what it takes to be a sufficiently strong manifestation of the belief in question to be protected. The ECtHR has rejected responsibility for defining the very concept of religion and falls back on the consensualist-justificatory track:

> The Court observes that the question whether or not Scientology may be described as a "religion" is a matter of controversy among the member States. It is clearly not the Court's task to decide *in abstracto* whether or not a body of beliefs and related practices may be considered a "religion" within the meaning of Article 9 of the Convention. In the absence of any European consensus on the religious nature of Scientology teachings, and being sensitive to the subsidiary nature of its role, the Court considers that it must rely on the position of the domestic authorities in the matter and determine the applicability of Article 9 of the Convention accordingly.[251]

Clearly, the reasoning of the ECtHR suggests that religious beliefs are typically those that engage the responsibility of the state rather than ecclesiastic bodies. Again, typical instances of interference involve curtailing access to places of worship and restricting the ability of adherent participants in religious observances.[252] However, the ECtHR has not said much about the foundations of such rights and, in particular, the link with the notions of "personal identity" and "conception of life"; as Marshall puts it, "this provision has been largely unsuccessful in upholding individuals' manifestation of their religious beliefs and the Court decisions have little to say about their connection with people's identity, particularly their identity formation".[253]

Second, the ECtHR tends not to recognize positive duties within the scope of Article 9, or it remains unclear of whether the duties require an active role on the part of the respondent State Party. In *Valsamis v. Greece*, which concerned the right of Jehovah's witnesses (and the pacifist beliefs associated with them) not to manifest and take part in the celebration of the National Day in Greece (held to commemorate the outbreak of war between Greece and Fascist Italy), the Commission did not require the state to adapt its activities to conform to the right-holders' beliefs and thoughts because those activities could not be taken as offending the beliefs of the right-holders:

> In the Government's submission, Article 9 (art. 9) protected only aspects of religious practice in a generally recognised form that were strictly a matter of conscience . . .

> The State was not under an obligation to take positive measures to adapt its activities to the various manifestations of its citizens' philosophical or religious beliefs . . .

---

251 *Kimlya and Others v. Russia*, App. Nos. 76836/01, 32782/03, 1 October 2009, para. 79.
252 *Cyprus v. Turkey.*
253 Marshall, *Personal Freedom through Human Rights Law?*, 141.

196 *Balancing and justification at the ECtHR*

> The Commission considered that Article 9 (art. 9) did not confer a right to exemption from disciplinary rules which applied generally and in a neutral manner and that in the instant case there had been no interference with the applicant's right to freedom to manifest her religion or belief.[254]

The ECtHR has derived a positive obligation for States Parties to ensure that individuals can foresee whether they can apply for the status of conscientious objector in the context of military service.[255] Moreover, when a State Party actively intervenes to mediate conflicts between communities within a single religion, the ECtHR does not require the State Party not to act positively in order to resolve the conflict. In *Supreme Holy Council of the Muslim Community v. Bulgaria*, the ECtHR found an interference with Article 9 on the ground that the State should not go beyond "neutral mediation".[256] Those justificatory grounds do not only reveal the prevalence of the requirement of *state neutrality vis-à-vis* individuals: the "State's role as the neutral and impartial organiser of the exercise of various religions, faiths and beliefs" that the ECtHR also grounds in the preservation of pluralism;[257] it also suggests that there is no stringent interest behind the right of religious groups to have their claims recognized and protected. In other words, while it is true that the ECtHR invokes pluralism as an important normative foundation, it neither specifies nor actively promotes it – as is the case in the practical reason of the ECtHR under Articles 10 and 11 and Article 3 Protocol 1.

Third, and most importantly, the ECtHR logically tends to accord a wider margin of appreciation to States Parties on sensitive issues pertaining to freedom of religion and, more broadly, on the "conception of morals". This directly echoes the lack of specification of the core interest that Article 9 protects. While the ECtHR reviews alleged violations of Article 10 with a high degree of rigour, it modifies the strictness of the scrutiny in the assessment of reasons for an interference of Article 9 rights. Again, this does not imply that such freedoms are not important in the eyes of the Court – they stand on an equal footing with others in the text of the ECHR – or that it does not protect important interests and values. Rather, it implies that the fixing of the scope of protection on sensitive issues is the resort of the States Parties on an important set of issues – while the ECtHR focuses only on a limited set of core duties. This restraint is not only salient in a number of cases; the ECtHR has also defended it as a principled normative claim. In *Wingrove v. United Kingdom*, it held:

> Whereas there is little scope under Article 10 para. 2 of the Convention (art. 10–2) for restrictions on political speech or on debate of questions of public interest . . ., a wider margin of appreciation is generally available to the

---

254 *Valsamis v. Greece*, App. No. 21787/93, 18 December 1996, para. 35.
255 *Tarhan v. Turkey*, App. No. 9078/06, 17 July 2012, para. 62.
256 *Supreme Holy Council of the Muslim Community v. Bulgaria*, App. No. 39023/97, 16 December 2004, para. 80.
257 Ibid., para. 96.

Balancing and justification at the ECtHR 197

Contracting States when regulating freedom of expression in relation to matters liable to offend intimate personal convictions within the sphere of morals or, especially, religion.[258]

Of course, the ECtHR does not explicitly hold that Article 9 is less central than Article 10 in serving the purpose(s) of the ECHR. Rather, it falls back on the consensualist absence of uniform conception in the field of religious beliefs:

> Moreover, as in the field of morals, and perhaps to an even greater degree, there is no uniform European conception of the requirements of "the protection of the rights of others" in relation to attacks on their religious convictions. What is likely to cause substantial offence to persons of a particular religious persuasion will vary significantly from time to time and from place to place, especially in an era characterised by an ever growing array of faiths and denominations. By reason of their direct and continuous contact with the vital forces of their countries, State authorities are in principle in a better position than the international judge to give an opinion on the exact content of these requirements with regard to the rights of others as well as on the "necessity" of a "restriction" intended to protect from such material those whose deepest feelings and convictions would be seriously offended.[259]

As I have argued earlier in the chapter, the consensualist method of interpretation is premised on the comparative analysis of the various national legislative instruments and conceptions across Europe in order to inductively generate the appropriate level of protection. In doing so, the ECtHR gives credence to the evolutive meaning and scope of the interests that the ECHR protects across Europe without bypassing the practices of States Parties. Such a move is not just a method of *interpretation* but also of *justification*; as we have explained, it is not a "method that actually yields the meaning of a Convention's provision, but instead is used to legitimate the Court's exercise of discretion".[260] It therefore exemplifies the *structural* use of the margin of appreciation doctrine; it is used to mask the judicial restraint of the ECtHR on the overriding grounds that actually justify the restriction.

Yet if this justificatory reasoning were to be consistent as a methodology, the ECtHR would apply it in the assessment of other ECHR rights. As I have argued, it is far from clear what kind of principled role consensualism plays in the adjudication of the ECtHR. When, for instance, the Court actively protects the duties correlative to Article 10, it does not use the consensualist method to justify its rigorous scrutiny and protective attitude; it explicitly appeals to a

---

258 *Wingrove v. United Kingdom*, App. No. 17419/90, 25 November 1996, para. 58.
259 Ibid.
260 Carozza, "Uses and Misuses of Comparative Law in International Human Rights: Some Reflections on the Jurisprudence of the European Court of Human Rights", 1225.

198 *Balancing and justification at the ECtHR*

normative conception of "democratic society" that it has itself specified – reflecting the prevalent *teleological* method of interpretation. The consensualist method is therefore not used as a justificatory device in this context. As I argue later in the chapter, this asymmetry has far-reaching consequences in our attempt to capture the overarching justificatory patterns of ECHR rights. The consensualist approach via the margin of appreciation doctrine refers to the *external* concept of sovereignty.

The most illustrative cases of the margin of appreciation accorded to States Parties under Article 9 perhaps pertain to the wearing of religious symbols – and, most famously, the issue of scarf wearing in schools and universities. It appears from the case law that the prohibition of such religious symbols amounts to an interference with the right to manifest religious beliefs. However, the ECtHR is very likely to recognize a certain margin of appreciation for the respondent State Party, on the ground that the State Party needs to prevent fundamentalist religious groups from exerting pressures on people that may amount to proselytic practices. In this case, when it held that the State Party "did not exceed their margin of appreciation and that the measure they took was therefore not unreasonable",[261] the ECtHR was using the *substantive* concept of the margin of appreciation, which addresses the relationship between individual and collective goals, and which actually "resolves" the balancing of conflicting interests. In *Leyla Şahin v. Turkey*, in which the applicant was prohibited from wearing a headscarf at university and thereby refused to attend classes, the ECtHR by contrast fell back on the consensualist-justificatory track, asserting that:

> Where questions concerning the relationship between State and religions are at stake, on which opinion in a democratic society may reasonably differ widely, the role of the national decision-making body must be given special importance . . . . It is not possible to discern throughout Europe a uniform conception of the significance of religion in society . . . and the meaning or impact of the public expression of a religious belief will differ according to time and context . . . . Rules in this sphere will consequently vary from one country to another according to national traditions and the requirements imposed by the need to protect the rights and freedoms of others and to maintain public order . . . . Accordingly, the choice of the extent and form such regulations should take must inevitably be left up to a point to the State concerned, as it will depend on the specific domestic context.[262]

It is, however, important to note that on this question the ECtHR makes a distinction between public space, on the one hand, and public schools or universities.[263]

---

261 *Dahlab v. Switzerland.*
262 *Leyla Şahin v. Turkey*, App. No. 44774/98, 10 November 2005, para. 80.
263 *Ahmet Arslan and Others v. Turkey*, para. 49.

8.6 Article 8 (Privacy)

I have shown above that cases brought before the ECtHR and the interests protected do not consistently receive similar scrutiny. This is concretely translated in the text of the case by the loose definition of the core interest protected by the provision, the absence of positive duties generated as well as a wider margin of appreciation accorded to States Parties in a significant set of cases – in particular, where the ECtHR assesses the conception of morals within the State Party in question and acknowledges the absence of consensus across Europe, which itself replaces the justificatory reasoning usually devoted to balancing. As I have explained earlier in this chapter, those are the cases where the consensualist method applies and, correlatively, where the margin of appreciation in the case of an absence of consensus is wide. Interestingly, a strikingly similar pattern can be seen in the Court's treatment of Article 8. In principle, the core interest protected by the provision has not been clearly specified. While the ECtHR has used more abstract and indeterminate notions such as "autonomy", it clearly refuses to determine the core interest protected by Article 8. Moreover, it usually accords the State Party a certain margin of appreciation. Nevertheless, the ECtHR has in some cases elaborated on the normative force of the provision against competing interests – more importantly, in the case of conflict between the right to reputation under Article 8 and the right to freedom of expression. In such cases, the ECtHR makes explicit the predominance of the latter over the former in relying on the normative conception that transpires from Articles 10 and 11 and Article 3 Protocol 1.

8.6.1 The interest protected

The text of the article states that the right is to respect private and family life, home and correspondence. Among other ECHR rights, the wording is particularly abstract and indeterminate and asks for specification. Is it limited negatively to the prohibitions of unwanted intrusion into a person's intimacy – usually defined as control over one's own body and health, one's sexual identity and life? Or does it encompass, for instance, the right to full knowledge of one's biological origins? In other words, what are the enabling conditions to properly exercise the right to privacy? The need for specification is reinforced by the concept of "family life" included in the provision that the ECtHR has examined in the relationships between single parents and their children, transsexuals and their partners or cohabitating homosexuals. Along the development of its case law, the ECtHR has taken a stand on all those issues, yet without being clearly willing to specify the core interest protected by the provision. The initial point of Article 8 as specified by the ECtHR was essentially that of protecting the individual against arbitrary interference by public authorities. However, the Court has quickly moved beyond this loose standard to incorporate an idea of moral and physical integrity. This was the case in *X and Y v. The Netherlands*, in which a violation was found following the failure of Dutch criminal law to provide effective protection for a mentally handicapped 16-year-old subjected to sexual assault:

200   *Balancing and justification at the ECtHR*

There was no dispute as to the applicability of Article 8 (art. 8): the facts underlying the application to the Commission concern a matter of "private life", a concept which covers the physical and moral integrity of the person, including his or her sexual life.[264]

Further, the provision encompasses the development of the fulfilment of one's personality – in particular, through relationships with other human beings. In *X v. Iceland*, the Commission held the following:

> For numerous Anglo-Saxon and French authors the right to respect for "private life" is the right to privacy, the right to live, as far as one wishes, protected from publicity . . . . In the opinion of the Commission, the right to respect for private life does not end there. It comprises also, to a certain degree, the right to establish and to develop relationships with other human beings, especially in the emotional field for the development and fulfilment of one's personality.[265]

In this case, the ECtHR had to decide whether a dog can fall within the scope of the provision, and did not find a violation. What the ECtHR has been keen to emphasize is that the concept of "private life" should not be restricted to the "inner circle" but should also encompass relationships with other human beings. In *Niemetz v. Germany*, the ECtHR held that:

> The Court does not consider it possible or necessary to attempt an exhaustive definition of the notion of "private life". However, it would be too restrictive to limit the notion to an "inner circle" in which the individual may live his own personal life as he chooses and to exclude therefrom entirely the outside world not encompassed within that circle. Respect for private life must also comprise to a certain degree the right to establish and develop relationships with other human beings.[266]

In the same vein, the ECtHR has extended the scope of the provision to "the sphere of imprisonment"[267] along the same lines. This jurisprudential development has given rise to some form of enthusiasm in the literature as to the existence of a right to personal autonomy. The ECtHR asserted *in Tysiac v. Poland* that "'private life' is a broad term, encompassing, inter alia, aspects of an individual's physical and social identity, including the right to personal autonomy, personal development and to establish and develop relationships with other human beings and the outside world".[268] As Marshall puts it, "the point of Article 8 has been

---

264 *X and Y v. The Netherlands*, App. No. 8978/80, 26 March 1985, para. 22.
265 *X v. Iceland*, App. No. 6825/74, 18 May 1976, p. 87.
266 *Niemetz v. Germany*, App. No. 13710/88, 16 December 1992, para. 29.
267 *McFeeley and Others v. United Kingdom*, App. No. 8317/78, 2 October 1984, para. 82.
268 *Tysiac v. Poland*, App. No. 5410/03, 23 March 2007, para. 107.

Balancing and justification at the ECtHR 201

described as involving not simply protecting people from the embarrassment of external scrutiny of their personal situations but also as respective of their dignity and sense of being valued".[269] True, the ECtHR has generated positive obligations, for instance, when the case involves core family relations such as the reunion of parents and children. Yet the Court has also made explicit that States Parties enjoy a margin of appreciation, as in the recent case of *Raw and Others v. France*:

> Cela étant, la Cour rappelle que, si l'article 8 de la Convention tend pour l'essentiel à prémunir l'individu contre des ingérences arbitraires des pouvoirs publics, il engendre aussi des obligations positives inhérentes à un "respect" effectif de la vie familiale. Dans un cas comme dans l'autre, il faut avoir égard au juste équilibre à ménager entre les intérêts concurrents de l'individu et de la société dans son ensemble; de même, dans les deux hypothèses, l'Etat jouit d'une certaine marge d'appréciation.[270]

However, the enlargement of the scope of a provision does not matter much if there is no clear statement, in the reasoning of the ECtHR, of the conditions under which it applies. The reluctance to capture the core interest and its association with the wide margin of appreciation the ECtHR accords in a majority of cases under Article 8 is indicative of judicial restraint. Accordingly, the Court extensively uses the consensualist approach, which replaces the justificatory reasoning usually devoted to balancing. As I explained earlier in the chapter, when enough "pan-European" commonality is not found, consensualism restricts the scope of the ECHR rights. In the seminal *Rees v. United Kingdom*, for instance, in which the ECtHR had to deal with non-recognition of a post-operative transsexual's new sexual identity as an alleged violation, the absence of consensus justified the use of the margin of appreciation doctrine:

> As the Court pointed out in its above-mentioned *Abdulaziz*, *Cabales* and *Balkandali* judgments the notion of "respect" is not clear-cut, especially as far as those positive obligations are concerned: having regard to the diversity of the practices followed and the situations obtaining in the Contracting States, the notion's requirements will vary considerably from case to case . . . . In other States, such an option does not – or does not yet – exist. It would therefore be true to say that there is at present little common ground between the Contracting States in this area and that, generally speaking, the law appears to be in a transitional stage. Accordingly, this is an area in which the Contracting Parties enjoy a wide margin of appreciation.[271]

The ECtHR revisited the case on several occasions over the years that followed until 2002 when, in *Goodwin v. United Kingdom*, it reversed its case law by

---

269 Marshall, *Personal Freedom through Human Rights Law?*, 70.
270 *Raw and Others v. France*, App. No. 10131/11, 7 March 2013, para. 78.
271 *Rees v. United Kingdom*, paras 36–7.

202 *Balancing and justification at the ECtHR*

giving priority to the interests of the applicant. By that time, consensus had become sufficient in the Court's eyes to grant protection to the applicant and restrict the State Party's margin of appreciation. The same reasoning applies to cases such as the Roma community's right to live in caravans when the ECtHR later stated that Article 8 does not give "a right to be provided with a home",[272] and further that "there is no explicit right under the Convention to a clean and quiet environment".[273]

8.6.2 The limits of Article 8

As in the case of Article 9, the specification of the interest by the ECtHR may not be successful in drawing a clear line between what falls within the scope of the provision and what does not. Under Article 8, it seems that such restraint is willingly assumed. It is true that, as under Article 9, the ECtHR may scrutinize the state's justification only in limited cases in which it applies the standard of the effect on personal autonomy. As the ECtHR held in the recent case of *Lashin v. Russia*, "where the measure under examination has such a drastic effect on the applicant's personal autonomy as in the present case . . ., the Court is prepared to subject the reasoning of the domestic authorities to a somewhat stricter scrutiny".[274]

However, the ECtHR has repeatedly refrained from providing a comprehensive definition of "private life". Another way of noting this indeterminacy is when the ECtHR explains that the distinction between positive and negative obligations does not lend itself to a precise definition. This goes in tandem with the Court's repeated assertion that in such matters States Parties enjoy a certain margin of appreciation. In *White v. Sweden*, the ECtHR makes those points explicit:

> The boundary between the State's positive and negative obligations under this provision does not lend itself to precise definition. The applicable principles are, nonetheless, similar. In both contexts regard must be had to the fair balance that has to be struck between the competing interests of the individual and of the community as a whole; and in both contexts the State enjoys a certain margin of appreciation.[275]

Yet the ECtHR does sometimes strike a balance and justifies its reasoning. It remains therefore to see how the ECtHR strikes the balance between the two rights in its *ad hoc* approach. As I outlined above, one part of my argument is that the justificatory reasoning of the ECtHR helps it to resolve conflicts between rights that formally stand on an equal footing in the text of the ECHR. This is clear, for instance, in the justificatory reasoning that prevails for Article 10 and its implications when it conflicts with the right to reputation under Article 8. In an article on the history of the conflict, Stijn Smet notes that "the effect of this recognition on the

---

272 *Chapman v. United Kingdom*, App. No. 27970/02, 24 June 2008, para. 99.
273 *Hatton and Others v. United Kingdom*, para. 96.
274 *Lashin v. Russia*, App. No. 33117/02, 22 January 2013, para. 81.
275 *White v. Sweden*, App. No. 42435/02, 19 September 2006, para. 20.

Balancing and justification at the ECtHR 203

legal reasoning of the Court under Article 10 has been minimal".[276] Why does the ECtHR tend not to recognize the conflict and favours preferential framing? In principle, the circumstances in which the interest in reputation may take precedence over the interest in expression on issues of public interest are particularly narrow. For instance, it occurs when the views expressed are not capable of being proven or supported by facts. In *Ivanova v. Bulgaria*, the ECtHR held that the more serious an allegation, the more solid the factual basis must be. This relates to the journalistic ethic promoted by the ECtHR, outlined earlier in the chapter:

> The Court must further examine whether the research done by the applicant before the publication of the untrue statement of fact was in good faith and complied with the ordinary journalistic obligation to verify a factual allegation. The Court's case law is clear on the point that the more serious the allegation is, the more solid the factual basis should be.[277]

Such an ethic was emphasized by the ECtHR in *Novaya Gazeta and Borodyanskiy v. Russia* in which the Court dwells on sociological considerations:

> These considerations play a particularly important role nowadays, given the influence wielded by the media in contemporary society: not only do they inform, they can also suggest by the way in which they present the information how it is to be assessed. In a world in which the individual is confronted with vast quantities of information circulated via traditional and electronic media and involving an ever-growing number of players, monitoring compliance with journalistic ethics takes on added importance.[278]

Interestingly, however, the demand for factual support is less stringent in the context of a lively political debate. This is precisely where the interest protected by Article 10 comes into play and deploys its normative force. In those cases, the ECtHR accords wide freedom to criticize even when the statements in question lack factual support. As I have argued above, the Court's attachment to the protection of freedom of the press is vital to an effective democracy in the role of transparently forming the opinions of individuals on issues of public interest. In *Lombardo v. Malta*, the ECtHR held:

> The Court would in any event observe that the distinction between statements of fact and value judgments is of less significance in a case such as the present, where the impugned statement is made in the course of a lively political debate at local level and where elected officials and journalists should enjoy a wide freedom to criticise the actions of a local authority, even where the statements made may lack a clear basis in fact.[279]

---

276 Smet, "Freedom of Expression and the Right to Reputation", 235.
277 *Ivanova v. Bulgaria*, App. No. 52435/99, 12 April 2007, para. 64.
278 *Novaya Gazeta and Borodyanskiy v. Russia*, App. No. 14087/08, 28 March 2013, para. 42.
279 *Lombardo v. Malta*, App. No. 7333/06, 24 April 2007, para. 60.

204 Balancing and justification at the ECtHR

More precisely, whenever there is a potential conflict of rights in defamation cases, the ECtHR places great emphasis on the presence of a public interest. As Smet puts it, "the Court links any public interest in hearing the statement to the public right to receive information on matters of public interest".[280] In turn, this public interest corresponds with the individual interest in being informed on issues of public interest – most importantly, the information related to elected representatives. In *Standard Verlag GmbH v. Austria*, the protection of a politician's reputation was clearly outweighed by the interest of being informed as to his credibility. This is another instance of the predominance of the right to freedom of expression and the interest to convey information on issues of public interest more broadly defined. This is clearly the case in *Romanenko v. Russia*, which involved allegations against a public servant:

> Both publications in the applicants' newspaper concerned the unlawful felling of trees and undocumented sale of timber to Chinese companies, a matter of intense public interest for residents of the Primorskiy region, where the timber industry was one of the main employers . . . . As the Court has held on many occasions, reporting on matters relating to management of public resources lies at the core of the media's responsibility and the right of the public to receive information. However, there is no evidence in the domestic judgments that the courts performed a balancing exercise between the need to protect the plaintiffs' reputation and the right of the members of the press to impart information on issues of general interest.[281]

Conversely, when an issue of general interest is not present, the right to reputation may prevail. This was the case, for instance, in *Karhuvaara and Iltalehti v. Finland*, in which the press was convicted for mentioning the name of a politician in an article on criminal proceedings against her husband:

> On the other hand, it is to be noted that the subject matter of the impugned reporting did not have any express bearing on political issues or any direct links with the person of Mrs A. as a politician. Consequently, the articles in question did not pertain to any matter of great public interest as far as Mrs A.'s involvement was concerned. However, the public has the right to be informed, which is an essential right in a democratic society that, in certain special circumstances, may even extend to aspects of the private life of public figures, particularly where politicians are concerned . . . . In this connection, the Court notes the District Court's opinion that the conviction of the spouse of a politician could affect people's voting intentions. In the Court's opinion this indicates that, at least to some degree, a matter of public interest was involved in the reporting.[282]

280 Smet, "Freedom of Expression and the Right to Reputation", 223–4.
281 *Romanenko v. Russia*, para. 42.
282 *Karhuvaara and Iltalehti v. Finland*, App. No. 53678/00, 16 November 2004, para. 45.

Balancing and justification at the ECtHR 205

Therefore, the ECtHR found a violation of Article 10. Clearly, the public interest at stake here is defined by the interdependence of Article 10 and Article 3 Protocol 1: criticism towards politicians – in particular, when they are candidates competing for election – is subject to wider protection and more intense scrutiny by the ECtHR, given the interest in the free circulation of information in pre-electoral periods.

More generally, in the conflict between the interest in expressing opinions on issues of public interest and the interest in reputation, the former takes precedence over the latter only in particular circumstances. One instance is precisely when there is no public interest to be protected. This is the case when the ECtHR finds that the criticisms serve no other purpose than to satisfy the curiosity of a certain readership, as in *Leempoel v. Belgium* where the publication in question criticized a judge's personality:

> La Cour a affirmé à plusieurs reprises que l'élément déterminant, lors de la mise en balance de la protection de la vie privée et de la liberté d'expression, doit résider dans la contribution que l'article publié apporte au débat d'intérêt général. Or force est de constater qu'en l'espèce cette contribution fait défaut.[283]

Even when allegations of criminal conduct impinge on the principle of the presumption of innocence, the public interest in information may take precedence over the right to reputation, as in *White v. Sweden*, in which newspaper articles ascribed criminal offences, including the murder of Prime Minister Olaf Palme, to the applicant. Another instance where Article 8 outweighs Article 10 is when applicants do not respect the Court's self-defined ethic of journalism. This was the case in *Alithia Publishing Company v. Cyprus*, which involved a civil defamation conviction for publishing a newspaper article accusing the former Minister of Defence of corruption:

> The applicants relied on the defence of fair comment, which required them to prove the alleged factual basis on which their statements had been based. The Court considers that it is not, in principle, incompatible with Article 10 to place the onus of proving, to the civil standard, the truth of the factual basis on which a value judgment was based.[284]

A final instance where the right to reputation takes precedence over Article 10 is when an attack on a person's reputation reaches a certain level of gravity and is considered to undermine that person's integrity. This concerned, for instance,

---

283 *Leempoel S.A. Ed. Ciné Revue v. Belgium*, App. No. 64772/01, 9 November 2008.
284 *Alithia Publishing Company Ltd and Constantinides v. Cyprus*, App. No. 17550/03, 22 May 2008, para. 69.

206 *Balancing and justification at the ECtHR*

the publication of photographs of the Princess of Monaco's everyday life[285] – in which the ECtHR made explicit that the criterion again is that the Princess does not play any official role in the government of the Principality – as well as the press disclosure of a private person's HIV-positive status.[286]

---

285 *Von Hannover v. Germany*, App. No. 59320/00, 24 June 2004, paras 62–5.
286 *Armonienė v. Lithuania*, App. No. 36919/02, 25 November 2008, para. 42.

9 Conclusion

Constructing the normative foundations of the ECHR

In the last chapter, I examined the exercise of balancing by the ECtHR in respect of Articles 8 to 11 and Article 3 Protocol 1. At this stage of the review, the ECtHR addresses the reasons provided by the parties and authoritatively settles the dispute. I concluded that despite the *prima facie* opaqueness of the interpretation stage, both the balancing stage and, more specifically, the third step of "democratic society" play a crucial role in striking the balance. I further argued that there is a salient *practical reason* – a set of powerful reasons by which state and individual actions are judged – that governs the Court's balancing of those Articles. Three instances of this practical reason were found. First, the ECtHR identifies the right-holders whose contribution to the realization of "democratic society" is particularly central. Their prominence leads the Court to review their claim(s) with particular scrutiny and rigour. Conversely, it identifies right-holders that do not play such a crucial role and do not qualify for such treatment. On this point, I concluded that there is a salient interdependence, in the Court's reasoning, between Article 3 Protocol 1 (free elections), Article 10 (freedom of expression) and Article 11 (freedom of assembly) in the reasons that justifies the nature and scope of the duties correlative to those rights (including positive duties). In a nutshell, this interdependence is governed by the search for an informed debate on issues of public interest and its representation in the elected parliament. In those instances, the ECtHR is not only protecting individuals from state interference – the classical requirement of state neutrality. It is openly promoting a conception of "democracy" and "democratic society".

Second, the more the alleged interference by the respondent State Party endangers those core democratic interests, the more the ECtHR restricts the margin of appreciation. In this situation, the Court is using the *substantive* concept of the margin of appreciation. This is the case, most prominently, with opinions and ideas on issues of public interest that deserve special protection in the case law and justifies scrutinizing, for instance, the political programme of an Islamist party and comparing it with discourses held by its leaders. The consensualist-justificatory approach is contingent upon this standard as well. For instance, the very fact of exercising the right of sexual minorities may be subject to it, but the right to campaign for those rights cannot be. The ECtHR has made a special effort to specify the reasons for protecting the free circulation and expression of ideas and opinions

208   *Conclusion*

on issues of public interest. Conversely, there are ECHR rights the core interest of which is not specified – the ECtHR openly refuses to define it – and that lend themselves to rather modest scrutiny. Those rights are freedom of thought and religion (Article 9) and the right to private life (Article 8). Moreover, those rights are more subject to the consensualist framework: the absence of consensus on the given matter justifies a wider margin of appreciation – even for the positive duties that such rights may imply. In this case, the ECtHR is using the *structural* concept of the doctrine in which it refrains from arbitrating the reasons provided by the litigants.

Third, this practical reason helps in striking a balance in that prominent rights outweigh other rights in the event of conflict. This is the case, most clearly, with the conflict between the right to reputation under Article 8 and the right to freedom of expression under Article 10. If the reasons for both determining the normative basis of the right and giving it enough outweighing power in the event of conflict are the same, it follows that those reasons should be privileged for the task of normative evaluation.

Finally, I have used the concept of *sovereignty* in its internal and external senses to illuminate the asymmetry of the reasoning of the ECtHR between Articles 10 and 11 and Article 3 Protocol 1, on the one hand, and Articles 8 and 9, on the other. *Internal* sovereignty implies the self-limitation of state power, while *external* sovereignty implies state freedom from external interference. Of course, one may say that the internal sense of sovereignty also pertains to the particular legal organization of public life within states. I merely want to suggest that while the rights that best serve the "democratic society" of the ECtHR reveal the *internal* concept of sovereignty, the rights shaped by the consensualist approach via the margin of appreciation reflect the *external* concept of sovereignty. The concept of internal sovereignty is normative and needs to be specified as such. This preliminary distinction just helps to conceptualize the too-often criticized use of the margin of appreciation doctrine.

Pro memoria, what was the initial project of addressing the reasoning of the ECtHR specifically? First, it has to do with the abstract and indeterminate nature of human rights *qua* legal norms in need of concretization through judicial practice. Adjudication is therefore crucial for the characterization of the practice of the ECHR in that it specifies the normative content of those rights. The second reason has to do with the broader constructivist framework adopted for this investigation. Constructivism claims that the normative principles we should accept and follow are, in rough terms, those that would obtain if we were to engage in an idealized process of justification from within our collectively sustained practices. We aim for a moral conception that justifies the role that ECHR rights play as public norms. Because the authoritative role of ECHR rights in domestic legal orders is shaped by the ECtHR's supreme adjudication, I suggest applying the constructivist procedure to the "democratic society" of the ECtHR given the predominant justificatory role the notion plays. Chapter 8 therefore corresponded with the second stage of our constructivist roadmap, complementing the first stage on the status of the ECHR in national legal orders. I noticed, however, that the respondent State Party may execute only the decisional content of the judgment (*res judicata*) and not its interpretative content (*res interpretata*). In both cases, however, the right-based reasoning of the ECtHR remains crucial. While the role of ECHR rights is captured by the concept of authority in a descriptive sense, the normative basis that serves the role is located in the reasoning of the ECtHR. Those two dimensions of the normativity of the ECHR must be synchronically examined.

However, the attention paid to the localized reasoning of the ECtHR does not make full sense if we do not replace it within the more abstract and normative discussion located in human rights theory. In order to see this more clearly, let me go back to the initial objective of my investigation outlined in Chapter 1. In a nutshell, I argued that there is room for the reconciliation of the ethical and the political conceptions of human rights when one examines the legal and judicial dimension of human rights practice. I argued that the very fact that human rights play a practical (and international) role, captured by both international and national law, does not necessarily preclude one from researching and justifying human rights in moral terms. I can now deliver a better account of what this reconciliation consists of. Three steps in this final chapter can be distinguished, all of which are necessary to fully reach the goal of reconciliation.

9.1 Three steps towards reconciliation

In this reconciliation, I first reconstruct the status assigned to the ECHR in national legal orders as well as the limited function of the ECtHR. As explained in Chapter 4, constructivists assign priority to the practical and social roles of public norms. ECHR rights are concretized in law both through implementation in national legal orders and the judicial powers of the ECtHR through adjudication. I therefore argued that this step asks for a specification of the political conception of human rights from within the conceptual framework of international law. International law is here *political* only in the Beitzian sense that its normative dimension is captured in *functional* terms as giving reasons for action in certain circumstances. Overall, the ECHR gives reasons for national authorities to surrender the right to rule over the way in which those authorities treat their subjects on a number of fundamental issues pertaining to public life. In this respect, I show justice to Beitz's seminal claim that human rights are hardly captured without close attention to their role in international practice, to the optimal guarantor of human rights, and to the importance of individual interests that underlie them.

Second, it is clear that one cannot fully capture the normativity of ECHR law without grasping how the ECtHR generates and justifies the duties correlative to those rights. Hence, turning to the adjudication of the ECHR, I argue that it can be illuminated and justified by a unifying moral conception of democracy *qua* internal sovereignty. Again, I am not implying that such a conception captures the social object that law is. I imply that the reasoning in the balancing of the ECtHR in specific circumstances can itself be justified by appealing to a unifying moral

210   *Conclusion*

conception in the constructivist sense. I distinguish between two interrelated aspects of this conception with the concepts and models we find in normative democratic theory: *equality in deliberation* and *sovereignty in representation.* While the former captures an abstract moral concept, the latter determines its concrete institutional implications – and therefore helps us to distinguish the sense in which the ECHR contributes to the internal sovereignty of States Parties. Although I distinguish the two aspects for analytical clarity, both are grounded in one and the same conception of political equality in normative democratic theory. Both for the role and the content of ECHR rights, the constructivist procedure can be applied in exploring what may follow from a given practical standpoint.

Third, I turn more specifically to the decisive claim of the reconciliation thesis. How, and to what extent, are the two conceptions reconciled? The reconciliation obtains by focusing on the concept that unifies the role and content of ECHR rights: democracy *qua* internal sovereignty. The centrality of democracy *qua* internal sovereignty in our political morality gives reasons not only to establish a legal system of international human rights that preserves it – that is, an authoritative process of adjudication that may provide its subjects with a moral reason to coordinate their behaviour on issues of public concern; it also supports how the ECtHR conducts its balancing of Articles 8 to 11 and Article 3 Protocol 1. In that very sense, the moral conception *justifies* both the prominent function that ECHR rights play in national legal orders and the reasoning of the ECtHR. As Besson puts it, "it follows from the moral-political nature of human rights that the law is an important dimension of their recognition and importance".[1]

In his recent overview of human rights theories, Buchanan argues that Beitz "does not explain why the need to protect against such horrors took the form of international legal rights of individuals rather than legal duties of states".[2] I argue that democracy *qua* internal sovereignty can explain the prevalence of individuals by relying on the notion of equal political status and its place in the democratic procedure. Such a notion does not only ascribe a particular status to individuals in the procedure; it also implies that our legal and political institutions are designed accordingly. As I have already indicated, the case law under Article 3 Protocol 1 sheds light on the limited implications that the ECtHR draws in this respect.

It must be clear that the normative order places the moral foundations of sovereign equality – the status of individuals in the political community – *before* the role it plays in both the national legal orders and the status it holds in the adjudication of the ECtHR. The reasoning of the ECtHR and the duties generated are justified by a moral conception that itself justifies the role that those rights play in the national legal orders of States Parties and the prominent status its holds in the adjudication of the ECtHR. Further, it must be clear that the reconciliation thesis also aims to justify the duties that the ECtHR has recognized in its reasoning. This is the unifying function of the normative conception of democracy *qua* internal sovereignty. The interdependence, in the Court's view,

---

1 Besson, "Human Rights and Democracy in a Global Context", 24.
2 Buchanan, "Human Rights", 283.

Conclusion 211

of Article 3 Protocol 1 with Article 10 (freedom of expression) and Article 11 (freedom of association) constitutes the web of normative claims upon which the conception is based.

If this is correct, then we can further specify the normative basis through the constructivist procedure. My argument is better stated as follows. As far as the role of ECHR rights is concerned, we can infer that the ECHR as an international human rights treaty is central to the ordinary legal and political life of each of the States Parties. This is a *functional* account that is limited to the role that ECHR rights and ECtHR judgments play in national legal orders. On this point, I agree with Besson's definition of the function of international human rights as "an external minimal guarantee and pressure on domestic law".[3] Moreover, when one adds to this functional account the jurisprudential layer of reasons, one can infer that ECHR rights implemented by States Parties protect the basic conditions for the democratic procedure of collective decision-making in those legal and political orders. In more abstract terms, the ECtHR makes sure that collectively binding decisions on issues of public interest are made contingent upon the standards of political equality as specified in democratic normative theory. Through the constructivist procedure, I therefore offer a conception that *justifies* the role that ECHR rights play in practice. However, I do not want to terminate my argument just on an abstract and academic note. The best illustration to support it is to return to the reasoning of the ECtHR for a final push and address what the Court has held on the alleged right to self-determination. The sustained refusal of the ECtHR to recognize the right to self-determination under the right to elections (Article 3 Protocol 1) and the reasons that it gives for it illustrates the role of the ECHR as guaranteeing and consolidating the internal sovereignty of the people *within* the state. As such, ECHR rights *qua* human rights aim to protect their status of political equals in the democratic order – a status that only humans can have.

9.2 Step one: the resources of the political conception

In my first chapter, I contended that the combination of Griffin's and Beitz's models contain essential but insufficient resources to develop a practice-responsive theory of the ECHR. First, the Beitzian conception of human rights certainly helps us to think about the concept of human rights as they are concretized in the practice of the ECHR. Beitz made a seminal contribution to the field of normative human rights theory in arguing that constructing a conception of human rights cannot be achieved without close attention to their role(s) in international political practice and the pattern of international concern. It is worth returning to the structure of his argument and his three-pronged model. In the face of an absent supranational judicial organ or appellate review of findings, Beitz rightly identifies a set of paradigms of implementation that have come to constitute the core of the emergent practice of global human rights. Beitz relies heavily on the diverse normativity of human rights (accountability, inducement, assistance, domestic contestation and

3 Besson, "The 'Erga Omnes' Effect of the European Court of Human Rights", 155.

212   *Conclusion*

engagement, compulsion and external adaptation[4]) to construct his model. It is important for Beitz to emphasize the distinctively *political* nature of those practices. Although human rights were originally confined to international treaties, the reasons for action that have developed until now are *political* rather than *legal*: "neither the charter-based nor the treaty-based component of the UN human rights system have evolved effective mechanisms for the appellate review of findings or for the juridical application of sanctions".[5] Beitz infers from this that we can resist calling the emerging global human rights practice a "regime".

9.2.1 The limits of Beitz's global standpoint

At this point of the argument, I want to rehearse a critical remark I made about Beitz's account in Chapter 3. "Global political life", as Beitz calls it, is not the *only* standpoint one may take when reflecting on the practice of human rights. It is one thing to notice that the practice of international human rights lacks anything close to a supranational judicial organ in charge of their enforcement, or even no supranational judicial review mechanism, and that human rights give reasons for a number of distinctively political actions. Yet it does not follow that human rights operate in a legal and judicial vacuum either. True, Beitz notices that the legal and judicial practice of human rights is restricted to mechanisms of consultation and reporting, but he fails to account for the nature and scope of this practice, such as the *interpretative practices* of UN treaty bodies. It is the *authority* of the rights enshrined in treaties and the views and recommendations of UN treaty bodies in national legal orders that Beitz targets. Beitz's claim that "the human rights system is notable for the weakness and unevenness of its capacities for adjudication and enforcement"[6] is not only contingent and incomplete on a global scale but is also misguiding for interpreting the legal and judicial practice of the ECtHR.

Irrespective of this first corrective critique, Beitz's model is marked by a problematic practice-dependent character. Once the prevalent aspects of the practice of human rights are identified, Beitz's project is to construct a "facially reasonable conception of the practice's aim formulated so as to make sense of as many of the central normative elements as possible within the familiar interpretative constraints, coherence, and simplicity".[7] Using conceptual analysis, Beitz develops the following conception of human rights in distinguishing three components. The first component concerns the *interest* protected by human rights. According to Beitz, it must be "sufficiently important when reasonably regarded from the perspective of those protected that would be reasonable to consider its protection to be a political priority".[8] However, in light of the heterogeneity of those actions correlated with the heterogeneity of underlying interests, Beitz concludes that "it

4 Beitz, *The Idea of Human Rights*, 33–44.
5 Ibid., 40.
6 Ibid., 43.
7 Ibid., 108.
8 Ibid., 137.

Conclusion 213

does not seem necessary to identify a list of relatively specific interests or values to serve as the grounds or subject-matters of human rights".[9] The second component concerns the *advantageous protector* of the potential interest, that is, the institutional resources of the state. This component of the model is derived from "more-or-less substantial empirical generalizations about human social behavior and the capacities and dynamics of social institutions".[10] Finally, any plausible human right "must be a suitable object of international concern".[11] This third condition will further constrain the set of possible interests: "whatever its importance regarded from the perspective of potential beneficiaries and however appropriate it would be as a requirement for domestic institutions, a protection cannot count as a human right if it fails to satisfy a requirement of this kind".[12] Now it is crucial to note that the standards used to identify standards are obtained not by an independent moral idea but by facing and interpreting the practice itself. The crucial implication of the model, directed to Griffinians, is that human rights "do not appear as a fundamental moral category . . . . Human rights operate at a middle level of practical reasoning, serving to organize these further considerations and bring them to bear on a certain range of choices".[13]

9.2.2 The relevance of Beitz's three-pronged model

How is Beitz's conception useful in reconstructing the legal and judicial practice of the ECHR? I contend that the three components are useful in the basic conceptual resources they provide but that they fail to account for normative practice in some crucial aspects. Let me address them in turn and try to distinguish what needs to be preserved. First, the interest to be protected has to be sufficiently important when regarded from the perspective of those protected. Since Beitz contends that we cannot apprehend or specify those interests by referring to a deeper layer of moral reasoning, we are left with an explanatory gap when we seek to account for the reasons-giving force of those interests. This, in Beitz's view, is because of the distinctively heterogeneous nature of human rights practices. Beitz's practice is *sui generis* in this very respect and "one may have expected to learn from Beitz how human rights differ from law as normative practice or how at least their legal dimension relates to their broader normative nature".[14] However, as explained in Chapter 3, "global political life" is not the *only* standpoint one may take when reflecting upon the practice of human rights. In the European human rights context the existence of an accomplished judicial organ, authoritatively settling disputes, implies that the interests underlying rights are further specified (in the case law) and this specification, I have suggested, lends itself to a moral reconstruction.

---

9 Ibid., 138–9.
10 Ibid., 139.
11 Ibid., 140.
12 Ibid.
13 Ibid., 127–8.
14 Besson, "Human Rights *qua* Normative Practice: *Sui Generis* or Legal?", 131.

214 *Conclusion*

The second standard is fully relevant too. ECHR rights protect individual interests against the institutions of the state as primary guarantor. In this regard, Beitz is certainly correct: the primary addressees of international human rights are state institutions (legislative, executive, judicial). As Besson puts it, "states are the primary subjects that are legally bound to by both the duty to obey those international law norms and by the right-based duties contained in those norms".[15] However, this standard must be further specified with the help of international law and the concept of *subsidiarity* – in its jurisdictional, substantive and remedial dimensions. As a result, the standard of the state *qua* primary addressee of human rights is neither sufficient to account for the complementary role that ECHR rights play *vis-à-vis* the constitutional rights of the State Party, nor to account for their normativity in national legal orders. More importantly, the normativity of ECHR rights and ECtHR judgments in national legal orders is unique in international law in that most of its 47 States Parties have given *direct effect* to ECHR rights and ECtHR judgments. *Direct effect* means, in concrete terms, that such rights and judgments are binding within national law without any legislative step and are invocable by individuals *vis-à-vis* all state institutions, whether legislative, executive or judicial. International law is therefore needed to explain the conditions for the ECHR to have any role to play in the ordinary legal and political life of States Parties.

The third and final standard is fully relevant but also needs to be specified in the context of the ECtHR. Beitz argues that any plausible human right must be a suitable object of international concern. Since Beitz's standpoint is the global political practice of human rights and his account is practice-dependent, there cannot be some rights that are *a priori* subject to international concern by virtue of international law. This depends on the practice at hand, but this is precisely what ECHR rights are by virtue of the international obligations *qua* States Parties to the ECHR. All ECHR rights are legally suitable objects of international concern. How does the legal practice make this explicit? Beyond the very binding force that is entrenched in the treaty itself and their direct effect, the right of individual petition (Article 46 ECHR) plays the triggering role between the domestically defined relationship with the ECHR and the ECtHR as a subsidiary and authoritative judicial organ – provided that internal remedies have been exhausted. There is, in principle, no legal obligation stemming from the ECHR to execute a judgment of the ECtHR. Moreover, if it does, *remedial subsidiarity* implies that the state chooses the appropriate measures to respond to the Court's judgment. As a result, international concern needs to be specified here again by the subsidiary function of the ECtHR in its jurisdictional dimension.

So much for the Beitzian-functional framework. I hope that it is clear now that if Beitz provides us with the basic structure of the function that human rights play, his account falls short of illuminating the normativity of the ECHR in some crucial aspects. This does not invalidate Beitz's scrupulous analysis of the political

15 Besson, "Human Rights: Ethical, Political . . . or Legal? First Steps in a Legal Theory of Human Rights", 236.

Conclusion 215

practice of human rights, of course. The point is that it falsely conveys the idea that the global political practice of human rights is all that there is to the normativity of international human rights law. In envisioning the scope of this role, it appears that ECHR rights enjoy a much wider normativity than that suggested by Beitz. By analogy with a constitutional court, the ECtHR determines the ways in which States Parties may treat individuals in their jurisdictions. In that sense, human rights violations are not just *pro tanto*, political reasons to act, but *conclusory* reasons of a legal kind. Moreover, what is clearly missing in a Beitzian-functional framework is an account of the adjudication of the ECtHR and the additional layer of reasons that it provides for the interpretation of the practice of human rights. This is where another kind of interpretation of the practice of ECHR rights – the ethical one – is needed.

9.3 Step two: the resources of the moral conception

Griffin has made a central contribution to human rights theory through his account of personhood. Griffin seminally argued that we lack a normative standard to settle our disputes involving human rights claims. Those old-fashioned Enlightenment concepts inherited from the natural law tradition will simply not do: "we agree that human rights are derived from 'human standing', or 'human nature', but virtually no agreement about the relevant sense of these two criteria-providing terms".[16] This is the "justificatory deficit" of human rights. The need for a standard of human rights is reinforced, Griffin argues, by the pre-eminence of *structural* theories of rights developed most (Feinberg's rights as *claims*, Dworkin's rights as *trumps* and Robert Nozick's rights as *side-constraints*): "the largely structural and legal-functional accounts are short on explanatory power".[17] Not only does the personhood account determine the human rights we have, but it also pervades the very structure of rights in determining their correlated duties, and serves as a standard of criticism to "clean" the conventional lists of human rights in international law.

I have suggested in Chapter 2 that the form of justification developed by Griffin operates from a practice-independent moral standpoint. This is because for Griffin "human rights" speaks for a fundamental moral category that requires an independent form of reasoning. In this way, personhood fills a vacuum in our moral repertoire. This is also why Griffin almost exclusively focuses on the *interests* and *values* that those rights may protect. Moral conceptions, I have suggested, identify a stringent moral interest or value and then navigate with it from the moral to the political and the legal dimensions of human rights. In this sense, I have suggested, Griffin's account is *practice-independent*. I have specified the *internal*, *external* and *right-based* critiques of the personhood account at length in Chapter 2 and showed how a constructivist account can incorporate those critiques in Chapter 4. I want to focus here on how Griffin's conception can help

16 Griffin, *On Human Rights*, 16.
17 Ibid., 21.

216 *Conclusion*

us to reflect on the foundations of ECHR rights as concretized in the reasoning of the ECtHR. Let me come back to the powerful argument against personhood made by Raz:

> There is nothing wrong in singling out the capacity for normative agency, or more broadly the capacities which constitute personhood, as of special moral significance . . . . The problem is the absence of a convincing argument as to why human rights practice should conform to their theories.[18]

I follow Raz and Besson in that rights have a particular structure, which Griffin neglects. The structure of rights implies a *threshold* between the interest(s) and the right(s). As Besson puts it in her modified interest-based conception, "they are moral interests recognized by the law as sufficiently important to generate moral duties".[19] The threshold from rights to duties consists of the kind of *pro tanto* response to which their violation gives rise – *categorical* and *exclusionary*, as Raz puts it. Tasioulas precisely argues that Griffin takes "rights out of human rights". Rights trigger some special kind of reason for action.

Yet I contend that there is a point at which Griffin's modality of reasoning is needed to account for the practice. True, Griffin's value of personhood does not help in singling out the conception of ECHR rights as inhering in a "democratic society". Griffin's distinctive aim is to account for the idea that human rights are those rights we have in a pre-institutional state of affairs. However, institutions can recognize and enforce rights that protect distinctively human status and capacities that only *they* can have. As Buchanan forcefully explains:

> "[S]imply by virtue of being human" here only means that these moral rights are ascribed to all individuals independently of any further gender, racial, ethnic, or other qualifications, such as social contribution; it does *not* preclude the possibility that the ascription of some (or all) human rights depends on assumptions about institutional context. It also does not imply that these rights are to be deduced *a priori* from a concept of human nature or that they exist pre-institutionally in a state of nature.[20]

Instead of fetishizing the contradiction that human rights cannot be both an institutional construct and inhere in our condition of human beings in the state of nature, I suggest asking whether the degree of institutionalization of rights can hold without implying the protection and the consolidation of a moral status that only human beings can have. As Besson forcefully puts it, "human rights are not merely a consequence of the equal status of individuals; they are also a way of

---

18 Raz, "Human Rights Without Foundations", 328–9.
19 Besson, "Human Rights: Ethical, Political . . . or Legal? First Steps in a Legal Theory of Human Rights", 236.
20 Buchanan, "Human Rights", 282.

Conclusion 217

actually earning that equal status and consolidating it".[21] Also, Griffin's substantive account does not help us to shed light on the normative role that ECHR rights and ECtHR judgments play in national legal orders. This is precisely the *external* critique that promoters of the political conception have put forward: the personhood account is not apt to account for the fact that human rights trigger, on the supply side, some international concern. However, such a functional account is not enough to accommodate the authoritative adjudication of the ECtHR either. True, the respondent State Party may execute only the decisional content of the judgment (*res judicata*), and not its interpretative content (*res interpretata*), but in both cases we cannot have an informed picture of the normativity of the ECHR without addressing those two dimensions synchronically.

This is where we need, I contend, another kind of philosophical resource to account for the practice of ECHR rights – the ethical one – but it has to be *legislated*, as the constructivists put it, by the standards found within the relevant practical standpoint. When one addresses the specific structure and content of the reasoning in the case law of the ECtHR – how the Court interprets ECHR rights, how it addresses the justification given by the respondent State Party and how it arbitrates conflicts of rights – there is enough, I argue, to capture a *practical reason* – a set of powerful reasons by which the actions of states and individuals are judged – to govern the reasoning on those Articles. In setting the scope of ECHR rights – that is, in attributing normative content to those rights – the ECtHR is led to reflect on their existence conditions and the reasons that are sufficient for authoritatively deciding cases. The reasons that the ECtHR gives for the recognition, specification and allocation of duties under Articles 8 to 11 and Article 3 Protocol 1 originate in the Court's "democratic society" clause as the decisive normative standard to decide the merits of a case. As I have already mentioned, this claim should not be viewed from the standpoint of analytic legal theory. I do not contend that capturing and illuminating the practical reason of the ECtHR on those Articles contradicts a positivist theory of ECHR law – a statement that would target the nature of the reasoning and its possible confinement to legal sources or facts sociologically defined, be it the Razian "source thesis" or the Hartian "rule of recognition".

I contend that the reasoning of the ECtHR lends itself to and can be justified by normative political theory irrespective of its specific nature *qua* law. Again, this judicial arena matters insofar as the States Parties diligently follow the Court's case law. I here follow Waldron in that:

> We have to remember that a lot of what we call moral thought is not devoted to the establishment of a moral order analogous to a legal order, but is in fact oriented to the evaluation of and criticism of the legal order itself.[22]

21 Besson, "Human Rights: Ethical, Political . . . or Legal? First Steps in a Legal Theory of Human Rights", 233.
22 Waldron, *Dignity, Rank, and Rights*, 67. This argument also transpires from Waldron's analysis of the role of judges in Waldron, "Judges as Moral Reasoners".

218 *Conclusion*

It is rather the reasons given to justify a range of duties and how those reasons weigh against others in the reasoning of the ECtHR under Articles 8 to 11 and Article 3 Protocol 1 that matter. The propositional content of the case law is authoritative. This is where the sense of *justification* comprised not in law *qua* legal reasoning but in political theory prevails – that is, the liberal enterprise of reconciling our freedoms with the post-national institutional structures in which we find ourselves. To recall, we assumed that "a moral conception has a *social role*, to provide beings like us with a *public basis for justification* regarding our moral, social, political relations".[23]

9.3.1 Equality in deliberation

There are two aspects of the practical reason of the ECtHR that support the justification of ECHR rights in democratic terms. The first aspect of the conception is what I call *equality in deliberation*. While *sovereignty in representation* focuses on the practical and institutional implications of the conception, equality in deliberation concerns the moral foundations and depicts in abstract terms the status ascribed to individuals who hold those rights. Of course, in terms of justification, deliberation *precedes* representation and thereby justifies it. It is only when we get a grasp of the moral significance of equality in deliberation that equality in representation matters. Moreover, both instances *publicly* realize equality in that individuals can see that they are treated as equals. Not surprisingly, freedom of expression under Article 10 prevails and morally justifies the right in a principled sense (1), and more specifically, its correlative those duties (2), but also its overriding force when it conflicts with other rights in given circumstances (3).

In so doing, I am using the constructivist approach in that I articulate and unify a restricted number of normative statements held by the ECtHR on Article 10. The right to democracy, if one may wish to assert its normative existence, is therefore not a right *stricto sensu* but a democratic interest founded on sovereign equality the moral force of which is deployed throughout the rights and the range of duties correlative to those rights. As Besson explains, "the phrase 'human right to democracy' can only be used therefore as shorthand for a human right to a given democratic interest".[24] The normative basis lies, I argue, in normative democratic theory and, in particular, in the *egalitarian* argument for democracy, which holds that democracy is *inherently* valuable in that it respects each person's point of view on matters of public interest by giving each an equal say when there is deep disagreement about what to do. It addresses the conditions that ought to be met for determining the terms of association and the institutions that structure social interactions. As Christiano puts it, "democratic decision-making is the unique way to publicly embody in collective decision-making under the circumstances of pervasive conscientious disagreement in which we find ourselves".[25]

---

23 Freeman, "Constructivism, Facts, and Moral Justification", 49.
24 Besson, "The Human Right to Democracy – A Moral Defence with a Legal Nuance", 14.
25 Christiano, *The Constitution of Equality: Democratic Authority and Its Limits*, 75–6.

Conclusion 219

9.3.2 The scope of disagreement

There are two important steps in the defence of *equality in deliberation*. First, there is a premise about the circumstances of modern political deliberation: egalitarian democrats assume that there are deep conflicts of conviction on how to define terms of association in society. The conflict may concern what the real issues are and the solutions to those issues, as well as designing the agenda. Christiano insists on the background facts of *diversity, disagreement, cognitive bias* and *fallibility* when individuals determine their conception of the common good. Second, egalitarian democrats assume that such conflicts cannot be solved by rational persuasion over the terms on how to organize society by which they will be bound. As Christiano argues, "they acknowledge fundamental conflicts of interests and convictions in society and assert that because of this lack of consensus, each person may demand an equal share in political rule".[26] Note here that the egalitarian argument for democracy attacks the liberty-based justification of democracy on the assumption of the amount of consensus that may be within reach. The liberty-based argument assumes that democratic society is justified by its capacity to provide terms of arrangements that correspond with individual judgment of what is best. However, if consensus were easily within reach, there would be no point in the maintenance of the institution of voting and election. As Waldron puts it, "on an account like this, any need for voting must seem like an admission of failure".[27]

9.3.3 The normative claim in the face of disagreement

Second, there is a normative claim that precisely accommodates the force of pluralism: equality in deliberation *demands* that when there is some kind of social and political arrangement that is imposed on the life of individuals, and when there is deep disagreement about defining the terms of the arrangement, we should treat those individuals as having an equal say in the decision-making process. Given the background facts of *diversity, disagreement, cognitive bias* and *fallibility*, equality in deliberation allows individuals to see that they are *publicly* treated as equals. If the society is regulated by principles one cannot endorse, then "it gives one good reason to think that the dominant interests are being advanced and that one's own interests are not being advanced".[28] The principle of *publicity* is therefore grounded in equality.[29] It is crucial to the egalitarian argument for democracy that individuals are equally entitled to participate in the process of deliberation in order for them to see that they are treated as equals.[30] When this requirement of equality in deliberation is publicly respected, it gives reasons for

---

26 Christiano, *The Rule of the Many: Fundamental Issues in Democratic Theory*, 47.
27 Waldron, *Law and Disagreement*, 92.
28 Christiano, "A Democratic Theory of Territory and Some Puzzles about Global Democracy", 84.
29 Christiano, *The Constitution of Equality: Democratic Authority and Its Limits*, 56–66.
30 Ibid., Chapter 5.

220 *Conclusion*

us to accept the terms of association and the imposition of obligations upon us. As Christiano puts it:

> The thought is that when an outcome is democratically chosen and some people disagree with the outcome, as some inevitably will, they still have a duty to go along with the decision because otherwise they would be treating the others unfairly.[31]

This is the idea behind the democratic conception of political authority and its *content-independent* dimension: the decision of the majority gives a reason to comply and replaces the reason on which one would have acted if there were no democratic ruling.[32] In that very sense, treating individuals as equals in deliberation on issues of public interest publicly respects those pervasive disagreements. "Equal say" implies the equal right to have one's own judgment about what to do taken equally into account. ECHR rights protect the interests in making a judgment about social and political arrangements. It is the basic and generative moral basis of equality in deliberation within my broader conception of democracy *qua* internal sovereignty.

Again, I do not ascribe particular importance to the distinction between protecting the individual *interests* that should be equally advanced and protecting the *judgments* of individuals when they exercise the rights the interests of which are protected.[33] I assume that interests, in the wording of the ECtHR, can be interpreted as protecting the status of agents – following the constructivist approach – if we address the practical reason on specific ECHR rights and not *a priori*. While the concept of interest helps us in capturing the general conceptual structure of rights in their "non-speciesist quality",[34] I argue that when we get to the localized reasoning of the ECtHR on the provisions examined, the concept of *status* is helpful in the constructivist project of justification. The *deontological* nature of the moral right to democratic participation is, however, clearly assumed and remains the central premise. As Besson rightly puts it, "all persons have by reason of their equal status a claim to equal participation in the most important political decisions that concern them".[35] Besson also understands equal political status as the "point of passage"[36] from a general and fundamental interest to a human right, but since she wants to maintain her concept of human rights sufficiently wide to accommodate a wide variety of interests in a broad range of contexts, this point of passage remains too abstract in my view and the argument

31 Christiano, "Authority".
32 For a brief analysis, see also ibid., Section 7.
33 For Christiano's distinction, see Christiano, *The Rule of the Many: Fundamental Issues in Democratic Theory*, 53–6. Christiano's second book on equality and democracy does not make this distinction as strong as it is in the first: Christiano, *The Constitution of Equality: Democratic Authority and Its Limits*, 58.
34 Besson, "The Egalitarian Dimension of Human Rights", 28.
35 Besson, "The Human Right to Democracy – A Moral Defence with a Legal Nuance", 10.
36 Besson, "Human Rights and Democracy in a Global Context", 22.

Conclusion 221

loses its illuminative power. If one pays attention to the practical reason of the ECtHR, then one must notice that some rights are privileged over others for some reasons, and such ordering cannot be left unexplained or unspecified by the broad concept of "interest". I have used the concept of right between interest and duties as a heuristic device to distinguish the practice of ECHR rights among other forms of normative practice – in addition to the fact that the ECtHR uses the language of interests and duties in its case law – but I do not believe that relying on the concept of *interest* can account for the normative breadth of human rights, at least those specified by the ECtHR on which I have focused.

Turning now to the practical reason of the ECtHR as concretizing this normative basis, the two steps just outlined have been clearly endorsed by the Court and govern the reasoning. First, as we saw in Chapter 8, it is a *leitmotif* of the practical reason of the ECtHR that the right to express views on issues of public interest is foundational to "democratic society". This is best seen in the special effort made by the ECtHR to identify whether there is an issue of public interest in the case brought before it. Not surprisingly, this is where Article 10 plays its central role. The ECtHR is very attached to finding whether an alleged interference pertains to the expression of views on issues of public interest. In the recent case of *Yordanova and Toshev v. Bulgaria*, the ECtHR held that "the Court must firstly have regard to whether the publication has made a contribution to a debate of general interest".[37] This echoes the original statement in *Lingens v. Austria*, in which the ECtHR held that "more generally, freedom of political debate is at the very core of the concept of a democratic society which prevails throughout the Convention".[38] As the Court also held in *Dupuis v. France*:

> The promotion of free political debate is a fundamental feature of a democratic society. The Court attaches the highest importance to freedom of expression in the context of political debate and considers that very strong reasons are required to justify restrictions on political speech. Allowing broad restrictions on political speech in individual cases would undoubtedly affect respect for freedom of expression in general in the State concerned.[39]

Second, I detailed in the last chapter the Court's view of pluralism as a necessary characteristic of "democratic society". The ECtHR makes explicit that one's views on issues of public interest should be *informed* by the public, transparent and adversarial discussion of views on issues of public interest. As the ECtHR puts it, "a person opposed to official ideas and positions must be able to find a place in the political arena".[40] In other words, not only does the Court acknowledge the existence of pluralism in modern politics, but it insists on the necessity of actively

---

37 *Yordanova and Toshev v. Bulgaria*, App. No. 5126/05, 2 October 2012, para. 49.
38 *Lingens v. Austria*, App. No. 9815/82, 8 July 1986, para. 42.
39 *Dupuis and Others v. France*, App. No. 1914/02, 7 June 2007, para. 40.
40 *Piermont v. France*, App. Nos. 15773/89, 15774/89, 24 July 1995, para. 76.

222 Conclusion

promoting a pluralistic debate on issues of political or public interest. It therefore assumes that the adversarial character is an additional and qualitative requirement of "democratic society" – echoing the need for public debate premised on the background facts of cognitive bias, diversity, disagreement and fallibility that pervade modern politics within the state. This requirement is clearly derived in the case law from the more abstract recognized *right of the public to be informed* on issues of public interest. In *Erdoğdu and İnce v. Turkey*, for instance, the ECtHR held that "domestic authorities in the instant case failed to have sufficient regard to the public's right to be informed of a different perspective on the situation in south-east Turkey, irrespective of how unpalatable that perspective may be for them".[41] It therefore seems that the ECtHR assumes that the confrontation of views is beneficial for "democratic society".

It is therefore central to understand the role(s) that pluralism plays in the egalitarian argument for democracy. The appeal to procedural forms of democracy and majority voting results from the assumption of the irremediable diversity and incommensurability of views on issues of public interest. Accordingly, if individuals are treated and seen as equals in the process of deliberation, this gives them reasons to accept the terms of association, although they may still profoundly disagree with them. As Cohen puts it, "it is natural to suppose that by excluding a comprehensive consensus on values the fact of reasonable pluralism leads to a procedural conception of democracy".[42] It is important to note here that the authority of democracy contrasts with the Razian *instrumentalist* concept of authority.[43] The result of majority voting is binding because there are genuinely moral reasons to abide by it and those reasons lie in the public and equal incorporation of views and opinions – the "equal advancement of interests" in Christiano's words. Neither is the authority of democracy justified upon commitment to relativism about moral truth. As Waldron explains, "respect has to do with how we treat each other's *beliefs* about justice where none of them is self-certifying, not how we treat the truth about justice itself".[44]

However, the scope of pluralism is more disputable. One may stipulate an *epistemic* virtue in that listening to other views helps in getting to the right answer, or a *moral* virtue in that individuals are forced to accommodate the interest of others. In both cases, this would grant "democratic society" an *instrumental* value that discontinues from the *normative* value based on sovereign equality *qua* moral status. Conversely, pluralism may be promoted precisely as an expression of a requirement of political equality. Pluralism is a natural fact of modern society and politics. This would fit with the *leitmotif* of the ECtHR, as stated in *Gorzelik and Others v. Poland*, that "the implementation of the principle of pluralism is impossible without an association being

---

41 *Erdoğdu and İnce v. Turkey*, App. Nos. 25067/94, 25068/94, 8 July 1999, para. 51.
42 Cohen, "Procedure and Substance in Deliberative Democracy", 18.
43 Christiano, *The Constitution of Equality*, 232–5.
44 Waldron, *Law and Disagreement*, 111.

Conclusion 223

able to express freely its ideas and opinions",[45] or recently in *Eweida v. United Kingdom*, in which the ECtHR held that pluralism in religious faith has two distinct functions:

> This is a fundamental right: because a healthy democratic society needs to tolerate and sustain pluralism and diversity; but also because of the value to an individual who has made religion a central tenet of his or her life to be able to communicate that belief to others.[46]

However, the clearest instrumental instance of the role of pluralism is social cohesion. As the ECtHR held in *Alekseyev v. Russia*, concerning the right of the gay community in Russia to campaign:

> It is only through fair and public debate that society may address such complex issues as the one raised in the present case. Such debate, backed up by academic research, would benefit social cohesion by ensuring that representatives of all views are heard, including the individuals concerned.[47]

In view of the normative roles that pluralism plays in the justificatory reasoning of the ECtHR, the concept has an instrumental and non-contradictory function of helping individuals in deepening their own views and opinions on issues of public interest and in putting their views against the views and opinions of others (including those who may be marginalized). It may be the case not only that individuals have not fully understood the issues pervading their society and the interests they have in it, but also that they may be biased about what others think about their own interests, and vice-versa. This is a function on which deliberative democrats very much insist.[48]

This point illuminates the positive duties generated by the ECtHR to promote pluralism and the recurrent objective of "social cohesion", which it asserts. It is the broadly *cognitive* function of deliberation and discussion in the context of pluralism that could be viewed as instrumentally beneficial for "democratic society" normatively construed. We learn about issues of public interest and what we have to do about them by confronting our opinions in discussion with others.

This is a point that the egalitarian argument for democracy can fully endorse. As Christiano explains, "the process of discussion and deliberation ought to be thought as instrumental in acquiring understanding about one's interests and one's society".[49] At the same time, "the person can identify with the larger projects of

---

45 *Gorzelik and Others v. Poland*, App. No. 44158/98, 17 February 2004, para. 91.
46 *Eweida and Others v. United Kingdom*, App. Nos. 48420/10, 36516/10, 51671/10, 59842/10, 15 January 2013, para. 94.
47 *Alekseyev v. Russia*, App. Nos. 4916/07, 25924/08, 14599/09, 21 October 2010, para. 86.
48 See the contributions in Parkinson and Mansbridge (eds), *Deliberative Systems: Deliberative Democracy at the Large Scale*.
49 Christiano, *The Rule of the Many: Fundamental Issues in Democratic Theory*, 41–2.

224   *Conclusion*

the society as a whole as well as the particular projects of parts of society".[50] The rights to be informed and to receive information are therefore not only predicated on the accountability and publicity of the state or on the capacity to improve the understanding of one's own interests, but also to prevent the marginalization of minorities in the debates on issues of public interest. As Christiano puts it:

> If people judge the justice of an arrangement where a minority or even a majority assumes for itself the right to rule for others, they will judge that it advances the interests of the ruling class at the expense of the others. Hence, they will judge that it is profoundly unjust from an egalitarian standpoint.[51]

When the ECtHR held in the seminal case of *Young, James and Webster v. United Kingdom* that "democracy does not simply mean that the views of the majority must always prevail" and that "a balance must be achieved which ensures the fair and proper treatment of minorities and avoids any abuse of a dominant position",[52] it seems to endorse this very point. Freedom of expression contributes greatly to fulfilling this requirement and plays a specific role. Respect for individuals' freedom of expression enables them to attain true and justified beliefs on issues of public interest. Since each person's views are to some extent biased, expressing views allows individuals to confront the Millian process of "trial and error" in the search for improved beliefs on issues of public interest. As Christiano puts it, "one benefits just from the process of having to clarify one's thought to others. And one benefits by hearing the responses of others and having to think of replies to them".[53] By the same token, freedom of expression *publicly* realizes equality. The normative force of the right to freedom of association (Article 11) is justified on the same grounds.

In this vein, there is one further implication of democratic theory that I want to emphasize at this stage and that may also illuminate the reasoning of the ECtHR on pluralism, although to a lesser extent. The more specific view of *deliberative democracy* within the egalitarian defence for democracy demands that the reasons we give for our social and political arrangements are grounded in principles that *everyone can reasonably accept*. Joshua Cohen is a prominent defender of this approach:

> In such a procedure participants regard one another as equals; they aim to defend and criticize institutions and programs in terms of considerations that others have reasons to accept, given the fact of reasonable pluralism and the assumption that those others are reasonable.[54]

Note that such a demanding view of democracy is contested in democratic theory, in particular, in that it assumes that some consensus on justification can be

---

50 Christiano, *The Constitution of Equality: Democratic Authority and Its Limits*, 90.
51 Ibid.
52 *Young, James and Webster v. United Kingdom*, App. Nos. 7601/76, 7806/77, 13 August 1981, para. 63.
53 Christiano, *The Constitution of Equality: Democratic Authority and Its Limits*, 151.
54 Cohen, "Procedure and Substance in Deliberative Democracy", 21.

Conclusion 225

reached for all individuals involved in deliberation, an assumption that concerns both the motivational powers of agents and the epistemic powers of deliberation. True, upon deliberation there may be a conflict of interests that can reach a solution that is equally satisfactory for all the parties. This is *compromise*. However, as Christiano puts it, "this instance of compromise does not tell us how to resolve disagreements at all".[55] This is what egalitarian arguments for democracy-based individual *interests*, such as those of Christiano, assert. They contend that the cost of that consensus, or the cost of having to find reasons acceptable to all involved, may be too high: why should it be the case that one's effort to justify one's claims are detrimental to one's very right to express one's own view? It is therefore true that the "deliberative conception requires more than the interests of others be given equal consideration; it demands, too, that we find politically acceptable reasons – reasons that are acceptable to others, given a background of differences of conscientious conviction".[56] In his more recent book, Christiano also argues against deliberative democracy on the ground that respect for the free exercise of reason of individuals overrides the standard of epistemic reasonableness: "no single moral point of view or set of ideas is justified *simpliciter*".[57]

Those distinctions matter for democratic theorizing, but there is no basis in the case law that may help us to strike the balance beyond a few rather indicative claims about the necessity of a pluralistic debate in a democratic society to reinforce social cohesion. As a result, I do not go further in the philosophical discussion of their pros and cons. The closest instance of deliberative democracy is, for instance, when the ECtHR held in *United Communist Party of Turkey and Others v. Turkey*:

> There can be no justification for hindering a political group solely because it seeks to debate in public the situation of part of the State's population and to take part in the nation's political life in order to find, according to democratic rules, solutions capable of satisfying everyone concerned.[58]

Satisfaction seems to suggest that although one does not fully agree with the arrangement, one does find the costs not too prohibitive, although there is not enough to assess the implications of the Court's reasoning. The same indeterminacy is found in *Yazar and Others v. Turkey* when the ECtHR held:

> Even if proposals inspired by such principles are likely to clash with the main strands of government policy or the convictions of the majority of the public, it is necessary for the proper functioning of democracy that political groups should be able to introduce them into public debate in order to help find solutions to general problems concerning politicians of all persuasions.[59]

---

55 Christiano, *The Rule of the Many: Fundamental Issues in Democratic Theory*, 49.
56 Cohen, "Procedure and Substance in Deliberative Democracy", 24.
57 Christiano, *The Constitution of Equality: Democratic Authority and Its Limits*, 208.
58 *United Communist Party of Turkey and Others v. Turkey*, App. No. 29400/05, 19 June 2012, para. 57.
59 *Yazar and Others v. Turkey*, App. Nos. 22723/93, 22724/93, 22725/93, 9 April 2002, para. 58.

226 *Conclusion*

Yet the reasoning remains underdeveloped and does not lend itself to a rigorous reconstruction.

Turning now to the scope of the duties that are justified by the normative basis, it is best illustrated by the "public watchdog" role ascribed to the press and, in particular, by the role it plays in conveying information on issues of public interest. As the ECtHR made clear in *Editions Plon v. France*, "the national margin of appreciation is circumscribed by the interests of a democratic society in enabling the press to exercise its vital role of 'public watchdog'".[60] The generative force of the normative basis is here again deployed. The ECtHR explicitly justifies the right to receive such information and the duty to convey it on the same substantive grounds. In *Özgur v. Turkey*, the Court held the following:

> While the press must not overstep the bounds set, inter alia, for the protection of the vital interests of the State . . ., it is nevertheless incumbent on the press to convey information and ideas on political issues, even divisive ones. Not only has the press the task of imparting such information and ideas; the public has a right to receive them. Freedom of the press affords the public one of the best means of discovering and forming an opinion of the ideas and attitudes of political leaders.[61]

True, in this case, we can hardly explain the normative force of democracy *qua* internal sovereignty without adding the role played by the subject of criticism – that is, elected representatives – and this pertains to the conceptual interdependence of Article 10 and Article 3 Protocol 1, to which I return later. However, the main point is this: equality in deliberation demands that individuals should be provided with *equal resources* to conceive and elaborate their own views on issues of public interest. If we ascribe individuals a value in having equal rights to express their views, it seems that the same egalitarian argument also requires that they should be provided with equal resources to develop their own views and opinions on those issues. As Christiano puts it, "inasmuch as everyone has interests in making these decisions, the ideal of equality of resources ought to be applied to the collective decision-making procedures".[62] The institution of deliberation in public debate is justified in protecting the individual's opportunity to learn more about public issues: "egalitarian institutions are charged with the task of disseminating understanding widely so that the individuals have the means of informing themselves of how to advance their interests and convictions".[63]

This is where several prominent right-holders identified in Chapter 8 appear as central. Beyond the privileged role of the press, political parties crucially matter. The ECtHR has developed a significant case law on the role of political parties in

---

60 *Editions Plon v. France*, App. No. 58148/00, 18 May 2004, para. 43.
61 See also *Lingens v. Austria*, App. No. 9815/82, 8 July 1986, para. 41 and *Fressoz and Roire v. France*, App. No. 29183/95, 21 January 1999, para. 45.
62 Christiano, *The Rule of the Many: Fundamental Issues in Democratic Theory*, 70.
63 Ibid., 85.

Conclusion 227

their vital contribution to the search for political pluralism and informed political debate. As Christiano puts it, "parties play a role in social discussion during the electoral period, and they play a role in legislative decision-making as delegates to their constituencies".[64] In *Refah Partisi and Others v. Turkey*, the ECtHR held:

> It is in the nature of the role they play that political parties, the only bodies which can come to power, also have the capacity to influence the whole of the regime in their countries. By the proposals for an overall societal model which they put before the electorate and by their capacity to implement those proposals once they come to power, political parties differ from other organisations which intervene in the political arena.[65]

Similarly, the role that elected representatives play in informing the electorate about issues of public interest is another obvious case. As I have argued in Chapter 8, the protection of those right-holders is framed as a vehicle for informing the public. In *Castells v. Spain*, freedom of the press "gives politicians the opportunity to reflect and comment on the preoccupations of public opinion; it thus enables everyone to participate in the free political debate which is at the very core of the concept of a democratic society".[66] Here, too, the duties generated in the practical reason of the ECtHR are justified by the concept of equality in deliberation in that the wide scope of the right to freedom of expression relies on the necessity to have a fuller understanding of their own views and opinions on issues of public interest. As Christiano explains, "discussion and deliberation thus contribute importantly to egalitarian democratic institutions, and the principle of equality provides a rationale for distributing the resources for deliberation equally".[67] The abstract right to be informed, recognized by the ECtHR, is here fully justified. Accordingly, there cannot be a wide margin of appreciation in those matters. The duty of the public to receive information is correlative to the clear recognition by the ECtHR that the press's "duty is to impart – in a manner consistent with its obligations and responsibilities – information and ideas on all matters of public interest".[68] The normative basis is the same for other persons or entities that perform the same role in society, such as audio-visual companies[69] and NGOs.[70] As Christiano puts it, "interest groups provide citizens with the opportunity to hear developed and articulated views about their interests . . . . Interest groups have uniquely informed perspectives on essential parts of the society".[71]

---

64 Ibid., 246.

65 *Refah Partisi (The Welfare Party) and Others v. Turkey*, App. Nos. 41340/98, 41342/98, 41343/98, 41344/98, 13 February 2003, para. 87.

66 *Castells v. Spain*, App. No. 11798/85, 23 April 1992, para. 43.

67 Christiano, *The Rule of the Many: Fundamental Issues in Democratic Theory*, 86.

68 *Radio France and Others v. France*, App. No. 53984/00, 30 March 2004, para. 30.

69 *Radio Twist A.S. v. Slovakia*, App. No. 62202/00, 19 December 2006, paras 57–8.

70 *Vides Aizsardzības Klubs v. Latvia*, App. No. 57829/00, 27 May 2004, para. 42.

71 Christiano, *The Rule of the Many: Fundamental Issues in Democratic Theory*, 247.

228 *Conclusion*

Now, as we saw in Chapter 8, the ECtHR is very tolerant towards extremist or provocative views when those pertain to issues of public interest. Defending Sharia law or separatism falls within the scope of Article 10. The same is true for exaggeration, provocation and satire. The limits, in the eyes of the ECtHR, lie not in the *expression* of anti-democratic or separatist views, but whether the political project deemed detrimental to the values of the ECHR has a chance of being realized in the near future. As the ECtHR makes clear in *Refah Partisi v. Turkey*, about an Islamist party that was dissolved by the Constitutional Court of Ankara:

> The Court accordingly considers that at the time of its dissolution Refah had the real potential to seize political power without being restricted by the compromises inherent in a coalition. If Refah had proposed a programme contrary to democratic principles, its monopoly of political power would have enabled it to establish the model of society envisaged in that programme.[72]

The limits adduced to freedom of expression resonate in democratic theory in that the very reliance on equal say on issues of public interest cannot reach a point where it attains the very core of the interest on which it is founded. This is also true of other central democratic rights, such as the right of association and the right to elections. The internal limit of the authority of democracy arises because the normative basis used to justify democracy and its central rights may be violated by the same democratic process. As Christiano explains, "were the majority to strip some minority of its democratic rights, then this would be a publicly clear way in which it acted as if its interests were of superior worth to those of the minority".[73] Given the emphasis by the ECtHR on pluralistic debate on issues of public interest, we may infer that any promoted political regime that would threaten those conditions and which would have a chance of being implemented ought to be banned. This is a consequence of the egalitarian argument for democracy:

> Intuitively, if one dissents from an outcome that has been chosen and one attempts to bring about another outcome by means of revolution or intrigue or manipulating the system, one is acting in such way that cannot be thought of by others and in the light of the facts about judgment and the interests in respect for judgments, one is in effect expressing the superiority of one's interests over others.[74]

The same is true for incitement to violence, which the ECtHR considers as inherently detrimental to "democratic society". In *Zana v. Turkey*, for instance, regarding incitement to violence contained in the words of an activist in the Kurdish cause, the ECtHR held:

---

72 *Refah Partisi (The Welfare Party) and Others v. Turkey*, para. 108.
73 Christiano, *The Constitution of Equality: Democratic Authority and Its Limits*, 265.
74 Ibid., 99.

Conclusion 229

Those words could be interpreted in several ways but, at all events, they are both contradictory and ambiguous. They are contradictory because it would seem difficult simultaneously to support the PKK, a terrorist organisation which resorts to violence to achieve its ends, and to declare oneself opposed to massacres; they are ambiguous because whilst Mr Zana disapproves of the massacres of women and children, he at the same time describes them as "mistakes" that anybody could make.[75]

Note that, following the Court's attachment to the right in the first place, it carefully scrutinizes the ideas and opinions held by applicants and compares, for instance, political discourses and written political programmes, as we have seen. The interference with Article 10 should always be thoroughly supported by facts. Only when incitement to violence is established does the ECtHR leave it to the national courts to determine the scope of the need for interfering with the provision through the margin of appreciation.[76]

9.3.4 Equality in representation

The first aspect of sovereign equality in deliberation, just defended, relies on an abstract and substantive moral concept of equal status. The concept is able not only to generate specific sets of duties but also to arbitrate conflicts of rights. However, sovereign equality is not just an abstract moral concept that ascribes a particular status to individuals in collective decision-making. It also implies that our legal and political institutions in charge of enacting law ought to respect the equal moral status just posited. As Besson explains, "public or political equality implies that people can see that they are treated as equals by others and this takes the form of its recognition by the law and institutions".[77] In this very sense, democracy *qua* internal sovereignty *publicly* realizes political equality too. This is where the very concept of *sovereignty* takes it distinctive normative significance in designing the process of distributing institutionalized political power to enact laws – in short, the right to self-rule.

There are, of course, practical reasons for the establishment of representative democracy and for the division of labour between the people and their will, on one hand, and the elected representatives of the people, on the other. There is no hope in the possibility of an egalitarian legislative assembly of millions of individuals, or even an egalitarian assembly of thousands of representatives of millions of individuals. As Christiano explains, "most citizens would not have the time to devote to the complicated issues involved in making legislation. The process would be inevitably highjacked by elites".[78] Representative democracy permits, however, that disagreements among people find an expression

75 *Zana v. Turkey*, App. No. 18954/91, 25 November 1997, para. 56.
76 *Schwabe and M.G. v. Germany*, App. Nos. 8080/08, 8577/08, 1 January 2011, para. 113.
77 Besson, "The Egalitarian Dimension of Human Rights", 31.
78 Christiano, *The Constitution of Equality: Democratic Authority and Its Limits*, 105.

230 *Conclusion*

in the legislative body. In the words of Waldron, legislative assemblies are "structured in a way that represents (or claims to represent) the more serious and substantial disagreements that there are in society about the way society is organized".[79] The legislative body represents individuals and embodies the idea of *egalitarian self-rule*. If pluralism is inherent in modern political debate and if such pluralism results from equal rights, then legislative bodies ought to appropriately represent such diversity. Equality is therefore publicly realized when it comes to making legislation. As a result, the concept of equality in representation demands that when individuals are subject to the same laws, those individuals have an equal right to determine their representatives. As Waldron puts it, "we value the integrity of a deliberative process that ends in *voting* so that there is a fair basis for determining which among the various contributions that have been made in debate are to count as law and which are not".[80] Note here that Christiano diverges from Waldron about the point at which respect for individual judgment has to end.[81]

Here, again, I argue that this more concrete, institutional and methodological aspect of the broader conception of democracy *qua* internal sovereignty can justify (1) the normative basis, (2) the duties generated, as well as (3) the scope of the duties, of the ECtHR. However, an important *caveat* is in order: while the abstract concept of sovereign equality provides for the moral foundations, the concrete concept of representation addresses its limited practical, institutional and methodological implications, which help us to grasp the distinction between the normative role of ECHR rights *qua* international human rights and a broader and more demanding normative ideal that we may want to ascribe to democracy *tout court* or to the domestic concretization of ECHR rights. This is a general point about the legal and political dimension of international human rights: "complete justifications need not be given by international human rights law and its application, which only protect fundamental interests but leave the balancing between those interests and their concretisation to national legal orders".[82]

This is where the right to regular elections (Article 3 Protocol 1) takes its distinctive role. The moral, justificatory link between the two aspects of the conception is as follows. Democracy gives individuals equal abilities to advance their concerns on issues of public interest; therefore each individual should be provided with a vote of equal value in deciding the outcome of an election. By the same token, all can see that they are treated as equals. Majority rule is therefore obtained. As Christiano explains, "majority rule is a genuinely egalitarian rule because it gives each person the same chance as every other to affect the outcome".[83] Note that majority as a method for making the final choice is important

---

79 Waldron, *Law and Disagreement*, 23.
80 Ibid., 41. See also Christiano, *The Constitution of Equality: Democratic Authority and Its Limits*, 246.
81 Christiano, ibid., 285–6. See also Christiano, "Waldron on Law and Disagreement".
82 Besson, "The Authority of International Law – Lifting the State Veil", 377.
83 Christiano, *The Rule of the Many: Fundamental Issues in Democratic Theory*, 55.

Conclusion 231

in the egalitarian pedigree. The alternatives of *unanimity* and *supermajority* are inegalitarian in that they will favour the status quo and therefore only the interests of those favoured by the status quo.[84]

More precisely, let us come back to the reasoning of the ECtHR when it concretized the right and specified its interest in the first cases brought before the Commission. As I argued in Chapter 8, the interest captured by the ECtHR is also salient when the Court specifies what "regular election" implies – that is, the requirement of representation of the prevailing opinions of the electorate in the legislative body. Not only does the ECtHR hold that the conditions for elections "must reflect, or not run counter to, the concern to maintain the integrity and effectiveness of an electoral procedure aimed at identifying the will of the people through universal suffrage",[85] but it also sets limits on the institutional design that is deemed sufficient to guarantee its realization.

First, on the abstract normative level, why is the regularity of free and fair elections important? In *Timke v. Germany*, the Commission held:

> The Commission finds that the question whether elections held at reasonable intervals must be determined by the reference to the purpose of parliamentary elections. That purpose is to ensure that fundamental changes in prevailing public opinion are reflected in the opinions of the representatives of the people. Parliament must in principle be in a position to develop and execute its legislative intentions – including longer term legislative plans. Too short an interval between elections may impede political planning for the implementation of the will of the electorate. Too long an interval can lead to the petrification of political groupings in Parliament which may no longer bear any resemblance to the prevailing will of the electorate.[86]

Clearly, the ECtHR is protecting the expression of the opinion of the electorate through the right to free, fair and regular elections. This has been a constant justificatory ground of the Court. In *Lykourezos v. Greece*, the ECtHR held that conditions for elections "must reflect, or not run counter to, the concern to maintain the integrity and effectiveness of an electoral procedure aimed at identifying the will of the people through universal suffrage".[87] There must be a regular *test* of representation between the opinions of the represented electorate and the representative legislative body. This is clearly a realization of the *public equality* of individuals. This emphasis on the protection of "prevailing public opinion" also allows us to envision the conceptual interdependence, in the Court's view, of Article 3 Protocol 1 with Article 10 (freedom of expression) and Article 11 (freedom of association) through the overarching political morality they serve. Of course, if they form part of a continuum, they certainly do not play the same

---

84 Christiano, *The Constitution of Equality: Democratic Authority and Its Limits*, 103.
85 *Lykourezos v. Greece*, App. No. 33554/03, 15 June 2006, para. 52.
86 *Timke v. Germany*, App. No. 27311/95, 11 September 1995, p. 160.
87 *Lykourezos v. Greece*, para. 52.

232 *Conclusion*

specific role. Freedom of expression, we have seen, is prevalent in pre-electoral periods in the deliberation process whereas the right to elections sanctions or concretizes it: "the stage of voting and bargaining represents the end stage of the democratic process".[88]

Turning to the duties correlative to the right (3), the ECtHR has made clear that when representatives are elected, they can be subject to wider criticism:

> The limits of permissible criticism are wider with regard to the Government than in relation to a private citizen, or even a politician. In a democratic system the actions or omissions of the Government must be subject to the close scrutiny not only of the legislative and judicial authorities but also of the press and public opinion.[89]

Also, the ECtHR has made clear that the right does not simply justify the electoral process. It is crucial that the elected parliamentarian can actually hold office for the mandate. In *Sadak and Others v. Turkey*, the ECtHR made clear that the election must effectively lead to the elected politician sitting in office[90] and cannot be subject to arbitrariness in the designation of the seat, as in the fairly recent case of *Grosaru v. Romania*.[91] Furthermore, the ECtHR went on to find a principle of "legitimate expectation", according to which the elected parliamentarian must serve the interests of his or her constituents. This is clear from the important case of *Lykourezos v. Greece*, which concerned the disqualification by the Special Supreme Court of a Greek parliamentarian for exercising a profession; the ECtHR found a violation of such principle. In *Ahmed and Others v. United Kingdom*, the ECtHR held:

> Members of the public also have a right to expect that the members whom they voted into office will discharge their mandate in accordance with the commitments they made during an electoral campaign and that the pursuit of that mandate will not flounder on the political opposition of their members' own advisers.[92]

Another illustrative subject area assessed by the ECtHR concerns public officials (civil servants, police officers, the judiciary, etc.). In general, the Court is reluctant to restrict this right, given the role it serves in a democratic society.[93] However, as we have seen, Article 3 Protocol 1 is certainly not absolute. My hint here is that the very moral foundations of equality in deliberation can account for the core interests protected by the ECtHR as limited to the expression of

---

88 Christiano, *The Rule of the Many: Fundamental Issues in Democratic Theory*, 87.
89 Ibid., para. 46.
90 *Sadak and Others v. Turkey (No. 2)*, App. Nos. 25144/94, 26149/95, 26150/95, 26151/95, 26152/95, 26153/95, 26154/95, 27100/95, 27101/95, 11 June 2002, para. 33.
91 *Grosaru v. Romania*, App. No. 78039/01, 2 March 2010, para. 47.
92 *Ahmed and Others v. United Kingdom*, App. No. 22954/93, 2 September 1998, para. 53.
93 *Kavakçı v. Turkey*, App. No. 71907/01, 5 April 2007, para. 45.

the opinion of the electorate in the legislative body without specifying various requirements that may be associated with it. It does not protect this interest beyond a certain scope that the legal reasoning determines. The threshold is that the conditions for elections "must reflect, or not run counter to, the concern to maintain the integrity and effectiveness of an electoral procedure aimed at identifying the will of the people through universal suffrage".[94] At the level of concrete institutional design, the ECtHR, for instance, does not require States Parties to conform with a specific system of election and representation (proportional, majority, etc.) or the "specific electoral administration bodies",[95] as long as the core interest is effectively protected, and the Court therefore accords a wider margin of appreciation to States Parties in those matters. As the ECtHR held in the seminal case of *Mathieu-Mohin v. Belgium*:

> Article 3 (P1-3) provides only for "free" elections "at reasonable intervals", "by secret ballot" and "under conditions which will ensure the free expression of the opinion of the people". Subject to that, it does not create any "obligation to introduce a specific system" . . . such as proportional representation or majority voting with one or two ballots. Here too the Court recognises that the Contracting States have a wide margin of appreciation, given that their legislation on the matter varies from place to place and from time to time.[96]

There are several instances of this judicial restraint which corroborate this threshold. The same is true in *Py v. France* when the ECtHR held:

> The rules on granting the right to vote, reflecting the need to ensure both citizen participation and knowledge of the particular situation of the region in question, vary according to the historical and political factors peculiar to each State. The number of situations provided for in the legislation on elections in many member States of the Council of Europe shows the diversity of possible choices on the subject. However, none of these criteria should in principle be considered more valid than any other provided that it guarantees the expression of the will of the people through free, fair and regular elections.[97]

The issue of proportionality of representation of constituencies is another case in point. In *Bompard v. France*, where the ECtHR had to assess whether population differences infringed the principle of equal suffrage of constituencies in France, the Court also clearly confines its assessment to the core interest of the protected right:

---

94 *Lykourezos v. Greece*, para. 52.
95 *Georgian Labour Party v. Georgia*, App. No. 9103/04, 8 July 2008, para. 103.
96 *Mathieu-Mohin and Clerfayt v. Belgium*, App. No. 9267/81, 2 March 1987, para. 54.
97 *Py v. France*, App. No. 66289/01, 11 January 2005, para. 46.

234 *Conclusion*

In view of the foregoing, the Court considers that the introduction of such a system of electoral boundaries ensured that the right to vote was granted under conditions that reflected the need to ensure both citizen participation and knowledge of the particular situation of the region in question, fully in accordance with Article 3 of Protocol No. 1 . . . . In particular, those conditions could not in themselves have had the effect of impeding the "free expression of the opinion of the people in the choice of the legislature.[98]

In this respect, the right to elections as specified by the ECtHR focuses on the election of the legislative body, but not beyond. The Court generates positives duties for States Parties to meet this threshold. As it reiterated in *Yumak and Sadak v. Turkey*: "the State is under an obligation to adopt positive measures to 'organise' democratic elections 'under conditions which will ensure the free expression of the opinion of the people in the choice of the legislature'".[99] We may mention here the early rejection by the ECtHR of the right to a referendum mentioned in Chapter 8. We may also mention the absence in those positive obligations of strict equal media coverage for the 2003 presidential election campaign in *Communist Party of Russia and Others v. Russia*. The ECtHR relied on the following facts:

The applicants did obtain some measure of access to the nation-wide TV channels; thus, they were provided with free and paid airtime, with no distinction made between the different political forces. The amount of airtime allocated to the opposition candidates was not insignificant. The applicants did not claim that the procedure of distribution of airtime was unfair in any way. Similar provisions regulated access of parties and candidates to regional TV channels and other mass media. In addition, the opposition parties and candidates were able to convey their political message to the electorate through the media they controlled.[100]

Those limited duties shed light on the distinctive role of the ECtHR in safeguarding democracy *qua* internal sovereignty. The ECtHR does not design the constitutional arrangements of States Parties and their model of democracy in their specific detail in order to realize a strong form of political equality in society, but only a set of core safeguards that preserve the core idea of democracy *qua* internal sovereignty – that is, the representation of the prevailing public opinion in the legislature. There is a margin of appreciation, the ECtHR systematically holds, on the more specific duties that the States Parties have in those respects. As the ECtHR recalled in the recent case of *Scoppola v. Italy*:

There are numerous ways of organising and running electoral systems and a wealth of differences, inter alia, in historical development, cultural diversity

---

98 *Bompard v. France*, App. No. 44081/02, 4 April 2006, p. 9.
99 *Yumak and Sadak v. Turkey*, App. No. 10226/03, 8 July 2008, para. 106.
100 *Communist Party of Russia and Others v. Russia*, App. No. 29400/05, 19 June 2012, para. 126.

Conclusion 235

and political thought within Europe which it is for each Contracting State to mould into its own democratic vision.[101]

This is where the egalitarian argument in democratic theory demands much more than that which the ECtHR consents to protect under Article 3 Protocol 1. For instance, it would ask to scrutinize the role of legislators and the sphere of freedom they have in choosing the best means to reach the end they think appropriate to the common will. Democratic theorists disagree over the discretion that legislators should have without informing voters. Following the egalitarian argument of equality, it seems unclear why legislators could change the aims worthy of being pursued if voters have debated those aims. As Christiano puts it, "giving legislators authority to change aims would be an arbitrary infringement of the right of citizens to be equal members of the political community".[102]

Similarly, the ECtHR does not explain how we should specifically understand the relationship between interest groups and voters. The egalitarian argument would require that interest groups, such as NGOs, "do not advance their own aims by means of financing campaigns and lobbying the legislature; they are to serve the citizenry by contributing to its understanding of the issues".[103] Yet the ECtHR does not state any particular obligations on such grounds.

As a result, the moral significance of ECHR rights *qua* human rights should not be equated with what one may expect from other moral concepts that prevail in our ordinary political discussion within the state, such as *social justice*, and therefore with determinate principles on how to allocate the benefits and burdens of social and economic interaction. Social justice is far richer as it concerns "the kinds of claims people can make against each other in determining the appropriate balance of benefits and burdens".[104] One may defend an egalitarian conception of democracy and ascribe a minimal role to distributive justice in this respect.[105] However, this is not the core of the conception precisely because disagreement pervades the discussion of such matters. It is true that ECHR rights overlap with the ideal of justice in that both are founded on the basic principle of equality of advancement of individuals' interests and in that "a person whose judgment about society is never taken seriously by others [and] is treated in effect like a child or a madman"[106] and therefore as an inferior. However, their scope varies significantly. The ECHR rights *qua* human rights do not, therefore, advance the search for a richer account of equality among people, such as *equality of well-being* or an *equality of resources*, which are models with significant distributive implications. Christiano's account of equality that democracy realizes, for instances, requires an economic minimum in order to publicly treat individuals as equals.[107]

---

101 *Scoppola v. Italy (No. 3)*, App. No. 126/05, 22 May 2012, para. 39.
102 Christiano, *The Rule of the Many: Fundamental Issues in Democratic Theory*, 217.
103 Ibid., 257.
104 Christiano, *The Constitution of Equality: Democracic Authority and Its Limits*, 47.
105 Ibid., Chapter 2.
106 Ibid., 63.
107 Ibid., 272–4.

236 *Conclusion*

Nor should ECHR rights *qua* human rights be conceived as protecting a richer account of *political equality*. The ECtHR does not protect *equality of opportunity* in running for election, however central elections are to its own practical reason.[108] This is the blurry area in which we can characterize the distinctive role – following Beitzian standards – of ECHR rights *qua* international human rights. The ECHR, therefore, is not to be equated with the constitutional rights of national legal orders. Constitutional rights refer to the detailed legal organization of a state's internal sovereignty. Again, on the moral, justificatory level, this role may be served by a conception of the status of individuals in political morality – that of sovereign equals – but the scope of the normative ideal is again more modest. It also does not furnish, as we have seen, equal resources to understand and elaborate one's interest as the egalitarian argument for democracy may itself require. It does not require, as Christiano does, that laws and policies issued by the legislative body do not violate political equality.[109] ECHR rights *qua* human rights pose the minimal conditions for the possibility of democratic ruling in that they guarantee the process by which everyone's interests are considered equally, and the prevailing opinions are represented in the legislative body.

In this sense, democracy is a non-instrumental requirement of ECHR rights in that they do not specify the more particular arrangements of social justice or simply the realization of some end. At least, this is what the legal and judicial practice of ECHR rights suggests. As Christiano forcefully puts it, "this equality of decision-making cannot be justified by reference to any further substantive equality in law and politics because there is pervasive disagreement on these and because each has fundamental interests in advancing his or her judgment".[110] The only specific standards that may be required are those that aim to mitigate the effects of social status in furthering individual interests. The reasoning of the ECtHR and the restriction of the right to run for election are among such standards.[111] Yet they can be confined in justificatory terms to the conception of sovereign equality.

9.4 Step three: the reconciliation thesis

I can now get to the core of my argument by incorporating both the role that ECHR rights play in the ordinary legal life of Europeans *and* the reasoning of the ECtHR in specifying the content of those rights. In doing so, I strictly follow the constructivist procedure in that normative principles hold only when they survive the web of normative claims held by the ECtHR that serve the prominent role of ECHR rights in national legal orders. More precisely, the reconciliation is achieved by focusing on the concept that unlocks the discontinuity between *role* and *substance*: democracy *qua* internal sovereignty. The centrality of the concept of democracy *qua* internal sovereignty in our political morality gives reasons not

108 Ibid.
109 Christiano, *The Constitution of Equality: Democratic Authority and Its Limits*, 276.
110 Ibid., 96.
111 *Gitonas and Others v. Greece*, App. Nos. 18747/91, 19376/92, 19379/92, 1 July 1997, para. 40.

Conclusion 237

only to establish a system of international human rights but also to be prominently deployed in the adjudication of those abstract norms. The moral conception *serves* the practical role that the rights play in legal and judicial practice – both in national legal orders and the duties generated within the adjudication of the ECtHR – and thereby morally justifies them. One aspect of it can be expressed in functional, Beitzian terms, via the direct effect granted to ECHR rights and ECtHR judgments as well as the emerging *interpretative* or *persuasive* authority of the judgments in national legal orders. True, Beitz cannot account for the distinctively legal role that ECHR rights play. This is because he neglects the distinctively legal normativity of international human rights law and their normativity in States Parties as well as the structuring role of subsidiarity. As I argued in Chapter 3, one may wonder whether the *global standpoint* should be recommended as a practical standpoint to grasp the normativity of international human rights. The *subsidiarity* of international human rights implies that their legal and judicial practice is primarily to be found at the level of internal state practices. This has been done by examining the normative role of ECHR rights and ECtHR judgments in national legal orders.

Another aspect of the conception is expressed through the reasoning of the ECtHR via the prevalent balancing it has developed in respect of Articles 8 to 11 and Article 3 Protocol 1. The key question is whether the applicant's claims fall within the search for an informed debate on issues of political interest (Articles 10 and 11). Further, the ECtHR requires that legislative and executive power should be exercised in the name of the sovereign people only through regular elections tests (Article 3 Protocol 1). The centrality of democracy *qua* internal sovereignty as a normative quest in moral terms, *pace* Griffin, can therefore account for the role of the ECHR in legal practice, *pace* Beitz. The two conceptions, the ethical and the political, are therefore both necessary but not sufficient to account for the normativity of the ECHR. The continuum of function and substance is nicely put forward by Besson: "public institutions are necessary for collective endeavour and political self-determination, but they may also endanger them. Human rights enable the functioning of those institutions in exchange for political equality and protection from abuse of political power".[112] The attribute of subsidiarity, neglected in Beitz's account, is also thereby justified.

In other words, the final core argument is that ECHR rights *qua* international human rights (with special reference to Articles 8 to 11 and Article 3 Protocol 1) *consolidate* democracy *qua* internal sovereignty and, by the same token, reinforce the commitment to our status of equals in the legal and political orders of the States Parties. As such, democracy *qua* internal sovereignty falls within the range of *non-instrumental* justification for democracy. In that limited sense, we need the resource of moral conceptions and its appeal to a deeper moral layer of reasons if we do not want to leave this crucial aspect of the normative practice of

---

112 Besson, "Human Rights: Ethical, Political . . . or Legal? First Steps in a Legal Theory of Human Rights", 235.

238   *Conclusion*

ECHR rights in the dark. A final illustration to support it is to return to the reasoning of the ECtHR for a final push and address what it has held on the alleged right to self-determination. The sustained refusal of the Court to recognize the right to self-determination under the right to elections (Article 3 Protocol 1) and the reasons that it gives for it illustrate the role of the ECHR in guaranteeing and consolidating the internal sovereignty of the people *within* the state.

Indeed, if the overall point of ECHR rights is to consolidate the status of political equality *within* the state, they cannot by the same token protect the right to secede from the state. Rather, they aim to consolidate the responsiveness of the state already there with the demands of the people and their interests in having an equal say on the important issues that affect them. As the ECtHR held in *Refah Partisi v. Turkey*, "democracy requires that the people should be given a role. Only institutions created by and for the people may be vested with the powers and authority of the State".[113] This is not to say that self-determination is morally foreign to democratic values, of course. The ECtHR itself held that it "accepts that the principles supported by the HEP, such as the right to self-determination and recognition of language rights, are not in themselves contrary to the fundamental principles of democracy".[114] However, the ECtHR goes, it does not fall within the mandate of a human rights court – established by states and for states – to evaluate such a demand. This sheds light on another facet of the distinction between a richer normative ideal of democracy and that which is *co-original* with ECHR rights. As Besson forcefully explains, "the re-qualification of the human right to democracy also makes clear that democracy remains a distinct and autonomous value and principle, which can be used to criticize or provide a richer normative guidance in the interpretation of the right to democratic participation".[115]

The ECtHR has faced the issues of self-determination in a growing number of cases in treating them as the demands of "ethnic" or "national" minorities. While the Court places emphasis on the protection of the rights of such minorities to express their political views and their association – this is precisely an instance of their right *qua* sovereign equals – this protection ends when the claims reach the point of separatism and self-determination. ECHR rights *qua* international human rights protect the rights of individuals against the state, not the right to leave the state. The clearest instance in the case law lies in two paragraphs in *Gorzelik v. Poland*:

> A pluralist and genuinely democratic society should not only respect the ethnic, cultural, linguistic and religious identity of each person belonging to a national minority, but also create appropriate conditions enabling them to express, preserve and develop this identity. Indeed, forming an association in order to express and promote its identity may be instrumental in helping a minority to preserve and uphold its rights . . . .

---

113 *Refah Partisi (The Welfare Party) and Others v. Turkey*, para. 43.
114 *Yazar and Others v. Turkey*, para. 57.
115 Besson, "The Human Right to Democracy – A Moral Defence with a Legal Nuance", 14.

Conclusion 239

Freedom of association is not absolute, however, and it must be accepted that where an association, through its activities or the intentions it has expressly or implicitly declared in its programme, jeopardises the State's institutions or the rights and freedoms of others, Article 11 does not deprive the State of the power to protect those institutions and persons.[116]

It is important not to get the normative order wrong: the morality of democracy *qua* sovereign equality justifies its authority in national legal orders and its prominence in the adjudication of the ECtHR. Because of the stringency of their moral basis, those rights and their interests are also privileged in the case of conflicts with other ECHR rights, as we have seen. Our commitment to the status of equal sovereigns justifies their prevalent overriding power in adjudication too. It is also important to note briefly that when the ECtHR safeguards the core idea of representative democracy as " an electoral procedure aimed at identifying the will of the people through universal suffrage",[117] the will of the people is just one way of talking about the addition of individual claims to equal political standing. The ontology of democracy is a consequence of its morality. As Waldron puts it, "we can still adopt an individualist view of what democracy is, even if we concede that its success presupposes a certain social background".[118]

The overall consequence of this investigation is that there is no reason to think that ECHR rights *qua* human rights, in light of their embodiment within the legal and political orders of 47 States Parties across Europe and within the adjudication of the ECtHR, is a *sui generis* concept that political theory and the history of political ideas cannot understand and justify. The central question I addressed in this last chapter is the *extent* to which it is continuous with our political morality and with underlying traditions in political thought. To capture this threshold, it is necessary to address the very localized and specific circumstances of their practice and the justificatory reasoning found in that same practice (such as the generative force of Article 10) to the concrete legal and institutional implications (such as the limited scope of Article 3 Protocol 1). Human rights are just too wide as a moral concept to be apprehended independently of their concretization in law and politics. However, the emphasis on their concretization cannot, in turn, remain unaccounted for if they play such a role as public norms in domestic legal and political orders.

It is true that, because ECHR rights *qua* international human rights are an international legal creation and operate in complementing constitutional rights, their function is certainly novel in the legal and political practice of the post-1945 era in the additional, supranational safeguards for democracy they provide. However, it does not follow that the *reasons* for establishing and developing such practice, together with the broad conception of individuals it embodies, must be novel too. That being said, I am not claiming that the conception of sovereign equality in

---

116 *Gorezlik and Others v. Poland*, App. No. 44158/98, 17 February 2004, paras 93–4.
117 *Lykourezos v. Greece*, para. 52.
118 Waldron, "Democracy", 191.

240 *Conclusion*

the democratic tradition is the *only* conceptual framework that can be used for the philosophical elucidation of the ECHR as concretized in law. I want to suggest, however, that such an enterprise cannot be disconnected from the conceptual and normative frameworks we contemplate *within* the modern state – not only in functional and concrete terms about the role that human rights play in law and politics, but also in moral and abstract terms about the status of individuals in our political morality. At least, this is what the practice of the ECHR encourages us to do.

In relying on the constructivist view of justification, I have defended a conception of the normative foundations of ECHR rights – with particular reference to Articles 8 to 11 and Article 3 Protocol 1 – that inheres in three distinct layers of reasons that conceptually reinforce each other. Following constructivist standards, the reasoning of the ECtHR is privileged and sets standards by which other reasons may be endorsed. I therefore have searched for a moral conception that justifies the standards set by the practice as well as the role that ECHR rights have in national legal orders. Those standards are congruent with the ethical and political theories of human rights on the one hand, but they are clearly insufficient. Rather, I showed that the role of ECHR rights and their concretization in the case law are best justified by a conception of egalitarian democracy. Surely, this enterprise remains an ongoing investigation as much as law itself is an ongoing normative practice, but I hope to have paid enough attention to the localized legal and judicial practice of ECHR rights so that the conception does not leave us with the Razian worry of the "absence of a convincing argument as to why human rights practice should conform to their theories".[119] My response is constructivist in that the theorizing starts with a firm grip within the legal and judicial practice of the ECHR. It is a moral justification of the legal justification of ECHR rights by the ECtHR and the prominent role they hold in the ordinary legal and political life of 47 European states. As such, this investigation contributes to a political theory of the ECHR.

---

119 Raz, "Human Rights Without Foundations", 328–9.

Bibliography

Akira, Iriye, Petra Goedde and William I. Hitchcock, eds. *The Human Rights Revolution: An International History*. Oxford: Oxford University Press, 2012.

Arai-Takahashi, Yutaka. *The Margin of Appreciation Doctrine and the Principle of Proportionality in the Jurisprudence of the ECHR*. Antwerp: Intersentia, 2002.

——. "Disharmony in the Process of Harmonisation? – The Analytical Account of the Strasbourg Court's Variable Geometry Decision-Making Policy Based on the Margin of Appreciation Doctrine". In *Theory and Practice of Harmonisation*, edited by Mads Andenas and Camilla Baasch Anderson. Cheltenham: Edward Elgar, 2012.

Bagnoli, Carla. "Constructivism in Metaethics". In *The Stanford Encyclopedia of Philosophy*, edited by Edward N. Zalta. Winter 2011, available at http://plato.stanford.edu/archives/win2011/entries/constructivism-metaethics/.

Bates, Ed. "The Birth of the European Convention on Human Rights". In *The European Court of Human Rights Between Law and Politics*, edited by Jonas Christoffersen and Mikael Rask Madsen. Oxford: Oxford University Press, 2011.

Baynes, Kenneth. "Constructivism and Practical Reason in Rawls". *Analyse & Kritik* 14 (1992): 18–32.

——. "Discourse Ethics and the Political Conception of Human Rights". *Ethics & Global Politics* 2, no. 1 (2009): 1–21.

Beitz, Charles. "What Human Rights Mean". *Daedalus* 132, no. 1 (2003): 36–46.

——. "Human Rights and the Law of Peoples". In *The Ethics of Assistance: Morality and the Distant Needy*, edited by Deen Chatterjee. Cambridge: Cambridge University Press, 2004.

——. *The Idea of Human Rights*. New York: Oxford University Press, 2009.

BENEFRI. *La Cour européenne des droits de l'homme après le Protocole 14: premier bilan et perspectives/The European Court of Human Rights after Protocol 14: Preliminary Assessment and Perspectives*, edited by Samantha Besson. Genève: Schulthess, 2011.

Benvenisti, Eyal. "Margin of Appreciation, Consensus, and Universal Standards". *The NYU Journal of International Law & Politics* 31, no. 4 (1999): 843–54.

Bernardt, Rudolf. "Thoughts on the Interpretation of Human-Rights Treaties", quoted in Alastair Mowbray, "The Creativity of the European Court of Human Rights", *Human Rights Law Review* 5 (2005): 57–79, 60.

Besson, Samantha. "The Reception Process in Ireland and the United Kingdom". In *A Europe of Rights: The Impact of the ECHR on National Legal Systems*, edited by Alec Stone Sweet and Helen Keller. New York: Oxford University Press, 2008.

——. "The Authority of International Law – Lifting the State Veil". *Sydney Law Review* 31, no 3 (2009): 343–80.

242   *Bibliography*

——. "Human Rights *Qua* Normative Practice: *Sui Generis* or Legal?" *Transnational Legal Theory* 1, no. 1 (2010): 127–33.

——. "Les effets et l'exécution des arrêts de la Cour européenne des droits de l'homme – le cas de la Suisse". *EMRK und die Schweiz*, edited by Bernhard Ehrenzeller and Stefan Breitenmoser. St-Gallen: Institut für Rechtspraxis, 2010.

——. "The Human Right to Democracy – A Moral Defence with a Legal Nuance". In *Souveraineté et droits de l'homme*, Collection Science et Technique de la Société, Strasbourg: Editions du Conseil de l'Europe (2010), available at www.venice.coe.int/webforms/documents/?pdf=CDL-UD%282010%29003-e.

——. *Droit international public: abrégé de cours et résumés de jurisprudence*. Abrégé Stämpfli. Berne: Stämpfli, 2011.

——. "European Human Rights, Supranational Judicial Review and Democracy – Thinking Outside the Judicial Box". In *Human Rights Protection in the European Legal Orders: Interaction Between European Courts and National Courts*, edited by Patricia Poepelier, Catherine Van de Heyning and Piet Van Nuffel. Cambridge: Intersentia, 2011.

——. "Human Rights and Democracy in a Global Context: Decoupling and Recoupling". *Ethics & Global Politics* 4, no. 1 (2011): 19–50.

——. "Sovereignty, International Law and Democracy". *European Journal of International Law* 22, no. 2 (2011): 373–87.

——. "The 'Erga Omnes' Effect of the European Court of Human Rights". In *La Cour européenne des droits de l'homme après le Protocole 14: premier bilan et perspectives/ The European Court of Human Rights after Protocol 14: Preliminary Assessment and Perspectives*, edited by Samantha Besson. Genève: Schulthess, 2011.

——. "Human Rights: Ethical, Political . . . or Legal? First Steps in a Legal Theory of Human Rights". In *The Role of Ethics in International Law*, edited by Donald Earl Childress. Cambridge: Cambridge University Press, 2012.

——. "The Egalitarian Dimension of Human Rights". *Archiv für Sozial- und Rechtsphilosophie Beiheft* (2012), available at http://doc.rero.ch/record/203061/files/BESSON_S._-_The_Egalitarian_Dimension_of_Human_Rights.pdf.

——. "The Extraterritoriality of the European Convention on Human Rights: Why Human Rights Depend on Jurisdiction and What Jurisdiction Amounts To". *Leiden Journal of International Law* 25, no. 4 (2012): 857–84.

Besson, Samantha and John Tasioulas. "The Emergence of the Philosophy of International Law". In *The Philosophy of International Law*. New York: Oxford University Press, 2010.

Boillat, Philippe. "Le passé et l'avenir de la réforme". In *La Cour européenne des droits de l'homme après le Protocole 14: premier bilan et perspectives/The European Court of Human Rights after Protocol 14: Preliminary Assessment and Perspectives.*, edited by Samantha Besson. Zürich: Schulthess, 2011.

Brems, Eva. "The Margin of Appreciation in the Case Law of the ECHR". *Zeitschrift für Ausländisches Öffentliches Recht und Völkerrecht* 56 (1996): 230–314.

Brownlie, Ian. *Principles of Public International Law*. 7th edn. Oxford: Oxford University Press, 2008.

Buchanan, Allen. *Justice, Legitimacy, and Self-Determination: Moral Foundations for International Law*. Oxford: Oxford University Press, 2004.

——. "Equality and Human Rights". *Politics, Philosophy & Economics* 4, no. 1 (2005): 69–90.

Bibliography 243

———. "Human Rights and the Legitimacy of the International Order". *Legal Theory* 14, no. 1 (2008): 39–70.

———. "The Egalitarianism of Human Rights". *Ethics* 120, no. 4 (2010): 679–710.

———. "The Legitimacy of International Law". In *The Philosophy of International Law*, edited by Samantha Besson and John Tasioulas. New York: Oxford University Press, 2010.

———. "Human Rights". In *The Oxford Handbook of Political Philosophy*, edited by David Estlund. New York: Oxford University Press, 2012.

Caflisch, Lucius. "Le juge unique et les comités". In *La Cour européenne des droits de l'homme après Le Protocole 14: premier bilan et perspectives/The European Court of Human Rights after Protocol 14: Preliminary Assessment and Perspectives*, edited by Samantha Besson. Zürich: Schulthess, 2011.

Carozza, Paolo. "Uses and Misuses of Comparative Law in International Human Rights: Some Reflections on the Jurisprudence of the European Court of Human Rights". *Notre Dame Law Review* 73, no. 5 (1998), 1217–38.

Christiano, Thomas. *The Rule of the Many: Fundamental Issues in Democratic Theory*. Boulder: Westview Press, 1996.

———. "Waldron on Law and Disagreement". *Law and Philosophy* 19, no. 4 (2000): 513–43.

———. "A Democratic Theory of Territory and Some Puzzles About Global Democracy". *Journal of Social Philosophy* 37, no. 1 (2006): 81–107.

———. *The Constitution of Equality: Democratic Authority and Its Limits*. New York: Oxford University Press, 2010.

———. "Authority". In *The Stanford Encyclopedia of Philosophy*, edited by Edward N. Zalta. Spring 2013, available at http://plato.stanford.edu/archives/spr2013/entries/authority/

Christoffersen, Jonas and Mikael Rask Madsen, eds. *The European Court of Human Rights Between Law and Politics*. Cambridge: Cambridge University Press, 2011.

Cohen, Daniel G. "The Holocaust and the 'Human Rights Revolution': A Reassessment". In *The Human Rights Revolution: An International History*, edited by Akira Iriye, Petra Goedde and William I. Hitchcock. New York: Oxford University Press, 2012.

Cohen, G.A. "Facts and Principles". *Philosophy & Public Affairs* 31, no. 3 (2003): 211–45.

Cohen, Joshua. "Procedure and Substance in Deliberative Democracy". In *Philosophy and Democracy: An Anthology*, edited by Thomas Christiano. New York: Oxford University Press, 2003.

Council of Europe. *Collected Edition of the "Travaux Préparatoires" of the European Convention on Human Rights: Preparatory Commission of the Council of Europe, Committee of Ministers, Consultative Assembly, 11 May–8 September 1949*. Leiden: Brill, 1975.

Craven, Matthew. "Legal Differentiation and the Concept of the Human Rights Treaty in International Law". *European Journal of International Law* 11, no. 3 (2000): 489–519.

De Schutter, Olivier and Françoise Tulkens. "Rights in Conflicts: The European Court of Human Rights as a Pragmatic Institution". In *Conflicts Between Fundamental Rights*, edited by Eva Brems. Oxford: Intersentia, 2008.

Ducoulombier, Peggy. "Conflicts Between Fundamental Rights and the European Court of Human Rights". In *Conflicts Between Fundamental Rights*, edited by Eva Brems. Oxford: Intersentia, 2008.

———. *Les conflits de droits fondamentaux devant la Cour européenne des droits de l'homme*. Bruxelles: Emile Bruylant, 2011.

Dworkin, Ronald. *Taking Rights Seriously*. London: Duckworth, 2005.

244   Bibliography

Edmundson, William A. *An Introduction to Rights*. Cambridge: Cambridge University Press, 2012.

Elster, John. "Constitutional Bootstrapping in Philadelphia and Paris". In *Constitutionalism, Identity, Difference and Legitimacy*, edited by M. Rosenfeld. Durham, NC: Duke University Press, 1994.

European Movement. *European Movement and the Council of Europe*. London: Hutchinson, 1949.

Feinberg, Joel and Jan Narveson. "The Nature and Value of Rights". *The Journal of Value Inquiry* 4, no. 4 (1970): 243–60.

Flauss, Jean-François. "L'effectivité des arrêts de la Cour européenne des droits de l'homme: du politique au juridique et vice-versa". *Revue trimestrielle des droits de l'homme* 77 (2009): 27–72.

Føllesdal, Andreas, Johan Karlsson Schaffer and Geir Ulfstein, eds. *The Legitimacy of International Human Rights Regimes*. New York: Cambridge University Press, 2013.

Forowicz, Magdalena. *The Reception of International Law in the European Court of Human Rights*. New York: Oxford University Press, 2010.

Forst, Rainer. "The Basic Right to Justification: Towards a Constructivist Conception of Human Rights". *Constellations* 6, no. 1 (1999): 35–60.

——. "The Justification of Human Rights and the Basic Right to Justification: A Reflexive Approach". *Ethics* 120, no. 4 (2010): 711–40.

Freeman, Samuel. "The Burdens of Public Justification: Constructivism, Contractualism, and Publicity". *Politics, Philosophy & Economics* 6, no. 1 (2007): 5–43.

——. "Constructivism, Facts, and Moral Justification". In *Contemporary Debates in Political Philosophy*, edited by Thomas Christiano and John Christman. Malden: Wiley-Blackwell, 2009.

Gardbaum, Stephen. "Human Rights as International Constitutional Rights". *The European Journal of International Law* 19, no. 4 (2008): 749–68.

Gerards, Janneke. "Judicial Deliberations in the European Court of Human Rights" (2008), available at http://papers.ssrn.com/sol3/papers.cfm?abstract_id=1114906.

Gerards, Janneke and Hanneke Senden. "The Structure of Fundamental Rights and the European Court of Human Rights". *International Journal of Constitutional Law* 7, no. 4 (2009): 619–53.

Gewirth, Alan. "Rights and Virtues". *The Review of Metaphysics* 38, no. 4 (1985): 739–62.

Green, Leslie. "Legal Obligation and Authority". In *The Stanford Encyclopedia of Philosophy*, edited by Edward N. Zalta. Winter 2012, available at http://plato.stanford.edu/archives/win2012/entries/legal-obligation/

Greer, Steven. "Constitutionalizing Adjudication under the European Convention on Human Rights". *Oxford Journal of Legal Studies* 23, no. 3 (2003): 405–33.

——. "Balancing and the European Court of Human Rights: A Contribution to the Habermas-Alexy Debate". *The Cambridge Law Journal* 63, no. 2 (2004): 412–34.

——. *The European Convention on Human Rights : Achievements, Problems and Prospects*. New York: Cambridge University Press, 2006.

——. "What's Wrong with the European Convention on Human Rights". *Human Rights Quarterly* 30 (2008): 680–702.

——. "Europe". In *International Human Rights Law*, edited by Daniel Moeckli, Sangeeta Shah and Sandesh Sivakumaran. New York: Oxford University Press, 2011.

——. "The New Admissibility Criterion". In *La Cour européenne des droits de l'homme après le Protocole 14: premier bilan et perspectives/The European Court of Human*

Rights after Protocol 14: Preliminary Assessment and Perspectives, edited by Samantha Besson. Zürich: Schulthess, 2011.
Griffin, James. *Value Judgement: Improving Our Ethical Beliefs*. New York: Oxford University Press, 1998.
——. "Discrepancies Between the Best Philosophical Account of Human Rights and the International Law of Human Rights". *Proceedings of the Aristotelian Society* 101, no. 1 (2001): 1–28.
——. *On Human Rights*. New York: Oxford University Press, 2008.
——. "Human Rights and the Autonomy of International Law". In *The Philosophy of International Law*, edited by Samantha Besson and John Tasioulas. New York: Oxford University Press, 2010.
Geuss, Raymond. *History and Illusion in Politics*. Cambridge: Cambridge University Press, 2001.
Harmsen, Robert. "The Reform of the Convention System". In *The European Court of Human Rights Between Law and Politics*, edited by Jonas Christoffersen and Mikael Rask Madsen. New York: Oxford University Press, 2011.
Helfer, Laurence. "Consensus, Coherence and the European Convention on Human Rights". *Cornell International Law Journal* 26, (1993): 133–65.
——. "Redesigning the European Court of Human Rights: Embeddedness as a Deep Structural Principle of the European Human Rights Regime". *The European Journal of International Law* 19, no. 1 (2008): 125–59.
Helfer, Laurence and Anne-Marie Slaughter. "Toward a Theory of Effective Supranational Adjudication". *Yale Law Journal* 107, no. 2 (1997): 273–391.
Helfer, Laurence and Erik Voeten. "International Courts as Agents of Legal Change: Evidence from LGBT Rights in Europe". *International Organization* 68, no. 1 (2014): 77–110.
Jacquemot, Florence. *Le standard européen de société démocratique*. Montpellier: Université de Montpellier, 2006.
James, Aaron. "Constructing Protagorean Objectivity". In *Constructivism in Practical Philosophy*, edited by James Lenman and Yonatan Shemmer. Oxford: Oxford University Press, 2012.
——. "Constructivism, Moral". In *The International Encyclopedia of Ethics*, edited by Hugh Lafollette. Hoboken, NJ: Wiley-Blackwell, 2013.
——. "Political Constructivism". In *A Companion to Rawls*, edited by Jon Mandel and David A. Reidy. Hoboken, NJ: Wiley-Blackwell, 2013.
——. "Political Constructivism: Foundations and Novel Applications", available at http://philpapers.org/rec/JAMPCF
Keller, Helen and Alec Stone Sweet. "Assessing the Impact of the ECHR in National Legal Systems". In *A Europe of Rights: The Impact of the ECHR in National Legal Systems*, edited by Helen Keller and Alec Stone Sweet. New York: Oxford University Press, 2010.
Keller, Helen and Geir Ulfstein. "Introduction". In *UN Human Rights Treaty Bodies: Law and Legitimacy*, edited by Helen Keller and Geir Ulfstein. Cambridge: Cambridge University Press, 2012.
Korsgaard, Christine. *The Sources of Normativity*. Cambridge: Cambridge University Press, 1996.
——. "Realism and Constructivism in Twentieth-Century Moral Philosophy". In *The Constitution of Agency*, APA Centennial Supplement to *The Journal of Philosophical Research*, Charlottesville: The Philosophy Documentation Center (2008), 302–46.

246   Bibliography

Krisch, Nico. *Beyond Constitutionalism: The Pluralist Structure of Postnational Law*. Oxford: Oxford University Press, 2012.

Lambert Abdelgawad, Elisabeth. *L'exécution des arrêts de la Cour européenne des droits de l'homme*. Council of Europe, 2008, available at http://hal.archives-ouvertes.fr/hal-00377500

——. "L'exécution des arrêts de la Cour européenne des droits de l'homme". In *Revue trimestrielle de droits de l'homme* (2012), 861–86.

Lécuyer, Yannick. *Les droits politiques dans la jurisprudence de la Cour européenne des droits de l'homme*. Paris: Dalloz, 2009.

Lenman, James and Yonatan Shemmer. "Introduction". In *Constructivism in Practical Philosophy*, edited by James Lenman and Yonatan Shemmer. Oxford: Oxford University Press, 2012.

Lester, Anthony. "The European Court of Human Rights after 50 Years". In *The European Court of Human Rights Between Law and Politics*, edited by Jonas Christoffersen and Mikael Rask Madsen. Cambridge: Cambridge University Press, 2011.

Letsas, George. "Two Concepts of the Margin of Appreciation". *Oxford Journal of Legal Studies* 26, no. 4 (2006): 705–32.

——. *A Theory of Interpretation of the European Convention on Human Rights*. New York: Oxford University Press, 2009.

——. "Strasbourg's Interpretive Ethic: Lessons for the International Lawyer". *The European Journal of International Law* 21, no. 3 (2010): 509–41.

Lord Lester of Herne Hill. "Universality Versus Subsidiarity: A Reply". *European Human Rights Law Review* 1 (1998): 73–81.

Madsen, Mikael Rask. "From Cold War Instrument to Supreme European Court: The European Court of Human Rights at the Crossroads of International and National Law and Politics". *Law & Social Inquiry* 32, no. 1 (2007): 137–59.

——. "The Protracted Institutionalization of the Strasbourg Court". In *The European Court of Human Rights Between Law and Politics*, edited by Jonas Christoffersen and Mikael Rask Madsen. New York: Oxford University Press, 2011.

Mahoney, Paul. "Marvellous Richness of Diversity or Invidious Cultural Relativism". *Human Rights Law Journal* 19 (1998): 1–6.

Marmor, Andrei. *Interpretation and Legal Theory*. Oxford: Clarendon Press, 1992.

——. "On the Limits of Rights". *Law and Philosophy* 16, no. 1 (1997): 1–18.

Marshall, Jill. *Personal Freedom through Human Rights Law? Autonomy, Identity and Integrity under the European Convention on Human Rights*. Leiden: Brill, 2009.

Matscher, Franz "The Methods of Interpretation of the Convention". In *The European System for the Protection of Human Rights*, edited by Ronald St. John Macdonald, Franz Matscher and Herbert Petzold. Dordrecht: Martinus Nijhoff, 1993.

——. "La Cour européenne des droits de l'homme, aujourd'hui et demain, du lendemain de son cinquantième anniversaire: regards d'un ancien juge de la Cour". *Revue trimestrielle des droits de l'homme* 20, no. 80 (2009): 901–21.

Mazower, Mark. *No Enchanted Palace: The End of Empire and the Ideological Origins of the United Nations*. Princeton, NJ: Princeton University Press, 2009.

McCrudden, Christopher. "Human Dignity and Judicial Interpretation of Human Rights". *European Journal of International Law* 19, no. 4 (2008): 655–724.

McHarg, Aileen. "Reconciling Human Rights and the Public Interest: Conceptual Problems and Doctrinal Uncertainty in the Jurisprudence of the European Court of Human Rights". *The Modern Law Review* 62, no. 5 (1999): 671–96.

Bibliography   247

Moravcsik, Andrew. "The Origins of Human Rights Regimes: Democratic Delegation in Postwar Europe". *International Organization* 54, no. 2 (2000): 217–52.

Morsink, Johannes. *Inherent Human Rights: Philosophical Roots of the Universal Declaration*. Philadelphia: University of Pennsylvania Press, 2010.

Mowbray, Alastair. "The Creativity of the European Court of Human Rights". *Human Rights Law Review* 5, no. 1 (2005): 57–79.

——. "A Study of the Principle of Fair Balance in the Jurisprudence of the European Court of Human Rights". *Human Rights Law Review* 10, no. 2 (2010): 289–317.

Moyn, Samuel. "The Last Utopia: Human Rights in History". *The Nation*, 11 August 2010, available at www.thenation.com/article/153993/human-rights-history

Nagel, Thomas. *Equality and Partiality*. New York: Oxford University Press, 1991.

Neuman, Gerald. "Human Rights and Constitutional Rights: Harmony and Dissonance". *Stanford Law Review* 55 (2003): 1863–1900.

Nickel, James. *Making Sense of Human Rights*. Malden, MA: Blackwell, 2007.

Nickel, James and David A. Reidy. "Philosophy". In *International Human Rights Law*, edited by Daniel Moeckli, Sangeeta Shah and Sandesh Sivakumaran. New York: Oxford University Press, 2010.

Nollkaemper, André. *National Courts and the International Rule of Law*. New York: Oxford University Press, 2011.

Nussbaum, Martha. "Capabilities and Human Rights". In *Global Justice and Transnational Justice*, edited by Ciaran Cronin and Pablo de Greiff. Cambridge, MA: The MIT Press: 2002.

O'Neill, Onora. "Political Liberalism and Public Reason: A Critical Notice of John Rawls, Political Liberalism". *The Philosophical Review* 106, no. 3 (1997): 411–28.

——. "Constructivism vs. Contractualism". *Ratio* 16, no. 4 (2003): 319–31.

——. "Constructivism in Rawls and Kant". In *The Cambridge Companion to Rawls*, edited by Samuel Freeman. Cambridge: Cambridge University Press, 2003.

——. "The Dark Side of Human Rights". *International Affairs* 81, no. 2 (2005): 427–39.

Ost, François. "The Original Canons of Interpretation of the European Court of Human Rights". In *The European Convention on Human Rights: International Protection vs. National Restrictions*, edited by Mireille Delmas-Marty. Dordrecht: Kluwer, 1992.

Parkinson, John and Jane Mansbridge. *Deliberative Systems: Deliberative Democracy at the Large Scale*. Cambridge: Cambridge University Press, 2012.

Perry, Michael. *Toward a Theory of Human Rights: Religion, Law, Courts*. Cambridge: Cambridge University Press, 2008.

Pogge, Thomas. "The Incoherence Between Rawls's Theories of Justice". *Fordham Law Review* 72, no. 5 (2004): 1739–59.

——. *World Poverty and Human Rights: Cosmopolitan Responsibilities and Reforms*. Cambridge: Polity Press, 2008.

Polakiewicz, Jörg. "The Status of the Convention in National Law". In *Fundamental Rights in Europe: The ECHR and Its Member States 1950–2000*, edited by Robert Blackburn and Jörg Polakiewicz. New York: Oxford University Press, 2001.

Rawls, John. *A Theory of Justice*. Cambridge, MA: Belknap Press of Harvard University Press, 1971.

——. "Kantian Constructivism in Moral Theory". *The Journal of Philosophy* 77, no. 9 (1980): 515–72.

——. *Political Liberalism*. New York: Columbia University Press, 1993.

——. *The Law of Peoples: With "The Idea of Public Reason Revisited"*. Cambridge, MA: Harvard University Press, 2001.

248 Bibliography

Raz, Joseph. "Legal Rights". *Oxford Journal of Legal Studies* 4, no. 1 (1984): 1–21.
——. "On the Nature of Rights". *Mind* XCIII, no. 370 (1984): 194–214.
——. *The Morality of Freedom*. New York: Oxford University Press, 1988.
——. "Interpretation Without Retrieval". In *Law and Interpretation: Essays in Legal Philosophy*, edited by Andrei Marmor. New York: Oxford University Press, 1995.
——. "Rights and Politics". *Indiana Law Journal* 71, no. 1 (1995): 27–44.
——. "On the Nature of Law". *Archiv. für Rechts-und Sozialphilosophie* 82, no. 1 (1996): 1–25.
——. "The Problem of Authority: Revisiting the Service Conception", *Minnesota Law Review* 90 (2006): 1003–44.
——. "Human Rights Without Foundations". In *The Philosophy of International Law*, edited by Samantha Besson and John Tasioulas. New York: Oxford University Press, 2010.
——. "Human Rights in the Emerging World Order". *Transnational Legal Theory* 1, no. 1 (2010): 31–47.
Ress, George. "The Effect of Decisions and Judgments of the European Court of Human Rights in the Domestic Legal Order". *Texas International Law Journal* 40, no. 3 (2004): 359–82.
Risse, Thomas and Kathryn Sikkink. "The Socialization of International Human Rights Norms into Domestic Practices: Introduction". In *The Power of Human Rights: International Norms and Domestic Change*, edited by Thomas Risse, Steven C. Ropp and Kathryn Sikkink. Cambridge: Cambridge University Press, 1999.
Ronzoni, Miriam and Laura Valentini. "On the Meta-ethical Status of Constructivism: Reflections on G.A. Cohen's 'Facts and Principles'". *Politics, Philosophy & Economics* 7, no. 4 (2008): 403–22.
Rosen, Michael. *Dignity: Its History and Meaning*. Cambridge, MA: Harvard University Press, 2012.
Scanlon, T.M. *What We Owe to Each Other*. Cambridge, MA: Harvard University Press, 2000.
——. "Rawls on Justification". In *The Cambridge Companion to Rawls*, edited by Samuel Freeman. Cambridge: Cambridge University Press, 2003.
Schlütter, Birgit. "Aspects of Human Rights Interpretation by the UN Treaty Bodies". In *Human Treaty Bodies: Law and Legitimacy*, edited by Helen Keller and Geir Ulfstein. Cambridge: Cambridge University Press, 2012.
Shany, Yuval. "Toward a General Margin of Appreciation Doctrine in International Law?" *European Journal of International Law* 16, no. 5 (2005): 907–40.
Shaw, Malcolm. *International Law. Vol. 6*. Cambridge: Cambridge University Press, 2008.
Shue, Henry. *Basic Rights: Subsistence, Affluence, and U.S. Foreign Policy*. Princeton, NJ: Princeton University Press, 1996.
Simmons, A. John. "Justification and Legitimacy". *Ethics* 109, no. 4 (1999): 739–71.
Simpson, Alfred William Brian. *Human Rights and the End of Empire: Britain and the Genesis of the European Convention*. New York: Oxford University Press, 2004.
Smet, Stijn. "Freedom of Expression and the Right to Reputation: Human Rights in Conflict". *American University International Law Review* 26 (2010): 183.
Song, Edward. "Rawls's Liberal Principle of Legitimacy". *The Philosophical Forum* 43, no. 2 (2012): 153–73.
Stone Sweet, A. and Helen Keller. "The Reception of the ECHR in National Legal Orders". *Faculty Scholarship Series* Paper 89 (2008), available at http://digitalcommons.law.yale.edu/fss_papers/89

Bibliography   249

Stone Sweet, Alec. "On the Constitutionalisation of the Convention: The European Court of Human Rights as a Constitutional Court", Faculty Scholarship Series Paper 71 (2009), available at http://digitalcommons.law.yale.edu/fss_papers/71/

Street, Sharon. "Constructivism About Reasons". In *Oxford Studies in Metaethics*, edited by Russ Shafer-Landau. Vol. 3. Oxford: Oxford University Press, 2008.

——. "What Is Constructivism in Ethics and Metaethics?" *Philosophy Compass* 5, no. 5 (2010): 363–84.

Tasioulas, John. "In Defence of Relative Normativity: Communitarian Values and the Nicaragua Case". *Oxford Journal of Legal Studies* 16, no. 1 (1996): 85–128.

——. "Human Rights, Universality and the Values of Personhood: Retracing Griffin's Steps". *European Journal of Philosophy* 10, no. 1 (2002): 79–100.

——. "The Moral Reality of Human Rights". In *Freedom from Poverty as a Human Right*, edited by Thomas Pogge. New York: Oxford University Press, 2004.

——. "Are Human Rights Essentially Triggers for Intervention?" *Philosophy Compass* 4, no. 6 (2009): 938–50.

——. "Taking Rights out of Human Rights". *Ethics* 120, no. 4 (July 2010): 647–78.

Teitgen, Pierre-Henri. "Establishment of a Collective Guarantee of Essential Freedoms and Fundamental Rights", Doc. 77, 5 September 1949, available at http://assembly.coe.int/nw/xml/XRef/Xref-XML2HTML-en.asp?fileid=36&lang=en

Toma, Ramona. *La réalité judiciaire de la Cour européenne des droits de l'homme*. Baden-Baden: Nomos Verlagsgesellschaft, 2003.

Valentini, Laura. "Global Justice and Practice-Dependence: Conventionalism, Institutionalism, Functionalism". *Journal of Political Philosophy* 19, no. 4 (2011): 399–418.

——. "Human Rights, Freedom, and Political Authority". *Political Theory* 40, no. 5 (2012): 573–601.

——. "In What Sense Are Human Rights Political? A Preliminary Exploration". *Political Studies* 60, no. 1 (2012): 180–94.

Van Alebeek, Rosanne and André Nollkaemper. "The Legal Status of Decisions by Human Rights Treaty Bodies in National Law". In *UN Human Rights Treaty Bodies*, edited by Helen Keller and Geir Ulfstein. Cambridge: Cambridge University Press, 2012.

Waldron, Jeremy. "A Right-Based Critique of Constitutional Rights". *Oxford Journal of Legal Studies* 13, no. 1 (1993): 18–51.

——. *Law and Disagreement*. New York: Oxford University Press, 2001.

——. "The Core of the Case Against Judicial Review". *The Yale Law Journal* (2006): 1346–406.

——. "Judges as Moral Reasoners". *International Journal of Constitutional Law* 7, no. 1 (2009): 2–24.

——. "The Rule of International Law". *Harvard Journal of Law and Public Policy* 30, no. 1 (2010): 15–30.

——. "Democracy". In *The Oxford Handbook of Political Philosophy*, edited by David Estlund. New York: Oxford University Press, 2012.

——. *Dignity, Rank, and Rights*, edited by Meir Dan-Cohen. New York: Oxford University Press, 2012.

——. "Political Theory: An Inaugural Lecture". *Journal of Political Philosophy* 21, no. 1 (2013): 1–23.

Weiler, Joseph. "The Geology of International Law – Governance, Democracy and Legitimacy". *Heidelberg Journal of International Law* 64 (2004): 547–62.

Wheatley, Steven. "On the Legitimate Authority of International Human Rights Bodies". In *The Legitimacy of International Human Rights Regimes*, edited by Andreas Føllesdal,

250   *Bibliography*

Johan Karlsson Schaffer and Geir Ulfstein. Cambridge: Cambridge University Press, 2013.

White, Robin, Claire Ovey and Francis Jacobs. *The European Convention on Human Rights*. Vol. 5. New York: Oxford University Press, 2010.

Wildhaber, Luzius. "The European Convention on Human Rights and International Law". *International and Comparative Law Quarterly* 56, no. 2 (2007): 217–32.

Yourow, Charles Howard. *The Margin of Appreciation Doctrine in the Dynamics of European Human Rights Jurisprudence*. International Studies in Human Rights. The Hague: Kluwer Law International, 1996.

Index

accessibility of law 141
agnosticism 137, 189, 193
authority 1, 11, 13, 14, 16, 23, 27, 40, 46, 50, 62, 74, 84, 85, 86, 90, 94, 95, 96, 97, 99, 107, 108, 109, 110, 111, 116, 117, 118, 119, 120, 143, 146, 163, 203, 209, 212, 220, 222, 240, 235, 237, 238, 239
autonomous concepts 122, 127, 129
autonomy 3, 5, 26, 32, 33, 38, 42, 45, 61, 87, 100, 154, 158, 193, 199, 200, 202

balancing 26, 27, 85, 121, 122, 125, 138, 139, 140, 145, 147, 148, 149, 150, 151, 152, 168, 187, 199, 201, 204, 209, 2010, 130, 237

cognitive bias 219, 222
common social practice 71, 73
conception of life 189, 190, 193
conception of morals 146, 189, 196, 199
consensualism 98, 120, 123, 130, 131, 132, 133, 134, 140, 152, 153, 175, 188, 195, 197, 198, 199, 201, 207, 208
constructivism 17, 18, 24, 25, 27, 29, 44, 46, 64, 65, 66, 67, 68, 69, 70, 71, 72, 73, 74, 75. 76, 92, 94, 101, 120, 137, 138, 139, 153, 208, 209, 210, 211, 215, 217, 218, 220, 236, 240
content-dependence 94
content-independence 94, 120

democratic society 26, 69, 135, 139, 140, 142, 149, 150, 151, 153, 154, 155, 156, 158, 159, 160, 161, 162, 164, 170, 171, 174, 178, 180, 181, 186, 190, 190, 191, 192, 193, 198, 204, 207, 208, 216, 217, 219, 221, 222, 223, 225, 226, 227, 228, 232, 238

deontologism 29, 36, 45, 143, 150
dignity 1, 2, 3, 9, 22, 25, 33, 35, 39, 46, 48, 57, 190, 191, 201
direct effect 16, 26, 74, 92, 93, 96, 104, 105, 106, 107, 108, 109, 111, 112, 113, 114, 120, 214, 237
disagreement 4, 6, 12, 14, 16, 30, 50, 122, 134, 218, 219, 220, 222, 225, 229, 230, 235, 236
dualism 103, 104, 106

egalitarian self-rule 230
equality in deliberation 27, 210, 218, 219, 220, 226, 227, 229, 232
equality in representation 27, 218, 229, 230
erga omnes effect 117, 188
evolutive interpretation 26, 122, 123, 125, 126, 129, 130, 131, 132, 133, 134, 139, 197
external sovereignty 130, 208
extraterritoriality 95, 96

fair balance 139, 141, 150, 150, 152, 202
fictitious author 123, 125, 134
foreseeability of law 141
forum internum 193, 194
freedom of association 82, 129, 141, 144, 149, 174, 175, 177, 178, 179, 180, 182, 185, 191, 193, 201, 207, 211, 218, 219, 220, 222, 223, 224, 234, 238, 239
freedom of expression 2, 5, 6, 32, 43, 55, 77, 82, 122, 139, 140, 141, 144, 148, 149, 154, 155, 156, 157, 158, 159, 161, 162, 164, 165, 166, 167, 168, 169, 170, 171, 172, 174, 175, 176, 177, 178, 179, 180, 181, 183, 185, 186, 187, 191, 192, 193, 197, 198, 199, 203, 204, 205, 207,

252 *Index*

208, 211, 218, 221, 222, 224, 227, 228, 229, 231, 232, 233, 234

freedom of religion 61, 139, 141, 144, 149, 166, 170, 189, 190, 191, 192, 193, 194, 195, 196, 198, 204

global political life 12, 19, 55, 212, 213

human right to democracy 218, 238

implicit basis of agreement 69
incitement to violence 172, 173, 228, 229
intentionalism 120, 125, 127, 128, 130, 136
inter partes regime 95, 108, 118
interest-based theory 10, 11, 37, 216
internal sovereignty 27, 208, 209, 210, 211, 220, 226, 229, 230, 234, 236, 237, 238
international intervention 6, 60, 212
intuitionism 66

judicial activism 86, 90, 116, 230
judicial dialogue 15, 112
judicial restraint 146, 196, 197, 201, 202, 233

Kantian constructivism 67, 68

legal diplomacy 85, 86
legislative body 79, 182, 185, 186, 230, 231, 233, 234, 236
legitimacy 14, 20, 23, 24, 46, 53, 61, 74, 93, 98, 99, 100, 101, 102, 103, 108, 130, 131, 134, 190
legitimate aim 142, 151, 153
legitimate authority 95, 99

margin of appreciation 13, 20, 26, 27, 74, 98, 108, 120, 130, 131, 133, 134, 140, 141, 142, 143, 144, 145, 146, 147, 148, 149, 150, 151, 152, 153, 54, 155, 159, 162, 172, 175, 186, 187, 188, 189, 190, 191, 196, 197, 198, 199, 201, 202, 207, 208, 223, 224, 226, 227, 229, 233, 234
materials of construction 17
monism 103, 104, 106
moral conception of human rights 4, 5, 6, 8, 11, 21, 25, 28, 28, 62, 215, 237
moral truth 17, 68, 72, 73, 121, 124, 127, 133, 135, 137, 138, 222

Normal Justification Thesis 94
normative agency 4, 32, 33, 35, 41, 42, 45, 216

normative legitimacy 15, 20, 98, 99, 100, 101, 190
normativity 10, 17, 20, 22, 26, 48, 51, 52, 54, 55, 57, 58, 62, 65, 73, 76, 89, 92, 93, 94, 95, 96, 99, 103, 104, 107, 111, 113, 120, 209, 211, 214, 215, 217, 237

objectivity 17, 66
originalism 123, 127, 136

paradigm of implementation 19, 40, 52, 63, 86, 211
personal identity 190, 195
personhood 4, 5, 6, 9, 11, 25, 28, 29, 30, 31, 32, 33, 34, 35, 36, 37, 38, 39, 40, 41, 42, 43, 44, 45, 48, 57, 58, 59, 63, 72, 75, 215, 216, 217
pilot judgment 90, 116
pluralism 154, 155, 156, 158, 166, 170, 172, 174, 176, 177, 178, 189, 190, 191, 193, 196, 219, 221, 222, 223, 224, 227, 230
political conception of human rights 4, 11, 12, 14, 19, 22, 24, 25, 27, 28, 46, 47, 48, 62, 64, 66, 70, 73, 75, 76, 92, 93, 120, 139, 209, 211, 217
political equality 27, 210, 211, 222
political morality 67, 73, 2010, 233, 236, 239, 240
positive duties 37, 74, 154, 189, 195, 199, 219, 208, 223
positivism 101, 121, 217
practicalities 34, 36, 37, 38, 41
practice-dependence 11, 12, 25, 45, 47, 48, 56, 60, 62, 75, 212, 214
practice-independence 11, 25, 28, 31, 38, 40, 43, 45, 48, 63, 75
preferential framing 148, 153, 158
pressing social need 139, 142, 150
pro tanto reasons 10, 14, 16, 56, 57, 74, 215, 216, 235
proportionality 143, 151, 152, 186, 187, 233
Protocol no. 11 15, 82, 88, 89, 108, 110, 111, 115
Protocol no. 14 90, 116
public interest 140, 143, 145, 146, 150, 151, 154, 155, 156, 157, 158, 159, 160, 161, 162, 163, 164, 166, 167, 168, 169, 170, 171, 172, 173, 174, 175, 176, 177, 180, 185, 191, 182, 193, 196, 203, 204, 205, 207, 208, 211, 218, 220, 221, 222, 223, 224, 226, 227, 228, 230
public morals 146, 151, 153
public reason 61, 62

realism/anti-realism 66
relativism 66, 153, 222
res interpretata 95, 118, 209, 217
res judicata 95, 118, 209, 217
restitutio in integrum 114, 116, 120
restricted set of normative judgments 70, 71
right to free elections 4, 139, 164, 165, 171, 180, 181, 185, 186, 187, 231, 233
right to individual petition 76, 77, 82, 83, 84, 85, 86, 88, 107, 111, 112, 113, 139
right to private life 82, 133, 141, 143, 144, 164, 165, 167, 168, 169, 175, 188, 192, 199, 200, 202, 204
rule of law 51, 87, 124, 125, 127, 130, 136
rule of recognition 217

source thesis 217
state neutrality 154, 190, 196, 207
subsidiarity 13, 14, 15, 20, 22, 74, 97, 98, 108, 111, 120, 112, 113, 116, 130, 134, 151, 195, 214, 237

target set of normative judgments 69, 71, 153
teleological interpretation 26, 120, 121, 123, 125, 127, 129, 133, 134, 198
textualism 120, 123, 125, 128, 130, 136
tolerance 60, 85, 155, 162, 165, 190, 191

utilitarianism 36

voluntarism 66, 96